TOWARDS FULL AND
DECENT EMPLOYMENT

TOWARDS FULL AND DECENT EMPLOYMENT

Edited by
José Antonio Ocampo
and
Jomo K. S.

Orient Longman

Zed Books
London and New York

TWN
Third World Network

Published in association with the UNITED NATIONS

Towards Full and Decent Employment was first published in 2007.

Published in association with the United Nations

Published in the Indian Subcontinent, South East Asia (except Malaysia and Singapore) and Africa by
ORIENT LONGMAN PRIVATE LIMITED
Registered Office: 3-6-752 Himayatnagar, Hyderabad 500 029 (A.P.), India
Email: info@orientlongman.com *Website:* www.orientlongman.com
Other Offices: Bangalore, Bhopal, Bhubaneshwar, Chennai, Ernakulam, Guwahati, Hyderabad, Jaipur, Kolkata, Lucknow, Mumbai, New Delhi and Patna

Published in the UK, Europe, USA, Canada and Australia by
ZED BOOKS LIMITED
7 Cynthia Street, London N1 9JF, UK and
Room 400, 175 Fifth Avenue, New York, NY 10010, USA
www.zedbooks.co.uk
Distributed in the USA on behalf of Zed Books by
Palgrave Macmillan, a division of St Martin's Press, LLC
175 Fifth Avenue, New York, NY 10010, USA

Published in Malaysia and Singapore by
THIRD WORLD NETWORK
131 Jalan Macalister, 10400 Penang, Malaysia
www.twnside.org.sg

Published worldwide by the United Nations and distributed worldwide
via the UN specialized network of agents
United Nations Publications
2 United Nations Plaza Room DC2-853, New York, NY 10017, USA
https://unp.un.org *Email:* publications@un.org

United Nations' sales number: E.07.IV.6
ISBN: 978 81 250 3239 7 Pb (Orient Longman)
ISBN: 978 1 84277 882 1 Hb (Zed Books)
ISBN: 978 1 84277 883 8 Pb (Zed Books)

A catalogue record for this book is available from the British Library
US CIP data is available from the Library of Congress

Cover and book design by Orient Longman Private Limited 2007
Typeset in Minion Pro 10.5/13 by OSDATA, Hyderabad 500 029, India
Printed in India by Graphica Printers, Hyderabad 500013

Contents

Acknowledgements

The September 2005 World Summit, reiterating the goal of 'full employment and decent work for all', reinstated one of the key objectives set by the World Summit for Social Development held in Copenhagen in 1995. The Copenhagen Summit had placed employment – together with poverty reduction and social integration – at the centre of the international social development agenda.

Following up on the decisions of the 2005 World Summit, the United Nations Economic and Social Council focused on full employment and decent work for all in its deliberations in 2006, as will the Commission for Social Development in 2007–2008. This will also be the theme of the United Nations' *Report on the World Social Situation* in 2007.

UN Under-Secretary-General for Economic and Social Affairs José Antonio Ocampo convened the second UN Development Forum on 8–9 May 2006 on the theme of 'productive employment and decent work'. The chapters in this volume include abridged versions of papers by the invited participants. Longer and more technical versions of many of them have been published as working papers by the Department of Economic and Social Affairs (DESA).

This book would not have seen the light of day if not for the contributions and revisions of the authors themselves as well as the untiring efforts of Dominika Halka, Suzette Limchoc and Ivan Foo. Saroja Douglas, Mary Jane Holupka, Mary Nolan and Cheryl Stafford worked conscientiously to copy-edit these chapters for publication.

Sergei Kambalov, Leslie Wade, Aliye Celik, Paul Simon and other colleagues contributed to making a success of the May 2006 UN Development Forum. Leslie Wade prepared a report on the May forum which became the basis for the introduction to this volume. Donald Lee and Carl Gray led a team including Sarangerel Erdembileg, Anke Green, Alex Julca, Renata Kaczmarska, Cornelia

Kaldewei, Malinka Koparanova, Felice Llamas, Julie Pewitt, Victoria Saiz-Omenaca, Patience Stephens, Joop Theunissen and Sergio Vieira in preparing comprehensive reports of the presentations and the ensuing discussions.

The editors are grateful to all of them for their contributions.

Jomo K. S.

List of Tables

x • *List of Tables*

List of Figures

Preface

Employment and the UN Development Agenda

José Antonio Ocampo

The 2005 World Summit firmly put the goal of *full and productive employment and decent work for all* back at the forefront of the United Nations Development Agenda. The Summit showed a solid global consensus that employment and decent work need to be at the centre of economic and social policies aimed to achieve the primary Millennium Development Goal (MDG) – to cut poverty in half by 2015. Moreover, it led world leaders to conclude that the MDGs and the whole array of internationally agreed development goals may not be reached in many parts of the world under prevailing employment and labour market conditions.

This decision brought back one of the central objectives set by the World Summit for Social Development held in Copenhagen in 1995, which placed employment, together with poverty reduction and social integration, at the centre of the world social agenda. As a follow-up to the decisions of the 2005 World Summit, the United Nations Economic and Social Council placed full and productive employment and decent work for all at the centre of its deliberations in 2006. The Commission for Social Development will do likewise in its biennial cycle in 2007–2008, and this will also be the central topic of the United Nations' *Report on the World Social Situation* in 2007.

Major trends

To reflect on the policies needed to achieve this central goal of the international community, it is useful to begin by highlighting five significant global trends, dealing with job creation and its relations to economic growth, income inequality, and international migration.

First, over the decade since the World Summit for Social Development, unemployment has risen, rather than fallen. According to the most recent ILO's *Global Employment Trend Brief*, the number of unemployed worldwide reached new heights in 2005 – nearly 192 million people, equivalent to 6.3 per cent of the population force, over the 6.0 per cent reached in 1995. Furthermore, the employment to population ratio has declined over the last decade, from 62.8 per cent in 1995 to 61.4 per cent in 2005. Although the term 'jobless growth' – commonly used to describe the weak pattern of job creation that has characterized the world – is no doubt imprecise to describe such a trend, it brings attention to the fact that the link between global economic growth and job creation has been weak throughout the world. Furthermore, 'jobless growth' is not an inappropriate term to characterize certain episodes of growth in several countries, particularly when we take into account the quality of employment. We could add that, all over the world, most of the creation of employment has taken place in the service sector. This is somewhat paradoxical in terms of the links between globalization and employment creation: although services are increasingly traded internationally, most employment is created in what economists characterize as 'non-tradables', i.e., activities not directly linked to the global economy.

Second, underemployment, characterized by low productivity and inadequate income, remains pervasive and is probably increasing; half of the world's labour force still does not earn enough to lift themselves and their families above the global poverty line of US$2 per day. While unemployment poses the major challenge in many industrial economies, in most developing countries, poverty results less from unemployment than from the inability of the employed to secure decent incomes. This is particularly so in the agricultural sector and in the urban informal economy, which together account for the major share of employment in most developing countries, and especially in least-developed countries (LDCs). Moreover, in those countries and regions where growth has not been very dynamic, most growth in employment has taken place in low-productivity services, which have served as the activity that absorbs the surplus labour generated by both the traditional reduction in agricultural employment and the more recent and fairly widespread process of de-industrialization.

Third, globalization and other related economic processes have widened disparities in incomes among the employed, particularly between skilled and unskilled workers. Taken with two other trends – the rising share of profits and, in some countries, growing regional or urban-rural disparities – this explains the fairly widespread trend towards rising income inequality *within* countries over recent decades. On the other hand, while there seems to be a fairly widespread trend towards a reduction in gender gaps, such gaps remain very large – not only in terms of income, but also of employment opportunities and the higher levels of open unemployment and informality that affect women in almost every corner of the world.

Fourth, employment opportunities, both within and among countries, are showing significant change. Shifting production across the world – such as in the shift of labour-intensive manufactures or the off-shoring of services to developing countries – may have net job creation effects, though evidence of this is unclear. Similarly, trade liberalization may bring efficiency gains. Yet, all these phenomena bring little comfort to those who lose their jobs. More generally, the world seems to be experiencing a long-term trend loss in what people perceive as 'secure employment', whether in the private or public sectors. And this perception is strengthened by persistent calls for more 'labour flexibility'. The upshot is a broad-based and growing sense of economic and social insecurity, with social problems on the rise as people feel increasingly insecure within their jobs or, in fact, lose them.

Fifth, international migration is also reshaping the global labour market, giving rise to both xenophobia and racism, but also to unprecedented mass mobilizations of migrants, and even revolts. Such migration has had some adverse effects on the less-skilled segments of the labour markets in receiving countries, in terms of income and/or employment, which in many industrial countries is largely made up of prior migrants. However, hard evidence seems to indicate that these effects are relatively small, as low-skilled migrants generally occupy occupations for which there is insufficient supply of domestic workers. Moreover, the additional demand and growth that migration brings to recipient countries may swamp any negative labour market effects. The fact, however, that restrictions on labour mobility have forced the demand for such low-skilled labour to be filled with irregular flows means that migrants are in a vulnerable situation. This vulnerability may spill over into the less-skilled segment of the labour markets of natives and prior migrants, feeding into the sense of labour market insecurity. In any case, there are significant asymmetries in the mobility of factors of production and goods in the global economy. Capital and goods are more mobile than labour, and skilled labour is more mobile than unskilled labour. This may generate a distributional bias against the less mobile factor – i.e., unskilled labour – contributing to the adverse distribution trend.

THE POLICY AGENDA

Against this backdrop, the United Nations Economic and Social Council has challenged us to consider how to create "*an environment at the national and international levels conducive to generating full and productive employment and decent work for all, and its impact on sustainable development*". In tackling this theme, we should focus on three key dimensions:

- First, designing domestic policies and creating an environment at the national level conducive to full and productive employment and decent work;
- Second, ensuring that the work opportunities available to the poor contribute to lifting the burden of poverty; and
- Third, ensuring that the economic environment at the international level – especially in the critical areas of trade, finance, investment, technology and international migration – supports the goal of full employment and decent work for all.

Enhanced international cooperation in addressing macroeconomic and trade-related issues is essential to generating more and better jobs. Particularly important is a more balanced and coordinated international strategy for sustainable global growth and full employment, based in part on equitable sharing of responsibility for maintaining high levels of effective demand in the global economy.

Patterns of international investment, the growth of trade and cross-border movements of workers all affect jobs, incomes, security and the rights of workers. Therefore, better-coordinated international policies in all of these areas are needed to improve the prospects for achieving productive employment and decent work for all. This also means better-coordinated policies in the UN system[1] and the wider international community.

Notwithstanding these international dimensions, the responsibility to create the conditions for full and productive employment and decent work rests first and foremost with national governments. This requires summoning the political will to make employment generation a key priority – not only of social development strategies, but also, and perhaps mainly, of *economic* strategies and policies, at both the macroeconomic and sectoral levels.

Two essential ingredients of such strategies are sound macro-economic policies and an overall national development strategy conducive to dynamic employment generation. Economic growth is important, but even more so is its quality, measured particularly in terms of its capacity to generate quality jobs. So employment should be a key objective of macroeconomic authorities, including independent central banks. The idea that macroeconomic policies aim to promote full employment used to be a fundamental tenet of economic analysis, so much so that "the promotion and maintenance of high levels of employment" was enshrined in the IMF's first Articles of Agreement. But this idea has often been abandoned due to monetary policy's shift in focus to the single objective of achieving and maintaining low levels of inflation. Exchange rate policies are also crucial for employment generation in developing countries, particularly as trade liberalization has reduced policy space to adopt proactive industrial policies. And the fiscal space for public expenditures should also be preserved, especially in situations of economic recession that may necessitate counter-cyclical macroeconomic policies.

For many developing countries, the agricultural sector is still the main employer, particularly in sub-Saharan Africa and South Asia. Accordingly, more concerted action is needed on rural development, aimed at expanding market access, employment and productivity.

More broadly, the prevalence of the working poor in the developing world points to the importance of creating employment sufficiently productive to yield a decent income. For this reason, employment generation and productivity growth must be pursued jointly. A comprehensive strategy for achieving them together over the long run would entail investing in dynamically growing sectors of the economy; promoting micro and small enterprises, where most employment is generated today in many countries; and building strong linkages between dynamic sectors and small firms. It is in this context that promoting entrepreneurship plays an essential role, by making it easier to start and nurture small enterprises that provide more and better jobs.

Around the world, the evident restructuring of firms, sectors and even whole regional and national productive structures has put in even sharper relief the crucial role that investments in education and training play in ensuring a skilled and adaptable workforce in a global economy. Beyond that, the rising sense of job insecurity must be managed through strengthened social protection systems. In developing countries, where the link between employment and social protection historically has been weak, this will require increased State responsibility for providing social protection through fiscal mechanisms not tied to social security contributions.

Indeed, an effort to balance labour market flexibility with social protection must be at the centre of the global development agenda. This also includes avoiding excessive rotation of personnel that, according to existing evidence, reduces productivity. It is important as well to take into account alternatives to traditional labour market flexibility to facilitate adaptation to technological change and global competition. This could involve institutions that enhance labour-employer cooperation for adapting to changing circumstances, at national and local levels and within firms: that is, "social dialogue" in the language of the ILO. And, above all, flexibility should never be treated as a substitute for adequate macroeconomic policies. For we know that, in an unstable macroeconomic environment, additional flexibility may lead to a sharp deterioration in the *quality* of employment, while yielding often dubious benefits in terms of the *quantity* of "formal" employment, its primary objective.

National policies should also take into account the fact that, aside from the effects on the quantity and quality of employment, labour market institutions affect income distribution and social integration. For this reason, some analysts cite labour flexibility as one of the major forces behind the broad-based trend towards worsening income distribution in the world, with centralized wage bargaining operating in a few countries as a defence against this trend. Labour unions are also a major means of social participation. Social dialogue that engages labour unions and employers' associations can thus help to ensure that policies are balanced and enjoy wide public support, and to enhance broader social integration.

Finally, the growing emphasis on productive employment and decent work within the drive to fully implement the United Nations Development Agenda should lead to development of specific instruments to link national policies and international commitments. Thus, as part of the follow-up to the World Summit for Social Development and the 2005 World Summit, countries may consider developing guidelines and benchmarks, along with peer review processes, in order to strengthen country-level implementation and accountability for achieving full and productive employment and decent work for all.

NOTE

1 This is already been reflected in UN agencies, funds and programmes, the international financial institutions, and donor and lending agencies increasingly placing employment issues at the centre of their activities. In the case of the UN, effective mainstreaming of employment policies into national development and growth strategies should figure prominently at the country level, particularly through the incorporation of the ILO's Decent Work Country Programmes into the UN Development Assistance Frameworks (UNDAFs).

1
Towards Full Employment and Decent Work: An Introduction

JOMO K. S.

The 2005 World Summit put the goal of full and productive employment, and decent work for all at the forefront of the United Nations development agenda. It reiterated the core commitments of the World Summit for Social Development held in Copenhagen in 1995 to achieve the inclusive goals of poverty eradication, social integration and full employment – including the centrality of employment in policy formation.

Employment issues are cross-cutting and involve economic and social policies that have far-reaching implications. If the first Millennium Development Goal of reducing poverty by half by 2015 is to be achieved, full employment and decent work need to be the focus of economic and social policies, and such policies need to be pursued in an integrated way. Social development should not be treated as an addendum to macroeconomic or economic development policies, and social development policies should be mainstreamed into a broad and coherent concept of macroeconomic stability and development, including a universal approach to social protection (instead of targeting). Such mainstreaming of employment policies should be tailored to country conditions, needs and institutional environments.

Since the 2005 World Summit, the United Nations Economic and Social Council (ECOSOC) has prioritized full and productive employment and decent work for all in its deliberations during 2006. This will be the theme of the United Nations' *Report on the World Social Situation* in 2007, as well as the Commission for Social Development in 2007–2008. In support of these efforts, the UN Department of Economic and Social Affairs (DESA) convened the second UN Development Forum on 8–9 May 2006 on the theme of 'productive employment and decent work'. This book captures the major work presented at the forum, while this introduction seeks to locate the chapters in the context of the discussion and debate.

Structural Reform and Employment

The early chapters in this volume explore ways in which broad structural reforms, including macroeconomic policies, have affected employment opportunities in developing countries and suggest ways to mitigate those effects. Structural reforms have had, by and large, negative impacts on employment. There is now a general consensus on the weak link between trade liberalization and economic growth in most developing countries (see Hoekman and Winters, 2007; Lee, 2007). Increased trade openness in many developing countries has resulted in large adjustment costs, including increased income inequality, unemployment and limited creation of decent jobs. Initial conditions, including the quality of institutions, have also affected the impact of trade liberalization on investment, growth and employment creation.

Financial liberalization has also been encouraged with the expectation that it would provide more capital for investment, economic growth and employment creation in developing countries. This objective has largely been unmet because financial flows have been increasingly volatile and, in many cases, have disrupted the productive sectors of these countries. Indeed, the volatility of capital flows has left many developing countries more vulnerable to financial crises, which have resulted in increased unemployment, growth of the informal sector, lower wages, and increased poverty. Moreover, developing countries experienced lags in the recovery of real wages and employment after financial crises.

Financial and trade openness have thus often imposed constraints on developing countries. First, governments *are* compelled to reduce fiscal expenditures to keep inflation down and retain the confidence of foreign investors, even in the presence of underutilized capacity and large-scale unemployment. Policies have often turned out to be deflationary, prompting reductions in consumption and hindering employment creation. Second, economies have become more dependent on externally-determined technological change and sources of productivity growth. In many cases, these factors have led to a decrease in the demand for labour in developing countries, causing growth in the labour force to exceed growth in the demand for labour. In addition, surges of capital inflows have been as damaging as capital outflows, as their impacts on exchange rates and the opportunity cost of maintaining increased reserves have been high.

Rolph van der Hoeven and Malte Lübker note that external financial liberalization has contributed to a surge in international capital flows since the early 1990s. While the direct growth benefits of financial openness are doubtful, many developing countries have experienced greater economic volatility and financial crises since the early 1990s. These crises have had a considerable impact on GDP and long-term growth prospects; labour has suffered disproportionately as labour market indicators typically lag economic recovery, with labour's share in national income typically eroded by financial crises. Recent crises have led some developing countries to engage in costly reserve accumulation on an unprecedented scale, financing the growing US current account and budget deficits.

Policy options in developing countries have been constrained by the conventional 'macroeconomic policy trilemma', with countries unable to simultaneously maintain an open capital account, stable exchange rates and an independent monetary policy regime. The standard neoclassical solution to this problem has been abandonment of one of these constraints. A different approach would not seek 'corner solutions', but rather intermediate ones, including managed exchange rates aiming at a stable, but competitive, real exchange rate and associated fiscal and monetary policies, based on a social pact among government, workers and employers, to keep inflation at bay.

In this context, there is the need for some degree of capital control or capital account management. Such capital controls should discriminate between foreign direct investment and financial capital inflows, considering the potential of different types of flows to contribute to employment creation. Governments can also adopt short-term and long-run policies to mitigate the adverse impacts of economic opening. In the short-run, governments can increase public-sector expenditures where underutilized capacity exists, particularly in rural areas where unemployment levels may be highest, in order to generate employment and increase incomes. Supply-side management (provision of grains and other essential commodities from stocks, for example) can be used to offset potential inflationary pressures from increased expenditures. In the long-run, the introduction of labour-saving technologies and potentially destabilizing capital flows should be monitored and controlled appropriately by the authorities to prevent increases in unemployment.

An international financial system consistent with employment objectives should provide liquidity when needed, stability for global markets, and enough space for policy autonomy for all countries. Policy coherence is needed at three levels – policies in industrialized countries, multilateral rules, and policies in developing countries – for an international financial system more conducive to growth and employment.

Prabhat Patnaik notes that problems of unemployment and underemployment have been increasingly pervasive in recent decades, both in developing as well as OECD countries. Ironically, the problem of unemployment has also been accentuated in some developing countries experiencing high growth. Strong economic growth in some parts of the world may have involved relocation of existing or even fewer jobs from some parts of the world to others, rather than the net creation of new employment worldwide. It is also doubtful that greater labour market flexibility has led to employment creation, as greater flexibility has contributed to reduction of domestic demand, with negative effects for employment. The low level of employment creation worldwide is also due to slowing world demand growth and the rapid increase in global labour productivity.

Diane Elson observes that though women's labour force participation is still below that of men, their formal unemployment rate is generally still higher. Because of the 'discouraged worker effect', official unemployment rates tend to underestimate female unemployment, while women are overrepresented among the working poor, as a result of their overrepresentation in informal employment with low earnings and no social protection. Women, of course, account for a much higher share of unpaid domestic work.

Research shows that women's higher unemployment rates are a result of demand side factors, not just supply side factors. 'Deflationary bias' in macroeconomic policies interacts with biased social norms that ascribe 'breadwinning' to men and 'care work' to women, to put women at the back of the job queue when unemployment is high. Recent research suggests that 'contractionary' inflation reduction policies not only cause employment to fall relative to the long-run trend, but also adversely affect women's employment disproportionately. On the other hand, 'expansionary' inflation reduction causes employment to rise relative to the long-run trend, and is not associated with a disproportionate impact on women's employment. Also, maintaining a competitive exchange rate in periods of contractionary inflation reduction has been shown to offset the disproportionately negative effects on women. To promote gender equality in employment, policy should therefore avoid contractionary inflation reduction with uncompetitive exchange rates in line with a broader set of central bank policy goals and a wider range of instruments. In addition to appropriate macroeconomic policy, there is need to eliminate discrimination against women in labour markets, to invest in public infrastructure and services that lessen the burden of unpaid work, and introduce measures that promote more equal sharing between women and men of both earning and caring.

Gerald Epstein notes that employment creation has dropped off the direct agenda of most central banks. The current 'global best practice' approach to central banking does not focus on economic growth or employment generation, but rather on keeping inflation in the low single digits. However, the record shows that employment generation and economic growth are rarely, if ever, by-products of inflation-focused central bank policy. His chapter argues for a return to the historical norm of central bank policy in which employment creation and more rapid economic growth join inflation and stabilization more generally as key goals of central bank policy. To support this argument, he summarizes major lessons of a multi-country research project which shows feasible alternatives to inflation targeting that focus more on important social and real sector outcomes such as employment generation and poverty reduction.

Central banks currently contribute little, if anything, to employment creation. In the worst cases, they even create obstacles to more and better employment. With their widespread focus on inflation targeting (both implicit and explicit), current central bank policies are principally concerned with keeping inflation low. Available evidence from emerging market countries suggests that moderate inflation – below 15 or 20 per cent – does not necessarily have negative effects on growth, and may be good for alleviating inequality and poverty. In addition, external (international) and internal financial liberalization reduces the range of monetary policy tools, leaving the short-term interest rate as the main, if not the only tool. Monetary policy 'obsessed' with low inflation tends to create an environment of high real interest rates, which is often detrimental to growth and employment generation. In conjunction with tight fiscal policies, austere monetary policy reduces demand for productive loans, investments and growth, thus adding to global employment problems.

Central bank policies can affect aggregate demand for exports through the real exchange rate, and domestic demand by reducing the cost and increasing the availability of credit. Improving the quality of jobs and maintaining sustainable growth in real wages through public and private investment and improved export possibilities are also affected by the real exchange rate, cost and availability of credit, and credit allocation to different sectors. Central bank policy for employment creation should therefore focus on enabling expansion of aggregate demand, making credit available for sustainable investment and maintaining a stable and competitive real exchange rate to support export demand.

Research on alternatives to inflation targeting highlights the need for country-specific targets and policy instruments as well as related institutions. A one-size-fits-all inflation-targeting approach that has only one major target cannot be appropriate. The research points to a set of broad goals – such as employment generation, investment promotion, productivity enhancement, and a stable and competitive real exchange rate – besides attaining moderate inflation. Allowing central banks to promote growth and employment generation may increase the risk of supply-side shocks, triggering runaway inflation, as with the oil price shocks during the 1970s. Possible remedies include tripartite bargaining among social partners to avoid inflationary spirals, and directed credit allocation to employment generating sectors and firms. The latter could protect employment from the effects of a general credit crunch that would be triggered if policy were to rely solely on the rather blunt instrument of interest rate hikes.

Over the past two decades, there has been a major shift in development paradigm and development policy towards market liberalization, with a reduced role for government in setting economic and social policies. Only East and South Asia experienced sustained economic growth in this period, with the best growth performers not pursuing liberal market policies. Despite rapid growth in some economies, performance in terms of reducing inequality and advancing social development has been mixed.

Aziz Khan identifies three different employment trajectories experienced by developing countries. First, industrialization has been characterized by a rapid decline in the share of agricultural employment and significant shifts of workers into industry and services. Rapid growth and a high output elasticity of employment can thus be conducive to growth highly effective in alleviating poverty, as in some East Asian economies from the 1960s. Despite their high economic growth rates, China and India have not quite achieved this type of growth, since both countries have been unable to generate employment as rapidly. Recent reforms of the old state-owned enterprises have resulted in the shedding of 'excess' workers. In India, jobs created (e.g., in the information and communication technologies (ICT) sector) have not employed the poor, but mainly the educated.

A second type of transformation has seen the development of rural non-farm industries, as exemplified by Bangladesh. This type of transition has had a strong disequalizing effect on income distribution because the income generated has mainly accrued to the relatively well-off within the rural sector. A third scenario has seen a rise in the agricultural share of employment, as experienced by seven of the thirteen case study countries. This type of transition occurs when there are no incentives to industrialize, and people move into agriculture for survival.

In the past four decades, most countries have liberalized their trade and financial markets, made important efforts to control runaway inflation and privatized many public assets. In recent decades, most of the world has witnessed democratization and a related growth of civil society organizations. The last few decades have also seen the diversification of economies and fast growth experienced by some formerly low-income countries. Except for Africa, all other regions of the world are now less dependent on agriculture. The emergence of other sectors has varied greatly with country and time. The resilience of countries and people to crises and shocks has also varied.

In sub-Saharan Africa, economies were relatively stagnant for almost three decades until recently. Jobless growth in Latin America has contributed to rising inequality, and in other fast-growing regions, including China and South Asia, inequality has been increasing. Many traditional livelihoods are not sustainable, due to market penetration, which has been eroding livelihoods. Countries with weak infrastructure and institutions are unable to attract investment, and even in countries with relatively better infrastructure, the poor have less access to infrastructure and services, due to spatial inequalities, exclusion and prohibitive cost. Basic education alone is no longer sufficient to secure jobs as skill demands also increase in the job market.

The role of government has not been as positive as desired. Force has rarely been used for the benefit of people. In most places of the world, trust in public institutions has declined. Weaker governments have been subject to elite capture and corruption, and in many countries, public actions, such as re-classification of public assets and licensing, have been important sources of wealth creation for government officials.

Janvier Nkurunziza observes that poverty in Africa has been increasing over the last three decades. As poverty on the continent is largely rural, it should be addressed through the creation of decent jobs in rural areas. This objective can be achieved by developing agriculture, particularly food production, and expanding rural non-farm activities. Refocusing resource allocation on the rural economy

– by ensuring greater financial support for rural investment, creating a long-term rural investment fund using excess liquidity, bolstering microfinance and revitalizing development banking – will be key to implementing this programme.

One of the root causes of persistent poverty lies in the inability to create enough decent jobs to cope with the fast-increasing labour force. Despite higher economic growth after 2002, growth has failed to generate much employment. Even the fastest-growing economies in Africa were not able to create jobs, causing rapid economic growth to coexist with high poverty. Political declarations on employment creation as key to fighting poverty have not been translated into action. Analysis of 21 Poverty Reduction Strategy Papers (PRSPs) reveal their weak employment content. The fact that most development strategies do not consider job creation a priority helps explain why the employment intensity of the growth process is very weak.

LABOUR MARKET FLEXIBILITY

During the 1960s, the experiences of developed economies seemed to point to the compatibility of the institutionalization of workers' rights and an extended welfare state with fast and stable growth. However, this view was challenged from the 1970s, when there was a slowdown in economic growth accompanied by mass unemployment. A new conventional wisdom emerged that there is a trade-off between economic efficiency and social justice. It was argued that labour market rigidities were detrimental to job creation, growth and innovation, and therefore, reform of labour market institutions was needed to increase labour market flexibility to provide incentives for job-creation. The pressure to make labour markets more flexible has been reinforced by the transfer of production and jobs to emerging economies, especially in Asia.

Gerry Rodgers considers the challenges of advancing the decent work agenda in the face of pressures for greater labour flexibility. Employment protection legislation seems easier to implement than unemployment insurance since it requires firms to pay for the unemployment they generate. Unemployment insurance, on the other hand, is more demanding institutionally and can encourage labour turnover, putting much more pressure on the state besides pooling risks among all workers. Employment protection legislation tends to reduce the creation of formal sector salaried jobs, increase the size of the informal sector, and slow investment and output growth.

Thus, the promotion of worker security may simultaneously improve overall welfare as well as macroeconomic performance. Each country faces specific structural and institutional obstacles to advancing decent work and worker security. Thus, each country has to follow its own path to more decent work and better security for workers, including finding its own mix of security and flexibility. Country-specific situations warrant the adoption of specific approaches for which there will always be trade-offs associated with each approach.

In recent decades, market economies have generated more employment risk, both destroying and creating jobs, with higher rates of turnover in smaller firms. Competition is also a source of growth, forcing existing firms to become more productive or perish. For various reasons, developing countries face higher unemployment risks while lacking many of the institutional arrangements to mitigate such risks. There are usually little or no unemployment insurance, few services helping workers to find jobs or training, and limited collective bargaining. Most are characterized by limited welfare state provisions, offering little protection for the unemployed.

However, the supposed trade-off between economic efficiency and worker security may not be as commonly depicted. There are good reasons to believe that balancing flexibility and security may deliver better macroeconomic performance and employment growth than maximum flexibility. Low wages and poor working conditions for workers may not be desirable for encouraging work, commitment, intensity and productivity, all desired by firms. Fairer labour contracts – which provide employment stability, unemployment benefits and rights to training and education – may enhance worker commitment and productivity to improve both firm profitability and worker welfare.

Robert Boyer challenges the conventional wisdom that the dynamism of employment is always contradictory to the enforcement of some forms of security for workers. Contemporary theorizing now recognizes the specificity of the wage-labour nexus. Consequently, some security is required for good economic performance by firms and national economies. Comparative analysis of OECD countries shows that the extended security promoted by welfare systems has not been detrimental to growth, innovation and job creation.

Further, contrary to the expectation that the countries with the most deregulated labour markets would perform better in terms of job creation, innovation and growth, evidence from OECD countries suggests that countries that have adopted 'flexicurity' – a combination of labour flexibility with worker security – actually delivered better outcomes than conventional labour flexibility. In most developing countries, the expected links among fast output growth, employment growth and poverty reduction have generally been weak. Indeed, many studies show that low wages and poor working conditions do not necessarily attract multinationals to relocate in developing countries. Instead, ensuring basic worker rights may well be a precondition for successful growth strategies, rather than the outcome of economic reforms to increase efficiency. Although security will be costlier in the short run, it represents an investment with considerable beneficial side effects.

Formalizing the Informal Sector?

As the chapters by Chen and Tokman note, the informal sector is large, very heterogeneous and a significant source of employment in developing countries, particularly for women and youth. The costs and benefits of participation in the informal economy, as well as the incentives and disincentives to formalization must be carefully considered before seeking to formalize the informal sector. Several different approaches define and address informality. For many, the definition includes self-employed persons in small, unregistered or unincorporated enterprises, such as employers, own account operators and unpaid family workers, as well as wage workers without legal protection in formal and informal firms, or households, or those with no fixed employer.

Numerous benefits accrue to those operating informally including tax and regulatory avoidance, flexibility and convenience. The costs of informality may include other taxes or charges incurred by those outside the formal sector; less access to and higher costs of borrowing; poorer access to utilities and infrastructure; lack of social and legal protection, training or mobility prospects; and limited bargaining power. Formalization can ensure enforceable contracts; access to formal financial and other services; legally recognized rights; better access to public utilities, infrastructure, services, social protection; and membership in formal associations, providing 'voice'.

Government policies towards informality have so far ranged from persecution to support. There is a need for a new approach towards informality focused on regulations to meet people's needs. This may require different regimes modifying the common system in relation to labour standards. One solution could be progressive compliance, encouraged by inspections, instead of sanctions. In such a scenario, legal requirements would be goals, with progress subject to monitoring, oversight and rewards.

Formalization is a way to achieve inclusion. Options to achieve such inclusion could involve introducing dual regimes; improving business accounting; simplifying bureaucratic procedures; extending legal protection; recognizing labour relations; and promoting better practices, better and easier access to credit, and special considerations for unique working conditions, e.g., of street vendors. An alternative approach could shift focus from the interests of insiders to the benefits of outsiders, and from employer obligations to (informal) worker entitlements.

Explanations for persistent and growing informality range from globalization and the weakening capacity of the state to enforce regulations to the emergence of new forms of organization from below. Informality can be addressed broadly or sector-specifically. The pervasiveness of the informal sector reflects the failure of existing regulatory approaches, as well as economic models. The realization of citizen and worker rights can empower people and offer a path to formalization. For many, however it is cheaper to stay informal, while advancing decent work requires more formal working conditions and social protection. Formalization of the informal economy may require transparent governance, a strong state and well-developed rule of law which recognizes property rights and enforces contracts. The informal sector greatly contributes to economic growth, development and employment creation. Remittances sent home by immigrants often come from the informal sector.

As formalization has many meanings, many incremental steps can be taken to extend the benefits of formal employment to informal workers before fully integrating them into the formal economy, e.g., by sequencing benefits before compliance. Labour market regulations should create incentives for socially responsible employment practices and provide basic benefits and rights for informal workers. Mechanisms and financing arrangements should be created to provide social protection to all workers. Informal entrepreneurs should be included in policy-making processes, and rules-setting institutions should recognize and promote the needs of informal entrepreneurs and informal wage workers. A new approach towards informality should focus on regulations adapted to people's needs, e.g., different regimes in relation to labour standards. Finally, attention should be given to tolerance and compliance with fundamental labour rights, freedom of association and collective bargaining, reduction of entry costs for all to the formal economy, simplification of rules and procedures and redesign of mechanisms of access to formality.

More and better incentives are needed to encourage informal enterprises to formalize. To be attractive, formalization should minimize the costs and disadvantages of working informally, and maximize the converse. Formalization should also help increase the productivity and competitiveness of informal enterprises, while offering protection and rights that most workers in the informal sector do not have. Meanwhile, labour market regulations should create incentives for socially responsible employment practices and provide basic worker benefits and rights to informal workers. Financing mechanisms and arrangements should be created to provide social protection to all workers. Participatory policy processes and inclusive rule-setting institutions – that include representatives of informal entrepreneurs and informal wage workers – should be promoted as well.

SOCIAL PROTECTION

Cichon, Hagemejer and Woodall focus on providing social security for all as a crucial investment for poverty eradication. Social protection and social security are understood as a set of formal or informal income transfers in cash or kind to improve access to health and social services as well as provide basic income security to cope with vulnerability due to loss of income. Social security has significantly reduced poverty in OECD countries. Only two percent of global GDP is needed for social protection to eradicate poverty. However, social security provision is still underutilized in national anti-poverty and development strategies.

The first common argument against extending social security is the affordability argument, i.e., the supposed equity-efficiency trade-off implies that a large welfare state is not compatible with a competitive economy; social protection expenditures are too expensive for developing countries; ageing poses an insurmountable problem and related social provision expenditures will become unmanageable in the future. However, there has been a positive correlation between social expenditure per capita and productivity in OECD countries. Although the causality is unclear, the correlation challenges the conventional presumption of an equity-efficiency trade-off. Evidence from two African countries shows, that child benefits and pensions have reduced poverty by one-third to 40 per cent at a cost of less than 5 per cent of GDP. The relative cost of a basic package of social protection should decline over time. Development aid can be used to complement domestic resources for social protection to ensure that it focuses where it can achieve the most. The challenge of an ageing labour force for social security systems can be ameliorated by increasing the labour force, e.g., by raising the retirement age.

The claim that globalization limits fiscal space and will lead to a 'race to the bottom' also poses a challenge to social security. While levels of pensions and health benefits have been declining, there is little reason to assume that fiscal capacity will collapse completely. A sustained reduction in real pension levels would increase old-age poverty in the European welfare states.

Since the trade-off between equity and efficiency is dubious, some level of social security is affordable at any level of economic development. As social security reduces poverty and inequality, social security should be seen as an investment in people, and not as a burden. This shift in perspective regarding social protection – from cost to investment – needs to be accompanied by a change in paradigm from exclusive social protection, which covers only civil servants and formal private sector employees, to 'progressive universalism' covering all population groups. To achieve this, one could start with basic health care for all; child benefits conditional on schooling; self selective targeted social assistance; and universal benefits for the aged, disabled and in the event of loss of breadwinner. Evidence has shown, for example, that old-age assistance to grandmothers, in particular, has benefited entire families.

Thandika Mkandawire summarizes recent UNRISD research on social policy in a development context, suggesting a continuum between 'distributionist' and 'productivist' welfare regimes. A sole focus on the redistributive aspects of social policy would ultimately be economically unstable while a productivist approach would inevitably encounter opposition, generating instability, and ultimately undermining growth. Recent research indicates that welfare measures could be introduced at fairly low levels of national income, supporting the principal affordability claim of the previous chapter. Finally, the evidence is clear that the countries likely to halve extreme poverty by 2015 have adopted unorthodox macro-economic policies. He goes further to suggest the transformative potential of social policy in relation to both economic development and political democracy, as suggested by recent UNRISD research findings.

Carmen Pagés argues workers generally now face higher risks of unemployment that cannot be easily mitigated by the market. Hence, the state must develop and maintain instruments, programs and policies to protect workers against such risk. While workers in developing countries are especially vulnerable, their governments are poorly equipped to handle the challenge. Pagés assesses the relative merits and costs of different instruments and options. Governments should provide better job intermediation services for unemployed workers, improve training and retraining facilities, and be willing to provide flexible public works employment in the face of the likely persistence of unemployment. No single scheme fits all countries, and governments should be willing to experiment in protecting workers against unemployment.

Huck-ju Kwon argues that the rise of a more inclusive developmental welfare state in some parts of East Asia since the 1997-1998 economic crises has permitted reconsideration of the supposed trade-off between economic development and social security. The reform of their developmental welfare states is associated with the shift of economic development strategy from an 'extensive' to a more competitive production system, after the crisis. Although social policy continues to be subordinated to economic development strategy, the developmental welfare state has become more inclusive, universalizing access to social services while enhancing capabilities to strengthen competitiveness in the face of global competition.

The inadequacies of the old developmental welfare state model in the face of the Asian crisis also inspired the reforms. Before the economic crisis, the developmental welfare system, built on the idea of maintaining full employment and discouraging dependency on the state, did not cover many needs and contingencies. Social insurance, mainly for formal workers, only provided social benefits to contributors. As the number of unemployed was small, the 'protection' of this select group was not considered a major problem. However, with the crisis, the increase in unemployment challenged this exclusive social system as the welfare state did not adequately help many who lost their jobs. In response, new public assistance programmes were introduced, recognizing entitlement to benefits as a social right and increasing benefits to the vulnerable.

Democratization also contributed to more inclusive social policy. The earlier developmental welfare states were sustained by authoritarian governments which suppressed dissent. With democratization in the Republic of Korea, the new government organized a tripartite committee – the Employees-Employers-Government Committee – in 1997 to forge a social consensus for reform. This broad social basis for reform created a package of social protection measures for the unemployed. In contrast, the welfare state remained relatively unchanged in Singapore and the Special Administrative Region of

Hong Kong where economic policy was not similarly reoriented and politics did not become significantly more democratic. Lastly, Kwon argues that the experiences of Korea and Taiwan Province of China refute the conventional assertion that the role of social policy is minor in economic development.

Finally, Michael J. Piore and Andrew Schrank acknowledge that though the notion of 'decent work' is an ambiguous concept, it holds greater promise of rising above the bare minimum suggested by the currently popular 'core labour standards'. While problems of child labour and forced labour persist, even in advanced developed economies, they argue for a renewed focus on labour-market regulation, touching the daily lives of most workers in the formal economy and beyond. They urge the tripartite ILO to reclaim its core mission, arguing that renewed attention to labour inspection can serve not only to advance decent work, but also equitable economic development more generally. Viewing such initiatives as necessary responses to offset the consequences of recent economic liberalization and globalization, they do not seek to impose a single labour standard, opting instead for mutual collective learning from a variety of appropriate home-grown experiments.

A Double Movement for the Early 21ˢᵀ Century

After twenty-five years of the Washington Consensus, a worldwide 'social protection' counter-movement is emerging in response to the consequences of the trend towards economic globalization and liberalization. One focus of this counter-movement is the promotion of full and decent employment. A historical antecedent for such a 'double movement' was described in Polanyi's *The Great Transformation*, first published in 1944. In the late 19th and early 20th centuries, economic transformation was inspired by a liberal market philosophy, while social protection initiatives emerged in response to the disruptive effects of the market on community.

While the liberal market approach was promoted by the rigid economic mechanisms of the gold standard in the past, it is now facilitated by a network of multinational institutions. The countervailing social movements in the past often involved violent reactions, contributing to the rise of communism and fascism as well as social democracy and the welfare state. In the middle of the 20th century, Keynesian economics seemed to provide the basis for a viable alternative from a social development perspective, allowing the reconciliation of market forces and social imperatives. Today, such a conciliatory framework is lacking, and there is an urgent need for international discussion and consensus on a new alternative that would balance social needs with economic growth. In this context, the role of labour market interventions to ensure social protection while allowing sufficient economic flexibility is considered crucial.

Against this background, the full employment and decent work policy agenda has a particularly urgent relevance, and involves a number of important dimensions. There is a need to improve the international economic environment, in areas such as trade, finance, investment, technology and migration to support the goal of full employment and decent work for all. These international dimensions should not, however, reduce the responsibility of national governments to create favourable conditions through sound macro-economic policies and an overall national development strategy conducive to dynamic employment generation.

There must be an effort to balance labour market flexibility with social protection as part of the global development agenda. Interventions in labour markets do not necessarily lead to unemployment, while social protection as well as other social expenditure also need to be seen as investments, and not merely as costs or burdens. There is also a need for enhanced flexibility involving closer labour-employer cooperation to adapt to technological changes and increased global competition. Investments in education and training have played a role in ensuring a skilled and adaptable workforce. The rising sense of job insecurity should be managed through strengthened social protection. Thus, social dialogue can help ensure that policies are balanced and enjoy wide public support.

More and better employment is key to poverty reduction. However, growth does not necessarily lead to employment creation, much less good jobs. Recent growth associated with globalization has also been associated with greater risks, including higher job-turnovers. The widespread prevalence of the working poor in the developing world points to the urgent need to create employment sufficient to yield decent incomes. Investing in rural development remains important, together with more support for micro, small and medium enterprises as well as entrepreneurship.

There is a growing debate over the core assumptions regarding employment levels, labour standards and labour markets. Previously accepted trade-offs – between employment protection and employment levels, between labour market interventions and employment levels, between equity and efficiency, between labour standards and attracting foreign direct investment, and between development and stabilization – have also been challenged. The presumption that social protection and other labour market interventions are not affordable has also been increasingly disputed by major new initiatives in some of the least developed countries of the world.

Some specific policy recommendations for mainstreaming the full employment and decent work objectives which emerged from the debate at the May 2006 forum include the following:

- Social pacts should include employment and income-distribution objectives in the design of fiscal, monetary and exchange rate policies to increase the policy space to address employment objectives in developing countries. Nonetheless, such social pacts cannot replace social investment and development objectives, to address the root causes of financial instability.
- Policies should be tailored to specific economic realities and institutional settings. Thus, a 'one-size-fits-all' approach will not be appropriate.
- The international community should support the re-emergence of national development banks, for credit allocation and employment creation. Besides providing 'patient capital', they can lend managerial support to small and medium enterprises.
- Research on the role of unpaid work and on how to reconcile paid and unpaid work should be supported.
- Demand- and supply-management policies should more effectively address employment problems in developing

countries. Such policies are more likely to work in countries with significant underutilized capacity.

- Significant complementarities among economic, financial, social and labour-market policies for employment creation should be coordinated to reduce the adverse impacts of increased volatility of capital flows and trade openness on employment.

- The perceived trade-off between labour market flexibility and worker security is less pronounced than previously posited. In fact, maximum flexibility does not necessarily mean optimum efficiency, and a balance between employer or firm flexibility and worker security can promote productive employment. This balance needs to be tailored to existing conditions.

- The decent work agenda offers a framework for social policy that goes beyond the issues raised in the flexibility-security debate. It incorporates other widely-shared, broad social policy goals. In so far as there are tradeoffs between security and employment, for example, then it is necessary to find institutional and policy frameworks that address both.

- Labour market regulations should create incentives for socially responsible employment practices and provide basic benefits and rights for informal workers.

- Mechanisms and arrangements should be financed to provide social protection to all workers. Informal entrepreneurs should be included in policy-making processes, and rules-setting institutions should recognize and promote the needs of informal entrepreneurs and informal workers.

- A new approach should focus on adapting regulations to diverse needs, with different regimes modifying labour standards accordingly.

- In the informal economy, attention should be given to compliance with fundamental labour rights, freedom of association and collective bargaining, reduction of formal sector entry costs for all, simplification of rules and procedures and redesign of mechanisms for access to formality.

- The financial crisis of the late 1990s prompted structural reforms in the economy and structural changes in the social protection strategies of some countries in East Asia. Democratic transitions resulted in changes in social protection from exclusive to more inclusive systems. The requirements of more inclusive developmental welfare systems need to be elaborated.

- Social security systems often have underutilized potential for achieving poverty reduction. The affordability of these systems in developing countries has undermined the widespread belief that globalization, increased international competition, and demographic changes would make those systems unaffordable.

2

Financial Openness and Employment: The Need for Coherent International and National Policies*

ROLPH VAN DER HOEVEN AND MALTE LÜBKER

The consequences of mistakes in financial markets, where capital is volatile and mobile globally, far exceeds the consequences of mistakes in the labour markets, where labour is largely immobile across national lines.

Richard Freeman (2003)

The current wave of globalization is characterized by a more liberal policy stance at the international and national levels. While policy for trade liberalization dominated the international agenda since the 1960s, policies for financial liberalization have been of a much more recent vintage. They have been applied in the wake of stabilization and adjustment policies which marked the 1980s and early 1990s. The major expected result from financial liberalization was that it would allow (developing) countries to utilize resources better and to increase capital formation, through stimulating foreign direct investment (FDI) and other international capital flows such as private portfolios investment. A more open national financial system was seen as a necessary complement to the lifting of impediments to international capital flows. Over the past two decades, many countries have liberalized their capital accounts (see Lee and Jayadev, 2005) and almost all policy measures related to foreign direct investment favoured a more open regime (see van der Hoeven and Luebker, 2006: Annex Figures 1 and 2).

As a consequence, capital has become globally mobile – in contrast to labour, whose movement is still highly restricted.[1] International capital flows accelerated especially since the mid-1990s. Worldwide gross private capital flows (the sum of the absolute values of foreign direct, portfolio, and other investment inflows and outflows) have been equal to more than 20 per cent of world GDP for the past seven years, compared to less than 10 per cent of world GDP before 1990. Worldwide FDI flows, a sub-category of private capital flows, also rose substantially during the 1990s and equalled 4.9 per cent of world GDP in 2000. They have since declined, but they are still well above the level of the 1970s or 1980s. Yet, despite this substantial increase in capital flows, a number of worrying trends remain:

During the surge in foreign capital flows since the 1990s, actual investment into new infrastructure and productive capacity stagnated. Gross fixed capital formation (the most commonly used measure for physical investment) equalled 22.0 per cent in 2000 (the year when international capital flows peaked), only marginally above the level of the early 1990s (see Figure 2.1). This divergence in trends can in part be attributed to the fact that much FDI was spent on mergers and acquisitions, and did not go into new factories or machinery.[2] Despite the widespread perception of an investment boom during the 1990s, increased cross-border flows have not increased the overall level of investment. Gross fixed capital formation was on average actually lower since 1990 than in the 1980s or the 1970s.[3] It is thus not surprising that world GDP growth, too, was slower than in previous decades (see also Figure 2.2).

Cross-border capital flows are still largely a phenomenon of developed countries. In 2004, gross private capital flows equalled 28.4 per cent of GDP in high-income countries, but only 11.9 per cent of GDP in low- and middle-income countries. While there was a positive balance between in- and outflows for developing countries as a group, these flows by-and-large bypassed the poorest countries since the early 1990s as over 90 per cent of the net inflows went to middle-income countries. FDI, as well, is highly concentrated among industrialized countries and a small group of middle-income countries (see van der Hoeven and Luebker, 2006: Annex Figure 3). Low-income countries therefore still draw, to a large extent, their foreign resources from official development assistance which, despite lofty statements at various international fora, has not increased in the past 15 years.[4]

International capital movements have led to greater economic volatility, a trend that has been well documented (Diwan, 2001; Prasad and others, 2003; 2004; Cerra and Saxena, 2005). Most research points to the direction that volatility in turn has lead to more frequent financial and economic crises in developing countries (while this is not necessarily the case for industrialized countries) (see Easterly, Islam and Stiglitz, 2001; Singh, 2003). Such crises have negative effects on growth, investment and incomes, not only in the short term, but also in the long run (Diwan, 1999; 2001; Cerra and Saxena, 2005). Hence, volatility and financial crises that are caused by financial integration should be seen as a serious problem for enterprises and labour – contrary to earlier views that, with proper national institutions and so-called safety-net programmes, countries would be able to withstand the medium- and long-term negative aspects of volatility and crises.

In the light of these trends, the purpose of this chapter is to review the effects of financial liberalization on employment and incomes. The chapter will concentrate on the effects of volatility and crises on labour that is primarily associated with debt and portfolio equity flows, and less with FDI flows.[5] The chapter is motivated by the concern expressed by the World Commission on the Social Dimension of Globalization that '[g]ains in the spheres of trade and FDI run the risk of being set back by financial instability and crisis' (WCSDG, 2004: 88). It draws the conclusion that volatility in international financial markets is currently perhaps one of the most harmful factors for enterprises and labour in developing countries, particularly in the middle-income countries that have been most prone to financial turmoil. Hence, the chapter suggests how greater policy coherence between international and national economic and employment policies can give greater attention to employment and incomes.

In discussing the rules, conditions and behaviour at international financial markets, different authors use different terms to describe recent developments. In this chapter, the following terms are employed: Financial openness[6] is used as an umbrella term that includes both financial integration and financial liberalization. Financial liberalization in turn incorporates the liberalization of the capital and financial account[7], but also other elements such as less or different supervision and regulation of the banking sector and often a liberalization of the foreign exchange rate regime. The difference between financial integration and financial liberalization is that the former describes a situation in which a country is more integrated in the world financial markets (i.e., through higher FDI/GDP ratio), while financial liberalization means changes in laws and regulations, which may (or may not) lead to greater financial integration.[8]

FIGURE 2.1

World FDI and investment as share of GDP (1970–2004)

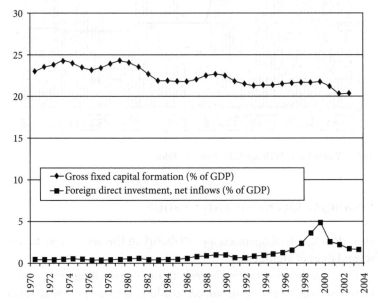

Source: World Bank, WDI, online database, as of May 2006.

Since this chapter focuses on private capital flows (i.e., those private international transactions that are recorded under the balance of payments' financial account), it will only make reference in passing to other important sources of foreign financing – such as official and private development assistance, income generated from exports and workers' remittances. Although the latter are a genuinely private form of financial flows, they do not establish an investment position and are, therefore, recorded under the current account.

FIGURE 2.2
World GDP Growth, 1961–2004

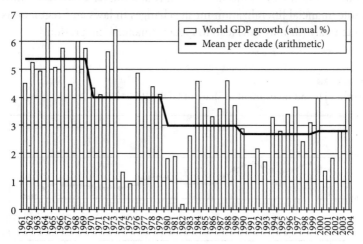

Source: World Bank, WDI 2003, 2005 on CD-Rom.

FINANCIAL OPENNESS AND LABOUR

How does financial openness affect labour? In this section, we follow several lines of argument.

First, we briefly review the effects of liberalization on growth. Here, two arguments are advanced: In addition to the potential direct positive effect of capital flows on growth (as countries gain additional resources that can be invested), there can also be an indirect negative effect on growth. In particular, financial liberalization forces countries to hold a larger amount of foreign reserves which reduces incomes and growth potential. If financial flows have, on balance, a positive impact on growth, this would be generally beneficial for labour, while slow growth is usually disadvantageous for labour. However, even in the case of fast or steady growth, the distributional impact on different categories of labour needs to be taken into account. Labour might be benefiting less than appropriate and necessary for long term institutional and human capital development.

Secondly, we look into the effects of international financial flows on volatility, and their role in provoking financial crises. If financial crises become more frequent, their negative consequences for growth (both in the short and long run) could cancel out any benefits from financial liberalization, or even lead to a net negative effect of financial openness on growth. Moreover, financial crises can have impacts on labour that go over and above their general economic impact. Since, as indicted above, volatility and the frequency of financial crises have increased, we review their direct impact on employment. This is followed by a discussion of wage shares, and how they have evolved during crises, and a summary of the main findings.

FINANCIAL OPENNESS AND GROWTH

Direct Effects on Growth

A recent study by IMF researches (Prasad and others, 2004) has confirmed the main findings of earlier studies such as those undertaken in UNCTAD (2001): it is difficult to establish a robust causal relationship between financial integration and growth. In general, growth is more depending on the quality of domestic institutions and careful macro-economic management. Edison and others (2004) argue in the same direction and demonstrate that the findings of previous research (that found a positive association between capital account openness and growth) crucially depended on the country coverage, the choice of time periods and the indicator for capital account openness. They also find evidence for a suggestion that was first made by Rodrik (1998), namely that conventional indicators for capital account openness closely proxy the reputation of a country's government. If governance is controlled for, capital account openness has no significant effect on economic performance (Edison and others, 2004: 243ff.). By contrast, Tornell, Westermann and Martínez (2003) study a sub-set of countries with functioning financial markets (thus excluding the majority of developing countries) and argue that switching to a regime of *de facto* financial openness will ease credit constraints, which leads to higher growth but also increased risk of financial crises. By their account, the growth effect outweighs the cost of crises. This result runs counter to the findings presented by Lee and Jayadev (2005) who use a *de jure* measure of capital account liberalization (rather than a *de facto* measure that reflects the success in attracting inflows). For the period from 1973–1995 (i.e., even when excluding the negative impact of the East Asian crisis), they find no positive effect on growth rates and, contrary to theory, some indication that openness reduces the investment share in GDP.

The conflicting results could in part be caused by differences in country coverage, but also by differences between the indicators employed in the literature. Prasad and others (2004) and Collins (2005) highlight the crucial difference between 'de jure' or 'de facto' measures of financial openness. 'De jure' financial openness (or financial liberalization) includes abolishment or changes in rules and regulations concerning foreign capital, as it is often required as part of the conditionality for financial support by the International Financial Institutions. Many countries in Latin America fall under this category. By contrast, 'de facto' financial openness (or financial integration) relates to increases in a financial openness indicator, irrespective of whether rules have changed or not (India and China, but also other Asian countries fall into this category). In the latter case, the causal relationship between financial openness and growth is more difficult to establish. Did financial integration lead to higher growth or did higher growth induce financial integration? Rodrik (2003) and Singh (2003) argue that especially for India and China, growth induced greater financial integration. Policy discussions should therefore emphasize firstly appropriate growth strategies, and, in the light of those, consider various variants of liberalization. Tokman (2003), for example, argues that slow growth cum liberalization in Latin America has led to a greater informalization of the work force, persistent poverty and greater inequality.

Another factor to explain the difference in results could be the different impact of financial openness across countries. As Edison and others (2004) argue, capital account liberalization can be beneficial to middle-income countries under certain conditions, while low-income countries with a poor regulatory framework and inadequate institutions have little to gain. The importance of institutions and the policy framework as a pre-condition for capital account liberalizations is also pointed out by Gilbert, Irwin and Vineset (2001). They conclude that "[b]y itself, capital account liberalisation will deliver relatively little" while leaving poor countries more vulnerable to crisis (Gilbert, Irwin and Vineset, 2001: 121). An even more pessimistic view emerges from the study by Lee and Jayadev (2005) who find that even when the most commonly mentioned pre-conditions are met, capital account liberalization has, overall, no positive effect on growth.

While the argument that the impact of financial flows depends on country characteristics is most frequently applied to portfolio equity and short-term debt flows, it has also been made for FDI. Ghose (2004) found that the effects of FDI on the host country crucially depended on country specific circumstances, in particular whether they met an unmet demand for investment finance (e.g. to build up export-oriented manufacturing industry). However, FDI does not always add to the productive capacity of the recipient country, but can also crowd out domestic investment when foreign entrepreneurs seize upon investment opportunities that would have otherwise been taken up by domestic enterprises (Ghose, 2004).

Indirect Growth Effects Through Increased Reserve Holdings

As a consequence of financial openness and of the instability of the current international financial system, developing countries have been increasingly building up foreign reserves since the early 1990s. For some countries these reserves were created by surplus on the current account, while others built up reserves through capital inflows which were not spent on foreign goods. As Feldstein (1999) argues, increasing international liquidity is an effective 'self help' strategy in the absence of an international lender of last resort. However, while giving countries some protection against financial crises, holding large international reserves is also a costly strategy as foreign reserves are held in low interest bearing instruments such as US treasury bills, rather than earning much higher returns on the capital market or through investment into human or physical capital. Baker and Walentin (2001) estimate that the increased reserve level of the late 1990s compared to that common in the 1960s implies an annual cost of around 1 per cent of GDP in most regions, and of between 1.2 and 2.5 per cent in East Asia and the Pacific. They argue that the gains of trade liberalization in terms of higher GDP growth were actually 'eaten up' for most countries in the 1990s by the earning forgone on holding higher reserves (Baker and Walentin, 2001). In a more recent study, Rodrik (2006) estimates that the cost of increased reserve holdings is 1 per cent of GDP on average for developing countries. While imposing costs on developing countries, increased reserve holdings are indirect subsidy to the countries in whose currency the reserves are held (see Stiglitz, 2000).

What is striking, however, is that the trend of the 1990s has accelerated in the first years of the current century to a somewhat alarming level (see Figure 2.3). Overall, reserves held by low- and

FIGURE 2.3
Reserve holdings by developing countries, 1970–2004 (% of GNI)

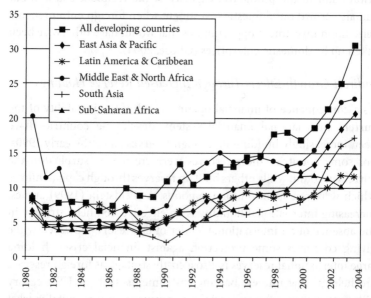

Source: World Bank (2005b) Global Development Finance, 2005, online database (as of May 2006); based on series 'International Reserves (US$)' and 'Gross National Income (US$)'.

middle-income countries were equal to 20.7 per cent of their GNI in 2004, compared to 6.9 per cent in the first half of the 1990s – a threefold increase.[9] The substantial increase took place in low- and in middle-income developing countries alike, and across regions.

FINANCIAL OPENNESS, VOLATILITY AND CRISES

Growth Effects of Volatility and Crisis

Prasad and others (2004) made also another pertinent observation, namely that financial liberalization in developing countries is associated with higher consumption volatility and increased GDP volatility than in developed countries. This observation is consistent with those of many other researchers (see e.g. Kose, Prasad and Terrones, 2003; Levchenko, 2005), and especially with those who emphasize the need for stronger institutions as a precondition for development. Kaminsky, Reinhart and Végh (2004) pointed out that the absence of sound financial regulation, both at the national and international levels, makes developing countries much more vulnerable to negative impacts of capital flows. When institutions with the ability to manage greater volatility are absent or not fully effective, the generally pro-cyclical nature of international capital flows ('when it rains it pours'-syndrome) adds to the effects of fiscal policies, and, to a certain extent, also macroeconomic polices, that tend to be pro-cyclical in most developing countries. Such pro-cyclical behaviour deepens and prolongs a crisis.

Financial crises typically have a large impact on the real economy. In the five countries most affected by the East Asian crisis of 1997/98, GDP per capita fell between 2.8 per cent (Philippines) and 14.8 per cent (Indonesia). In Latin America, the Mexican crisis of 1994/95 led to a decline in incomes by 7.8 per cent, and the Argentinean crisis of 2001/02 reduced the country's per capita incomes by 16.3 per cent.[10] A recent study by Hutchison and Noy (2006) documents that so-called 'sudden stop' crises (a reversal in capital flows and a simultaneous currency crisis) have a particular harmful effect on output – over and above that of 'normal' currency crises. On average, they cause a cumulative output loss of 13 to 15 per cent of GDP over a three-year period. One important factor behind this trajectory is often the disarray financial crises cause in the banking sector. Burdened with non-performing loans, the domestic banks fail to perform their function of providing credit at a time when it is most needed. An extreme case of a prolonged credit crunch is Mexico, were real credit continued falling until 2002 – eight years after the crisis of 1994 (see Tornell, Westermann and Martínez, 2003: 54ff.).

FIGURE 2.4

Typical growth path after financial crisis in rich and poor countries

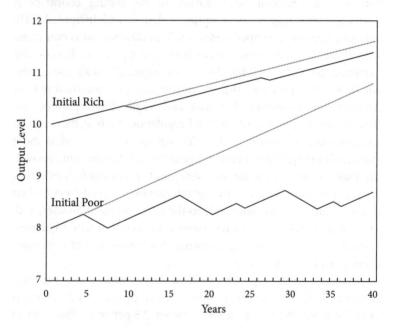

Source: Cerra and Saxena (2005: 24)

Financial crises can therefore have long-term implications, although there is some controversy about how big and permanent the costs of financial crises are. Tornell, Westermann and Martínez (2003: 23) argue that crises 'are the price that has to be paid in order to attain faster growth', and that that it is possible for GDP growth to recover rapidly from a crisis (although this need not happen and actually did not happen in Mexico, the case they study in more detail). The view that crises pose only a temporary set-back is challenged by Cerra and Saxena (2005), who deconstruct what they call the 'myth of recovery' by using panel data for broad datasets of countries. They document that recessions are typically not followed by high-growth recovery phases, either immediately following the trough, over several years of the subsequent expansion, or even over the complete subsequent expansion that follows a complete recession (see Figure 2.4). Indeed, for most countries, growth is significantly lower in the recovery phase than in an average expansion year. Thus, when output drops, it tends to remain well below its previous trend. As they argue,

> political and financial crises are costly at all horizons. Financial crises contribute to half of the episodes of negative growth, and there is no evidence that they typically lead to economic reforms or policy adjustments that restore output to trend. Change to a more democratic government system, on the other hand, improves the rebound from a recession. We also find evidence that while trade liberalization increases the long-run growth rate, it can weaken recovery from recession. However, such weak recoveries tend to occur in combination with liberalized capital account regimes (Cerra and Saxena, 2005: 24).

Another important point the authors make is that frequent crises and instabilities prevent a smooth convergence process as the neoclassical growth literature indicates:

> When shocks derail growth, incomes [between countries] diverge. Poor countries have respectable expansions, and therefore do not appear to be stuck in a poverty trap. However, many poor countries do appear to be mired in a crisis trap. Countries that experience many negative shocks to output tend to get left behind and their long-term growth suffers. Thus, while standard growth theory may work well in explaining expansions, a fruitful direction for future research would be to explain the proclivity to wars, crises, and other negative shocks (Cerra and Saxena, 2005: 24).

This is related to the point Rodrik (2003) makes, namely that policies for stimulating growth are different from policies to sustain growth and that frequent crises require frequent policy regime switches.

Effects of Financial Crises on Employment

Financial crises are generally not only associated with an economic decline, but also with severe social costs. These are most prominently felt in terms of rising open unemployment, falling employment-to-population ratios, falling real wages, or a combination of the above (see e.g. Lee, 1998). Moreover, the social costs can usually be felt longer than the economic impact: Even when GDP per capita has recovered to pre-crisis level, the other indicators usually lag behind. This pattern can be observed in a majority of countries that were most affected by the financial crises of the past decade. Mapping the observed trends against a counterfactual with limited financial openness and no financial crises would, from an analytical perspective, of course be the empirical strategy of choice. However, such a counterfactual is excessively difficult to construct.

Figure 2.5 demonstrates clearly the consequences of financial crises on employment. In all but one case the unemployment rate, even three years after the crisis, had not returned to its pre-crisis level. A higher post-crisis unemployment rate could be the consequence of sluggish growth after the crisis, but van der Hoeven and Luebker (2006), reviewing several crises in Latin American and East Asian countries and in Turkey, demonstrate that after the crisis, in almost all cases, GDP recovered much faster than employment—in other words, the recovery of output was not accompanied by a return to pre-crisis levels of unemployment. The worrying conclusion is that financial crises affect employment more than temporarily and may lead to unwarranted structural changes in the long term creation of employment.

Effects of Financial Crises on Labour Shares

Contrary to the conventional wisdom that sees the labour share in GDP as constant, research by Diwan (2001) and Harrison (2002) shows that the proportion of GDP that goes into wages and other labour income is variable over time. Using a data set from 1960 to 1997, Harrison (2002) splits her sample of over 100 countries into two even groups (based on GDP per capita in 1985). Her data show that, in the group of poorer countries, labour's share in national income fell on average

FIGURE 2.5
Unemployment rates before, during and after financial crises

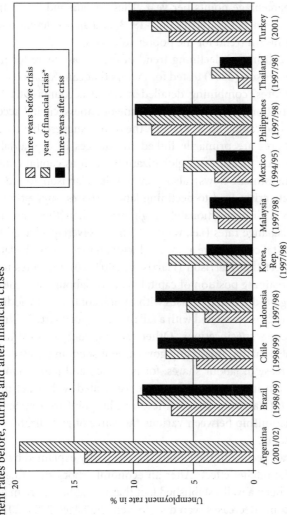

* If a financial crisis extended into a second calendar year, the unemployment figure refers to the later year where the economic impact of the crises usually peaked.
Note: The unemployment figures for Argentina refer to urban areas only; the pre-crisis unemployment rate for Indonesia refers to 1996.
Source: International Labour Office, *Key Indicators of the Labour Market,* 4th edition.

by 0.1 percentage points per year prior to 1993. The decline in the labour share was more rapid after 1993, when it started to fall by an average by 0.3 percentage points per year. In the richer sub-group, the labour share grew by 0.2 percentage points prior to 1993, but then fell by 0.4 percentage points per year. These means indicate a trend reversal for the richer countries post-1993, and an acceleration of an already downward trend for the poorer sub-group.

After establishing a declining trend of the labour share for many countries, Harrison (2002) tested for factors that can explain changes in labour shares, combining detailed national accounts data from the United Nations with measures of trade openness, capital account restrictions and capital flows. Overall, the results suggest that changes in factor shares are primarily linked to changes in capital/labour ratios. However, measures of globalization (such as capital controls or direct investment flows) also play a role. Harrison found that exchange rate crises lead to declining labour shares, suggesting that labour pays a disproportionately high price when there are large swings in exchange rates (i.e., wages are more severely affected than GDP).[11] Capital controls are associated with an increase in the labour share, an effect that Harrison (Harrison, 2002: 20) attributes to the stronger bargaining position of capital vis-à-vis labour since the cost of relocating production increases with capital controls.[12] In addition, increasing trade is associated with a fall in the labour share. This result is robust across specifications. Other factors, such as government spending, also matter. Increasing government spending is associated with an increase in labour shares, for both rich and poor countries. Finally, foreign investment inflows are associated with a fall in the labour share (Harrison, 2002). These results point to a systematic negative relationship between various measures of globalization and the labour share.

The overall decline in the labour share is partly explained by what some call the ratchet effect: After an economic shock or a financial crisis, it has been a well-established fact that the labour share in gross national income decreases (van der Hoeven and Saget, 2004: 201). In the 1980s, some authors argued that the decline in labour share after the economic shocks was, in effect, the consequence of a too high labour share before the crisis in the 1980s and thus partly blaming labour for the build-up of the crisis. However, only in a minority of cases have financial crises been caused by bidding up wages and labour shares. In most cases, the crisis was caused by external events or rent-seeking behaviour of capital owners (Amsden and van der Hoeven, 1996: 522).

THE EFFECTS OF FINANCIAL OPENNESS ON LABOUR: SUMMARY OF MAIN FINDINGS

On balance, the capital account liberalization that many developing countries embarked upon in the 1990s has delivered disappointing results. This disappointment is well summarized in a recent World Bank report that reviews the growth performance of the 1990s: "Contrary to expectations, financial liberalization did not add much to growth, and it appears to have augmented the number of crises." (World Bank, 2005b: 21)

The preceding discussion, too, has shown that capital account liberalization fell not only far short of expectations, but did serious harm to some countries and had a disproportionately negative effect on labour. Six main conclusions emerge:

1. In the absence of adequate institutions, the capital account liberalization has had little direct benefits for growth. This is especially true for poor countries where the institutional gap is greatest, but also for middle-income countries where capital inflows were not used to fill unmet investment needs.

2. However, capital account liberalization – even if managed prudently – has its cost to developing countries. In order to cushion the effects of sudden outflows, developing countries have sterilized inflows and built up large reserves. Since these are mainly held in low-yield treasury bonds issued by industrialized countries, the opportunity cost of doing so is large.

3. Nonetheless, capital account liberalization has left developing countries vulnerable to crisis. These are often not triggered by a sudden deterioration of a country's so called fundamentals, but are an inherent property of the international financial system. The output losses associated with such crises are large, and even

a subsequent recovery is usually insufficient to bring a country back onto its old growth path.

4. The negative effects of financial crisis on the labour market can be detected in a number of indicators. Open unemployment typically rises substantially during a crisis, but the impact can also be seen in a fall of real wages, rising underemployment and shifts of workers from the formal sector towards the informal economy and agriculture.

5. Moreover, labour markets typically lag the economic recovery by several years. Even when GDP per capita has reached its pre-crisis level, the consequences of the crisis are normally still evident from the employment indicators. This lag means that labour pays a disproportionate cost.

6. Tracking the evolution of the labour share in national income also shows that crises are particularly harmful for labour. As recent research indicates, financial crises have a permanent negative effect on the share of labour compensation in GDP. They are thus a factor behind the long-term trend decline in the labour share that can particularly be observed from the early 1990s onwards.

FINANCIAL OPENNESS AND EMPLOYMENT: THE NEED FOR GREATER POLICY COHERENCE

The preceding sections made clear that concerns for growth, labour and employment should be more explicitly taken into account in the current financial system in order for it to perform better. Adelman (2000) argues that it might be advisable to restore a global financial environment which carries some of the characteristics of the so-called Golden Age – steady development for developing countries, combined with high stable growth for industrialized countries – while maintaining some of the virtues of a more liberalized trading and investment climate (Adelman, 2000: 1058). In order for such a system to function more efficiently in terms of growth and employment, it must have three different sets of properties:

- *Firstly, it should provide liquidity in the international system.* Liquidity is needed to respond to demands for foreign exchange and for foreign investment. In effect the downfall of the original Bretton Woods system was in part due to illiquidity of the system as a whole and the reliance on only one currency to provide liquidity.
- *Secondly, an international system should provide stability for global markets.* As indicated above the absence of stability during the last decade has caused severe and, as some have argued, even irreparable damage to the growth potential of a number of developing countries.
- *Thirdly, an international financial system should provide a large degree of policy autonomy for participating countries.* This is extremely important as countries not only have different factor endowments (capital, labour, and technology) but also different socio-economic systems. In order to find equilibrium between various policies to satisfy different economic and social demands, each country and society must be able to use the policy instruments and work with institutions which are best fitted to the country. This relates both to current conditionality as well as to difficulties countries have in applying monetary and fiscal instruments in order to achieve nationally determined economic and social goals.

The major question is, therefore, whether these required properties are compatible with each other. There is no automatism in that different sets of policies would automatically achieve all three requirements (Tinbergen's rule that the number of policy instruments must at least be equal to the number of policy targets remains as relevant as 50 years ago; see Tinbergen, 1970 [1952]). *A greater sense of policy coherence is therefore called for. We can distinguish policy coherence at, and between, three different levels in order to achieve an international financial system that is more cogent of concerns for employment and labour as discussed above,* namely: (i) policies in industrialized countries; (ii) the set of multilateral rules that has been developed since the Second World War; and (iii) policies in developing countries.

Policies in Industrialized Countries

Despite the success of emerging economies such as India and China, policies in industrialized countries and their outcomes circumscribe the economic and social policies of developing countries. Hence, even if the focus of concern is to increase the importance of employment and labour in the process of development, policies in industrialized countries need to be part of such considerations. For example, the WCSDG (2004) has indicated the following set of policies to be extremely relevant:

More coherent economic policies between the G3 (Europe, Japan and the United States): Uncoordinated fiscal, monetary and foreign exchange policies have created a highly volatile and instable system which is not geared towards growth and of which the spill-over effects for developing countries are serious.

There is almost unanimous agreement that the US economy cannot be the eternal engine of growth for the rest of world. Japan and Europe should give greater reflection to growth through better coordination of fiscal and monetary policies and their effects on employment and growth and not rely only on export growth. This would enable the United States to reduce its double deficit in a soft landing without serious repercussions for growth. Many argue that there are more structural impediments to boosting growth in the EU, but tight monetary and fiscal policies are not an answer to existing structural impediments. The effect of the deficit rules of the European Stability and Growth Pact (SGP) have thus been under much public debate. As Annett and Jaeger (2004) argue, an ideal fiscal rule would combine medium-term fiscal discipline with short-term fiscal flexibility. Assessing the SGP against this yardstick, they conclude that, generally speaking, "the pact proved conducive to fiscal discipline" and helped to bring the currency zone's structural deficit to less than half of that of the United States and less than one quarter of Japan's (Annett and Jaeger, 2004: 23f.). They also find that the GSP delivered a "high – but certainly not perfect – degree of fiscal flexibility during the downturn" (Annett and Jaeger, 2004: 24). Beetsma and Debrun (2005), who are, like Annett and Jaeger, IMF staff members, present an argument in favour of increasing the pact's procedural flexibility to improve welfare.

Allowing deviations from the 'letter of the rule' laid down in the SGP could minimize the additional negative consequences of demand side shocks during economic downturns. As the European Commission (2005: 157) lays out, demand disturbances have a potentially important impact on output and unemployment in the short- to medium-term. The Commission argues that "[t]his, together with the (consensual) finding that labour market outcomes, and the unemployment rate in particular, have high persistence, raises the important issue of macroeconomic policy stabilization" (European Commission, 2005: 161).

Apart from the specific consideration of growth and employment concerns in the Stability and Growth Pact, a greater concern for growth employment creation in general is called for from all three G3 areas. In combination with a more responsible attitude in the G3 countries for enhancing growth and reducing volatility for a better functioning international financial system, *the G3 has a third important responsibility, namely, in providing development assistance and in stimulating other sources of finance to enhance growth and development and so contribute to a more properly functioning international financial system* (see WCSDG, 2004: 103).

Rules of the International System

Such changes in G3 policy stances should be embedded in changes in multilateral rules and the functioning of international financial agencies. These are discussed in detail in the report of the WCSDG (2004: 88ff.), the principles of which are:

- Capital account liberalization should depend on a country's circumstance to maximize investment and to avoid volatility.
- In order to reduce volatility and contagion in emerging markets, the international system should have a greater resort to emergency financing.
- In order to make the international system more coherent, developing countries should be better integrated into it through:
  - greater involvement in the reform process of the international financial institutions (IFIs);

- o speeding up the process of reform;
- o removing barring caused by new codes to financial market access by developing countries;
- o providing a better system for debt reduction.

An important point in considering the rules of the international system and the policies applied by the IFIs is that the general context of the international financial landscape has changed considerably, this warrants different approaches from the decades of the 1980s and 1990s. One of the most salient points is that the continuous opening of trade, despite some recent setbacks, and the application of fairly drastic adjustment and stabilization policies in the 1980s and 1990s have dampened world wide inflationary tendencies (Akyüz, 2006). In some respect, inflation rates resemble those which were current during the Golden Age of development and growth. While a decade ago, many countries belonged to the group of countries with an inflation rate of 10 per cent or higher, today very few countries belong to this group.[13]

Moreover, there are also few signs that inflation will re-emerge. The current opening of trade and the international agreements concluded between different countries make it unlikely for inflation to soar. Hence, prices are fairly stable. But, as we discussed in the previous section, greater monetary discipline and price stability have not resulted in financial and macro-economic stability, while financial liberalization has led to increasingly sharp business cycles and sharp fluctuations in economic activity.

It is, therefore, a logical step to argue that the focus of the international system should shift from concerns on price instability to concerns for asset instability. International policies have therefore to shift. This would require firstly a greater surveillance by the IMF on asset instability and secondly, a review of its approach to capital account liberalization, leading to an internationally accepted system of managed capital account liberalization. There are signs that the international policy agenda is shifting in this direction. This is evident from the World Bank (2005b) report cited above, but also from within the IMF. The Fund's Independent Evaluation Unit now sees the role played by the IMF in the past as follows:

Throughout the 1990s, the IMF undoubtedly encouraged countries that wanted to move ahead with capital account liberalization, and even acted as a cheerleader when it wished to do so, especially before the East Asian crisis. [...] In multilateral surveillance, the IMF's analysis emphasized the benefits to developing countries of greater access to international capital flows, while paying comparatively less attention to the risks inherent in their volatility (IMF Independent Evaluation Office, 2005: 5).

The same evaluation report also describes a gradual shift in emphasis:

> More recently, however, the IMF has paid greater attention to various risk factors, including the linkage between industrial country policies and international capital flows as well as the more fundamental causes and implications of their boom-and-bust cycles. Still, the focus of the analysis remains on what emerging market countries should do to cope with the volatility of capital flows (for example, in the areas of macroeconomic and exchange rate policy, strengthened financial sectors, and greater transparency) (IMF Independent Evaluation Office, 2005: 3).

Policies in Developing Countries

Changes in rules and policies at the international level and the current low level of inflation would also allow developing countries to undertake more coherent policies in order to stimulate development, employment and growth. A potential effective set of policies would combine a flexible system of capital controls with a managed real effective exchange rate (Diwan, 2001; World Bank, 2005b; Charlton and Stiglitz, 2004). The flexible system of capital controls would allow for more coherent national policies to be undertaken and reduce volatility which has, as we documented earlier, serious consequences not only in terms of short-term welfare losses but also in terms of reduced growth potential.

The aim of a system of a managed real effective exchange rate is to keep the industry and the economy in general at high levels of capacity utilization and so aim for full employment, as we discuss in the following paragraphs. However, before discussing the employment effects of a system of managed real effective exchange rates, we first need to address whether a coherent approach of social and economic policies is above all possible. This relates to the so-called 'policy trilemma' or 'unholy trinity' of international economic policies (see Mundell, 1963; Cohen, 1993; Obstfeld, Shambaugh and Taylor, 2004) which states that national policy space is circumscribed by the impossibility to pursue the following three policies simultaneously:

- open capital account,
- fixed exchange rates,
- an independent monetary policy,

and that only two out of these three policies can be combined. For example, under a system of an open capital account and fixed exchange rates, countries can not pursue an independent monetary policy since interest rates are determined by world interest levels. Conversely, if countries need to undertake an independent monetary policy, they have either to revert to flexible exchange rates or opt for a closed capital account.

However, some more recent research argues that the *policy trilemma*, which has been guiding national and international policy makers for several decades, *can be relaxed by avoiding corner solutions*. This would imply to go beyond the traditional alternatives of fixed versus flexible exchange rates, or open versus closed capital accounts, and to adopt intermediate options in these three policy domains – like a capital account management through the selective application of capital controls, or a managed real exchange rate (see Bradford, 2004). For example, in the case of China, research from the IMF argues that making the quasi-fixed exchange rate more flexible would allow the country to pursue a more independent monetary policy. The same paper also argues for a cautious approach to capital account liberalization, given institutional weaknesses of China's financial system (see Prasad, Rumbaugh and Wang, 2005). The argument could be extended to many other developing countries. Rather than abandoning capital controls altogether, they should therefore remain a policy tool that can be used selectively.

Although capital controls have, much like any other policy instrument, not always been fully effective in reaching their stated objectives (see Ariyoshi and others, 2000), they have contributed to regaining greater policy autonomy in several cases. For example, controls imposed on inflows have helped to reduce their level and to change the composition of inflows towards longer maturities in Chile, hence increasing the autonomy of monetary policy (Gallego, Hernández and Schmidt-Hebbel, 1999; see also de Gregorio, Edwards and Valdés, 2000). An important side-effect is that the level of international reserves can be reduced when the amount of short-term liabilities falls, lowering the opportunity cost of reserve holdings. An important lesson is that controls need to have comprehensive coverage and be forcefully implemented to be effective (Ariyoshi and others, 2000: 17). The more controversial issue is controls on outflows, but Edison and Reinhart (2001) argue that such controls have enabled Malaysia to stabilize exchange rates and interest rates during the East Asian crisis and to gain more policy autonomy. Kaplan and Rodrik (2001) conclude that the Malaysian approach has led to a faster economic recovery and smaller declines in real wages and employment than IMF policies would have.[14] More generally, if applied soundly, a *managed capital account* can help to avoid financial crises or contain their impact, and hence contribute to a stable investment climate, sustained growth and employment creation.

How could a system of a *managed real exchange rate*, the second element mentioned earlier, affect employment? Rodrik (2003) and Frenkel (2004) provide three channels. Active management of the real exchange rate:

- will allow for higher capacity utilization in times of unemployment, if it is applied in combination with the appropriate mix of macroeconomic and fiscal policies;
- will stimulate output growth and hence employment, if it is combined with appropriate industrial policies, as the experience in various Asian countries has shown (Amsden, 2001);
- will affect the sectoral composition of exports towards more labour intensive goods, and hence increase the employment elasticity of the economy, as a whole, compared to another system.[15]

Employing a policy mix with intermediate options such as a managed capital account and a managed real exchange rate requires more fine-tuning and coherence in policies rather than relying on rule-of-thumb policy interventions. While this can help to avoid corner solutions, it necessitates national institutions with explicit mandates and capabilities to achieve this. Another possible, supplementary element to relax the policy trilemma would be to include one or two additional policy instruments to complement the fiscal and monetary tools (see also Tinbergen, 1970 [1952]: 40f.). Bradford (2004) suggests, for example, social pacts or coordinated wage bargaining to hold down inflation and so to 'free up' other policies to aim at growth and employment creation. Also, a greater concern for inequity and a reduction of national inequalities could contribute to reducing inflationary pressure and could be added either as part of a social pact or as a stand-alone policy instrument (see van der Hoeven and Saget, 2004). This, too, requires institutional capability.

Building Institutions for Coherent Policies

The conclusion of these deliberations is that a coherent approach in national and international financial policies to stimulate employment growth is well possible, but requires different rules, better fine tuning of different components of national policies, and appropriate institutions. For national institutions to function well, one can point to two distinct national configurations: Theoretically, one configuration would be a repressive state with a strong and autonomous bureaucracy that is able to coordinate a well functioning and coherent set of policies. The other would be a national system of consensus and willingness for policy dialogue that can design a coherent set of policies that are acceptable to citizens, and can therefore be implemented without resort to authoritarian methods.

The authoritarian path is neither desirable nor viable in the long run; it would often mean the violation of basic human rights (such as freedom of speech and association), and would not be internationally accepted either (see the report of the Commission on Human Security, 2003). Hence, the configuration of an open and consensus prone society is the only feasible option in the long run. Building institutions that formulate policies in a consensus-driven and democratic way is neither a straightforward nor a simple task. But then, as the widespread failure of implementing structural adjustment policies has shown, neither are orthodox policy packages. One obstacle is that reaching consensus is particularly difficult in unequal societies. Hence, by giving more attention to distributional issues, policy can reduce inequality and lay the ground to the better implementation of economic policies and to greater policy coherence.

Labour market institutions can play an important role in achieving this objective. Van der Hoeven and Saget (2004) argue for three efficiency criteria to evaluate the efficiency of labour market policies, namely allocative efficiency (matching supply and demand to reduce unemployment), dynamic efficiency (quality of the future labour force) and equity efficiency (containing inequalities). Many neoclassical economists evaluate labour market systems only on the basis of allocative efficiency, but Freeman (2000) observes in evaluating labour market institutions in more advanced countries, that the first order result of labour market institutions is distributional and the second order result is economic efficiency. Therefore, societies do not have to decide, on economic efficiency grounds, what type of labour market system to adopt, and can let distributional considerations play an important role in designing an appropriate labour market system. Dagdeviren, van der Hoeven and Weeks (2002) demonstrate that these need not be a trade-off between redistribution and growth, and that national socio-economic structures should determine the proper mix of growth and redistributive policies. This point was recently underscored by the United Nations' Report on the World Social Situation (United Nations, 2005).

Notes

* The authors would like to thank for comments received from colleagues around the ILO and during seminars and discussions held in Washington, D.C. (Carnegie Endowment, April 2005), Geneva (Policy Coherence Initiative, December 2005), Brussels (European Commission, December 2005), Johannesburg (ILO sub-regional seminar, December 2005), St. Petersburg (Seventh Annual Global Development Conference, January 2006), The Hague (Institute of Social Studies, January 2006), Geneva (XXII G24 Technical Group Meeting, March 2006) and New York (DESA Development Forum on Productive Employment and Decent Work, May 2006). All errors are the authors'. A longer version of this chapter is also published as Policy Integration Working Paper No. 75 by the ILO, Geneva.

48 • Towards Full and Decent Employment

1   Although labour migration has gained importance, the world's approximately 86.3 million
    migrant workers accounted for only 3.1 per cent of the economically active population
    in 2000 (based on ILO 2004a, p. 7, and the ILO database Laborsta, EAPEP, Version 5
    [International Labour Office, Geneva]).
2   UNCTAD data show that the FDI boom was in part driven by mergers and acquisitions:
    From 1998 to 2001, total cross-border M&A sales were equal to more than 70 per cent
    of total FDI outward flows, up from less than 50 percent between 1992 and 1994. See
    UNCTAD (2004b: Annex Table B.7) and UNCTAD (2004a).
3   The respective figures are 21.7 per cent of GDP (1990s), 22.5 per cent of GDP (1980s)
    and 23.8 per cent of GDP (1970s). See World Bank (2005a); based series 'Gross fixed
    capital formation (% of GDP)'.
4   Official development assistance and official aid (ODA/OA) to all low- and middle-
    income countries actually declined through most of the 1990s, falling from 65.5 billion
    current US$ in 1991 to a low of 52.3 billion US$ in 1997. The recovery thereafter brought
    it back to 65.3 billion US$ in 2002 and to 76.2 billion US$ in 2003. Despite this nominal
    increase, ODA/OA was about equal to its 1991 level in real terms in 2003. See World
    Bank (2005a); based on series 'Official development assistance and official aid (current
    US$)'.
5   The latter is discussed in a recent ILO paper by Ajit Ghose (2004) and in two recent
    documents prepared for the ILO's governing Body (ILO 2002 and 2004b). Ghose
    concludes that the 'available empirical evidence in fact suggests that capital account
    liberalisation is neither necessary nor sufficient for inducing FDI inflows.' (Ghose 2004:
    23f.).
6   Prasad and others (2004) use another term, namely financial globalization; this is close to
    what others and this chapter call financial openness.
7   Congruent with the literature, we henceforth use 'capital account liberalization' as
    shorthand for the liberalization of the capital and financial account (while acknowledging
    that, strictly speaking, the relaxation of rules that refer to direct investment and portfolio
    flows should be called 'financial account liberalization'; for the standard presentation of
    the Balance of Payments, see IMF, 2004).
8   It should be noted that some countries have become more financially integrated, without
    or with little financial liberalization (e.g. China), while other countries have financially
    liberalized but have not become more financially integrated – either because of geopolitical
    circumstances, or because they have been ignored by the international financial markets
    (various African countries would fall into this category). See the discussion below.
9   By contrast, foreign reserves have remained at under 5 per cent of GDP in industrialized
    countries (Rodrik 2006: 15).
10 See World Bank (2005a); based on series 'GDP per capita (constant 2000 US$)'.
11 These findings confirm those by Diwan (2001). He reports, based on a large sample of
    countries, an average drop in the labour share of GDP per crisis of 5.0 percentage points,
    and a modest catch-up thereafter. In the three years after the crisis, labour shares were still
    2.6 percentage points below their pre-crisis average (Diwan 2001: 6). Given the fact that
    most countries have undergone more than one crisis, the cumulative drop in the wage
    share over the last 30 years is estimated at 4.1 per cent of GDP, and is especially large
    for Latin America where the figure reached 6.7 per cent of GDP over the period 1970s–
    1990s. Thus, since many countries have undergone more than one crisis, the decline of
    the wage share during the crisis and the partial recovery, after the crisis has led to a
    secular decline in the wage share.

[12] The weak bargaining position of labour under open capital accounts is also a causal mechanism explored by Lee and Jayadev (2005). They find that financial openness exerts a downward pressure on the labour share both in developed and developing countries for the period from 1973–1995. The effect is independent of the negative impact of financial crises.

[13] In 2001 and 2002, roughly 80 per cent of the ca. 180 countries with available data had inflation rates below 10 per cent, compared to less than 50 per cent of all countries during most of the mid- to late 1970s and early 1980s, and between 50 and 60 per cent of all countries during the first half of the 1990s (based on 123 to 180 countries with available data). Today, high inflation is thus a problem for only a relatively small number of countries, and conditions are not too dissimilar from the 1960s. Back then, 85 to 90 percent of the ca. 100 to 120 countries with available data had inflation rates below 10 per cent (see World Bank, 2005a: WDI 2005 on CD-Rom).

[14] For a detailed review of the Malaysian experience, see Jomo (2005). For a comprehensive discussion of the management of capital flows in developing countries and policy conclusions, see UNCTAD (2003).

[15] This is a comparative static argument comparing two equilibria under different policy regimes. This is independent of a secular decline of employment elasticity, which various observers have been discussing.

DATA SOURCES

ILO (2005). *Key Indicators of the Labour Market.* 4th edition. International Labour Office, Geneva.

ILO (2006). ILO database Laborsta, EAPEP, Version 5. International Labour Office, Geneva.

IMF (2004). *Balance of Payments Statistics Yearbook.* International Monetary Fund, Washington, DC.

UNCTAD (2004a). *Handbook of Statistics 2004.* United Nations Conference on Trade and Development, Geneva and New York. CD-Rom.

UNCTAD (2004b). *World Investment Report 2004.* United Nations Conference on Trade and Development, Geneva and New York.

World Bank (2005a). *World Development Indicators 2005.* World Bank, Washington, DC. CD-Rom.

World Bank (2005b). *Global Development Finance 2005.* World Bank, Washington, DC. Online database.

REFERENCES

Adelman, Irma (2000). Editor's introduction (Special section: Redrafting the architecture of the global financial system). *World Development* 28 (6): 1053–1060.

Akyüz, Yilmaz (2006). Issues in macro-economic and financial policies, stability and growth. Policy Integration Department working paper no. 73, International Labour Office, Geneva.

Amsden, Alice H. (2001). *The Rise of the Rest: Challenges to the West from the Late-Industrializing Economies.* Oxford University Press, Oxford.

Amsden, Alice, and Rolph van der Hoeven (1996). Manufacturing output, employment and real wages in the 1980s: Labour's loss until century's end. *Journal of Development Studies* 32 (4): 506–530.

Annett, Anthony, and Albert Jaeger (2004). Europe's quest for fiscal discipline. *Finance & Development*, June: 22–25.

Ariyoshi, Akira, Karl Friedrich Habermeier, Bernard Laurens, Inci Ötker, Jorge Iván Canales Kriljenko, Andrei Kirilenko (2000). Capital controls: Country experiences with their use and liberalization. IMF occasional paper no. 190, International Monetary Fund, Washington, DC.

Baker, Dean, and Karl Walentin (2001). Money for nothing: The increasing cost of foreign reserve holdings to developing nations. CEPR policy paper, November 13, Center for Economic and Policy Research, Washington, DC.

Beetsma, Roel M.W.J., and Xavier Debrun (2005). Implementing the stability and growth pact: Enforcement and procedural flexibility. IMF working paper no. 05/59, International Monetary Fund, Washington, DC.

Bradford, Colin I. Jr. (2004). Prioritizing economic growth: Enhancing macroeconomic policy choice. Paper presented at the XIX G24 Technical Group Meeting, Sept. 27–28, Intergovernmental Group of Twenty-Four, Washington, DC.

Capario, Gerard, and Daniela Klingebiel (2003). Episodes of systemic and borderline financial crises. Processed, World Bank, Washington, DC.

Cerra, Valerie, and Sweata Chaman Saxena (2005). Growth dynamics: The myth of economic recovery. IMF working paper no. 05/147, International Monetary Fund, Washington, DC.

Charlton, Andrew, and Joseph E. Stiglitz (2004). A development round of trade negotiations? In François Bourguignon and Boris Pleskovic (eds). *Proceedings from the Annual Bank Conference on Development Economics, 2004.* World Bank, Washington, DC.

Cohen, Benjamin J. (1993). The triad and the unholy trinity: Lessons for the Pacific region. In Richard Higgott, Richard Leaver, and John Ravenhill (eds). *Pacific Economic Relations in the 1990s.* Allen and Unwin, London: 133–158.

Collins, Susan M. (2005). Comments on *Financial Globalization, Growth and Volatility in Developing Countries* by Eswar Prasad, Kenneth Rogoff, Shang-Jin Wei, and M. Ayhan Kose. Processed, National Bureau of Economic Research, Cambridge, MA.

Commission on Human Security (2003). *Human Security Now: Protecting and Empowering People.* United Nations, New York.

Dagdeviren, Hulya, Rolph van der Hoeven, and John Weeks (2002). Poverty reduction with growth and redistribution. *Development and Change* 33 (3): 383–413.

de Gregorio, José, Sebastian Edwards, and Rodrigo O. Valdés (2000). Controls on capital inflows: Do they work? *Journal of Development Economics* 63 (1): 59–83.

Diwan, Ishac (1999). Labor shares and financial crises. Processed, World Bank, Washington, DC.

Diwan, Ishac (2001). Debt as sweat: Labour, financial crisis, and the globalization of capital. Draft as of July 2001. Processed, World Bank, Washington, DC.

Easterly, William, Roumeen Islam, and Joseph Stiglitz (2001). Shaken and stirred: Volatility and macroeconomic paradigms for rich and poor countries. In Boris Preskovic and Nicholas Stern (eds). *Annual Bank Conference on Development Economics 2000.* World Bank, Washington, DC: 191–212.

Edison, Hali, and Carmen M. Reinhart (2001). Stopping hot money. *Journal of Development Economics* 66: 533–553.

Edison, Hali J., Michael W. Klein, Luca Antonio Ricci, and Torsten Sløk (2004). Capital account liberalization and economic performance: Survey and synthesis. *IMF Staff Papers* 51 (2): 220–256.

European Commission (2005). *Employment in Europe 2005*. European Commission, Brussels.

Feldstein, Martin (1999). A Self Help Guide for Emerging Markets. *Foreign Affairs*, March-April.

Freeman, Richard B. (2000). Single peaked vs. diversified capitalism: The relation between economic institutions and outcomes. NBER working paper no. 7556, National Bureau of Economic Research, Cambridge, MA.

Freeman, Richard B. (2003). Responding to economic crisis in a post-Washington Consensus world: The role of labor. Paper presented at the ILO Meeting on Cooperation for Argentina, January 13-17, revised May 2003. Processed, International Labour Office, Buenos Aires.

Frenkel, Roberto (2004). Real exchange rate and employment in Argentina, Brazil, Chile and Mexico. Paper presented at the XIX G24 Technical Group Meeting, Sept. 27-28, Intergovernmental Group of Twenty-Four, Washington, DC.

Gallego, Francisco, Leonardo Hernández, and Klaus Schmidt-Hebbel (1999). Capital controls in Chile: Effective? Efficient? Central Bank of Chile working paper no. 59, Central Bank of Chile, Santiago de Chile.

Ghose, Ajit K. (2004). Capital flows and investment in developing countries. Employment strategy paper no. 2004/11, International Labour Office, Geneva.

Gilbert, Christopher L., Gregor Irwin, and David Vines (2001). Capital account convertibility, poor developing countries, and international financial architecture. *Development Policy Review* 19 (1): 121–141.

Harrison, Anne (2002). Has globalization eroded labor's share? Some cross country evidence. Processed, National Bureau of Economic Research, Cambridge, MA.

Hutchison, Michael M., and Ilan Noy (2006). Sudden stops and the Mexican wave: Currency crises, capital flow reversals and output loss in emerging markets. *Journal of Development Economics*, 79 (1): 225–248.

ILO (2002). Investment in the global economy and decent work. Governing body paper GB 285/WPSDG /2, International Labour Office, Geneva.

ILO (2004a). Towards a fair deal for migrant workers. International Labour Conference, 92nd Session 2004, Report VI, International Labour Office, Geneva.

ILO (2004b). Trade, foreign investment and productive employment in developing countries. Governing body paper GB 291/ESP/2, International Labour Office, Geneva.

IMF (1993). *Balance of Payments Manual*. 5th edition. International Monetary Fund, Washington, DC.

IMF Independent Evaluation Office (2005). *The IMF's Approach to Capital Account Liberalization*. International Monetary Fund, Washington, DC.

Jomo, K. S. (2005). Malaysia's September 1998 controls: Background, context, impacts, comparisons, implications, lessons. G-24 discussion paper series no. 36, United Nations, Geneva.

Kaminsky, Graciela L., Carmen Reinhart, and Carlos Végh (2004). When it rains, it pours: Procyclical capital flows and macro economic policies. NBER working paper no. 10780, National Bureau of Economic Research, Cambridge, MA.

Kaplan, Ethan, and Dani Rodrik (2001). Did the Malaysian capital controls work? NBER working paper no. 8142, National Bureau of Economic Research, Cambridge, MA.

Kose, M. Ayhan, Eswar Prasad, and Marco Terrones (2003). Financial integration and macroeconomic volatility. *IMF Staff Papers* 50: 119–142.

Lee, Eddy (1998). *The Asian Financial Crisis. The Challenge for Social Policy*. International Labour Office, Geneva.

Lee, Kang-kook, and Arjun Jayadev (2005). Capital account liberalization, growth and the labor share of income: Reviewing and extending the cross-country evidence. In Gerald Epstein (ed.). *Capital Flight and Capital Controls in Developing Countries*. Edward Elgar, Cheltenham: 15–57.

Levchenko, Andrei A. (2005). Financial liberalization and consumption volatility in developing countries. *IMF Staff Papers* 52 (2): 237–259.

Mundell, R.A. (1963). Capital mobility and stabilization policy under fixed and flexible exchange rates. *Canadian Journal of Economics and Political Science* 29 (4): 475–485.

Obstfeld, Maurice, Jay C. Shambaugh, and Alan M. Taylor (2004). The trilemma in history: Tradeoffs among exchange rates, monetary policies, and capital mobility. NBER working paper no. 10396, National Bureau of Economic Research, Cambridge, MA.

Prasad, Eswar, Kenneth Rogoff, Wei Shang-Jin, and M. Ayhan Kose (2003). Effects of financial globalization on developing countries: Some empirical evidence. Processed, International Monetary Fund, Washington, DC.

Prasad, Eswar, Kenneth Rogoff, Wei Shang-Jin, and M. Ayhan Kose (2004). Financial globalization, growth and volatility in developing countries. NBER working paper no. 10942, National Bureau of Economic Research, Cambridge, MA.

Prasad, Eswar, Thomas Rumbaugh, and Wang Qing (2005) Putting the cart before the horse? Capital account liberalization and exchange rate flexibility in China. IMF policy discussion paper no. 05/1, International Monetary Fund, Washington, DC.

Prasad, Eswar, and Wei Shang-Jin (2005). The Chinese approach to capital inflows: Patterns and possible explanations. IMF working paper no. 05/79, International Monetary Fund, Washington, DC.

Rodrik, Dani (1998). Who needs capital-account convertibility? *Princeton Essays in International Finance* 207: 55–65.

Rodrik, Dani (2003). Growth strategies. NBER working paper no. 10050, National Bureau of Economic Research, Cambridge, MA.

Rodrik, Dani (2006). The social cost of foreign exchange reserves. NBER working paper no. 11952, National Bureau of Economic Research, Cambridge, MA.

Singh, A. (2003). Capital account liberalization, free long-term capital flows, financial crisis and development. *Eastern Economic Journal* 29 (2): 191–216.

Stiglitz, J. (2000). Capital market liberalization, economic growth, and instability. *World Development* 28 (6): 1075–1086.

Tinbergen, J. (1970). *On the Theory of Economic Policy*. [First edition, 1952] North-Holland, Amsterdam.

Tokman, Víctor E. (2003). Towards an integrated vision for dealing with instability and risk. *CEPAL Review* 81: 79–98.

Tornell, Aaron, Frank Westermann, and Lorenza Martínez (2003). Liberalization, growth, and financial crises: Lessons from Mexico and the developing world. *Brookings Papers on Economic Activity* 2: 1–112.

UNCTAD (2001). *Trade and Development Report 2001*. United Nations Conference on Trade and Development, Geneva.

UNCTAD (2003). *Management of Capital Flows: Comparative Experiences and Implications for Africa*. United Nations Conference on Trade and Development, Geneva.

United Nations (2005). *Report on the World Social Situation 2005: The Inequality Predicament*. United Nations, New York.

van der Hoeven, Rolph, and Catherine Saget (2004). Labour market institutions and income inequality: What are the new insights after the Washington Consensus? In Giovanni Andrea Cornia (ed.), *Inequality, Growth, and Poverty in an Era of Liberalization and Globalization*. WIDER Studies in Development Economics, Oxford University Press, Oxford: 197–220.

van der Hoeven, Rolph and Malte Lübker (2006). Financial Openness and Employment: The Need for Coherent International and National Policies. Policy Integration Working paper no. 75, International Labour Office, Geneva.

World Bank (2005a). *Global Economic Prospects 2006: Economic Implications of Remittances and Migration*. World Bank, Washington, DC.

World Bank (2005b). *Economic Growth in the 1990s. Learning from a Decade of Economic Reform*. World Bank, Washington, DC.

WCSDG (2004). *A Fair Globalization: Creating Opportunities for All*. World Commission on the Social Dimension of Globalization, International Labour Office, Geneva.

3
Technology and Employment in an Open Underdeveloped Economy

PRABHAT PATNAIK

Nicholas Kaldor, the Cambridge economist, used the term 'stylized facts' to refer to certain factual generalizations which can be made in any particular context, and which are broadly correct if we ignore the minutiae. Let me accordingly begin with certain 'stylized facts' about our current context. First, China and India have been witnessing rates of growth of GDP, as conventionally defined, which are much higher than what prevail either in the first world or in the rest of the third world. Secondly, this high growth phase in both these economies has been associated with 'opening up' to international trade. Thirdly, in both these economies, there has been, precisely during this period, a remarkable increase in income inequalities. And fourthly, in the case of both countries, the rate of employment growth has been much lower in absolute terms in this phase of high output growth than was the case when the rate of output growth was lower. In the case of China, this is partly explained by the fact that in the pre-'reform' period she avoided having any open unemployment, in keeping with the prevailing practice in socialist economies; so, comparisons between pre- and post-reform China in this respect are beset with conceptual difficulties. Nonetheless, what is still striking about post-reform China is that extraordinarily high rates of output growth sustained over a long period of time have still not led to the exhaustion of her labour reserves, or even to any noticeable tightening of the labour market. The absence of any significant impact of growth on employment therefore appears to be a phenomenon common to both these economies.

Normally, each of these 'stylized facts' is seen separately, as being dissociated from the others. Indeed it is this separation which underlies such ideas as 'the trickle down effect', 'liberalization with a human face', and 'we-need-still-higher-growth-rates-to-overcome-unemployment'. I propose to argue instead that these 'stylized facts' are inter-related, that they are causally interlinked, *and therefore constitute one integrated totality.* I shall present this argument analytically, that is, in terms of certain inherent tendencies of an open underdeveloped economy with vast labour reserves. I shall first focus on a *capitalist* underdeveloped economy; the possible implications of the difference between *socialist* and *capitalist* third world economies will be taken up subsequently.

DETERMINANTS OF LABOUR DEMAND GROWTH

Technological progress, in the sense of the introduction of new processes and new products, occurs initially in the metropolitan capitalist countries and is then transmitted to the third world. Since the tastes and preferences of the third world 'elite' are strongly influenced by those in the metropolis, new products get adopted fairly soon in the third world economies, once the barriers to their entry into such economies are removed. New products necessarily come with new processes; but even when new processes are introduced for the production of some existing products, the outcome of a new process is rarely identical with the pre-existing product, because of which the distinction between new processes and new products is, to an extent, arbitrary. But even if we can think of a *pure* process innovation, it too typically gets introduced first in the metropolitan capitalist countries; if the third world countries are open to international trade and are not insulated from foreign competition, then the new process soon makes an appearance in the third world economies as well. *Thus technological progress, no matter of what sort, occurring in the metropolis, makes its way to open third world economies after a fairly short time lag.*

Technological progress in the metropolis, however, takes the form predominantly of an increase in labour productivity, whether at a given capital-output ratio as claimed by neo-classical growth theory or at a rising capital-output ratio as suggested by Marx. The fact of its being transmitted rapidly to the third world entails a correspondingly rapid increase in labour productivity within the 'modern sector' of open third world economies.

There is also an additional factor at work. The so-called 'modern sector' which experiences rates of labour productivity growth comparable to the metropolis, also increases over time its relative weight within the third world economies, if the share of the 'elite' in total income increases. To be sure, even if this share remains constant, traditional technology keeps getting replaced over time, i.e. the 'modern' sector's weight increases over time, but this process gets a boost if the share of 'elite' income in total increases.

All this has two important implications. First, once an underdeveloped economy has undertaken 'trade liberalization', it ceases to have any control over the rate of labour productivity growth within its frontiers. The rate of growth of labour productivity appears, for all practical purposes, as an exogenously determined variable in open underdeveloped economies. Secondly, the rate of growth of labour productivity is likely to be higher after the 'opening up' of such economies than before, for the simple reason that a *dirigiste* economy takes steps to defend employment in traditional activities, by putting curbs on technological and structural change, while the rolling back of *dirigisme*, which is what 'opening up' entails, makes any such defence of employment impossible. The rate of growth of labour productivity therefore increases noticeably after trade liberalization.

Now, let us see what happens to the growth rates of GDP in these economies. The GDP is the sum of three components, namely, private expenditure on consumption and investment, government expenditure, and the current account surplus on balance of payments[1], the determinants of its growth can be analyzed by looking at how these expenditure items behave. Let us assume, to start with, that income distribution within the economy is given, and that the consumption-GDP ratio, the tax-GDP ratio, and the import-GDP ratio remain constant over time in the open underdeveloped economy (they may be different from what they were during the *dirigiste* phase, but that does not concern us here) and that the government is constrained to maintain the ratio of its fiscal deficit to GDP at a low and constant level, in keeping with the caprices of globalized finance. Since the magnitude of private investment is itself determined by the growth of GDP, it follows that the *independent variable* which determines the growth rate of GDP is the growth rate of exports[2].

Now, suppose there were only two economies in the world, the 'metropolis' and the 'third world'. Then the rate of growth of exports from the latter would depend essentially upon the rate of growth of demand from the former. And if the commodities produced by the two were distinct, then the third world's export growth would depend upon the growth rate of the metropolis' demand *for those particular commodities* which are produced by it, and this demand would not be particularly responsive to the prices of these commodities. In fact however there is an activity overlap between the two worlds, so that relative competitiveness does matter for the third world's export growth.

There are however strict limits to the diffusion of activities from the metropolis: even if at any point of time there is an activity overlap, (the *particular* activities where there is an overlap may keep shifting over time as technological change occurs but an old 'overlap fringe' will be replaced by a new 'overlap fringe'), the activities open to the third world are always limited.

Within the 'overlap fringe' the market share of the third world will depend upon its competitiveness, a possible measure of which is the relative dollar wage per efficiency unit of labour. But since the 'fringe' itself is limited, for any given rate of growth of world trade, the third world's share in total world trade will flatten out beyond a point even as its relative dollar wage per efficiency unit of labour keeps declining. It follows then that the rate of growth of exports from the third world would be the same as the rate of growth of world trade for any *given* relative dollar wage per efficiency unit of labour. If the latter keeps declining, it would exceed the rate of growth of world trade by a small margin transitionally, but will eventually approximate the rate of growth of world trade. Thus, for any given configuration of real wage and labour productivity in the metropolis and the third world, and any given rate of growth of world trade, there is a certain rate of growth of its exports, and hence a certain rate of GDP growth.

So far, we have talked of the third world as if it consisted of a single entity. In fact it consists of several economies which compete fiercely against one another for capturing the metropolis' market. While such competition will tend to equalize the relative dollar wage per efficiency unit of labour across these economies (the mechanism for such equalization would be exchange rate depreciations in the less competitive economies, accompanied by non-compensation of workers for real wage loss), differences will persist in practice, allowing some third world economies to do better than the others. But the fact of some countries thus stealing a march over other similarly-placed countries can arise only if the latter are acquiescent in accommodating the exports from the former. Thus, the rate of growth of exports from an open underdeveloped economy depends upon the rate of growth of world trade and the extent to which its exports are accommodated by others, over neither of which it has any control.

It follows then that even the rate of GDP growth in an open underdeveloped economy is largely determined by factors upon which it has little control, and hence, can be taken as being exogenously determined. This does not mean that the country can do nothing to boost its growth rate, but the degree to which its efforts bear fruit is dependent on factors outside its control.

The rate of growth of labour demand is merely the difference between the rate of growth of GDP and the rate of growth of labour productivity. If at any given level of income distribution both these elements are determined by factors over which the country itself has little control, then the rate of growth of labour demand too becomes an exogenously determined variable. If the rate of growth of labour demand so determined falls short of the rate of growth of the work-force, then the unemployment rate in the economy will increase; and in the opposite case, it will decline. But the basic point is this: *in an open underdeveloped economy, the unemployment situation evolves spontaneously; it is outside any control by the State.* This fact has important implications.

Poverty Trap

If the exogenously determined rate of growth of labour demand (for any particular income distribution) equals or falls short of the rate of growth of the work force, then the labour reserves in the economy, instead of getting depleted, grow at least at the same rate as the work-force; or putting it differently, the ratio of the reserve army of labour to the active army does not fall. The real wages therefore remain more or less pegged to the subsistence level, defined not as a biologically-determined level, but as the level that prevails by convention. Notwithstanding the high rate of GDP growth and the high rate of growth of labour productivity, the bulk of the working population in such a case remains tied to the subsistence level. The working population gets squeezed in two ways: through declining job opportunities and through stagnant real wages at the subsistence level.

We thus have a peculiar 'trap' here. If the exogenously determined rate of growth of labour demand (at the base income distribution) exceeds a certain threshold level (given by the rate of growth of the work-force), then the reserve army shrinks relative to the active army and real wages increase, improving the condition of the workers through both these avenues. If on the other hand this exogenously determined rate of growth of labour demand falls below the threshold rate, then the relative size of the reserve army increases and real wages remain tied to the subsistence level. The working population loses on both counts and the relative magnitude of absolute poverty increases over time.

Now, it may be thought that if real wages remain constant while labour productivity keeps increasing, then the unit labour cost of the economy would be falling, which, by making it more competitive internationally, would raise its rate of growth of exports and hence its rate of GDP growth. This would raise the rate of growth of labour demand in this economy and thereby get it out of the 'trap' mentioned earlier.

But this argument is untenable. If other open underdeveloped economies are similarly placed, then the unit labour costs in all of them would be declining similarly over time. The question of any one of them stealing a march over the others and experiencing a higher rate of growth of exports at the expense of the others does not therefore arise. As for declining unit labour costs in all of them leading to a higher rate of growth of exports for all of them at the expense of producers in the metropolis, we have already seen that the effect of declining relative dollar wage per efficiency unit of labour is a limited one.

The 'trap' is thus a real trap; its effectiveness arises precisely because it applies to *every* open underdeveloped economy with labour reserves. No single third world economy can hope to get out of it as long as others are stuck in it, since competition from the others will always pull it down. The only hope for each of them is if all of them experience such high rates of growth of labour demand that their labour reserves begin to get depleted. But the rate of growth of the world economy does not permit this.

The fact that it does not is not a mere accident. The period of liberalization is marked by the hegemony of international finance capital, which alters the nature of the capitalist State, prevents the adoption of Keynesian demand management policies in every capitalist economy, except the leading one, and imposes policies of deflation of expenditure, especially of State expenditure, everywhere. It thereby also lowers the rate of growth of the world economy. Keynes, in his *General Theory*, had asked for the 'euthanasia of the rentier' as a means of ensuring high levels of activity and employment under capitalism. But the rise to hegemony of international finance capital, as a result of the immanent tendencies of capitalism itself, has brought about the 'euthanasia of Keynesianism', because of which the levels of activity, employment and growth in the capitalist world have come down compared to the period of the so-called 'Golden Age of capitalism' when Keynesian policies were in vogue. The possibility of the depletion of third world labour reserves under the 'neo-liberal' regime therefore is non-existent in this context; on the other hand however it is only this context which imposes the 'neo-liberal' regime on the third world. *Thus the very conditions that force an 'opening up' of third world economies also prevent a using up of their labour reserves.*

REALIZATION OF THE GROWING SURPLUS

If real wages remain unchanged while labour productivity increases over time, then the surplus produced per worker within the third world economy keeps increasing, and so does the surplus as a proportion of GDP. If State expenditure as a proportion of GDP does not increase (in fact neo-liberal regimes bring about a *reduction* in State expenditure as a proportion of GDP in deference to the caprices of finance capital), then there must either be an increase in the GDP of the share of capitalists' consumption, private investment and net foreign lending taken together, or a realization crisis. Such a crisis, even if we ignore its second-order effects, must entail a reduction in capacity utilization and *a further fall in the rate of growth of labour demand* (both of which will only be compounded by the second-order effects causing a downswing).

Now, net lending abroad, though sizeable in the case of China, cannot be considered a significant avenue for the absorption of the surplus. And even though the Indian economy has been a demand-constrained system with very low rates of growth of labour demand, the fact that the GDP growth rates, as conventionally measured, have been quite high, suggests the absence of any acute realization crisis. (The absence of a realization problem is even more true of China). This raises the familiar question asked by Baran and Sweezy (1966): how has the increasing surplus been realized? In China's case, the answer may lie partly in the high rates of investment and these have been possible because her economy is not capitalist. But this answer cannot hold for the Indian economy. Not only has the investment ratio refused stubbornly to register any increase, but it has even declined relative to what it was on the eve of liberalization. Besides, increasing investment as a means of absorbing a rising share of surplus in output is an altogether unrealistic proposition under capitalism, even though this had been the scenario visualized by the Russian economist Tugan-Baranovsky[3].

He had claimed, in conformity with the views of J. B. Say and David Ricardo, that capitalism could never be afflicted by any generalized over-production, since all surplus in the hands of the capitalists in excess of what they consumed was invested. To the argument that such investment would only worsen the problem in the next period, since there would be an even larger amount of surplus, not just in absolute terms, but even relative to GDP, seeking investment, Tugan-Baranovsky's answer was that this too would be invested. This view, which amounted to postulating 'production for production's sake', stretched to an extreme limit, where it became a caricature, of a genuine insight into capitalism, namely that this system is not concerned with consumption as such. But, this lack of concern *for consumption as such* should not be confused with a lack of concern on the part of capitalists with *demand prospects altogether* in deciding on their investment plans. Tugan-Baranovsky, however, perpetrated this confusion, as Ricardo had done earlier.

In arguing that the introduction of machinery, though harmful for employment in the short run, gave rise to a higher employment profile in the long run, Ricardo had assumed that, with real wages fixed at the subsistence level, the increase in labour productivity caused by the introduction of machinery would raise the share of profits and *hence the share of savings and investment in the economy's output*. This, under unchanged technology (if we considered only a one-shot introduction of machinery), would raise the growth rate of output and hence the growth rate of employment[4]. The time-profile of employment with machinery, would eventually therefore overtake the time-profile of employment without machinery. The fallacy of his argument, as with Tugan-Baranovsky, lay in the assumption that all unconsumed surplus value was automatically invested without any concern for prospective demand.

What has prevented a realization crisis of a serious magnitude in open underdeveloped economies like India is the increase, not so much in the direct consumption of the capitalists, but in the consumption of a whole mass of persons, which includes those engaged in the business of circulation of commodities and of transactions involving finance; those engaged in providing personal services to the capitalists, skilled workers and to other persons in the service sector; those engaged in providing 'professional' services to these groups; the various 'hangers on' of capitalists, of MNCs and of other representatives of metropolitan capital, and a whole new army of speculators, fixers, wheeler-dealers, middlemen and 'parasites'. These groups constitute the modern version of Struve's 'third persons'[5] and of Adam Smith's 'unproductive labourers'. Their economic weight increases tremendously with the shift from *dirigisme* to a 'neo-liberal' regime.

While their incomes relative to GDP increase greatly, their numbers, relative to the work-force, do not increase correspondingly, or indeed, to any significant extent. This is to be expected, for if their relative numbers did increase, then labour reserves in the economy would actually start getting depleted, giving rise to an increase in the wage rate which would prevent a rise in the share of surplus and hence a rise in the army of such 'third persons'. *Thus, if their relative numbers did increase significantly, then this fact itself would have negated the very basis of their existence.* It follows that they constitute a segment of the population which is, on average, higher paid than the working class, or even the older sections of employees within the service sector itself. This clearly means that income distribution gets worsened in an underdeveloped economy pursuing 'neo-liberal' policies: personal income distribution gets worsened because of the emergence of this class of highly-paid 'parasites', and class distribution of income gets worsened when we look at surplus inclusive of these incomes.

The cause of the increase in income inequality, no matter how we define it, lies, however, not in the emergence of this class *per se*, but in the fact of an acceleration in the growth rate of labour productivity in the context of stagnant subsistence wages. This not only increases inequality *in the transition from dirigisme to neo-liberalism*, but it continues to raise inequality *during the tenure of the neo-liberal regime itself.*

The increase in inequality, in the distribution of both personal and class incomes, which we have so far considered to be the *consequence* of the increase in the relative size of the labour reserves which the 'opening up' of an underdeveloped economy entails, becomes, in turn, an additional *cause* of this increase in labour reserves itself. This is because the increase in the rate of growth of labour productivity gets an additional boost owing to the rise in income inequalities, since the 'elite' consumption demand is much more influenced by what prevails in the metropolis than the demand of other sections of the population.

The really puzzling question however is this: Why does the income of the mass of 'third persons', whose consumption provides the way out of a realization crisis, arise at all? After all, the macroeconomic consequences of such a rise cannot constitute the reason for its occurrence; then why does it occur so conveniently, precisely at the time when the system otherwise is threatened with the prospects of a realization crisis? This question can be asked of the Baran-Sweezy argument as well in the context of advanced economies, where the answer is difficult. In the context of third world economies by contrast, the answer is more simple, namely the 'opening up' to world trade and financial movements also brings in its train an 'opening up' to practices, systems and structures prevailing in the metropolis. And since metropolitan economies have, over the years, come to be characterized by a large and increasing category of 'parasitic' incomes, emulation of these structures by the 'opened up' third world economies replicates in a fairly short time the same phenomenon within their own frontiers.

The argument presented so far should be contrasted with two other arguments to underscore its specificity. The first is the Samuelson-Stolper theorem of conventional trade theory (Samuelson, 1970), which states that 'opening up' for trade should *increase the share of wages* in an economy whose comparative advantage lies in the labour-intensive good. According to this theory, the share of wages should be *increasing* in underdeveloped economies after they have 'opened up' to international trade flows, *which is the exact opposite of what is being argued here and which flies in the face of reality.* The reason for this difference lies in the obvious fact that we have avoided making such palpably untenable assumptions as full employment, an aggregate production function, and trade being governed by 'comparative advantage'.

The second argument is the one advanced by W. Arthur Lewis (1954), who also emphasized that the development of the third world hinged crucially on using up its labour reserves, which could only occur if the third world protected herself from international trade and ushered in her own agricultural and industrial revolutions by using the State as an instrument. The difference between the Lewis position and what is argued above lies in our explicit recognition of the fact that imitative technological change, introduced as a consequence of 'opening up', is a development-retarding factor.

Socialist Economies?

There is a long tradition in radical economics which argues that it is not the pace of technological change and of productivity growth per se that impinges adversely on the living conditions of the people, but the social formation within which such change occurs. Let us examine this view.

When we talked of the rate of growth of labour demand above, that referred to the demand for labour-time, not to the number of *labourers*. If we have a socialist economy with a work-sharing, product-sharing ethic, then, the same number of labour hours can be distributed among a larger number of labourers, indeed among all the members of the work-force, in which case unemployment as we know it, would cease to exist. Each worker would have a larger number of labour hours to pursue his or her creative interests, free from the drudgery of work. Such freedom moreover would not entail any material deprivation, since the total output, including what otherwise accrues to the class of 'third persons' and 'parasites', would now be distributed among the entire work-force on some appropriate principle of equity.

An example will clarify the matter. Suppose to start with 1000 units of output are produced by 100 workers, each of whom works for 10 hours during the unit period and obtains a wage-rate of 8 units during this period; the remaining 200 units of the product are used for investment and looking after those not in the work-force. Now, if in the next unit period, both output and labour productivity increase by 10 percent (both being determined from 'outside') and the work-force by 5 percent. In this new situation in a socialist economy each worker would work for 9.5 hours and obtain 8.4 units of the product (or to be precise 9+11/21 hours and 8+8/21 units respectively), which means a 5 percent increase in income and a 5 percent reduction in work for each worker. There would still be full employment and 20 percent of output would still be kept aside for investment and social expenditure.

We can express this formally as follows. If the growth rate of output is denoted by q, of productivity by b, of the work-force by n, of the hours of work by h, and of the wage rate by w, then, assuming that the proportion set aside for investment and welfare expenditure remains unchanged (and taking continuous time) we have the following two identities:

$$h = q - b - n \ \ldots \ (1) ; \quad \text{and} \quad w = q - n \ldots (2).$$

The very fact of the right-hand side of (1) being negative which is a 'problem' in capitalist countries can become an asset in socialist countries since in lieu of unemployment there can be greater leisure. Even so, as (2) shows, the wage rate can increase at the same rate as per capita output.

The real issue however is whether an immediate end to unemployment and underemployment, such as is implicit in the 'work-sharing, product-sharing ethic', is practicable, especially in an 'open' underdeveloped socialist economy. In general, the more the time taken to overcome unemployment and underemployment, the greater is the danger that the contradiction between the employed and the unemployed will get ossified: if the rate of growth of labour productivity is high relative to the growth rate of output, and the size of the labour reserve and the rate of growth of the work-force are large, then even with the persistence of subsistence wages it would take a long time for the labour reserves to get used up and during this period pressure would mount for an increase in the wage rate among the employed, especially since productivity growth happens to be quite high.

The problem gets compounded in an 'open' underdeveloped socialist economy, since its very 'openness' to trade flows creates pressures for a similar 'openness' to capital flows, which, if successful, would compromise the autonomy of the socialist State and jeopardize the existence of the system by exacerbating fissures within it. (This is in addition to the fact that 'openness' makes the economy vulnerable to 'international demonstration effects', and more crucially to pressures from outside to subvert socialist values). It is instructive that the only successful examples of using up labour reserves till date are the Soviet Union and the Eastern European countries which were not 'open' and which controlled the rate of technological change and hence the rate of growth of labour productivity.

In the case of capitalist underdeveloped countries, the problem of course is far more serious since there is no question of a 'work-sharing, product-sharing ethic'. Here 'openness' necessarily produces a dualistic structure not just with growing *income* inequalities, but with absolute worsening of the conditions of the vast labouring mass accompanying growing affluence on the part of a small stratum consisting of the local agents of the MNCs, the speculators, the capitalists and their 'hangers on'. Since the bourgeoisie which had earlier embarked upon a process of relatively autonomous development has itself given up this path and is pursuing 'neo-liberalism' instead, the idea of a 'closed' capitalist system with a controlled pace of technological change has little relevance in today's context. *The process of extricating the economy from this dualism therefore has to be a part of an alternative trajectory of development which leads towards socialism.*

But since any regime that puts in place this alternative trajectory cannot hope to realize a 'work-sharing, product-sharing ethic' in the immediate future, unrestricted technological change will have to be eschewed if the prospects of a recreation of dualism which undermines this alternative trajectory are to be avoided. It follows that restrictions on the rate of technological change would have to be enforced and these in turn require not autarky, of course, but a degree of control over trade, and complete control over financial flows.

There is a view, not just among 'bourgeois liberals', but even in sections of the Left, that any such restrictions on free commerce and capital flows necessarily entail curbs on the democratic rights of the people. This view is unfounded. There are, no doubt, many authoritarian regimes which keep their countries hermetically sealed from the outside world; but at the same time there are numerous regimes pursuing 'neo-liberal' policies which attenuate democracy in order to facilitate this pursuit. Indeed, one can argue that 'neo-liberalism' *necessarily* entails an attenuation of democracy in a way that relatively closed *dirigiste* regimes do not: nobody in India can possibly argue for instance that Nehruvian India, which saw the apogee of *dirigisme,* entailed an attenuation of democracy compared to the India of the 'neo-liberal' 1990s. And in any case, to talk of democratic rights of the people being ensured by a regime that produces dualism leading to the growth of affluence at one pole and absolute poverty at the other is sheer travesty of the truth. Democracy under all circumstances requires for its protection the struggle of the people, and such struggles are best carried on when the people are economically empowered, which constitutes, besides, a hallmark of democracy itself.

SUMMARY OF ARGUMENT

Let me summarize the argument. The 'opening up' of an underdeveloped economy to trade and capital flows implies that the pace of technological and structural change within the economy gets linked to what prevails in the advanced capitalist world. This implies an increase in the rate of growth of labour productivity compared to what prevailed under *dirigisme*. At the same time, the rate of GDP growth becomes dependent upon the rate of growth of exports, which, unless the underdeveloped countries eat into each other's market share, gets linked to the rate of growth of world trade, which is essentially outside the country's control. If the rate of growth of labour demand, which is the result of these two phenomena, falls short of the rate of growth of the work force, then the ratio of labour reserve to work-force increases, which means a constancy of the wage rate of workers at the subsistence level and increase in absolute poverty for a larger section of the work force. At the same time, the rise in surplus per worker has the effect of sustaining a larger income share for a group of 'parasites' and 'hangers on' of the MNCs, of international finance and of domestic capitalists. Their demand pattern, influenced by the life-styles prevailing in the metropolis, has the effect of increasing the pace of technological change still further, thus creating a vicious circle. (The demand for FDI in retail trade is an obvious example of the manner of its working.)

In a socialist economy, technological change need not result in unemployment; indeed, under a 'work-sharing, product-sharing ethic', it can benefit the workers through both greater leisure and higher incomes. But an 'open' socialist economy may find it difficult to introduce such an 'ethic'. When it comes to an 'open' capitalist underdeveloped economy, it certainly has little prospect of escaping the fate outlined above. Any alternative trajectory of development in such an economy must therefore involve a transition towards socialism, with control over the pace of technological change, brought about through trade and capital controls.

NOTES

[1] Since we are talking about the GDP, the current account surplus should exclude net factor payments from abroad.

[2] The fact that in a situation where investment is determined by the growth of income itself, we have the operation of what Hicks (1950) had called the 'super multiplier' (Lange (1964) had called it the 'compound multiplier') and that the overall rate of growth is determined by the rate of growth of the exogenous stimulus (exports in this case) was emphasized by Kaldor (1979).

[3] For a discussion of Tugan-Baranovsky's views, see Luxemburg (1963) and Kalecki (1971).

[4] See Ricardo (1951) and Hicks (1967).

[5] For a discussion of Struve's views, see Luxemburg (1963).

REFERENCES

Baran, P.A., and P. M. Sweezy (1966). *Monopoly Capital.* Monthly Review Press, New York.

Hicks, J.R. (1950). *A Contribution to the Theory of the Trade Cycle.* Clarendon Press, Oxford.

Hicks, J.R. (1967). *Capital and Time.* Clarendon Press, Oxford.

Kaldor, Nicholas (1979). The case for regional policies. In *Essays on Economic Policy,* Volume 1. Duckworth, London.

Kalecki, Michal (1971). The problem of effective demand with Rosa Luxemburg and Tugan-Baranovsky. In *Selected Essays on the Dynamics of the Capitalist Economy.* Cambridge University Press, Cambridge.

Lange, Oskar (1964). *Papers on Economics and Sociology.* Pergamon Press, Warsaw.

Lewis, W.A. (1954). Economic development with unlimited supplies of Labour. *Manchester School,* 22.

Luxemburg, Rosa (1963). *The Accumulation of Capital.* Routledge Kegan Paul, London.

Samuelson, P.A. (1970). *Collected Scientific papers of P. A. Samuelson.* Oxford University Press, Delhi.

4

Macroeconomic Policy, Employment, Unemployment and Gender Equality

DIANE ELSON

It is good to see the new emphasis on employment issues in international development analysis and strategies. An example is the recommendation in the 2006 report of the UN Secretary-General that a new employment target be used to track progress towards Millennium Development Goal 1 (Eradicate Extreme Poverty and Hunger). The target is "full and productive employment and decent work for all, including for women and young people" (UN, 2006: 6).

It is important to consider the gender dimensions of employment and decent work because men and women experience both employment and unemployment differently; and macroeconomic policies have different impacts on men's and women's employment. Much of the research and policy development on gender equality in employment has been focused on measures to enable women to compete with men on an equal basis. These measures include both measures to improve women's access to education and training, credit, land and other assets; and measures to reform the governance of markets to create a 'level playing field' (see, for example, World Bank, 2001; 2006). These measures are important, but they are not sufficient. To the extent that they are successful, they will simply redistribute some jobs from men to women. This will reduce gender gaps, but not in a way that provides 'full and productive employment and decent work for all'. Most organizations campaigning for the goal of gender equality and women's empowerment want to see this realized in ways that 'equalize up', rather than 'equalize down', in ways that improve the well-being of all. This requires an expansion of the number of decent jobs, as well as an improvement of women's access to them.

However, employment has ceased to be a goal of macroeconomic policy. Instead, the focus is on financial variables, such as inflation, the fiscal deficit, and debt to GDP ratios. As is well known, rates of inflation have been brought down to much lower levels than in the 1980s, but in many regions, this has been at a huge sacrifice in public investment, economic growth and decent jobs (for evidence, see, for example, UNRISD, 2005: 30). Macroeconomic policy has been increasingly characterized by 'deflationary bias', with governments cutting expenditure and raising interest rates, reducing aggregate demand and stifling the growth of decent employment in both public and private sectors. 'Deflationary bias' is no more a sound policy than 'inflationary bias', as other chapters of this volume explain in more detail. Here, we note that an environment with a deficiency of aggregate demand is not supportive of reductions in gender inequality combined with improvements in well-being (UN, 1999: 46–54).

Feminist economics suggests that women are particularly likely to be disadvantaged by 'deflationary bias' because it interacts with other biases, such as 'male breadwinner bias', the assumption that men are more deserving of decent jobs because they are the principal economic support of families, while women's incomes are supplementary, and not essential to family well-being (Elson and Cagatay, 2000: 1354–1356). In fact, many women provide the principal economic support for families, and in many other families, women's earnings are critical for lifting families above the poverty line (see, for example, Moser, 1997; Sethuraman, 1998). Moreover, the right to work is equally a right of women and men, and non-discrimination in employment is one of the core labour standards set out in the ILO Declaration on Fundamental Principles and Rights at Work (June 1998). To ensure gender equality in productive employment and decent work, both deflationary bias and male breadwinner bias need to be addressed.

The issues noted above are explored in more detail in the rest of this chapter. The first section presents evidence on some key gender differences in work and unemployment, including unpaid work as well as paid work. The second section reviews some research findings on the neglected topic of gender differences in unemployment, paying particular attention to demand factors. The third section discusses a unique study that links gender differences in employment outcomes to macroeconomic policy instruments. The final section draws some conclusions for policy.

Gender Differences in Labour Force Participation, Employment, Unemployment and Unpaid Domestic Work

The ILO regularly publishes employment data that reveal the gender differences in labour force participation rates, employment to population ratios, and unemployment rates (see, for instance, ILO, 2004). Table 4.1 shows these differences for the global labour market. The labour force participation rate and employment to population ratio are higher for males than for females, but the unemployment rate is higher for females than males in both 1993 and 2003. In this decade, the gap in labour force participation rates narrowed slightly, as the rate rose for women and declined for men. Similarly, the gap in the employment to population ratio narrowed slightly, as the ratio rose slightly for women and declined slightly for men. The unemployment rate rose for both women and men, with the female rate remaining 0.3 percentage points higher than the male rate.

TABLE 4.1
Gender differences in employment and unemployment

	Female		Male		Total	
	1993	2003	1993	2003	1993	2003
Labour Force (millions)	1,006	1,208	1,507	1,769	2,513	2,978
Employment (millions)	948	1,130	1,425	1,661	2,373	2,792
Unemployment (millions)	58.2	77.8	82.3	108.1	140.5	185.9
Labour Force Participation Rate (%)	53.5	53.9	80.5	79.4	67.0	66.6
Employment-to-Population Ratio (%)	50.4	50.5	76.1	74.5	63.3	62.5
Unemployment Rate (%)	5.8	6.4	5.5	6.1	5.6	6.2

Source: ILO (2004: Table 1.1)

The global figures mask big regional differences. Table 4.2 shows male and female participation rates by region in 2003. While the gap between the male and female rates has decreased, it has not been eliminated in any region. The number of economically active females per 100 economically active males ranges from a high of 91 to a low of 36. The gap in participation rates is smallest in the formerly centrally planned Transition Economies; next comes East Asia; the Industrialized Economies are in third place. This reflects the fact that in the highest income countries, women spend more time in post-school education than they do in the rapidly growing economies of East Asia. The gap is widest in South Asia and the Middle East and North Africa, due to a combination of economic and cultural factors.

TABLE 4.2

Male and female labour force participation rates and gender gap, 2003

	Male LFPR (%)	Female LFPR (%)	Gender Gap in LFPRs, Females per 100 Males
World	79.4	53.9	68
Middle East and North Africa	76.8	28.2	36
South Asia	81.1	37.4	44
Latin America and the Caribbean	80.5	49.2	64
Industrialized Economies	70.3	50.5	76
Transition Economies	65.7	53.1	91
South-East Asia	82.9	60.5	75
Sub-Saharan Africa	85.3	63.2	77
East Asia	85.1	73.1	83

Source: ILO (2004: Table 2.1)

There was an upward trend in female labour force participation in the last 40 years of the 20th century, especially pronounced in the 1980s. The upward trend in the global female labour force participation rate had come to an end by 2005, while the global male participation rate continued to decline (ILO, 2006: 3). The trend in female labour force participation is the result of structural changes, including commercialization of agriculture, industrialization, and the replacement of unpaid provision of services by women in families and communities, with the paid provision of services by women employed in both the public sector and private firms. We should note that available statistics tend to exaggerate the extent of the changes in female labour force participation, because it is easier to measure the labour force in market-based production than in subsistence production. In addition, efforts have been made over the last twenty years to improve the extent to which censuses and surveys capture the real extent of women's labour force participation.

An exception to the general rising trend has been the fall in female participation rates in most formerly centrally planned economies over the 1990s. For instance, in Eastern Europe, female labour force participation fell from an average of 60.9 per cent in 1980 to 51.8 per cent in 2000 (Heintz, 2006: 16). This is related to the large-scale job loss that followed transition to the market (around one-third of jobs were lost) and the loss of services that facilitated combining paid employment with women's domestic responsibilities.

A reduction in the gap between male and female labour force participation is not the same as an increase in gender equality in the labour market. As the ILO points out, the labour force participation rate does not indicate anything about the likelihood of being employed, or of having decent work. In almost all regions, the female unemployment rate is higher than the male rates, occupations are sex-segregated and gender gaps persist in earnings (ILO, 2004).

For many women, engagement in paid employment does not take them out of the home. Women seem to be much more likely than men to undertake paid work within homes (UN, 2000: 123–124). Two types of paid employment of women take place within homes. Women may work in their own homes, as home-based workers (either in self-employment or as an employee under subcontract to a market-based enterprise). Women are often constrained to undertake this kind of employment because it is easier to combine with unpaid domestic work, especially in the absence of public sector provision of water, sanitation, electricity, child-care and care for frail elderly people.

Women also work in other people's homes, as paid domestic workers (i.e., as maids, cleaners, cooks, housekeepers, and carers for children and elderly people, etc). It is not easy to get comprehensive statistics on such employment. Available evidence suggests that home-based work is on the increase around the world, in both high income and low income countries, and that home-based workers are much more likely to be women than men (UN, 2000: 123–124; ILO, 2002: 43–49). The employment of paid domestic workers, most of whom are women, also appears to be on the increase, especially in parts of the world, such as North America and Western Europe, where it had decreased in the middle decades of the twentieth century (Young, 2001).

Even if they engage in work outside the home, women tend to remain segregated in occupations that are extensions of women's unpaid domestic work in their own homes.

Women work primarily in the service sector, except in economies with large agricultural sectors such as sub-Saharan Africa and Southern Asia (UN, 2000: 114). Women's work in agriculture is frequently bound up with their responsibilities for feeding their families; and a large proportion of their work is undertaken as 'unpaid family workers', without direct monetary remuneration, either because they produce for family consumption or because the monetary proceeds of selling the output go to the male members of the family (UNIFEM, 2000: 87). In paid employment in the service sector, women are concentrated in community, social and personal services, whereas men are concentrated in financial and business services (ILO, 2004: 12). In paid employment in industry, women are concentrated in food processing, and in textile and garment production.

Women's paid work outside the home is also more likely to be informal than that of men (ILO, 2002: 8). Informal employment is work that is relatively unregulated and unprotected, typically lacking job security, fringe benefits, social insurance, and representation or voice. It is best thought of not as a separate sector of small enterprises, distinct from a formal sector of large enterprises, but as a type of employment status that can be found throughout the economy (ILO, 2002: 8). It is difficult to capture fully the extent of this type of work, but available evidence suggests that it is significant and on the increase in both rich and poor countries (ILO, 2002; Chen and others, 2005;

Heintz, 2006). The conditions of informal employment perpetuate the financial dependency of women wage earners on male relatives and partners. Even though women are not completely dependent on men, they do not earn enough in informal employment to support themselves and any children they may have.

Women have made some gains in formal sector employment. For instance women's share of administrative and managerial positions increased in the 1980s and 1990s in every region of the world except South Asia, but everywhere, this share is considerably lower than women's share of the total labour force (UN, 2000: 130). Moreover, only a small percentage of women are in this category, even in the developed countries (UN, 2000: 129). A somewhat larger proportion of women are professional and technical workers, but women's share of such jobs has increased only very slowly (UN, 2000: 1129–1130). An ILO report calls progress "slow, uneven, and sometimes discouraging" (ILO, 2005: 17). It points out that "in female-dominated sectors where there are more women managers, a disproportionate number of men rise to the more senior positions, and in those professions normally reserved for men, women managers are few and far between" (ILO, 2005: 18). The women manager has become very visible in the USA, where women hold about 44 per cent of administrative and managerial positions, but the women's share is considerably lower in most other developed countries, and even lower in developing countries (UNDP, 2000: 165–166).

To summarize the global picture, women are relatively more concentrated than men in informal employment that lacks the characteristics of 'decent work'. "Women are not only in different and more precarious types of employment than men, but within a given category women's earnings are generally lower than men's." (Chen and others, 2005: 46). Informal employment is much more likely to yield poverty wages than formal employment, and a high proportion of informally employed people are part of the working poor, employed, but living in households whose income is below the poverty line. It is estimated that of the approximately 2.8 billion employed people in the world in 2005, nearly half did not earn enough to lift their families above US$2 a day, and almost a fifth did not earn enough to lift themselves and their families above US$1 a day (ILO, 2006:

11). It is important to recognize that the prevalence of low-paying informal employment is not only related to the supply side of the labour market, but also the demand side of the labour market. People are crowded into low-paying informal employment, not only because they lack much in the way of education and capital assets, but also because there is insufficient aggregate demand in the economies in which they work to support enough 'decent jobs'.

Insufficient aggregate demand is also a key factor in explaining the prevalence of unemployment. It is true that in countries that lack unemployment insurance, unemployed people are frequently not among the poorest people, but are among the better educated, who can afford to be openly unemployed for a time, while poor people are forced to undertake low-paying informal jobs. Nevertheless, unemployment of those who wish to be employed signals a waste of human resources, with adverse consequences, both for the individuals who are unemployed and for the societies is which they live. The global unemployment rate has fluctuated in the period 1995–2005, but the trend has definitely been upward (ILO, 2006: 1). The major increases in unemployment rates were in Latin America and the Caribbean, and the Central and Eastern Europe and Commonwealth of Independent States (CIS) region. The only regions with significant decreases were the Developed Economies and the EU.

As noted in Table 4.1, at the global level, in 2003, the female unemployment rate was slightly higher than the male rate; however, this is not true in every region. For instance, in the Middle East and North Africa, and Latin America and the Caribbean, the female unemployment rate was higher than the male. However, in sub-Saharan Africa and East Asia the reverse was true (ILO, 2004: 2). Within the OECD countries (in 1999), there is variation, with female rates much higher than male rates in some countries such as those around the Mediterranean, while in others, such as the English-speaking countries (except the USA), the male rate is higher than the female rate (Azmat, Guell and Manning, 2006: 2).

In many countries, female unemployment rates are likely to underestimate the true extent of women's unemployment because of the 'discouraged worker' effect. Discouraged workers are people who have sought employment in previous periods, but due to their failure to find jobs, cease to actively search for one, although they would like to have a job if one were available. Women are more likely than men to be discouraged workers because their responsibilities for unpaid domestic work constrain the time they have available to search for work, and also provide a sense of identity that men may lack, if they are without a job. A further factor, in countries that have social insurance for unemployed people, is that women are less likely to be eligible, and therefore have less incentive to demonstrate that they are actively looking for work (which is usually a condition for claiming unemployment benefits). A further complication is that women are more likely than men to respond to loss of formal employment, both their own and that of their spouses, by moving into informal employment, with lower productivity, lower pay, and shorter hours, than their formal employment. This is best characterized as 'underemployment', but data is not collected on a regular basis on underemployment. The discouragement and underemployment of women appear to have been significant in the aftermath of the Asian financial crisis in 1997–1998. For instance, in South Korea, the rate of job loss for women was higher than for men, but subsequently, male unemployment rates appeared to be higher than female rates, while a higher proportion of women than before were employed in various types of informal employment (UNRISD, 2005: 42).

As well as paid work, both men and women undertake unpaid domestic work. This unpaid work includes the inter-personal work of caring for other household members; and in countries that lack sufficient infrastructure, the work of collecting water and fuel for household needs. Though men and boys do contribute to this work, a socially constructed division of labour assigns the major responsibility for this work to women and girls. Care work, in particular, is widely regarded as especially 'feminine', even though men do undertake some of this work, so that one may speak of 'female carer bias', as a parallel to 'male breadwinner bias'. Just as male breadwinner bias assumes that men are bound to be the principal earners, with women's earnings just 'helping out a bit', female carer bias assumes that women are bound to be the principal carers, with men's participation in care merely 'helping out a bit'.

It is not possible to refer to global or regional statistics on gender differences in unpaid domestic work since no UN agency is charged with collecting and publishing this data, and it is not a core activity in data collection by national statistical offices. An increasing number of countries, developing as well as developed, have carried out time use studies, which show how much time males and females spend in different kinds of unpaid domestic work, but there is no up-to-date international compilation of this data. Table 4.3 shows sex-disaggregated data for a selection of developing countries for various years in the early twenty-first century. While males do spend some time carrying out unpaid domestic work, it is clear that females spend much more time doing this. The same is true in developed countries, as shown in Table 4.4.

TABLE 4.3
Gender division of unpaid domestic work in selected developing countries

Country	(Average Minutes per Day by Sex)			
	Male	Female	F − M	F + M
Mexico	228	330	102	558
South Africa	80	220	140	300
India	31	297	266	328
Benin	65	215	150	280
Madagascar	70	245	175	315
Mauritius	73	277	204	350

Sources: Mexico: Calculated from INEGI National Time Use Survey, 2002;
South Africa: Budlender and Brathaug (2005: Table 2); India: Calculated from Chakraborty (2005: Table 3);
Benin, Madagascar, Mauritius: Calculated from Charmes (2005: Table 13).

The female–male gap seems to be smaller for the developed countries than for the developing, and men in developing countries seem to spend a lot less time on unpaid domestic work than men in developed countries (with the exception of Mexico, which is a middle income country). However, the total time spent does not seem to be lower in developed than in developing countries. Caution must be used in drawing firm conclusions since the data in the two tables is not strictly comparable, as the same definitions and methods were not used. But it seems likely that the total time spent on unpaid domestic work does not dramatically fall as per capita gross national product increases. Rather, the composition of the work changes, with the elimination of time spent collecting water and fuel (significant for poor females in poor countries) and an increase in time spent in child-care. Comparative conclusions can be drawn about the European countries in Table 4.4, as the data was produced using the Harmonized European Time Surveys.

TABLE 4.4
Gender division of unpaid domestic work in selected developed countries

| Country | (Average Minutes per Day by Sex) | | | |
	Male	Female	F–M	F + M
Belgium	158	272	114	430
Germany	141	251	110	392
Estonia	168	302	134	470
France	142	270	128	412
Hungary	159	297	138	456
Slovenia	159	297	138	456
Finland	136	236	100	372
Sweden	149	222	73	371
UK	138	255	117	393
Norway	142	227	85	369

Source: EUROSTAT (2005: 5)

The picture that emerges from both tables is that, on average, women are spending 3 to 4 hours a day on unpaid domestic work, as compared to 1 to 2 hours by men. This difference puts extra constraints on women's labour force participation and employment. It tends to reduce the demand for female labour, all other things being equal, as employers regard domestic responsibilities of employees as additions to their costs, and disregard the long run benefits produced by this work for the economy as a whole (Folbre, 2001: 185). The difference between the domestic responsibilities of male and female workers is often invoked to justify a preference for male workers, so it is important to recognize that it can be reduced by appropriate public policies. It is noteworthy that the female-male gap is smallest in Sweden and Norway, which have extensive public provision of care services. The total time spent on unpaid domestic work is also lowest in these two countries.

In this section, we have discussed patterns of gender difference in different aspects of work. In the next section, we explore, in more detail, gender differences in unemployment, a topic that has been relatively neglected in comparison with gender differences in labour force participation and in earnings.

Explaining Gender Differences in Unemployment

Gender differences in unemployment cannot be attributed only to supply side factors, such as differences in education, skills, and reservation wages. Demand side factors also play a role. When there is a shortage of jobs in the economy, groups lower down the social hierarchy, or considered less deserving of employment, may be placed at the back of the job queue by employers. There is evidence that this is at the root of higher unemployment rates of African-Americans than White Americans (Shulman, 1991). Seguino (2003) argues that, similarly, women may be placed at the back of the job queue in a society in which men are perceived to be the rightful breadwinners, with a stronger claim on jobs. She explores the role of this and other factors in determining why women are much more likely to be unemployed than men in Barbados, Jamaica and Trinidad and Tobago, using data for the period 1980–1999. In these three countries, as in much of the Caribbean, the female unemployment rate is high and considerably higher than that of men, as shown in Table 4.5.

Seguino finds that women's higher unemployment rate cannot be explained in terms of women being less educated than men, since women have a higher unemployment rate than men with the same education. For instance, in Barbados in 1999, university educated women were more likely than men to be unemployed, with an unemployment rate more than two percentage points higher than men with the same education. In Trinidad and Tobago, women with a secondary education had a higher rate of unemployment than men with any level of education, including those with no education. Nor was it simply a matter of women being concentrated in sectors or occupations experiencing slower rates of grow, since the probability of women being unemployed was higher than that of men being unemployed in every sector and occupational group in all three countries.

TABLE 4.5
Selected Caribbean countries: Female and male unemployment rates (%)

	1980–1999 Mean	2001[a]
Barbados		
Females	20.6	11.7
Males	12.6	8.3
Ratio F/M	1.6	1.4
Jamaica		
Females	28.6	22.3
Males	12.2	10.2
Ratio F/M	2.3	2.2
Trinidad/Tobago		
Females	19.8	14.4
Males	14.3	8.6
Ratio F/M	1.4	1.7

Source: Seguino's calculations, Seguino (2003: Tables 1 and 3). Data from ILO (various years)
Note: [a] Data for Jamaica are for 2000

Seguino examines the impact of macroeconomic demand side factors through an investigation of how economic upturns and recessions affect gender differences in unemployment, controlling for other demand and supply side factors. Her independent variables are the female unemployment rate, the male unemployment rate and the ratio of female to male unemployment rates, and her explanatory variables are the deviation of the rate of GDP growth from its trend, a measure of foreign direct investment (since such investment is often argued to have a positive impact on the creation of jobs for women), a time trend (to allow for long run influences on male and female unemployment rates aside from the variables included in the model), and the change in the female share of the labour force (to control for the impact of changes in the relative size of the female labour supply). The analysis uses a pooled cross-sectional time series panel data set for 1980–1999, with a fixed effects model to allow for country-specific effects.

The analysis showed that both male and female unemployment rates fell in economic upturns, but the unemployment rate for women fell less than that for men, so that in the upturn, there was a rise in the ratio of the female to the male unemployment rate. Men benefited more than women from economic upturns, thus widening the gender gap in enjoyment of paid work. Over the period 1980–1999, both male and female unemployment declined at a statistically significant rate, but the ratio of the female to the male unemployment rates did not, indicating the persistence of gender inequality. Foreign direct investment had no significant effect on unemployment rates. A rise in the female share of the labour force was positively associated with a rise in the female to male unemployment ratio, consistent with the hypothesis that women and men are not full substitutes in the labour market, so that a relative increase in the female labour supply leads to crowding of women into a narrow range of job slots.

In an extension of the analysis, Seguino disaggregated the economy into four sectors – manufacturing, agriculture, industry and services. She found that expansion or recession in manufacturing and agriculture did not have any impact on the ratio of female to male unemployment rates. But increases in the output of services and industry were associated with an increase in the ratio of female to male unemployment rate. This was not surprising for industry, in which most employment is in male-dominated occupations, but was surprising for the service sector, in which women are relatively concentrated, and in which they have a high share of jobs.

Seguino's results are consistent with the hypothesis that women's higher unemployment rates may be related to employer preferences for male workers (due to both male breadwinner bias and female carer bias), as the econometric results show that male workers are the first to be hired in upturns, even in the female intensive service sector. Her study did not investigate the reasons for this, though she speculates that women's child care responsibilities lead employers to prefer men; and that women may be disadvantaged by systems of maternity leave in which all costs fall on the employer, rather than being met in whole or part from tax revenues. It is worth noting that there is a high prevalence of female-headed households in the three countries in the study, and many women are the de facto breadwinners for their households. Her conclusion is that policies to create more jobs by stimulating economic growth will not, by themselves, be enough to reduce the gender gap in unemployment. Not only deflationary bias, but also male breadwinner bias has to be addressed. Seguino's study appears to be the only cross-country study available on gender differences in unemployment in developing countries. One hindrance is the lack of sex-disaggregated time-series data on unemployment in developing countries.

Much more sex-disaggregated data on unemployment are available for developed countries. Even so, there has been relatively little research on gender differences in unemployment in developed countries. An exception is a study of the gender gap in employment rates in selected OECD countries (14 EU countries plus USA) by Azmat, Guell and Manning (2006), using micro-data sets from household surveys in the EU and the US Current Population Survey. (The size of the gap by country is shown in Table 4.6). The study covers the period 1994–1999, and focuses on flows from employment to unemployment and from unemployment to employment, estimating the probability that an individual will make these transitions, controlling for characteristics of the individuals and the jobs they do. The study examines both supply side and demand side factors.

TABLE 4.6

Gender gaps in unemployment rates among selected OECD countries

Country	All Working Age (15–64)			
	Male	Female	Difference	Ratio
Spain	11.00	22.91	11.91	2.08
Greece	7.56	17.92	10.36	2.37
Italy	8.67	15.71	7.04	1.81
France	9.66	12.96	3.30	1.34
Netherlands	2.74	4.49	1.75	1.64
Luxembourg	1.77	2.68	0.91	1.51
Germany	8.15	9.22	1.07	1.13
Denmark	4.69	6.54	1.85	1.39
Portugal	3.84	5.05	1.21	1.32
Finland	9.58	10.73	1.15	1.12
Sweden	7.50	6.76	−0.74	0.90
United States	4.05	4.33	0.28	1.07
Austria	3.69	3.85	0.16	1.04
Ireland	5.90	5.50	−0.40	0.93
United Kingdom	6.75	5.07	−1.68	0.75

Source: Azmat Guell and Manning (2006: Table 1)

It finds that domestic responsibilities do not play a large direct role in explaining why employed women become unemployed, and are no more significant in countries with a large gender gap than in those with a small (or negative) gender gap. What is significant are the characteristics of the jobs that men and women occupy. The key factor that differentiates the high and low gap countries is the degree to which employers make use of temporary contracts, in which women workers are over-represented. It is easier to fire women workers than men workers, if the former are more concentrated in jobs with temporary contracts and the latter in jobs with permanent contracts. Some of the high gap countries, such as France and Spain, do have two-tier labour markets of this kind. The study finds no support for the hypothesis that women in high gap countries who are unemployed are not as serious in their job search as men who are unemployed, or are more selective about the jobs they will take. Again, the key factors lie on the demand side.

Differences in the costs employers face in employing women in different countries as a result of differences in maternity leave costs were not found to be important. The Nordic countries, which have generous maternity leave provisions, have smaller gender gaps in unemployment than other countries in the sample. Using data from the, 1996 Eurobarometer Attitude Survey, support was found for the hypothesis that gender gaps are highest in countries in which more people believe that "When jobs are scarce, men should have more right to a job than women". Azmat, Guell and Manning (2006: 31) suggest that employers are influenced by such social norms when labour markets are slack: "putting prejudices into practice is easier when unemployment is high and there are long queues for jobs, as has been the situation in most of the high gap countries in the 1980s and 1990s". They test this by examining the impact on the gender gap in unemployment of the interaction of the male unemployment rate with the attitudinal variable, and find it positive and significantly different from zero.

The study reviewed here of gender differences in unemployment rates in selected OECD countries provides indirect support for the hypothesis that deflationary bias in macroeconomic polices interacts with existing forms of gender bias to intensify gender gaps in unemployment, though it does not directly investigate a link with specific macroeconomic policies. The study of gender differences in unemployment rates in selected Caribbean countries provides indirect support for the hypothesis that policies to promote growth of GDP will not necessarily be sufficient to overcome gaps in unemployment, though it does not directly investigate a link with specific macroeconomic policies. In the next section, we discuss the only available study that does directly link gender inequality in the labour market with macroeconomic policies.

GENDER INEQUALITY IN EMPLOYMENT AND MACROECONOMIC POLICIES

As noted in the introduction, achievement of full employment has ceased to be an objective of macroeconomic policies. Instead, the objectives have been financial. For instance, reducing the rate of inflation and keeping it very low has become the most important objective of monetary policy (as noted by Epstein in the next chapter). Policies of raising interest rates and reducing the money supply have been used in many countries to achieve this. In a pioneering and unique study, Braunstein and Heintz (2006) have investigated the link between these policies and gender equality in employment in 17 low and middle income countries in the period 1970–2003. The countries are Barbados, Brazil, Chile, Colombia, Costa Rica, India, Jamaica, Kenya, Malaysia, Mauritius, the Philippines, Singapore, South Korea, Sri Lanka, Taiwan, Thailand and Trinidad & Tobago. The choice of countries was restricted by the availability of time-series sex-disaggregated data on employment. The employment data used (from the ILO LABOURSTA on-line data base) are likely to cover formal employment much better than informal employment, but because of this, are better indicators of decent and productive work than more comprehensive data would be.

The first step in the analysis was to identify inflation reduction episodes in these countries in the time period selected, and to examine employment trends in these periods. Fifty-one such periods were identified, and it was found that in thirty-six of them, the growth of employment fell below its long run trend; these are therefore labelled 'contractionary inflation reduction episodes'. In the remaining fifteen episodes, employment expanded faster than the long run trend in employment growth; these episodes are therefore labelled 'expansionary inflation reduction episodes'. Since governments often use increases in positive real interest rates as an inflation reduction tool, Braunstein and Heintz examined the trends in long run positive real interest rates in relation to inflation reduction episodes in which real interest rates were positive. They found that in almost all the expansionary inflation reduction episodes, real interest rates were, on average, kept below their long-run trend. However, in most contractionary inflation reduction episodes, real interest rates were, on average, kept above their long run trend. (The presence of real interest rates above the long-run trend is often used an indicator of deflationary bias). Their results are consistent with the hypothesis that reducing inflation by increasing positive real interest rates above their long-run trend tends to sacrifice employment for inflation reduction. They also investigated inflation reduction episodes in which real interest rates were negative. In the majority of these cases, they found that negative interest rates were kept below the long run average, but nevertheless, employment grew more slowly than its long run trend. They conclude that this suggests that keeping interest rates negative and below the long run trend cannot be relied upon to increase employment. Braunstein and Heintz also investigated the relation between the real money supply and inflation reduction episodes. They found that in 67 per cent of the contractionary episodes for which data were available, the average annual growth rate of real money supply fell below its long-run trend; while in 60 per cent of the expansionary episodes, real money supply grew faster than its long-run trend. Thus, policies of raising positive real interest rates (relative to long run trend) and tightening real money supply (relative to long run trend) were more likely to be associated with contractionary inflation reduction episodes, in which inflation reduction was achieved at the expense of employment growth.

Braunstein and Heintz investigated whether these policies have gender-differentiated effects by disaggregating employment by sex and examining the behaviour of the female to male employment ratio in relation to its long run trend. They found that in 67 per cent of the contractionary inflation reduction episodes, the female to male employment ratio fell below its long run trend, indicating that women were disproportionately affected by the slowdown in employment. However, in expansionary inflation reduction episodes, there was no clear disproportionate affect on either women or men. The female to male employment ratio increased faster than trend in 53 per cent of cases, and at or below trend in 47 per cent of cases. Braunstein and Heintz conclude that a policy of responding to inflationary pressures by raising positive real interest rates above their long run trend, and reducing real money supply below its long run trend tended to be associated with a greater loss in female than in male employment (relative to long run trends in both).

They noted that in 33 per cent of cases, women's employment was not disproportionately affected by deflationary policies, and investigated whether there is a link between this and the behaviour of the real exchange rate. If women's employment is growing fastest in export sectors (as has been the case in many industrializing developing countries), then avoiding an appreciation of the real exchange rate may offer some protection to the growth of women's employment. They found that in the 33 per cent of contractionary inflation reduction episodes in which women's employment improved relative to its long run trend, the real exchange rate either depreciated or remained at its long run trend. They conclude that "maintaining a competitive exchange rate may offset some of the gender bias observed during contractionary inflation-reduction" (Braunstein and Heintz, 2006: 12).

This is a pioneering study because of the way that it makes a direct link between gender differences in employment outcomes and macroeconomic policies. It would be interesting to know what happened to unpaid work during the episodes of inflation reduction. Were these episodes accompanied by cuts in public expenditure that added to women's unpaid work more than to men's? If this happened, then even if women did not suffer a disproportionate loss of employment, they would have suffered a disproportionate increase in unpaid work, and their overall well-being may have declined, as their total hours of work increased. Unfortunately, the lack of time-series sex disaggregated data on time spent in unpaid domestic work means that it is not possible to provide a definitive answer.

Conclusions

The evidence reviewed in this chapter supports the view that women are particularly disadvantaged by deflationary bias in macroeconomic policy if this intersects with gender biases, such as male breadwinner bias and female carer bias. To realize 'full and productive employment and decent work for all, including for women and young people' requires a combination of employment-focused macroeconomic polices that avoid deflationary bias; public investment in infrastructure and care services that reduce women's unpaid domestic work; and specific measures to counteract female carer bias and male breadwinner bias, such as parental leave for both mothers and fathers, funded by general taxation; and rigorously enforced legislation on equal opportunities and equal pay for work of equal worth.

REFERENCES

Azmat, Ghazala, Maia Guell and Alan Manning (2006). Gender gaps in unemployment rates in OECD countries. *Labor Economics* 24 (1): 1–37.

Braunstein, Elissa, and James Heintz (2006). Gender bias and central bank policy: employment and inflation reduction. Working Paper, Project on 'Alternatives to Inflation Targetting', The Political Economy Research Institute, University of Massachusetts, Amherst.

Budlender, Debbie, and Ann Lisbet Brathaug (2002). Calculating the Value of Unpaid Labour: A Discussion Document. SSA Working Paper, 2002/1, Statistics South Africa, Pretoria. www.statssa.gov.za.

Chakraborty, Lekha (2005). Public Investment and Unpaid Work in India: Selective Evidence from Time Use Data. Paper presented to the Conference on 'Unpaid Work and the Economy: Gender, Poverty and the Millennium Development Goals', Levy Economics Institute, Annandale-on-Hudson, October 1–3, www.levy.org/undp-levy-conference/program_documents.asp

Charmes, Jacques (2006). Gender and time poverty in Sub-Saharan Africa: A review of empirical evidence from UN-sponsored surveys. In Q. Wodon and C.M. Blackden (eds). *Gender, Time Use, and Poverty in Sub-Saharan Africa*. World Bank. Washington, DC.

Chen, Martha, Joann Vanek, Francie Lund, James Heintz, Renana Jhabvala, and Christine Bonner (2005). *Progress of the World's Women, 2005: Women, Work & Poverty.* United Nations Development Fund for Women, New York.

Elson, Diane, and Nilüfer Çağatay (2000). The social content of macroeconomic policies. *World Development* 28 (7): 1347–1363.

Eurostat (2005). *Comparable Time Use Statistics – National Tables from 10 European Countries.* Office for the Official Publications of the European Community, Luxembourg.

Folbre, Nancy (2001). *The Invisible Heart.* The New Press, New York.

Heintz, James (2006). Globalization, economic policy and employment: Poverty and gender implications. Employment Policy Unit, International Labour Office, Geneva.

ILO (2002). *Women and Men in the Informal Economy: A Statistical Picture.* Employment Sector, International Labour Office, Geneva.

ILO (2004). *Global Employment Trends for Women, 2004.* International Labour Office, Geneva.

ILO (2005). *Women's Employment: Global Trends and ILO Responses*. ILO Contribution, 49th Session of the Commission on the Status of Women, United Nations, New York, 28 February – 11 March, International Labour Office, Geneva.

ILO (2006). *Global Employment Trends Brief*. International Labour Office, Geneva.

INEGI (National Institute of Statistics, Geography and Informatics) (2002). *National Time Use Survey*. INEGI, Mexico, DF.

Moser, Caroline (1997). Household responses to poverty and vulnerability. Urban Management Programme Policy Paper Nos 21, 22, 23, 24, World Bank, Washington, DC.

Seguino, Stephanie (2003). Why are women in the Caribbean so much more likely than men to be unemployed? *Social and Economic Studies* 52 (4): 83–120.

Sethuraman, S.V. (1998). Gender, informality and poverty: A global review. Background paper for World Bank, *World Development Report, 2000*, World Bank, Washington, DC.

Shulman, Steven (1991). Why is the black unemployment rate always twice as high as the white unemployment rate? In R. Cornwall and P. Wunnava (eds). *New Approaches to Economic and Social Analyses of Discrimination*. Greenwood, Westport, CT, and Praeger, London: 5–37.

United Nations (1999). *World Survey on the Role of Women in Development. Globalization, Gender and Work*. United Nations, New York.

United Nations (2000). *The World's Women, 2000*. United Nations, New York.

United Nations (2006). Report of the Secretary-General on the work of the organization. General Assembly, Sixty-first Session, Supplement No. 1 (A/61/1), United Nations, New York.

United Nations Development Fund for Women (UNIFEM) (2000). *Progress of the World's Women, 2000*. United Nations Development Fund for Women, New York.

United Nations Development Programme (UNDP) (2000). *Human Development Report, 2000*. Oxford University Press, New York.

United Nations Research Institute for Social Development (UNRISD) (2005). *Gender Equality: Striving for Justice in an Unequal World*. United Nations Research Institute for Social Development, Geneva.

World Bank (2001). *Engendering Development*. Oxford University Press, New York.

World Bank (2006). *World Development Report, 2006: Equity and Development*. Oxford University Press, New York.

Young, Brigitte (2001). The Mistress and the Maid in the Global Economy. In Leo Panitch and Colin Leys (eds). *Socialist Register 2001: Working Classes, Global Realities*. Monthly Review Press, New York: 315–328.

5

Central Banks as Agents of Employment Creation

GERALD EPSTEIN*

Ironically, employment creation has dropped off the direct agenda of most central banks just as the problems of global unemployment, underemployment and poverty are taking centre stage as critical world issues (Heintz, 2006a). The ILO estimates that in 2003, approximately 186 million people were jobless, the highest level ever recorded (ILO, 2004a). The employment to population ratio – a measure of unemployment – has fallen in the last decade, from 63.3 per cent to 62.5 per cent (ILO, 2004b). And as the quantity of jobs relative to need has fallen, there is also a significant global problem with respect to the quality of jobs. The ILO estimates that 22 per cent of the developing world's workers earn less than $1 a day and 1.38 billion (or 57 per cent of the developing world's workers) earn less than $2 a day. To reach the Millennium Development Goal of halving the share of working poor by 2015, sustained, robust economic growth will be required. The ILO estimates that, on average, real GDP growth has to be maintained at 4.7 per cent per year to reduce the share of $1 a day poverty by half by 2015, and significantly more than that to reduce the share of $2 a day poverty by half. According to the ILO, "of the seven regions under consideration in this paper, only the three Asian regions and the Middle East and North Africa region appear on track to meet the $1 target, and East Asia is the only region on track to reduce $2 working poverty by half" (Kapsos, 2004: v; Heintz, 2006a). In addition, IMF economists estimate that economic growth needs to be sustained at 7 per cent per year or more to reach the Millennium Development Goal of reducing poverty by half by 2015 (IMF, 2005: 8).

Yet, for the past decade or more, the so-called 'global best practice' approach to central banking has not focused on economic growth or employment generation; instead, it pursues formal or informal 'inflation-targeting', in which keeping a low rate of inflation – in the low single digits – has been proposed as the dominant and often exclusive target of monetary policy. In this inflation-focused monetary policy, other important goals, such as rapid economic growth and employment creation, are seen as inappropriate direct targets of central bank policy; rather, they are viewed as hoped for – even presumed – by-products of an inflation focused approach to monetary policy (Allen, Baumgartner and Rajan, 2006). Thus, according to this orthodox approach to monetary policy, the focus of policy is on 'stabilization', rather than 'growth' or 'development', with an implicit assumption that once 'stabilization' is achieved, economic growth, employment creation, and poverty reduction will follow.

This orthodox view not only specifies the appropriate target of monetary policy, but also the appropriate tools or instruments. The orthodox approach has emphasized indirect, market-based instruments of policy, such as short term interest rates, as the primary and often exclusive tool of monetary policy (Masson, Savastano and Sharma, 1997). This is in contrast to the 'direct', quantitative tools often used by central banks which have involved credit allocation methods, interest rate ceilings, and other ways to direct credit to priority economic sectors and goals. In short, the orthodox approach has narrowed both the goals and the tools of monetary policy.

After several decades of experience with this inflation-focused, market-based approach, the policy record has been rather disappointing for many countries. In a number of countries, inflation has come down, to be sure, but it is questionable to what extent the drop in inflation is due to changes in domestic monetary policy, rather than the overall global fall in inflation (Ball and Sheridan, 2003; Roger and Stone, 2005). But even if domestic monetary policy *has* reduced inflation, the hoped for gains in employment have, generally, *not* materialized; and, for many countries following this orthodox approach, economic growth has not significantly increased. The key point, then, is this: despite what the orthodox approach maintains, employment generation and economic growth, are *not* automatic by-products of 'stabilization-focused' central bank policy.

Yet, surprisingly, despite a disappointing record, this almost single-minded focus on inflation is gaining a more secure foothold in monetary policy circles, and the circles are widening to include an increasing number of developing countries. This is occurring even as inflation becomes less and less of a global problem while unemployment and underemployment become increasingly dire. According to a recent report by the International Monetary Fund (IMF), an increasing number of central banks in emerging markets are planning to adopt inflation targeting as their operating framework (see Table 5.1). An IMF staff survey of 88 non-industrial countries found that more than half expressed a desire to move to explicit or implicit quantitative inflation targets. More relevant to our concerns, nearly three-quarters of these countries expressed an interest in moving to 'full-fledged' inflation targeting by 2010 (Allen, Baumgartner and Rajan, 2006: 8). To support and encourage this movement, the IMF is providing technical assistance (TA) to many of these countries and is willing to provide more (Table 5.1, and further discussion below). In addition, the IMF is considering altering its conditionality and monitoring structures to include inflation targets. In short, despite little evidence concerning the success of inflation targeting in its promotion of economic growth, employment creation and poverty reduction, and mixed evidence at best that it actually reduces inflation itself, a substantial momentum is building up for full fledged inflation targeting in developing countries. Promotion efforts by the IMF and western-trained economists are at least partly responsible for this increasing popularity.

While it might seem obvious that price stabilization-focused central bank policy represents the only proper role for central banks, in fact, looking at history casts serious doubt on this claim. Far from being the historical norm, this focus by central banks on price stabilization to the exclusion of development represents a sharp break from historical practice, not just in the developing world, but also in the now developed countries as well (Epstein, 2006b). In many of the successful, currently developed countries, as well as in many developing countries in the post-Second World War period, development was seen as a crucial part of the central bank's tasks. Now, by contrast, development and employment have dropped off the priority 'to do' list of central banks in most developing countries.

TABLE 5.1

Inflation targeting countries, current and potential

Country	When adopted	Current Inflation Target (% p. a.)	Technical Assistance requested from and given by IMF
Current Targeters (in order of adoption)			
Emerging Markets			
Israel	1997	1–3	
Czech Republic	1998	3 (+/– 1)	
Poland	1998	2.5 (+/– 1)	
Brazil	1999	4.5 (+/– 2)	
Chile	1999	2–4	
Colombia	1999	5 (+/– .5)	
South Africa	2000	3–6	
Thailand	2000	0 – 3.5	
Korea	2001	2.5 – 3.5	
Mexico	2001	3 (+/–1)	
Hungary	2001	3.5 (+/–1)	
Peru	2002	2.5 (+/–1)	
Philippines	2002	5–6	
Slovak Rep.	2005	3.5 (+/–1)	
Indonesia	2005	5.5 (+/–1)	
Romania	2005	8.8	
Industrial Countries			
New Zealand	1990	1–3	
Canada	1991	1–3	
United Kingdom	1992	2	
Sweden	1993	2 (+/– 1)	
Australia	1993	2–3	
Iceland	2001	2.5	
Norway	2001	2.5	

(contd)

TABLE 5.1 *(contd)*

Country	When adopted	Current Inflation Target (% p. a.)	Technical Assistance requested from and given by IMF
Candidates for Inflation Targeting			
Costa Rica, Egypt, Turkey, Ukraine (4)	Near Term, 1–2 years		Yes
Albania, Armenia, Botswana Dominican Republic, Guatemala, Mauritius, Uganda (8)	Medium Term, 3–5 years		Yes
Angola, Azerbaijan, Georgia, Guinea Morocco, Pakistan, Paraguay (6)	Medium Term, 3–5 years		No
Belarus, China, Kenya, Kyrgyz Republic, Moldova, Serbia, Sri Lanka, Vietnam, Zambia (9)	Long term: more than 5 years		Yes
Bolivia, Honduras, Nigeria, Papua New Guinea, Sudan, Tunisia, Uruguay, Venezuela (8)			No

Source: Allen, Baumgartner and Rajan (2006: Tables 1, 2).

The theme of this chapter is that there should be a return to the historical norm of central bank policy: in particular, employment creation and more rapid economic growth should join inflation and stabilization more generally as key goals of central bank policy.

This chapter outlines why a shift away from inflation targeting, the increasingly fashionable but extremist and destructive approach to central bank policy, and a move back toward a more balanced approach is both feasible and desirable. Of course, the paper does NOT argue that stabilization, including a moderate inflation rate, is unimportant. Indeed, historically, some central banks went much too far in downplaying the stabilization role, sometimes with disastrous consequences. But this does not mean that the optimal policy is to go to the other extreme and ignore the developmental role entirely. As I try to show in this paper, balancing between the price stabilization and developmental roles is both desirable and feasible for many central banks. In this context, for many countries, a focus on employment creation is a desirable goal of monetary policy.

Of course, central banks need not, and indeed, *cannot* be the only institution having an employment generation role. But, in most developing countries, central banks need to cooperate with other institutions by doing much more than simply keeping inflation rates in the low single digits. To bring this about, many institutions will have to play a supporting role. Among them is the IMF, which by modifying its conditionality and monitoring program approach is enshrining inflation control as a dominant policy. The IMF should change its advice to a more balanced position between inflation control and employment generation and poverty reduction.

The rest of the paper is organized as follows. In the next section, we briefly survey the current structure and impacts of inflation focused monetary policy, including a discussion of inflation targeting. The third section discusses alternatives to inflation-focused central banks, concentrating on the results of a multi-country research project. This section shows that there are viable, socially productive alternatives to inflation targeting, including those that focus on employment generation, and make the case that these alternatives should be further developed. The fourth and penultimate section discusses the historical practice of central banking in developed and developing countries, and, in particular, its developmental role. The final section concludes.

Structure, Promise and Impacts of Inflation Focused Monetary Policy

According to its advocates, 'full fledged' inflation targeting consists of five components: absence of other nominal anchors, such as exchange rates or nominal GDP; an institutional commitment to price stability; absence of fiscal dominance; policy (instrument) independence; and policy transparency and accountability (Mishkin and Schmidt-Hebbel, 2001: 3; Bernanke and others, 1999). In practice, while few central banks reach the 'ideal' of being 'full fledged' inflation targeters, many others still focus on fighting inflation to the virtual exclusion of other goals. The overriding announced goal of inflation targeting central banks is typically 'price stability', usually defined to be an inflation rate in the low single digits (Bernanke and others, 1999: 99). In addition, inflation targeting is usually associated with changes in the law that enhance the independence of the central bank (Bernanke and others, 1999: 102; Mishkin and Schmidt-Hebbel, 2001: 8).

The major claims made by advocates of inflation targeting are that it will[1]:

- Reduce the rate of inflation
- Enhance the credibility of monetary policy
- Reduce the *sacrifice* ratio associated with contractionary monetary policy
- Help to attract foreign investment

The evidence on these claims is mainly in the negative. It is true that countries that adopt inflation targeting often achieve lower inflation rates. But there is strong evidence that this decline in inflation might not be due to inflation targeting itself, but rather to the general decline in worldwide inflation or to a simple reversion to a more normal inflation rate (Ball and Sheridan, 2003; for a contrary view, though, see Allen, Baumgartner and Sharma, 2006, further discussed below). In addition, most evidence indicates that inflation targeting central banks do not reduce inflation at any lower cost than other countries' central banks in terms of foregone output. That is, inflation targeting does not appear to increase the credibility of central bank policy and therefore, does not appear to reduce the 'sacrifice ratio' (see Bernanke and others, 1999, and Epstein, 2000, for detailed surveys of the literature). Typically, central banks that reduce inflation do so the old-fashioned way: by raising interest rates, causing recessions or slowing growth, and by throwing people out of work.[2] Moreover, there is no evidence that countries adopting inflation targeting manage to attract more usable foreign investment.

A recent study by IMF economists, using a complex econometric model and policy simulations, reports findings that inflation targeting economies experience reductions in the *volatility* of inflation, without experiencing increased *volatility* in real variables such as GDP. According to these estimates, inflation targeting central banks do enhance economic 'stability' relative to other monetary rules, such as pegged exchange rates and money supply rules (Allen, Baumgartner and Rajan, 2006). While intriguing, these results are only as strong as the simulation model on which they are based, and are only as relevant as the relevance of the questions they pose' moreover, they are only as broad as the alternatives they explore. On all these scores, these IMF results are problematic. First, they do not simulate the impact of inflation targeting relative to other possible policy regimes, such as the real targeting regime discussed below. Second, the model is based on estimates of potential output that are themselves affected by monetary policy (Tobin, 1980). Hence, if monetary policy slows economic growth, it also lowers the rate of growth of potential output, and therefore reduces the gap between the two, thereby *appearing* to *stabilize the economy*. But in fact, it does so at the expense of slowing growth or even generating stagnation. This highlights the third key point: even if it could be shown that inflation targeting does a good job at stabilization, it is crucial to remember that the stabilization role of monetary policy is only one of the tasks facing central banks; the other task is to contribute directly to economic growth, employment creation and poverty reduction, and the IMF study fails to look at the impact of inflation targeting on the rate of growth of employment, or on the quality of employment. Yet, these are the issues at stake here.

ASYMMETRIES AND MISSES IN INFLATION TARGETING REGIMES

Experiences with inflation targeting present another odd feature: inflation targets are frequently missed, and often by a great margin. Moreover, inflation rates are just as likely to be too low as too high, and sometimes, more so (see Table 5.2). In other words, monetary policy is often more likely to be too tight than too loose. Yet, despite often missing the targets, countries which have adopted inflation targeting do not give it up. This presents several asymmetries which are possibly costly for employment and growth. If under inflation targeting, inflation is often too low, that means that central banks may be keeping monetary policy *too tight*, with possible negative implications for employment and growth. Second, why do countries continue to adopt inflation targeting even though the targets are often missed? With a stunningly Panglossian faith, IMF economists surmise: "These misses do not seem to reflect 'bad' monetary policy; otherwise, the regime would surely have been abandoned or substantially modified" (Roger and Stone, 2005: 37).[3]

TABLE 5.2
Inflation outcomes of inflation targeting countries

| | Frequency of Deviations (%) | | |
	Total	Below	Above
All Countries	43.5	24.2	19.3
Stable Inflation Targets	32.2	21.7	10.6
Disinflation Targets	59.7	27.7	10.6
Industrial Countries	34.8	22.5	12.3
Emerging Market Countries	52.2	25.9	26.2

Note: These outcomes are measured relative to the edges of target ranges.
Source: Roger and Stone (2005: 22, Table 7)

Another more likely interpretation is that once countries adopt inflation targeting, they are locked into it. They feel they cannot abandon it for fear that abandoning inflation targeting will send the 'wrong' signal to investors and could prove costly in terms of 'investor confidence', leading perhaps to exchange rate instability and capital flight. If this 'fear of inflation' is true, then countries maintain the inflation targeting framework, even if they often miss the targets.

Some might argue that this means an inflation targeting regime is a 'paper tiger', and that it therefore cannot have significant effects for good or ill. But I believe this is a mistaken interpretation. For one thing, as just mentioned, inflation targeters are just as likely, if not more likely, to have a monetary policy that is too tight in the sense that inflation is too low. But second, as long as central banks have an inflation targeting framework, they can argue that they do not need to worry about other objectives *except insofar as they affect inflation*. But, of course, this absolves central banks entirely of their developmental obligations, and eliminates a key tool of macroeconomic policy from the developmental arsenal that attempts to expand good jobs, among other goals. Inflation targeting central banks can simply say: "Employment creation? That's not MY department!"

PRE-REQUISITES FOR INFLATION TARGETING

Even if it could be shown that, in theory, inflation targeting or inflation focused central bank policy are the appropriate policy for countries that could undertake such a regime, there is still the question of whether a country has the ability to successfully undertake inflation targeting. This issue has typically gone under the rubric of whether countries satisfy the structural and institutional 'pre-requisites' for inflation targeting.

There has been a substantial evolution in the IMF's attitude toward this question in recent years. Masson, Savastano and Sharma, (1997), in a widely cited IMF working paper, argued that the institutional pre-requisites for successful inflation targeting were: 1) the ability to carry out an independent monetary policy, that is free of fiscal dominance, or a commitment to another nominal anchor, like the exchange rate, and 2) a quantitative framework linking policy instruments, such as a short term interest rate, to inflation. They concluded that: "These pre-requisites are largely absent among developing countries, though several of them could with some further institutional changes and an overriding commitment to low inflation make use of an IT framework" (Masson, Savastano and Sharma, 1997: 1). This is not exactly a ringing endorsement of the possibilities of successful inflation targeting in the developing world.[4]

Fast forward ten years and one gets a very different assessment from IMF economists. In an IMF report, 'Inflation Targeting and the IMF', IMF economists revisit this question in a section entitled 'Are Developing Countries Good Candidates for Inflation Targeting?' Here, the IMF argues that the pre-requisites are too rigid and agree with those who argue that the "list of initial conditions is not meant to constitute strict prerequisites for IT" (IMF, 2006: 17). The IMF claims that: "Our findings also suggest the need for a more nuanced, less 'mechanical' view of necessary, as opposed to desirable, conditions for successful adoption of inflation targeting" (p. 17).

Hence, there has clearly been a shift in focus by the IMF, from raising serious concerns about whether inflation targeting is appropriate for most developing countries, to a view that suggests that virtually any central bank can adopt targets if the government simply has the "will to make it so". This implies a much stronger advocacy of inflation targeting by the IMF than seemed apparent in the past. This is also reflected in the IMF's changing views on conditionality.

INFLATION TARGETING AND IMF CONDITIONALITY

As indicated above, the promotion of inflation targeting has implications for the type of conditionality the IMF imposes in conjunction with its lending programs. As the IMF states, "Conditionality in Fund-supported programs is intended primarily to ensure that Fund resources are used to support adjustment toward sustained external viability, and thereby to safeguard the capacity to repay the Fund. Traditionally, monetary conditionality consists of limits on monetary aggregates – specifically, a floor is set for the level of net international reserves (NIR) and a ceiling is established on the net domestic assets (NDA) or on base money" (IMF, 2006).

The IMF is concerned, however, that this NDA-NIR approach could allow for higher inflation than they might like, if, for example, larger than necessary increases in net international reserves result from inflows of capital (see Epstein and Heintz, 2006; Allen, Baumgartner and Rajan, 2006). As a result, inflation targeting might require a further tightening of monetary conditions for countries undergoing IMF programs in order to maintain inflation rates in the low single digits. To the extent that such tightening slows employment growth even further, inflation targeting as part of IMF conditionality could have even more severe impacts on employment and poverty impacts for developing countries than the current NDA-NIR conditionality.

WHY THE FOCUS ON INFLATION?

There is a further, more basic problem with inflation targeting and the neo-liberal approach to central bank policy more generally. Why is there such a focus on fighting inflation to the exclusion of other goals? As reported in Bruno and Easterly (1998) and Epstein (2000), there is a great deal of evidence that moderate rates of inflation, inflation up to 20 per cent or even more, has no predictable negative consequences on the real economy: it is not associated with slower growth, reduced investment, less foreign direct investment, or any other important real variable that one can find.

Some IMF economists and others have argued more recently that earlier results are misleading. They claim that there are non-linearities, such as threshold effects, that imply that inflation begins to harm economic growth at much lower levels than claimed by Bruno (1995) and others (Ghosh and Phillips, 1998; Kahn and Senhadji, 2001; Burdekin and others, 2004). Some of these find that inflation begins to harm growth in developing countries at rates as low as 3 per cent. However, an even more recent paper by Pollin and Zhu (2006) finds that, taking into account non-linear impacts of inflation on economic growth, inflation and economic growth are sometimes positively related, especially when the cause of inflation is demand expansion. More generally, they find that for developing countries, inflation below about 15 per cent is not harmful for economic growth, and can, indeed be beneficial (Pollin and Zhu, 2006: 606). Hence, they conclude that, there is little justification, at least on growth grounds, to focus the economy on bringing inflation down to the low single digits, especially if such policy has economic costs.

Apart from growth effects, however, many economists have argued that inflation harms the poor more than the rich. Hence, on distribution grounds, inflation reduction into the low single digits should be a priority. While more research is necessary to fully investigate this claim, important recent work by Jayadev (2006a, 2006b) calls this conventional wisdom into question. Jayadev looks at survey data on people's preferences about inflation versus unemployment. Whereas previous researchers had asked if people disliked inflation, Jayadev investigated the more appropriate question: which is a bigger problem – inflation or unemployment? This question better reflects the idea that there is a trade-off between the two, at least in the short to medium term. When people are asked this trade-off question, interesting and highly relevant results emerge. Jayadev (2006a) finds that those in the lowest quintile of the income distribution are more likely to perceive unemployment as a more serious problem than inflation, while those in the top quintile are more likely to have the opposite view. Jayadev (2006b) finds similar results when he divides the sample by classes, rather than by income groups. He finds that workers, and in particular, low-skilled workers, on average, find unemployment a more serious problem than inflation (Jayadev, 2006b).

Of course, all agree that very high levels of inflation, above 40 per cent, can have very serious impacts on growth and, possibly, the distribution of income. But there appears to be very little justification for monetary policy oriented toward keeping inflation in the low single digits, especially when employment and poverty are significant problems.

In addition to these concerns, Braunstein and Heintz (2006) find that dis-inflationary monetary policy in developing countries, like that undertaken in connection with inflation-focused monetary policy regimes, has a disproportionately negative employment effect on women, relative to men. Their excellent work is highly suggestive that there may be important gender effects of monetary policy, suggesting that this area needs much more research than it is currently receiving.

CENTRAL BANK POLICY FOR EMPLOYMENT CREATION

One reason that 'inflation-focused monetary policy' has gained so many adherents is the common perception that there is no viable alternative monetary policy that can improve growth and employment prospects. There are three main factors accounting for this perception. First, many economists believe the pre-Keynesian natural rate – or, alternatively, the 'non-accelerating inflation rate of unemployment' (NAIRU) – view of the labour market that claims that, left to their own devices, market forces will automatically bring the economy to full employment and, furthermore, any attempt to reduce unemployment further will only result in ever worsening inflation.

However, there is substantial evidence that the NAIRU theory is not empirically well based. The natural rate, or NAIRU, if it exists, does not seem to be constant; importantly, it seems to be affected by macroeconomic policy itself; in some countries, its effects are asymmetric, with increases in unemployment reducing inflation, but reductions in unemployment not increasing inflation; and it no longer even seems central to the work of mainstream economics (see Eisner, 1997; Baker, 2000; Ball and Sheridan, 2003; Ball and Mankiw, 2002; Pollin, 2005; Hall, 2005).

Second, in an internationally financially integrated economy with high levels of international capital flows, monetary policy can be extremely challenging. In particular, it might be very difficult to gear monetary policy by targeting monetary aggregates, or by pegging an exchange rate along with trying to promote employment growth. This is often seen as the so-called 'trilemma' which says that central banks can only have two out of three of the following: open capital markets, fixed exchange rates, and an autonomous monetary policy geared toward domestic goals. While this so-called 'trilemma' is not strictly true as a theoretical matter, in practice, it does raise serious issues of monetary management (Frenkel and Taylor, 2006). From my perspective, the real crux of the problem turns out to be one leg of this 'trilemma', namely the fact that orthodox economists, by and large, have taken for granted that eliminating capital controls is the best policy, and that virtually complete financial liberalization with respect to the foreign sector is the optimal policy. Yet, recent evidence amply shows that open capital markets can create very costly problems for developing countries and that many successful developing countries have used a variety of capital management techniques to manage these flows in order, among other things, to help them escape this so-called 'trilemma' (Prasad and others, 2003; Ocampo, 2002 ; Epstein, Grabel and Jomo, 2005).

Third, few economists have developed and proposed concrete alternatives to inflation targeting monetary policy in the current context, so those searching for alternatives have trouble finding models. There is some truth to this last point, but economists are in the process of rectifying this problem, and I report on these efforts in this section. The main point of this section is this: there *are* viable alternatives to inflation-focused monetary policy (including inflation targeting), alternatives that can promote more and better employment and poverty reduction. Moreover, these alternatives are also responsive to the needs to keep inflation at a moderate level and to maintain an exchange rate that is not excessively volatile: in short, these alternatives are responsive to stabilization needs as well as developmental needs.

In this section, I report on country studies undertaken by a team of researchers working on a PERI/Bilkent project on alternatives to inflation targeting, as well as a United Nations (UN) sponsored study of employment targeting economic policy for South Africa.[5] The countries covered in this project are Argentina, Brazil, Mexico, India, The Philippines, South Africa, Turkey, and Vietnam. As will be illustrated by these studies, one size does *not* fit all. A range of alternatives were developed in these papers, all the way from modest changes in the inflation targeting framework to allow for more focus on exchange rates and a change in the index of inflation used, to a much broader change in the overall mandate of the central bank to a focus on employment targeting, rather than inflation targeting. Some of the alternative policies focus exclusively on changes in central bank policy, while for other countries, changes in the broad policy framework and in the interactions of monetary, financial and fiscal policy are proposed. Some incorporate explicit goals and targets, while others prefer more flexibility and somewhat less transparency. But all the studies agreed that the responsibilities of central banks, particularly in developing countries, while including maintaining a moderate rate of inflation, must be broader than that, and should include other crucial 'real' variables that have a direct impact on employment, poverty and economic growth, such as the real exchange rate, employment, or investment.[6] They also agree that in many cases, central banks must broaden their available policy tools to allow them to reach multiple goals, including, if necessary, the implementation of capital account management techniques (Ocampo, 2002 ; Epstein, Grabel and Jomo, 2005).

ALTERNATIVES TO INFLATION TARGETING: VARIATIONS ON A THEME

Modest, but Useful Adjustments to the Inflation Targeting Regime

Some of the country studies in the PERI/Bilkent project proposed only modest changes to the inflation targeting regime. In the case of Mexico, for example, the authors argue that the inflation targeting regime has allowed for more flexible monetary policy than had occurred under regimes with strict monetary targets or strict exchange rate targets (Galindo and Ros, 2006). They suggest modifying the IT framework to make it somewhat more employment friendly. In the case of Mexico, Galindo and Ros find that monetary policy was asymmetric with respect to exchange rate movements – tightening when exchange rates depreciated, but *not* loosening when exchange rates appreciated. This lent a bias in favour of an over-valued exchange rate in Mexico. So Galindo and Ros (2006) propose a 'neutral' monetary policy so that the central bank of Mexico responds symmetrically to exchange rate movements and thereby avoids the bias toward over-valuation without fundamentally changing the inflation targeting framework.[7]

In his study of Brazil, Nelson Barbosa-Filho also proposed extending the inflation targeting framework, but as we will see shortly, in a more dramatic way. He writes "because of Brazil's past experience with high inflation, the best policy is to continue to target inflation while the economy moves to a more stable macroeconomic situation.

So far the great gain from inflation targeting has been the increase in the transparency and accountability of monetary policy in Brazil" (Barbosa-Filho, 2006). But he goes on to say, "The crucial question is not to eliminate inflation targeting, but actually make it compatible with fast income growth and a stable public and foreign finance" (Barbosa-Filho, 2006). As discussed in the next section, in order to do that, Barbosa-Filho joins a number of the country case study authors in proposing a monetary policy to maintain a stable and competitive real exchange rate (SCRER) which, they argue, will have a number of significant benefits for many of these economies and their peoples.

A Competitive and Stable Real Exchange Rate

As just indicated, a number of authors, following the lead of Frenkel and Taylor (2006), Frenkel and Ros (2006) and Frenkel and Rapetti (2006), argue that central bank should maintain a moderate inflation rate *and* should maintain a competitive and stable real exchange rate. They note that the real exchange rate can affect employment, and the economy more generally, through a number of channels: (1) By affecting the level of aggregate demand (*the macroeconomic channel*) (2) By affecting the cost of labour relative to other goods, and thereby affecting the amount of labour hired per unit of output (*the labour intensity channel*) and by affecting employment through its impact on investment and economic growth (*the development channel*) (e.g. Frenkel and Ros, 2006: 634–637). While the size and even direction of these channel effects might differ from country to country, in many countries, including countries in Latin America, maintaining a competitive and stable real exchange rate is likely to have a positive employment impact through some combination of these effects. For example, Frenkel and Ros find that most Latin American countries experiencing increases in unemployment in the 1990s, were characterized by significant appreciations in their real exchange rate. As Frenkel and Rapetti (2006) show, following the economic crisis in Argentina, maintaining a competitive real exchange rate has proven to have a strong positive impact on the recovery in employment.

From the point of view of monetary policy, the challenge is how to design a policy to maintain a stable and competitive real exchange rate

(SCRER) so that it does not get undermined by massive speculative capital flows. The danger is that if the markets see the central bank trying to manipulate the exchange rate, then the exchange rate will be subject to attacks and such attacks will undermine the ability of the central bank to prevent the currency from excessively appreciating or depreciating (Frenkel and Rapetti, 2006; Frenkel and Taylor, 2006).

First, it should be noted that many developing countries already take exchange rate movements into account when formulating monetary policy, including implementation of inflation targeting (e.g. Ho and McCauley, 2003). So, the so-called bi-polar view of exchange rate regimes – in which countries either have perfectly floating exchange rates or adopt a foreign currency or a currency board as a 'hard peg' – does not seem accurate. Most developing countries find themselves having to manage their exchange rates to some degree or other. Ho and McCauley point out that many of these countries, especially many of the success stories of East Asia, use capital account management techniques to help them maintain a stable and competitive exchange rate.

Second, central banks can, and do, adopt various types of capital controls and other types of capital account management techniques, to help manage exchange rates in the face of speculative capital flows (Ocampo, 2002; Epstein, Grabel, Jomo, 2005). This is an example where central banks may need to expand their range of policy tools in order to incorporate multiple targets.

In the PERI/Bilkent project, a number of country study authors proposed a new framework for central banks in which they should include a "stable and competitive real exchange rate" (SCRER) as an "intermediate goal". These countries included Argentina, Brazil, Mexico, the Philippines and Viet Nam (see Frenkel and Rapetti, 2006; Barbosa-Filho, 2006; Galindo and Ros, 2006; Lim, 2006; Packard, 2006). In all these cases, the authors argued that such a policy would help their economies pursue a more employment oriented growth path, while maintaining inflation in check. They all suggested that the countries they studied might need to impose short-term capital controls and other capital account management techniques to help them manage the exchange rate while maintaining moderate inflation.

For the case of Brazil, Barbosa-Filho (2006) developed a more elaborate policy framework which includes, as in the papers mentioned above, a focus on a competitive and stable real exchange rate. But, in addition, given Brazil's large public debt, Barbosa-Filho also proposes that the central bank target a reduction in the real interest rate, which would reduce the Brazilian debt service burdens and help increase productive investment. In terms of the familiar targets and instruments framework, Barbosa-Filho proposes that the Brazilian central bank choose exports, inflation and investment as ultimate targets, and focus on the inflation rate, a competitive and stable real exchange rate and the real interest rate as intermediate targets. Barbosa-Filho also elaborates on the monetary policy tools that can be used to reach these intermediate and ultimate targets. To maintain the SCRER, Barbosa-Filho proposes an asymmetric managed floating exchange rate regime in which the Brazilian central bank places a (moving) ceiling on the appreciation of the exchange rate, and, when necessary implements tight macroeconomic policy to prevent speculative attacks leading to excessive depreciations. The central bank should also attempt to lower the real interest rate. In order to achieve these goals, the central bank can use direct manipulation of the policy interest rate, bank reserve requirements and bank capital requirements (Barbosa-Filho, 2006).

Brazil is not the only highly indebted country in our project sample. Turkey is another case with that problem. Developing an alternative to inflation targeting using a computable general equilibrium (CGE) model for the case of Turkey, Voyvoda and Yeldan simulated the impact of a shift in policy from a strict inflation targeting regime, to one which had a focus on the competitiveness of the real exchange rate.[8] They find that such a shift generates much more rapid growth and employment creation, but at the expense of some worsening of the government debt position, relative to the strict inflation targeting and fiscal surplus regime currently in place (Voyvoda and Yeldan, 2006).

Frenkel and Rapetti, in the case of Argentina, show that targeting a stable and competitive real exchange rate has been very successful in helping to maintain more rapid economic growth and employment generation. In the case of India, Jha also argues against an inflation targeting regime, in favour of one that "errs on the side of undervaluation of the exchange rate" with possible help from temporary resort to capital controls (Jha, 2006: 30–31). Jha argues that, to some extent, such a policy would be a simple continuation of policies undertaken in India in the past. In Vietnam, Packard concludes, "a strict inflation targeting (IT) regime is not appropriate for Vietnam. IT's rigid rules constrain policymakers to operate in a framework that requires inflation to take priority over more pressing development objectives.... I argue that a stable and competitive real exchange rate is (a) superior alternative, precisely because it sets as a target a key macroeconomic relative price that is realistic, sustainable, and growth enhancing" (Packard, 2006).

For Mexico, Galindo and Ros propose a more fundamental alternative to inflation targeting. They propose combining inflation targeting with real exchange rate targeting (Galindo and Ros, 2006). "More precisely, the central bank would promote a competitive exchange rate by establishing a sliding floor to the exchange rate in order to prevent excessive appreciation (an 'asymmetric band'). This would imply intervening in the foreign exchange market at times when the exchange rate hits the floor (i.e. an appreciated exchange rate) but allows the exchange rate to float freely otherwise" (Galindo and Ros, 2006). They point out that such a floor would work against excessive capital inflows by speculators because they would know the central bank will intervene to stop excessive appreciation. If need be, Galindo and Ros also propose temporary capital controls, as do some of the other authors from the PERI/Bilkent project.

More Comprehensive Alternatives to Inflation Targeting

Case studies on other countries propose more comprehensive policy alternatives to simple inflation-focused monetary policy, including inflation targeting. Joseph Lim proposes a comprehensive alternative to inflation targeting for the case of the Philippines. Lim argues that the Philippine government has been seeking to achieve a record of dramatically higher economic growth, but that its monetary policy has been inappropriate to achieving that goal. He therefore proposes an 'alternative' that "clearly dictates much more than just a move from monetary targeting to inflation targeting". Lim argues that any viable alternative for the Philippines must take into account several key constraints or realities: 1) Easier monetary policy, by itself, will not stimulate investment or growth because it is accompanied by weak financial confidence and stricter financial requirements on banks. 2) Fiscal policy is highly constrained because of a large public debt. 3) High economic growth, by itself, will not necessarily enhance the quality of growth – i.e., improving the growth of good jobs with good wages. 4) Volatile external accounts and foreign exchange rates undermine rapid and high quality growth.

Lim's proposals include: 1) Maintenance of a stable and competitive real exchange rate (SCRER), either by pegging the exchange rate or intensively managing it as in South Korea. 2) To help manage the exchange rate, capital account management techniques are likely to be needed. 3) This should include strong financial supervision to prevent excessive undertaking of short-term foreign debt, and tax based capital controls on short-term capital flows, as were used, for example in Chile, an explicit stating of output and employment goals, as the central bank transitions from a purely inflation-targeting regime. Lim argues that these policies can have beneficial impacts on the current Philippine problems of high fiscal deficits, lack of financial confidence and unemployment. 4) Incomes and anti-monopoly policies to limit inflation to moderate levels, and 5) Targeted credit programs, especially for export-oriented and small and medium sized enterprises that can contribute to productivity growth and employment.

These policy proposals in broad outlines are similar to those proposed by Epstein (2006a) for the case of South Africa, which, in turn, have been developed in a much broader framework and in more detail by Pollin and others (2006).

An Employment-Targeted Economic Program for South Africa

In March 2005, to pick one recent, indicative date, South Africa had an unemployment rate of anywhere from 26 to 40 per cent, depending on exactly how it is counted. South Africa's government has pledged to cut the unemployment rate by 50 per cent, bringing the official unemployment rate to 13 per cent by the year 2014 (see Pollin and others, 2006: xiii). Pollin and others (2006) developed an "employment-targeted economic program" designed to accomplish this goal, with a focus on monetary policy, credit policy, capital management techniques, fiscal policy and industrial policy. Here, 'employment targeting' replaces inflation targeting as the proposed operating principle behind central bank policy, and moderate inflation becomes an additional constraint which the central bank must take into account when formulating policy (Epstein, 2006a).

Under this framework, the central bank, along with other key government institutions, identify an employment (or, in this case, an 'unemployment rate') target. Then, on the basis of models and estimates of the South African macro-economy a set of monetary policy instruments are determined – *along with a number of other policy tools such as credit policy and fiscal policy* – which, together, can achieve the target unemployment rate, while maintaining a moderate inflation rate and an acceptable level of exchange rate variability. In the particular model developed by Epstein in Pollin and others (2006), a simulation model shows that if the South African Reserve Bank lowers the interest rate from 11 to 7 per cent and holds it at that level for 5 years, economic growth will increase, on average, by 0.5 per cent per year, inflation will go up by 1 percentage point and the increase in exchange rate variability will be quite modest. In combination with other policies, such as credit guarantees and subsidized credit for labour-intensive sectors, as well as capital management techniques and incomes policies if necessary, the unemployment rate can be halved by 2014, as proposed by the South African government.

Hence, in the case of South Africa, as part of a coherent economic program, an employment-targeting central bank apparently can plausibly achieve a significant reduction in unemployment, while keeping inflation and exchange rate variability in check (Epstein, 2006a; Pollin and others, 2006).

Summary

The major lesson of these case studies and auxiliary materials is that there are well thought out and plausibly viable alternatives to inflation targeting that can focus more on important social, real sector outcomes such as employment generation, poverty reduction, export promotion and investment enhancement. If inflation targeting is resilient as the 'big idea' of modern central bank policy because many perceive that there is no alternative, these case studies provide an antidote by showing that viable alternatives are plausible and can be further developed and implemented. Indeed, as I argue in the next section, doing so would be consistent with long-standing historical practice.

Central Banks as Agents of Economic Development

The employment-targeting approach to central bank policy described in the previous section might seem quite alien to those schooled in the orthodox tradition of inflation targeting and financial liberalization. In fact, policies like those described above have been quite common historically in both currently developed and developing countries (Epstein, 2006b). Over the years, central banks have been seen as agents of economic development, not just agents of economic stabilization. And while sometimes central banks have failed quite spectacularly in this mission, there have been other important success stories, including important periods in the US, UK, France, Germany, Japan, South Korea and India, to name just a few examples. In continental Europe, the banking system, often directed by the central bank in conjunction with the ministry of finance, helped to mobilize and direct credit for industrial development (Pollin, 1995; Grabel, 2000). Even in the US and UK these policies were used to direct policy to promote social sectors such as housing; in the US and the UK, central bank policy and regulations were used to promote the financial sector as well (Epstein, 2006b).

As for developing countries, Alice Amsden describes the key role that investment banks played in the industrialization success stories such as South Korea, Taiwan, Malaysia, Brazil, Argentina and others, in mobilizing and directing savings to key industrial sectors, and in particular those specializing in exports (2001). In many of these cases, central banks were a key part of the government apparatus that played a supporting role by maintaining low interest rates, maintaining capital controls to help stabilize exchange rates at competitive levels, and sometimes engaging in direct lending for preferred purposes.

In some countries, engaging in these developmental roles, using a wide variety of instruments, was widely seen as a key part of the central bank's mission. After the Second World War, there was a major transformation of central banking in the developing world. In many respects, these changes paralleled those in the developed world just described. But in developing countries, central banks were much more emphatically *agents of economic development* than in many richer countries (Epstein, 2006b). As described by the renowned monetary historian of the New York Federal Reserve, Arthur I. Bloomfield:

> During the past decade there has been a marked proliferation and development of central banking facilities in the underdeveloped countries of the world, along with an increasing resort to the use of monetary policy as an instrument of economic control. Since 1945, central banks have been newly established and pre-existing ones thoroughly reorganized, in no less than some twenty-five underdeveloped countries. In other cases the powers of pre-existing central banks have been broadened.... in large part the recent growth of central banking in the economically backward areas has also reflected a desire on the part of the governments concerned to be able to pursue a monetary policy designed to promote more rapid economic development and to mitigate undue swings in national money incomes (Bloomfield 1957: 190).

Bloomfield goes on to describe the functions, powers, and goals of these central banks:

> Many of the central banks, especially those established since 1945 *with the help of Federal Reserve advisers* (emphasis added), are characterized by unusually wide and flexible powers. A large number of instruments of general and selective credit control, some of a novel

character, are provided for. Powers are given to the central bank to engage in a wide range of credit operations with commercial banks and in some cases with other financial institutions..... These and other powers were specifically provided in the hope of enabling the central banks... to pursue a more *purposive* (emphasis added) and effective monetary possible than had been possible for most.... that had been set up... during the twenties and thirties... (that) for the most part (had) been equipped with exceeding orthodox statutes and limited powers which permitted little scope for a monetary policy *designed to promote economic development and internal stability* (emphasis added) (Bloomfield, 1957: 191).

Somewhat surprisingly, from the perspective of today's financial orthodoxy, the Federal Reserve Bank of New York helped to establish developing country central banks and encouraged them to have a broad range of monetary and credit powers, especially in contrast to the orthodoxy of the 1920s and 1930s. Of course, the Federal Reserve continued to be concerned about the importance of stabilization, controlling excessive credit creation and maintaining moderate inflation.

But (the central bank's) efforts need not, and in fact should not, stop here. The majority of central banks in underdeveloped countries have in actual practice adopted a variety of measures designed more effectively to promote the over-all development of their economies. Some of these measures are admittedly outside the traditional scope of central banking, but central banking in these countries should not necessarily be evaluated in terms of the standards and criteria applied in the more developed ones.... the central bank can seek to influence the flow of bank credit and indeed of savings in directions more in keeping with development ends (Bloomfield, 1957: 197).

Bloomfield describes the same tools of credit manipulation described earlier with respect to Europe, Japan and even the United States:

selective credit controls applied to the banking system, through help in establishing and supporting special credit institutions catering to specialized credit needs, and through influence over the lending policies of such institutions, it can help to some degree to re-channel real resources in desired directions, both between the public and private sector and within the private sector itself (Bloomfield 1957: 198).[9]

While many central banks in developing countries adopted a developmental mission, alongside their stabilization objectives, not all of them succeeded in balancing the two. By 1971, Andrew Brimmer of the US Federal Reserve Board revisited the issue of central banking in the developing world, and concluded that many of these countries had sacrificed too much stability for the developmental results achieved (Brimmer, 1971). To be sure, there are many cases where central banks in the developing world failed to prevent balance of payments crises and excessively high levels of inflation, indeed, even hyper-inflation.[10]

Still, there are plenty of examples of success stories, where central banks supported government developmental goals, while maintaining key stabilization requirements, often by using a variety of monetary instruments, including credit subsidies, capital controls, asset-based reserve requirements, and interest rate ceilings. Today, of course, these policies would need to be tailored to modern conditions, as described above. But doing so, far from being a novel procedure, would, in fact, be well in the established tradition of central banking in both the developed and developing world.

CONCLUSION

Mentioned earlier was the resilience of inflation targeting despite the common target misses; and also mentioned was the expressed desire of many developing countries to adopt inflation targeting despite its apparent lack of success in reducing inflation or promoting economic growth, employment creation or poverty reduction. This chapter has argued that this inflation targeting 'fad', supported with technical assistance by the IMF, is far from benign. It creates in central banks a *culture* of inflation focus, or even inflation obsession. Millions of dollars are spent studying every aspect of inflation, but few aspects of unemployment; thousands of hours of the time of highly scarce, skilled economists are spent pouring over complex models designed to show how to get inflation down from 8 to 4 per cent, but not on how to create more and better jobs; and if other government officials or those in civil society ask the central bank to do something about employment creation, the central banks can respond, "that's not our job".

More than anything else, the cost of inflation-focused monetary regimes is to divert the attention of the some of the most highly trained and skilled economists and policy makers in developing countries away from the tasks that previous generations of central bankers took for granted as being their main job: to help their countries develop, to create jobs, and to foster socially productive economic growth. It is time to return to an earlier generation of central banking where central banks were seen as agents of economic development, including as agents of employment creation. But, it is always crucial to keep in mind this modern lesson: Central banks must balance their developmental goals with the crucial task of macroeconomic stabilization. Otherwise, both stabilization and development will be lost.

NOTES

* The author thanks José Antonio Ocampo and Jomo K.S. for help, and all the members of the PERI/Bilkent Alternatives to Inflation Targeting Project, and PERI colleagues, including Robert Pollin, James Heintz, Leonce Ndikumana, Erinc Yeldan, Roberto Frenkel, and Arjun Jayadev, for many helpful discussions and Lynda Pickbourn for excellent research assistance. I also thank the funders of the PERI/Bilkent Alternatives to Inflation Targeting project, including UN-DESA, Ford Foundation, Rockefeller Brothers Fund and PERI for their support. Of course, remaining errors are mine alone.

1 See Bernanke and others (1999), Mishkin and Schmidt-Hebbel (2001) and Roger and Stone (2005) for recent surveys.

2 Clifton, Leon and Wong (2001) report some findings that inflation targeting might have improved the inflation/unemployment trade-off in OECD countries, but they do not look at emerging market countries.

3 They offer an alternative answer as well: "Another way to answer this question is to note the lack of alternative regimes" (Roger and Stone, 2005: 38). I will discuss this point more below.

4 Eichengreen and others (1999) and Eichengreen (2002), among other economists, have concurred with Masson, Savastano and Sharma (1997).

5 For the PERI/Bilkent project, see Epstein and Yeldan (eds), forthcoming; and Pollin and others (2006).

6 It is true that so-called 'Taylor Rules' that estimate policy rules governing monetary policy often find that central banks react to the deviation between 'potential output' and

Central Banks as Agents of Employment Creation • 119

actual output (the 'output gap'), but, far from implying that central banks care about unemployment, these results can be justified by noting that the output gap affects future inflation, so the central bank focusing solely on inflation might still be concerned with the output gap (Eichengreen, 2002).

[7] Galindo and Ros (2006) also propose shifting from a CPI target to a domestic inflation target which would purge the exchange rate impact on the 'target' inflation rate and further reduce the basis for the monetary policy bias toward exchange rate appreciation.

[8] Another important change was from a primary fiscal surplus to a more relaxed fiscal stance.

[9] Of course, Bloomfield (1957: 197) cautions that, "Such measures would for the most part be justified, however, only to the extent that they do not conflict with the overriding requirement of financial stability or involve the central bank in details of a sort that might distract its attention and energies from the effective implementation of a policy aimed at stability".

[10] See Maxfield (1997) and Fry (1995) for a discussion of some of these cases.

REFERENCES

Allen, Mark, Ulrich Baumgartner, and Raghuram Rajan (2006). Inflation targeting and the IMF. Prepared by Monetary and Financial Systems Department, Policy and Development Review Department and Research Department, March 16, International Monetary Fund, Washington, DC.

Amsden, Alice (2001). *The Rise of the Rest: Challenges to the West from Late-Industrializing Economies.* Oxford University Press, New York.

Baker, Dean (2000). NAIRU: Dangerous dogma at the Fed. *Financial Markets and Society.* Financial Markets Center, Washington, DC, December. www.fmcenter.org

Ball, Laurence, and N. Gregory Mankiw (2002). The NAIRU in theory and practice. NBER working paper no. 8940, National Bureau of Economic Research, Cambridge, MA.

Ball, L., and N. Sheridan (2003). Does inflation targeting matter? IMF working paper no. 03/129, International Monetary Fund, Washington, DC.

Barbosa-Filho, Nelson (2006). Inflation targeting and monetary policy in Brazil. PERI working paper, Political Economy Research Institute, University of Massachusetts, Amherst. www.peri.umass.edu

Bernanke, Ben S., Thomas Laubach, Adam S. Posen, and Frederic S. Mishkin (1999). *Inflation Targeting: Lessons from the International Experience.* Princeton University Press, Princeton, NJ.

Bloomfield, Arthur I. (1957). Some problems of central banking in underdeveloped countries. *The Journal of Finance* 12 (2), May: 190–204.

Braunstein, Elissa, and James Heintz (2006). Gender bias and central bank policy: Inflation and employment reduction. PERI working paper, Political Economy Research Institute, University of Massachusetts, Amherst. www.peri.umass.edu

Brimmer, Andrew F (1971). Central banking and economic development: The record of innovation. *Journal of Money, Credit and Banking,* 3 (4), November: 780–792.

Bruno, Michael (1995). Does inflation really lower growth? *Finance and Development,* September: 35–38.

Bruno, Michael, and William Easterly (1998). Inflation crises and long-run growth. *Journal of Monetary Economics* 41: 3–26.

Burdekin, R.C.K., A.T. Denzau, M.W. Keil, T. Sitthiyot, and T.D. Willett (2004). When does inflation hurt economic growth? Different nonlinearities for different economies. *Journal of Macroeconomics* 26: 519–532.

Clifton, Eric V., Hyginus Leon, and Chorng-Huey Wong (2001). Inflation targeting and the unemployment-inflation trade-off. IMF working paper WP/01/166, International Monetary Fund, Washington, DC.

Eichengreen, Barry, P. Masson, M. Savastano, S. Sharma (1999). Transition strategies and nominal anchors on the road to greater exchange rate flexibility. In Barry Eichengreen and others (eds). *Essays in International Finance.* International Finance Section, Department of Economics, Princeton University, Princeton, NJ.

Eichengreen, Barry (2002). Can emerging markets float? Should they inflation target? Processed, February, Department of Economics, University of California, Berkeley.

Eisner, Robert (1997). A new view of the NAIRU. In Paul Davidson and Jan Kregel (eds). *Improving the Global Economy: Keynesianism and the Growth in Output and Employment.* Edward Elgar, Brookfield, VT.

Epstein, Gerald (2000). Myth, mendacity and mischief in the theory and practice of central banking. PERI working paper, Political Economy Research Institute, University of Massachusetts, Amherst.

Epstein, Gerald (2006a). Employment targeting central bank policy in South Africa. Paper presented at the 'Alternatives to Inflation Targeting Monetary Policy for Stable and Egalitarian Growth in Developing Countries' conference, May 13–14, Centro de Estudios de Estado y Sociedad (CEDES), Buenos Aires.

Epstein, Gerald (2006b). Central banks as agents of economic development. WIDER working paper no. 2006-54, World Institute for Development Economics Research, United Nations University, Helsinki. http://www.wider.unu.edu/publications/rps/rps2006/rp2006-54.pdf

Epstein, Gerald, Ilene Grabel and Jomo K.S. (2005). Capital management techniques in developing countries: An assessment of experiences from the 1990s and lessons for the future. In Gerald Epstein (ed.). *Capital Flight and Capital Controls in Developing Countries.* Edward Elgar, Northampton, MA: 301–333.

Epstein, Gerald, and James Heintz (2006). Monetary policy and financial sector reform for employment creation and poverty reduction in Ghana. International Poverty Centre Country Study no. 2, Brasilia. http://www.undp-povertycentre.org/newsletters/CountryStudy002.pdf

Epstein, Gerald, and Erinc Yeldan (eds) (forthcoming). *Alternatives to Inflation Targeting for Stable and Egalitarian Growth.* Book manuscript. PERI, Political Economy Research Institute, University of Massachusetts, Amherst, MA

Frenkel, Roberto, and Martin Rapetti (2006). Monetary and exchange rate policies in Argentina after the convertibility regime collapse. PERI working paper, Political Economy Research Institute, University of Massachusetts, Amherst. www.peri.umass.edu

Frenkel, Roberto, and Jaime Ros (2006). Unemployment and the real exchange rate in Latin America. *World Development* 34 (4): 631–646.

Frenkel, Roberto, and Lance Taylor (2006). Real exchange rate, monetary policy, and employment: Economic development in a garden of forking paths. Working paper no.

19, February, Department of Economic and Social Affairs (DESA), United Nations, New York.

Fry, Maxwell J. (1995). *Money, Interest and Banking in Economic Development.* 2nd Edition. The Johns Hopkins University Press, Baltimore.

Galindo, L.M., and Jaime Ros (2006). Inflation targeting Mexico: An empirical appraisal. Paper presented at the 'Alternatives to Inflation Targeting Monetary Policy for Stable and Egalitarian Growth in Developing Countries', PERI Working Paper, Political Economy Research Institute, University of Massachusetts, Amherst.

Ghosh, A., and S. Phillips (1998). Warning: Inflation may be harmful to your growth. *IMF Staff Papers* 45 (4): 672–686.

Grabel, Ilene (2000). Savings, investment and functional efficiency: A comparative examination of national financial complexes. In Robert Pollin (ed.). *The Macroeconomics of Saving, Finance and Investment.* University of Michigan Press, Ann Arbor: 251–298.

Hall, Robert E. (2005). Separating the business cycle from other economic fluctuations. NBER working paper no. 11651, National Bureau of Economic Research, Cambridge, MA, September. www.nber.org

Heintz, James (2006a). Growth, employment and poverty reduction. DFID discussion paper, Department for International Development, London, and Political Economy Research Institute, University of Massachusetts, Amherst. Available at: www.umass.edu/peri

Ho, Corrinne, and Robert N. McCauley (2003). Living with flexible exchange rates: Issues and recent experience in inflation targeting emerging market economies. BIS working paper no. 130, Bank for International Settlements, Basel.

ILO (2004a). *Global Employment Trends, 2004.* International Labour Office, Geneva.

ILO (2004b). *Global Employment Trends for Women, 2004.* International Labour Office, Geneva.

IMF (2005). Monetary and fiscal policy design issues in low-income countries. Policy Development and Review Department and Fiscal Affairs Department, 8 August, International Monetary Fund, Washington, DC.

Jha, Raghbendra (2006). Inflation targeting in India: Issues and prospects. PERI working paper, Political Economy Research Institute, University of Massachusetts, Amherst. www.peri.umass.edu

Jayadev, Arjun (2006a). Differing preferences between anti-inflation and anti-unemployment policy among the rich and the poor. *Economics Letters* 91: 67–71.

Jayadev, Arjun (2006b). The class content of preferences: Towards anti-inflation and anti-unemployment policies. PERI working paper, Political Economy Research Institute, University of Massachusetts, Amherst. www.peri.umass.edu

Kahn, M.S., and A.S. Senhadji (2001). Threshold effects in the relationship between inflation and growth. *IMF Staff Papers* 48 (1): 1–21.

Kapsos, Steven (2004). Estimating growth requirements for reducing working poverty: Can the world halve working poverty by 2015? Employment strategy paper no. 2004/14, Employment Strategy Department, International Labour Office, Geneva.

Lim, Joseph (2006). Philippine monetary policy: A critical assessment and search for alternatives. PERI working paper, Political Economy Research Institute, University of Massachusetts, Amherst. www.peri.umass.edu

Masson, Paul R., Miguel A. Savastano and Sunil Sharma (1997). The scope for inflation targeting in developing countries. IMF working paper WP/97/130, International Monetary Fund, Washington, DC.

122 • Towards Full and Decent Employment

Maxfield, Sylvia (1997). *Gatekeepers of Growth; The International Political Economy of Central Banking in Developing Countries*. Princeton University Press, Princeton.

Mishkin, Frederic, and Klaus Schmidt-Hebbel (2001). One decade of inflation targeting in the world: What do we know and what do we need to know? NBER working paper no. 8397, July, National Bureau of Economic Research, Cambridge, MA.

Ocampo, Jose Antonio (2002). Capital-account and counter-cyclical prudential regulations in developing countries. WIDER Discussion paper, August, World Institute for Development Economics Research, United Nations University, Helsinki.

Packard, Tu Anh (2006). Monetary policy in Vietnam: Alternatives to inflation targeting. PERI Working Paper, Political Economy Research Institute, University of Massachusetts, Amherst. www.peri.umass.edu

Pollin, Robert (1995). Financial structures and egalitarian economic policy. *New Left Review* 214: 26–61.

Pollin, Robert (2005). *Contours of Descent*. Verso Press, London.

Pollin, Robert N., Gerald Epstein, James Heintz, and Leonce Ndikumana (2006). An employment-targeted economic program for South Africa. A study sponsored by the United Nations Development Program (UNDP), New York, and Political Economy Research Institute (PERI), University of Massachusetts, Amherst. www.peri.umass.

Pollin, Robert, and Andong Zhu (2006). Inflation and economic growth: A cross-country nonlinear analysis. *Journal of Post Keynesian Economics* 28 (4), Summer: 593–614.

Prasad, Eswar, Kenneth Rogoff, Shang-Jin Wei, and M. Ayhan Kose (2003). Effects of financial globalization on developing countries: Some empirical evidence. Occasional paper no. 220, International Monetary Fund, Washington, D.C.

Roger, Scott, and Mark Stone (2005). On target? The international experience with achieving inflation targets. IMF working paper WP/05/163, International Monetary Fund, Washington, DC.

Tobin, James (1980). Stabilization policy ten years after. *Brookings Papers on Economic Activity* 1: 19–71.

Voyvoda, E., and Erinc Yeldan (2006). Macroeconomics of twin-targeting in Turkey: A general equilibrium analysis. PERI working paper, Political Economy Research Institute, University of Massachusetts, Amherst. www.peri.umass.edu

6
Growth, Employment and Poverty

AZIZUR RAHMAN KHAN

This chapter explores the relationship between economic growth and poverty reduction with special focus on the role of employment in shaping the linkage. The empirical basis of the analysis consists of two recent sets of studies: nine UNDP country case studies on the macroeconomics of poverty reduction (hereafter referred to as the UNDP case studies) and seven ILO/SIDA studies on "Growth-Employment-Poverty Nexus" (hereafter referred to as the ILO/SIDA studies).[1]

The case studies belong to two distinct sets. The first set, by the UNDP, considers the relationship between macroeconomic policies and poverty reduction, while the second set, sponsored by the ILO and SIDA, looks at the role of employment in the growth-poverty linkage. Motivations behind the two sets of studies may have been quite disparate. The UNDP studies appear to have been designed to demonstrate how developing countries might pursue macroeconomic adjustment that is more consistent with the welfare of the poor than the policy regime that the Bretton Woods institutions have incorporated as part of their conditionalities for assistance in recent decades. The principal focus is on designing macroeconomic policies so that they help accelerate, rather than retard, growth, and on shaping the character of growth in ways that benefit the poor. The ILO/SIDA studies start with the concern that benefits of growth often bypass the poor; they are premised on the notion that "countries which attained high rates of employment growth alongside high rates of economic growth are also the ones who succeeded in reducing poverty significantly".[2]

Despite their apparently disparate motivation and different coverage of issues, the two sets of studies have a large common area of focus. To see this clearly, one needs to consider the process that links economic growth with poverty reduction. While broader indicators are often used by the case studies, the basic indices of poverty that are common to them all relate to shortfalls from some minimum acceptable level of income or consumption (the poverty threshold). A change in such an income/consumption poverty index is completely determined by: (a) the change in average income/consumption; and (b) the change in the distribution of income/consumption (hereafter, for brevity, reference will be made only to income and income poverty, but would equally apply to consumption and consumption poverty).

The first of the above two determinants of change in poverty, the growth of average income, is determined by the rate of growth of the economy. An economy's growth rate is usually measured by the rate of growth of per capita real GNP. Change in income for poverty indicators, however, needs to be measured by the change in per capita *personal* income, in terms of which the poverty threshold is defined. In addition to individuals, or members of households, there are other claimants to GNP, e.g., business and government. It is not necessary for the shares of the different claimants to remain unchanged. Thus, it is possible, indeed quite normal, for the rate of growth of personal income to differ from the rate of growth of GNP. This difference itself is an outcome of macroeconomic policies.

The second of the two determinants of change in the poverty indicator, the change in the distribution of income, is represented by the change in the Lorenz distribution curve of income. While this is usually captured by the change in summary indicators of income distribution, e.g., the Gini index, this is not necessarily the case. This is because what matters is the change in the relevant segment of the Lorenz distribution curve, which is the part that lies to the left of the point that indicates the proportion of the population living in poverty. The Gini index can fail to capture a change in this segment accurately if there is a (compensatory) change in the segment of the Lorenz distribution curve that lies to the right.

Where does employment feature in this nexus? Growth in employment can influence both determinants of change in poverty. Growth in employment and productivity can improve the growth rate of the economy. This is especially the case for a typical developing economy which has a large endowment of labour relative to other factors, such as capital. Productive utilization of this relatively abundant resource can make growth go faster.[3]

But the more powerful way that growth in employment and productivity can influence the growth-poverty linkage is by pushing up the relevant segment of the Lorenz distribution curve. Except for income transfers in favour of the poor – an instrument that has always been of limited scope in poor countries and has become even more so in the present era of emphasis on macroeconomic stability, encompassing the avoidance of budgetary imbalance – and institutional changes, such as land reform – which have rarely occurred in contemporary history. This can only come about by increasing employment and its remuneration.

Most of the poor, who are clustered on the left of the Lorenz distribution curve, are endowed with labour as their only significant resource. Even when a poverty-reduction strategy improves the access of these poor to other resources – e.g., land and capital: physical, financial, infrastructural and human – the process of poverty reduction does not depend on the creation of an entitlement to rent or annuity for the poor, but on the enhancement of opportunity for them to be employed more intensively, productively and remuneratively.

There are many aspects of the linkage between employment and poverty. The poor can escape poverty when they have: (a) an increase in wage employment; (b) an increase in the real wage; (c) an increase in self-employment; (d) an increase in productivity in self-employment; and (e) an increase in the terms of exchange of the output of self-employment.[4] Poverty declines if the aggregate of all these effects is favourable for the poor.

Now, one can identify three distinct ways in which macroeconomic policies can contribute to poverty reduction:

(a) They can promote higher growth which, given the gross output elasticity of employment (GOEE), increases employment and/ or the earnings of the poor, which alleviates poverty.

(b) They can change incentives in favour of more labour-intensive activities and techniques, thereby increasing employment and/ or the earnings of the poor, which alleviates poverty.

(c) They can directly improve the welfare of the poor, e.g., by changing the allocation of public expenditure to increase income transfer to the poor. Faster growth facilitates this process, but is neither necessary nor sufficient for it to happen.

In analyzing the role of employment in the linkage between growth and poverty reduction – the subject of the ILO/SIDA studies – the focus must primarily be on a faster rate of increase in labour demand which translates into a higher rate of increase in employment and/or labour remuneration. Policies are no longer limited to macroeconomic instruments, but also include microeconomic instruments and institutional reform. Once again, one can think of two avenues for pursuing this goal:

(a) Promoting higher economic growth to stimulate labour demand; increase employment and earnings of the poor; and reduce poverty. This effect is essentially the same as the first effect of macroeconomic policies for poverty reduction shown above, except that the instruments for the promotion of higher growth are broader.

(b) Increasing the labour-intensity of growth, essentially the same as the second effect of macroeconomic policies listed above, except that a much broader set of instruments can be in play.

Strictly speaking, there is nothing corresponding to the third channel listed above, through which macroeconomic policies influence poverty directly because, by definition, these studies (should) limit themselves to only those instruments that affect poverty by influencing employment and earnings from it. Thus, the common area covered by the two sets of studies encompasses: policies for higher growth to stimulate greater labour demand and policies for greater labour-intensity of growth.

It is fair to say that the UNDP studies are primarily preoccupied with the first of these two aspects. They often analyze the second aspect, but do not always make the employment link explicit. Instead, they subsume this effect under a broad analysis of the effect of the *character* of growth on poverty reduction. The primary focus of the ILO/SIDA studies is – or should have been – on the second of the two channels although, in varying degrees, they also focus on the first set of issues. The analysis of the first effect by the two sets of studies should, in principle, have been distinct: the UNDP studies focusing only on macroeconomic policies, and the ILO/SIDA studies focusing on the whole gamut of policies, including microeconomic policies and institutional reforms. But in practice, this distinction is blurred by the very flexible definition of macroeconomic policy that the UNDP studies adopt: not only does the definition include monetary policies, fiscal policies, policies concerning trade, exchange rates and capital movement, policies concerning the setting of domestic prices and regulation of distribution, labour market policies, and privatization, but also land reform and other institutional changes. As is well known, reforms of trade, monetary and fiscal regimes entail both macroeconomic aspects, affecting the level of aggregate demand, as well as microeconomic aspects, affecting the allocation of resources.

This chapter primarily limits itself to those parts of the two sets of studies that deal with these common issues. There are many other aspects of growth and poverty that these studies are concerned with. For example, they often have comprehensive discussions of poverty reduction policies, going beyond the common, employment-related issues. They often devote a great deal of effort to identifying the characteristics of the poor during particular time periods. These are not the primary focus here. This review generally limits itself to the analysis made in the case studies. It does not concern itself with the validity of their analysis except in the obvious cases of clear inconsistency and convincing contrary evidence. Nor does it extend their analysis except in the rare instances where it is possible to do so by using easily available information from closely related sources – such as another publication in the same UNDP or ILO series.

The next section summarizes the experiences of the 13 countries in two areas: relationship among economic growth, income distribution, employment and poverty, and the broad patterns of employment growth. The following section is concerned with the role of macroeconomic policies in determining economic growth and its character, which subsumes the effect of growth on distribution and poverty – the principal focus of the UNDP case studies. The next section discusses the role of the employment intensity of economic growth in the growth-poverty nexus, the principal focus of the ILO/SIDA studies. The final section concludes by highlighting a few important areas in which similar future studies could make further useful analysis.

SUMMARY OF COUNTRY EXPERIENCES

Tables 6.1 and 6.2 summarize some relevant information about the 13 countries. Table 6.1 presents the most recent information about population, income, income growth, distribution of expenditure and poverty incidence from World Bank sources. Table 6.2 qualitatively summarizes information in these countries.

Growth, Distribution, Employment and Poverty

Table 6.1 shows that the richest country (China) has 5.8 times the real per capita income of the poorest country (Ethiopia). The Gini ratio of per capita expenditure distribution ranges from a low of 0.29 in Kyrgyz Republic to 0.45 in China and Bolivia. Poverty estimates, made by the World Bank with a common poverty threshold of approximately PPP$1 per day per person, should be internationally comparable. The headcount index of poverty ranges from a low of less than 2 per cent in Kyrgyz Republic to more than 82 per cent in Uganda. It is worth noting that Kyrgyz Republic has the fourth lowest income among the countries, which means that its low poverty incidence must be explained by its low inequality, lowest among all the countries studied. There are other indications that the poverty level is driven more by the inequality of distribution than by the level of income. Thus, China has more than twice the poverty of Indonesia, even though its income is nearly one and a half times that of Indonesia. The explanation appears to be the much higher inequality in China. A crude estimate of the elasticities of headcount rate of poverty, based on the data in Table 6.1, shows that the partial elasticity with respect to the Gini ratio of expenditure is higher than the absolute value of the partial elasticity with respect to per capita PPP$ income. Unfortunately, the estimated elasticities are not as highly significant as one would want them to be, probably largely due to the poor estimates of PPP$ income and its distribution.[5]

TABLE 6.1
Basic features of the countries studied

Country	Population million in 2002	Per capita Income 2002 $	Per capita Income 2002 PPP$	Per capital GDP growth Per year: 1990–2002	Gini Ratio Expenditure	Poverty (PPP$1) HC	Poverty (PPP$1) gap
Bangladesh	136	380	1770	3.0	0.32	36.0	8.1
India	1049	470	2650	4.1	0.33	34.7	8.2
Nepal	24	230	1370	2.4	0.37	37.7	9.7
Cambodia	12	300	1970	4.3	0.40	34.1	–
China	1280	960	4520	8.6	0.45	16.6	3.9
Indonesia	212	710	3070	2.3	0.34	7.5	0.9
Mongolia	2	430	1710	-0.1	0.44	13.9	3.1
Vietnam	80	430	2300	6.1	0.36	17.7	3.3
Ethiopia	67	100	780	2.2	0.30	26.3	5.7
Uganda	25	240	1360	4.1	0.43	82.2	40.1
Armenia	3	790	3220	-0.8	0.38	12.8	3.3
Kyrgyzstan	5	290	1560	-3.5	0.29	<2	<0.5
Bolivia	9	900	2390	1.6	0.45	14.4	5.4

Notes: These data are from the *World Development Indicators* (World Bank, 2003; 2004). These are not necessarily the same as the data shown in the case studies. PPP$ income estimates are often based on indirect methods. Gini ratios are for per capita (consumption) expenditure distribution. Poverty indices are based on poverty thresholds defined in terms of per capita daily expenditure of 1.08 PPP$ at 1993 prices. The gap index of poverty is the proportionate poverty gap, which is the product of the headcount ratio and the average of the proportions by which the incomes of the poor fall below the poverty threshold.

Table 6.2
Basic features of performance in growth, distribution, employment and poverty

Country	Growth	Distribution/Inequality	Employment	Poverty
Bangladesh	Moderate	Rising inequality	Fairly rapid growth in RNF	Falling
India	High	Rising inequality*	Increased employment Growth: still slow	Falling
Nepal	Slow	Uncertain: may not have increased	Uncertain: probably slowing down of growth	Uncertain
Cambodia	High but narrow base	Stable with a question mark	Rapid growth in narrow sectors; slow overall	Increase overall & rural; fell in urban areas
China	High	Increasing rapidly	Growing slowly	Falling, but at a slower rate
Indonesia (Pre-crisis period)	High	Stable and low	Growing rapidly	Falling rapidly

(contd)

Table 6.2 (contd)

Country	Growth	Distribution/ Inequality	Employment	Poverty
Indonesia (Post-crisis period)	Slow	Stable (or getting more unequal)	Slow growth; fell in formal sectors	Initial rise, then fall, ending above initial level
Mongolia	Slow & partial recovery from deep fall	Increased*	Fell in industries; labour moved into agriculture	Sharp rise since Soviet era; no change recently
Vietnam	Rapid	Modest rise in inequality	Slow growth in industries and modern services	Fell
Ethiopia	Slow	Rural inequality fell urban inequality rose	Slow growth in industries, negative in agriculture (data implausible)	Unchanged overall, rise in urban, fall in rural
Uganda	Moderate until 2000, slow since	Stable until 2000, rise thereafter	Slow growth in industries. Agriculture absorbed a lot of labour with falling prod-uctivity per worker	Fell until 2000, rose thereafter

(contd)

Table 6.2 *(contd)*

Country	Growth	Distribution/ Inequality	Employment	Poverty
Armenia	Sharp fall till 1993; Moderate, but in-complete recovery since	Sharp initial rise in inequality, slow further rise later possible	Fall in industries & services; rise in agriculture	Sharp rise since Soviet era
Kyrgyzstan (Recovery period)	Slow	Non-increasing	Fell in industries & most services; sharp rise in agriculture	Fell
Bolivia	Slow (fall in per capita income since 1999)	Sharp (inexplicable) fall in rural Gini since 1997; urban Gini rose since 1999	Rapid growth till 1997, slow thereafter	Urban fell till 1999, then rose; rose in rural (!)

Note: * Indicates that these are based on an estimate, or on data from outside the case studies.

Actual trends are often more nuanced (see Khan, 2005: Annex) than can be summarized in one short table. Only changes during the major sub-periods are reported in Table 6.2 when there is more than one sub-period within the time period of a case study. Growth rates are classified into three categories. A high growth rate refers to an annual average growth in per capita GDP of 4 per cent or more. The logic of this is that it should translate into an annual average growth in per capita personal income of 2.5 to 3 per cent (or more), which should provide a reasonable base for poverty reduction in so far as it should be able to outweigh the adverse effect of a moderate increase in inequality (though not necessarily of a large increase in inequality). Moderate growth refers to a minimum of 2.5 per cent growth in per capita GDP, which hopefully translates into a minimum of 1.5 per cent annual growth in per capita personal income. This would not prevent an increase in poverty if the increase in inequality was not very modest. Low growth refers to annual growth in per capita income of 2.5 per cent or less. This is not a reliable basis for poverty reduction: it could provide so low a rate of growth in per capita personal income that its effect would be outweighed by even a very modest increase in inequality.

Four countries – China, Vietnam, India and Cambodia – achieved high growth. Pre-crisis Indonesia also belonged to this category. With the exception of pre-crisis Indonesia, they all had increased inequality in the distribution of income and consumption. China, Vietnam and India achieved significant reduction in poverty. The rate of decline of poverty in each case, with the exception of pre-crisis Indonesia, was below the *potential rate of decline*, the rate of poverty reduction that would have resulted from the actual growth of income if distribution had remained unchanged.[6]

In the case of China, the sharp increase in inequality resulted in a fragile poverty outcome despite the country's historically unprecedented rate of growth: urban poverty during 1988–1995 probably increased overall, and in many regions poverty failed to decline. The powerful effect of distribution on poverty in China is also demonstrated by a subsequent study, which showed that the poverty reduction effect of a per cent increase in personal income sharply increased during 1995–2002 – over 1988–1995 – because inequality stopped increasing during the second period as compared to the sharp increase in inequality in the first period (Khan, 2005). Furthermore, the increased inequality during 1988–1995 was associated with a serious worsening of the employment situation, particularly with rising urban unemployment without social protection. The stable distribution in the subsequent period was associated with improved rural employment and the institution of a partial system of protection for the urban unemployed.

In India, employment growth was faster during the 1990s, the period of the case study, than earlier. Still, the overall employment intensity of growth was not high. In Vietnam, slow employment growth was the major blemish on an otherwise good growth performance. Of the rapidly growing cases, Cambodia failed to achieve an overall reduction of poverty. Poverty increased for rural Cambodia and for the nation as a whole, while it fell for urban Cambodia. The evidence on income distribution is murky. The poverty outcome is principally explained by the very narrow base of growth. Employment growth was limited to the narrow base of a few urban industries and overall employment growth was very slow.

In the rapidly growing contemporary cases (i.e., excluding pre-crisis Indonesia), inequality increased and/or employment growth was too slow to enable the poor to have an adequate share of the increase in income. The result was a slower and less robust reduction of poverty than the high rate of growth should have made possible.

Two countries, Bangladesh and Uganda (until 2000), achieved a moderate rate of growth in per capita GDP. Inequality in Bangladesh increased steadily. The most important, though perhaps still tentative, explanation of poverty reduction in Bangladesh is the rapid increase in remunerative employment in rural non-farm (RNF) activities. Still, it has been shown by simulation exercises that poverty reduction was significantly lower than what would be possible if the poor had maintained their share of incremental income (Khan and Sen, 2004). In Uganda, industrial employment increased at a relatively slow rate. Agriculture absorbed labour at a very rapid rate (even though the statistical evidence seems quirky), rendered remunerative by a favourable movement in agricultural terms of trade. This helped stabilize the distribution of income and reduce poverty. After 2000, income growth became slow, agricultural terms of trade deteriorated, and inequality and poverty increased.

In the two moderately growing countries, the real earnings of the poor were kept from falling, despite otherwise non-egalitarian growth in one of them, by unorthodox sources of employment, RNF and agricultural production, without which the poverty outcome might have been worse.

The remaining seven cases achieved slow growth, negative growth or no growth during the 1990s. Three of these – Armenia, Kyrgyz Republic and Mongolia – are transition economies. Over the 1990s, they experienced a sharp fall in per capita income, a sharp rise in inequality, a large fall in employment due to de-industrialization and a big increase in the incidence of poverty. Interestingly, the pattern of recovery began in the mid-1990s. De-industrialization forced many urban workers to move to agriculture. In Kyrgyz Republic and Armenia, egalitarian land reform widened the access of the population to land, and economic recovery, concentrated in agriculture, did not increase inequality. Indeed, estimates for Kyrgyz Republic show that, in the late 1990s, the Gini ratio of per capita expenditure remained stable in rural areas, so that the growth of agricultural income helped reduce poverty. Urban poverty fell, partly due to the reduced population pressure on urban income sources. In Armenia too, poverty fell after 1996, although estimates there suffer from greater uncertainty. In Mongolia, poverty remained unchanged between 1995 and 1998 – the only period for which estimates are available – due to greater inequality generated by the privatization of urban industries, housing and herds.

During the recovery, Indonesia's per capita GDP increased at half the rate at which it had increased prior to the crisis. Possibly growth in personal income and consumption was slower than GDP growth in the post-crisis period due to the large claims made by external creditors. The case studies are sceptical about official estimates, which claim that distribution of income remained stable and that the incidence of poverty fell, though not yet to the pre-crisis level. Be that as it may, during this period, formal sectors of the economy reduced their share in employment, while those of agriculture and informal sectors increased. In the aftermath of the crisis, poverty increased for all categories of workers, but the *proportionate increase* in poverty was lowest for agricultural workers and far greater for those employed in industries and services. This, again, is an example of agriculture providing at least temporary protection from poverty *relative* to other sectors.

The remaining three cases are plagued with too many gaps and inconsistencies in data to permit any reasonably confident analysis. In Bolivia, slow growth occurred until 1998. The case study reports a stable urban Gini and reduction in urban poverty until 1999, when poverty rose as per capita income growth became negative and urban inequality rose. Employment growth, rapid until 1997, became slow thereafter. This, together with the decline in growth, helps explain urban poverty. For rural areas, the case study claims a massive fall in inequality of income distribution in 1999, for which no explanation is provided and none can apparently be found, and which had no effect on poverty, which, according to the case study, increased steadily after 1997. For Ethiopia, poverty estimates are available only for 1995/1996 and 1999/2000. Growth in per capita GDP was so slow that per capita personal expenditure fell by 4 per cent in rural areas and rose by a mere 3 per cent in urban areas. Poverty, determined by the change in inequality, fell slightly in rural areas and increased substantially in urban areas: rural poverty fell a little and urban poverty increased. It is difficult to relate the fall in rural poverty to the employment outcome, which was highly negative for agriculture. The employment intensity of industries was low as well. For Nepal, it is difficult to be certain about any of the magnitudes or even directions of change of the indicators. The only certainty is that the rate of growth was low.

In the countries growing slowly, poverty was mainly shaped by the low rate of growth. In the three transition economies and in Bolivia and Indonesia, agriculture absorbed a lot of labour, while industries and most other modern sectors failed to do so. Egalitarian agriculture in Armenia, Kyrgyz Republic and Indonesia – promoted by land reform in the first two and by predominantly peasant farming in the last – helped of survival, through large-scale absorption of labour displaced from other sectors. This resulted in a reduction in poverty in Armenia and Kyrgyz Republic in the late 1990s and some protection for the poor in Indonesia, at least relative to those in other sectors.

Elsewhere, in slow-growing countries, poverty declined slightly where forces of inequality were held in check, despite slow growth of income and lack of dynamism in employment growth, which failed to prevent a rise in poverty where inequality increased for institutional or other reasons.

Patterns of Employment Growth

The case studies reveal at least three distinct patterns of employment growth. Classical industrialization envisages a rapid increase in employment in industries and other modern activities, leading to a quick fall in agriculture's share of employment, which soon translates into an *absolute* fall in employment in agriculture. In contemporary development experience, this is best illustrated by the original East Asian tigers: in the Republic of Korea, for example, agriculture's share of employment fell from 34 to 17 per cent between 1980 and 1991. Over the same period, absolute employment in agriculture fell by nearly 40 per cent!

None of the 13 countries under review has achieved anything like this yet, even though China has been growing at a faster rate for nearly two decades than the East Asian tigers ever did, and the Indian growth rate during the 1990s has approached the East Asian rate. China and, to a lesser degree, India appear poised for this transition however. In these two countries, the proportion of the workforce employed in agriculture has been declining for quite some time. In China, absolute employment in agriculture peaked in 1991, when it started falling very slowly. In India, employment in agriculture remained stable during the last six years of the last century. The historically unprecedented rate of growth in China failed to induce more than a very slow decline in agricultural employment, while in India, decades of industrialization, leading to moderately high rates of growth, failed to initiate a decline in the absolute size of the agricultural labour force. In both countries, the gross output elasticity of employment in industry has been far lower than in East Asia at a comparable level of development.

A different kind of employment dynamic is credited by the UNDP case study to have been the principal source of poverty reduction in Bangladesh.[7] This consists of a reduction in agricultural underemployment, not by the classical expansion of industrial employment, but by the rapid expansion of remunerative and productive employment in RNF activities. This also appears to have been a major source of employment growth in Vietnam and India. The sustainability of this path to poverty reduction is subject to numerous questions dealt with below.

A third kind of employment dynamic is a variant of 'agricultural involution', an increase in agriculture's share of employment when industries and related modern activities fail to absorb labour, or even reduce the number employed – a perverse trend from the standpoint of development theory. And yet, in seven of the 13 countries – Armenia, Kyrgyz Republic, Mongolia, Uganda, Indonesia, Bolivia and Cambodia – this phenomenon can be observed to various degrees.[8] What is even more surprising is that, at least in Armenia and Kyrgyz Republic, with the help of egalitarian land redistribution, this process helped reduce poverty during the period of recovery. Elsewhere, the evidence suggests that poverty would have been worse if it was not possible for agriculture to absorb more labour. While this cannot be a sustainable method of poverty reduction, experience shows that it can serve as a useful survival mechanism for short periods, if appropriate institutions are in place.

ROLE OF MACROECONOMIC POLICIES IN DETERMINING RATE AND CHARACTER OF GROWTH

The preceding section identified two broad sets of poverty determinants. The first concerns the rate of economic growth and its broad character, subsuming all factors that determine the pattern of income distribution and the wellbeing of the poor. The second is concerned with the very different employment intensities of growth. The former was the principal concern of the UNDP case studies, while the latter was the central focus of the ILO/SIDA case studies. This section and the next deal with these two sets of issues.

Summaries of the relevant findings of the UNDP case studies are available (Khan, 2005: Annex). As already noted, these studies have a broadly uniform approach and represent alternatives to the adjustment programmes sponsored by the Bretton Woods institutions, recently featuring Poverty Reduction Strategy Papers (PRSPs). The UNDP studies take the view that macroeconomic policies can affect poverty, both by influencing the rate of income growth and by making growth more or less pro-poor by influencing the incremental income share of the poor. Both these channels of poverty reduction operate through their effects on employment, among others. A majority of, but not all, the studies make this linkage explicit. The overall evaluation of the case studies of macroeconomic policies in the nine countries can be classified into three categories:[9]

(a) In China and Vietnam, macroeconomic policies have largely been designed by national policymakers. These policies have, by and large, been helpful in promoting economic growth. But they have not succeeded in ensuring a more equitable distributional outcome. In particular, these policies have been unhelpful for the expansion of productive and remunerative employment and for the welfare of the workforce.

(b) In countries like Bangladesh and Cambodia, these policies, designed under the auspices of the Bank and the Fund, have been neutral for economic growth overall. There have been both favourable and unfavourable effects on the welfare of the poor. The three transition economies are Armenia, Mongolia and Kyrgyz Republic.

(c) In the remaining cases, the three transition economies, Nepal and post-crisis Indonesia, Bank-Fund sponsored macroeconomic policies have both exacerbated recent crises and adversely affected the recoveries. Their overall effects on employment and poverty have been negative.

One might start with the last category representing the largest number of countries. The critique by the UNDP studies of the macroeconomic policy package that Bank-Fund conditionality imposes in these countries, has a number of major themes:

(a) Macroeconomic policies in these cases generally overemphasize macroeconomic stabilization, which involves a drastic retrenchment of aggregate demand. Public expenditure is subject to huge reduction and credit expansion is severely restricted. Ungenerous debt rescheduling and sharply reduced net external resources force a current account surplus (as in Indonesia) that reduces the rate of investment well below the rate of domestic saving. Sometimes, dogmatic insistence on curtailing expenditure results in restricting investment, even though domestic savings, properly mobilized, could finance a higher rate of investment (as in Kyrgyz Republic).

(b) These policies have a doctrinaire antipathy to public investment, justified by the claim that public investment crowds out more efficient and productive private investment. The UNDP studies – for example, on Indonesia, Bangladesh and Nepal – argue that public investment has indeed had a 'crowding in' effect. These investments, concentrated in sectors providing broad externalities (as argued by Allyn Young and Rosenstein-Rodan), actually make private investment more profitable. The notion that public and private investments are competitors for scarce resources is often exaggerated by an extreme emphasis on stabilization and intolerance of inflation.

(c) Trade reform is often implemented without adequate precautions to enable existing industries, fostered in the past by a regime of import substituting industrialization, to make orderly adjustments to a more open trade regime. Instead, 'shock therapy', simultaneously implementing wholesale reforms of the trade and price regimes, as in the case of the three transition economies, led to wholesale de-industrialization that drastically reduced employment and unfavourably affected the welfare of the poor. In Nepal, trade reform allegedly eroded the competitiveness of industries and adversely affected employment and poverty.

(d) In a number of countries, the bias against agriculture, the sector that provides livelihoods to most of the poor, was aggravated by the reform package. The Nepal case study argues that the reduction of public investment in agriculture and the abolition of subsidies for fertilizers and irrigation resulted in the fall in agricultural growth in the 1990s.

(e) Drastic curtailment of public expenditure also reduced the ability of the government to directly assist the poor. The ability to fund public works programmes and publicly funded programmes of direct income and consumption subsidies to the poor is reduced. Even when the government maintains, or increases, the share of public expenditure for health, education and other services for the poor and working members of the population, their absolute levels can be threatened and, within each expenditure category, the proportion directed to the poor could decline, due to more intense competition from privileged groups.

The UNDP case studies do not take a universally negative position vis-à-vis the Bank-Fund type of macroeconomic policy packages. Thus, the case study of Bangladesh recognizes the favourable effect these policies had by creating macroeconomic stability, which promoted higher rates of saving and investment. It argues, however, that trade reform had both favourable and adverse effects on the poor: while it helped foster higher agricultural growth by liberalizing the import of irrigation equipment in the 1980s and stabilized consumer prices by liberalizing private imports of rice in the 1990s, import liberalization stifled the growth of domestic engineering and capital goods in the absence of countervailing support for these fledgling industries. Also, discriminatory tariffs on machine tools, used by small enterprises, hindered the development of the latter. Fiscal policy in Bangladesh has had a neutral effect on aggregate demand. Banking reform, on the other hand, by focusing on the de-regulation of interest rates and neglecting appropriate institutional reform, created huge loan defaults, which effectively made credit scarce for small borrowers, a phenomenon that also occurred in other countries. The Cambodia case study takes the view that, on balance, macroeconomic reforms under the auspices of the Bank and the Fund neither helped nor hindered economic growth, which they were meant to promote. The Bangladesh case study refers to the interesting appreciation in the real value of the country's currency relative to the competing neighbours, which hindered the diversification of exports. However, it appeared to recommend inaction, noting that the exchange rate is market determined in the reformed trade regime. This might sound like absolving macroeconomic policy reforms of any responsibility for real exchange rate appreciation. It is, however, possible to argue that the only way out is to expand aggregate demand, especially investment, so that the demand for foreign exchange increases faster and brings about a market-determined reduction in the real exchange rate. Clearly, the overt emphasis on stabilization has been an obstacle to this solution, a condition which, it seems, has also afflicted other countries (e.g., Nepal).

The UNDP studies are generally complimentary about the effect on economic growth of the autonomous macroeconomic policy regime in China and Vietnam, but are critical of its effects on employment and poverty. While China's macroeconomic policies have helped rapid growth, which has expanded the opportunities for poverty reduction, their benefits have been unequally distributed among regions and groups. China's trade liberalization, especially related to WTO accession, has seriously constrained government ability to protect vulnerable rural producers. The benefits of income and employment growth have been concentrated in richer coastal areas, leaving the poorer inland regions further behind. Foreign direct investment (FDI) inflows have had a similar effect. The decentralization of China's fiscal system, along with the fall in the tax/GDP ratio, has exacerbated inequality among regions by making interregional transfers far more difficult than in the past. The case study claims that restricted credit expansion has hurt small enterprises with inadequate access.[10] Reform of state and collective enterprises, without prior institution of a system of unemployment insurance, has created a serious problem of urban unemployment, which has contributed to worsening urban poverty in a period of unprecedented growth. Half-hearted tolerance of migration and continued discrimination against migrants have become serious obstacles to faster labour allocation that would better serve the objective of poverty reduction. In Vietnam, the UNDP case study notes that failure to rein in the forces of inequality is a major limitation of macroeconomic policies. Principal omissions include the absence of old-age pensions and the erosion of transfers and subsidies.

The policy recommendations that emerge from the UNDP case studies are suggested by the above critique. First, they reject the extreme preoccupation with stabilization measures that heavily curtail aggregate demand by deflationary methods. These studies strongly emphasize the supreme importance of avoiding and reversing the decline in the level and rate of investment that so many countries have experienced. While most of the studies argue in favour of more strenuous efforts to generate domestic resources to this end, several studies recognize that avoidance of extreme stabilization is often contingent on the cooperation of international donors. Countries like Indonesia simply could not find a way of avoiding deflationary policies while coping with a drastic reduction in net capital inflows and meeting international commitments to service debt. Thus, this is as much a policy recommendation for the countries concerned as for the international donor and financial community.

Secondly, the studies advocate a strong role for public investment in human resources and infrastructure. They argue that the 'crowding in' effect of such investment, through the creation of widespread externality, is beneficial for private investment.

Thirdly, these studies urge caution in the adoption of sudden and wholesale trade reform without a system of countervailing support for the existing industries that have good long-term prospects of survival after an orderly and gradual integration with the global economy. They reject the 'shock therapy' of simultaneous wholesale reforms of price and trade regimes, which drove many existing industries in transition economies into extinction. Several studies also argue in favour of retaining the option of pursuing industrial policies of promoting fledgling industries and exports by provision of support, as in East Asia. This is an area in which there is a distinct likelihood of conflict between desirable policies and WTO commitments, except possibly for the very poor countries.

Fourthly, these studies place great emphasis on avoiding growth that raises inequality, to ensure that the incomes of the poor increase as fast as the overall growth of income. Macroeconomic policies should direct resources to sectors that employ and provide livelihoods to the poor. Rapid employment generation is seen by the studies as a major instrument for poverty reduction. To this end, they recommend easy access to resources for agriculture and small-scale non-farm activities, i.e. labour intensive sectors. Often, the studies underline the importance of improving the terms of trade for peasant agriculture by appropriate trade, price and related policies. Several studies go beyond the range of the usual macroeconomic policy instruments to urge broader institutional reform to make growth more egalitarian and pro-poor. More equitable distribution of land and other physical assets is often strongly emphasized.

EMPLOYMENT INTENSITY OF ECONOMIC GROWTH

The employment intensity of economic growth is the principal link in the growth-poverty nexus that the ILO/SIDA case studies focus on. These studies employ the concept of gross output elasticity of employment (simply the output elasticity of employment in the vocabulary used by most studies), the ratio of the growth rate of employment to the growth rate of output or value-added.

The Indian case study contests the utility of this concept by arguing that output growth is just one of several determinants of employment growth, the principal one being the rate of change in the 'real' wage rate (nominal wage rate deflated by the price of the product that the worker is employed to produce, or the real wage cost). It introduces the concepts of partial elasticity of employment with respect to output (which has a positive sign in normal cases) and partial elasticity of employment with respect to wage cost (which has a negative sign).

The authors of the Indian study argue that the concept of gross output elasticity of employment "does not net out the impact of other variables and, hence, is inappropriate in our view" (Sundaram and Tendulkar, 2002). They are right only in so far as the partial elasticities quantify *causal* sources of employment growth under *ceteris paribus* assumptions. While the concept of gross output elasticity of employment *does not capture the effect of output growth on employment growth in a causal sense*, it serves as an *observed indicator of the actual degree of the labour intensity of growth*, which is the outcome of the overall incentive system affecting the choice of labour intensity from among alternative techniques. A high elasticity means that the overall incentive system is employment friendly. A low elasticity means that the overall incentive system is employment hostile. Thus, a certain expansion of a particular activity, with a given labour intensity from the technological standpoint (with a given 'isoquant' if one were to use a narrower concept than intended), can provide larger (smaller) employment if the overall system of incentives is employment friendly (employment hostile).

The Indian case study argues that the gross elasticity represents the aggregate of two distinct effects: the positive effect of output growth on employment (the positive partial elasticity with respect to output) and the negative effect of the wage cost of employment (negative partial elasticity with respect to wage cost). The partial elasticity of employment with respect to output – which, *ceteris paribus*, shows the correct effect of output growth on employment growth – could be high while the observed gross output elasticity of employment could be low because of a large rise in the wage cost of employment. Gross elasticity, as an indicator of the labour intensity of growth, captures the effect of any unwarranted increase in wage cost or, for that matter, any other unfavourable change in the incentive system that guides the choice of technique. Thus, for example, several studies refer to the high gross output elasticity of manufacturing employment in East Asia during the 1970s, which ranged from 0.7 to 0.8. This observed gross elasticity was measured for a period when the real wage rate was rising at roughly the same rate as per capita income. The overall employment friendliness of the incentive system outweighed this effect to yield a gross elasticity as high as the observed ones. As the case study shows, this was far from the case in India. During the 1990s, when real wage cost per worker increased at a much slower rate (2.62 per cent per year) than per capita income, gross elasticity was less than 0.3. Clearly, there were other elements of the incentive system that were still rather strongly employment hostile. The much higher rate of increase in real wage cost during the 1980s clearly indicates the even higher employment hostility of the incentive system in that decade.

Empirical estimation of gross output elasticity of employment suffers from numerous problems. In agriculture and traditional services employment, estimates are often very unreliable, and over time, the intensity of employment varies, both due to actual changes and differences in survey methods over time. That is why one encounters an estimated elasticity for agriculture of well over two and for services of over one in certain cases. Estimates of employment in modern manufacturing and services should be relatively free from these problems. And yet, there can be serious problems when industries are not organized on market principles. Thus, excess employment is widely observed in state enterprises. Even in private enterprises fostered under protection, facing little pressure of competition to limit employment to what efficiency would dictate, employment in manufacturing can be excessive. During the process of market reform, these phenomena are going through a transition and can easily give 'wild' estimates of gross elasticity (in several cases, negative elasticities have been reported). But then again, this kind of transition can be viewed as periods of employment hostility of the incentive system, although this is clearly desirable.[11] China's extremely low observed gross elasticity in industry during the 1990s falls in this category.

None of the case studies found the rate of employment growth satisfactory during the periods on which they primarily focus (even though overall employment growth in Uganda was very rapid, estimates of gross elasticity for industry are low, and for agriculture and services, quirky). Table 6.3 tries to provide a qualitative evaluation of the factors behind the inadequate growth in employment for six of the case studies. (The Bangladesh case study itself does not provide enough information for complete identification of the nature of the problem within the framework used in this section. Subsequent discussion with the authors of the case study, partly based on the results of their more recent research, made possible the interpretation that follows).

Except in the case of India and Vietnam, slow economic growth is the dominant cause of slow growth in employment. Even in India, the case study argues in favour of faster growth as a necessary condition for expanding increasingly productive employment, requiring a reduction or stabilization of employment in certain low-productivity sectors, as a condition for poverty alleviation. Thus, faster economic growth seems to be the dominant condition for rapid expansion of employment.

Employment-hostile incentives also appear to be the dominant cause of slow employment growth in two cases and a significant or possible cause in another two. The incentive system only seems to be sufficiently employment-friendly in Indonesia and Bolivia, although in the former case, the evidence is based on the pre-crisis period, and in the latter case, only on the estimated value of the gross output elasticity of employment.

TABLE 6.3
Cause of slow employment growth

Country	Degree of employment intensity of growth	Cause of slow employment growth
Bangladesh	Questionable in industries; Fairly good in informal activities	Less than robust growth and questionable incentives
Bolivia	Good; high GOEE	Slow growth
Ethiopia	Poor: low GOEE in industry; negative in agriculture	Slow growth and bad incentives
India	Improving but low GOEE	Bad incentives
Indonesia	Seems good; no estimate of GOEE for post-crisis period; Good in pre-crisis period	Slow growth
Uganda	Mixed: GOEE low in industries Greater than 2 (1) for agriculture	Slow growth; possibly bad incentives as well (services)
Vietnam	GOEE good in agriculture & RNF; Low in industries (recently improved)	Poor incentives

Note: GOEE – gross output elasticity of employment.

The Indian case study gives an account of recent improvements in the incentive system: reduced barriers to entry, relaxation of constraints on the private sector, reduction of distortions caused by arbitrary customs and excise duty rates, as well as the lowering of these rates. In Vietnam, recent improvements in the gross output elasticity of employment in industries have been attributed to the abandonment of the policy of arbitrary allocation of resources for investment in large capital-intensive public enterprises and a big shift in favour of private investment, often in smaller enterprises. This is an area in which the ILO/SIDA studies could have made greater effort. There are outstanding labour market irrationalities that plague many of these countries. The great difference between industrial wages and average rural earnings is many times greater than the difference in the original East Asian tigers, for example. The lack of mobility of labour out of declining industries, often involving very high costs in getting them relocated elsewhere, is another important issue.

Several case studies acknowledge the role of institutions in employment generation. Reform of the agrarian system receives most attention. Poverty reduction in Kyrgyz Republic, despite 'agricultural involution', was possible, largely as a consequence of land reform. Though less definitively documented, Armenia seems to have had a similar experience of protecting those living in extreme poverty.

Earlier, three distinct paths of poverty-alleviating employment growth were identified in the ILO/SIDA case studies and a number of questions were raised. The principal question about the path of classic industrialization, transferring labour from agriculture to industries and modern services, was concerned with the tardiness of the process in rapidly growing contemporary economies, like China and India. Employment in agriculture in China peaked in 1991, and fell by a mere six per cent in the next eleven years. In the Republic of Korea between 1980 and 1991, agricultural employment fell by nearly 40 per cent. In India, absolute employment in agriculture remained stable for the last six years of the last century without beginning a decline. This slow transition out of the sector with far lower output and income per worker than industry and services is one reason for the persistence of poverty, which has a far greater incidence among agricultural populations than other populations.

Much of the explanation for this slow structural change in the composition of employment in China is to be found in the public policies pursued in the past. For decades, China restricted the movement of labour out of rural areas by exercising strict residential control. This has contributed to a steady increase in the ratio of urban to rural per capita household incomes. At more than three, this ratio in China is among the highest in the world. In recent years, there has only been a half-hearted tolerance of 'floating migrants' in urban areas who are subjected to severe discrimination. The other side of the explanation for slow transition is to be found in the slow growth in urban industrial employment. This is not because the new industries in China have not been sufficiently labour intensive. Indeed, these industries have, by all indications, created a lot of employment. The problem is that the SOEs (state and collective enterprises) initially had a great deal of excess labour as part of China's past policy of putting people on the payroll of SOEs as a method of 'concealed unemployment insurance'. During the period of reform, this could not be sustained, as the SOEs were opened up to competition and started shedding labour at a rapid rate. The low observed gross output elasticity of employment in China's industries is the weighted average of two unobserved elasticities: a highly negative one for SOEs and a fairly decent positive one for new industries. The effect of this transition on urban poverty was exacerbated by China's failure to institute an open system of unemployment insurance before reducing employment in SOEs.

The large difference between the average urban wage and the average rural earnings in India suggests something similar, though smaller in magnitude. Such high differentials effectively means that the wages of urban industrial employees include an element of 'rent', buttressed by regulations limiting entry into and exit out of industrial employment. Quite apart from contributing to a rise in wage costs, this system restricts labour mobility from less productive sectors to more productive industries.

Thus, compared to those countries that started industrialization without the above types of irrationalities characterizing their labour markets – for example, the original East Asian tigers – the countries that have embarked on reform from typical import-substitution regimes will take much longer to bring about a structural change in the composition of their employment.

How attractive an alternative is the Bangladesh model of rapid increase in remunerative employment in the RNF sector, as hypothesized by the UNDP case study of that country? As noted in Khan (2005: Annex), this review considers the explanation a tentative, albeit highly interesting hypothesis in need of clearer evidence to establish its validity. Be that as it may, the case study itself raises a number of question marks on its viability. First, the Bangladesh case clearly establishes that RNF income has a disequalizing influence on distribution. The evidence from China and Cambodia also shows that, contrary to what many development policymakers hoped, RNF income is rather strongly disequalizing. The question is: can such a disequalizing source of income be a dynamic source of poverty-alleviating employment expansion? Something needs to be done to make this a more equalizing source of income. A second problem, at least specific to Bangladesh, is that these RNF activities are all in non-traded sectors. The Bangladesh case study hints that their growth would be adversely affected if the trade regime was too liberalized, but is doubtful whether this is either viable or desirable in the long run. The way for these activities to survive is probably to link them up with the export market, requiring a good deal of investment to provide the necessary services.

The third path, which involves an increased share of agricultural employment, is the most widely prevalent case among the 13 countries. Development theory has long viewed this as an indicator of retrogression that does not constitute a long-term solution to the problem of unemployment and poverty. Some case studies nevertheless show that appropriate institutional reform can improve the capacity of agriculture to productively absorb more labour, thereby giving a short-term boost to poverty reduction.

A final issue highlighted by some ILO/SIDA studies – especially on India and Bangladesh – is the case of the working poor, the large numbers of workers engaged in long, strenuous labour but with low levels of remuneration. The way out of poverty is to make employment more productive for them and to get the higher productivity reflected in higher remuneration. The kind of action needed to attain this would depend on the nature of the problem, and solutions would consist of one or more of many instruments encompassing investment, access to resources, improvement in terms of trade for afflicted groups and structural change in the composition of employment.

CONCLUDING OBSERVATIONS

No attempt will be made to summarize the findings of this review, except to confirm the presumptions of the UNDP and ILO/SIDA case studies in some principal areas. Rapid economic growth and containment of the forces of inequality are essential for healthy and sustained poverty reduction. Increased inequality can even offset the benefits of a rapid rate of growth as far as poverty reduction is concerned. But continued, or even improved, equality of income distribution is an uncertain guarantee against increased poverty when growth is weak and narrowly-based. Equality in this context means maintaining at least an unchanged share of incremental income for the poor, rather than holding down some overall indicator of income distribution. This kind of equality is best ensured by a rapid expansion in remunerative and productive employment. The case studies indicate that no country's employment growth equalled the kind of dynamic growth envisioned by development theory as the hallmark of success. Poor or less than potential performance in poverty reduction in rapidly growing countries can all be traced to employment performance falling that far short of the best historically observed cases. In most cases, however, inadequate economic growth itself has to be blamed for poor employment performance. Apart from slow growth, there have also been serious problems with incentives and institutions determining the labour intensity of production and investment. Macroeconomic policies in most of the countries have either hindered growth or been unhelpful in promoting growth. In the two cases of growth-promoting macroeconomic policies, the effect of the latter has been to exacerbate inequality and hinder employment growth.

The two sets of studies have made substantial contributions to our understanding in a vitally important area of policymaking. The UNDP case studies have sharpened the debate on policy reform in contemporary developing countries by presenting a clear alternative to the adjustment process implemented by Bank-Fund conditionalities. These concluding comments will highlight two areas in which these studies might go further.

The first relates to international cooperation envisaged by these studies. Quite a number of them propose international scenarios that postulate large-scale accommodations by the donor community. This is most clearly illustrated by the Indonesian case, in which a large reduction in debt service is seen as a precondition for the expansionary policy recommended by the study. It is well known that the donor community, led by the Bank and the Fund, will not endorse such a strategy. What should the country do in this case? Should a poverty reduction strategy await a change of heart by the international community? Should the country seek some method of augmenting domestic resources, as suggested by the Armenian and Mongolian studies? In the latter case, what kind of scenario can be visualized for the transition process? What are the political and economic implications of these alternatives?

A second issue relates to trade liberalization. The UNDP strategy differs from the typical Bank-Fund strategy in that it has strong reservations against unrestricted free trade. It often recommends some variant of the East Asian kind of industrial policy, involving careful nurturing and promotion of fledgling industries. This is a policy that needs to be clarified in operational detail. The East Asian kind of industrial policy would be inconsistent with current WTO agreements, which are binding for the developing countries, with the possible exception of the very poor countries. It is important for the UNDP studies to clarify the implications of their vision for the on-going round of WTO negotiations in which developing countries are engaged. These countries need to preserve the option of promoting worthwhile fledgling industries. Similarly, they need to preserve their freedom to avoid unviable liberalization of capital movements – another major theme of the UNDP studies. Furthermore, these studies should have delved deeper into WTO issues involving intra-developing country conflicts, e.g., the termination of the MFA and its successor. While this was projected to bring enormous benefits to China and India, the effects on Bangladesh, Cambodia and Nepal were going to be highly negative, with serious adverse consequences for employment and poverty. How can macroeconomic policies in these countries achieve poverty-alleviating growth in the face of these external shocks?

The ILO/SIDA studies have heroically explored an area in which the quality of statistical information is notoriously poor in developing countries. A number of their estimates bear the mark of this deficiency. Future studies along this line should make greater effort to both improve the quality of data and make more nuanced use of existing data, as did the case study on India. Few countries among those in which case studies have been carried out have as good data as India has on these aspects of the economy. Thus, for many countries, meaningful improvement in analysis must be preceded by improving the quality of data. In the meantime, care needs to be exercised in qualifying, and finding explanations for, implausible data.

The ILO/SIDA studies also need to devote greater attention to the incentive system affecting employment intensity. Very few studies have paid significant attention to this issue, which should have been the principal focus of analysis seeking explanation for variations in employment intensity.

Several indicators of labour market functioning and of the incentive system affecting factor proportions should receive careful attention. These include the difference between the wage rates in urban industries and rural employment, factors contributing to arbitrarily high wage costs (e.g., administered wages and obstacles to mobility), differences between large and small enterprises in access to credit and other resources, differences in transaction costs accrued by large and small enterprises, and elements of under-pricing of competing factors, such as capital.

CASE STUDIES

UNDP

Armenia: Griffin (ed.) (2002).
Bangladesh: Osmani and others (undated).
Cambodia: Beresford and others (2004).
Kyrgyz Republic: UNDP (2002).
Mongolia: Griffin (ed.) (2003).
Nepal: UNDP (undated).

Vietnam: Weeks and others (undated).

ILO/SIDA

Bangladesh: Rahman and Islam (2003).
Bolivia: Jemio and others (2003).
Ethiopia: Demeke and others (2003).
India: Sundaram and Tendulkar (2002).
Indonesia: Islam (undated).
Uganda: Kabananukye and others (2004).
Vietnam: Pham and others (2003).

Notes

[1] The UNDP studies cover Armenia, Bangladesh, Cambodia, China, Indonesia, Kyrgyz Republic, Mongolia, Nepal and Vietnam. The ILO/SIDA studies cover Bangladesh, Bolivia, Ethiopia, India, Indonesia, Uganda and Vietnam. An ILO/SIDA study (Islam 2004), which is itself an overview of the growth-employment-poverty nexus based on the seven case studies and a cross-sectional analysis of a larger number of countries, is also taken into account in this chapter. Individual papers are cited before the list of references.

   Altogether, 13 countries are covered by the two sets of studies as three each of the UNDP and the ILO/SIDA studies concern the same countries (Bangladesh, Indonesia and Vietnam). Ten of the countries are located in Asia: three in South Asia, four in East and South-East Asia, one in the Caucasus, and two in Central Asia. Of the three non-Asian countries, two are in sub-Saharan Africa and one in Latin America. The countries range in population size from the two largest countries of the world at one end to five small countries, with populations ranging from two to twelve million, at the other end. In between are the fourth and the eighth largest countries of the world, two medium-sized, and two relatively small-sized countries. Three of them (China, Bolivia and Armenia) are lower-middle income countries according to the World Bank classification, while the rest are low-income countries. Note, however, that Indonesia, classified as a low-income country since the Asian crisis, has a higher real per capita income (PPP$ income) than does Bolivia, a lower-middle income country. Five of the countries – Bangladesh, Nepal, Cambodia, Ethiopia and Uganda – are in the category of least-developed countries, according to the UN classification. Note, again, that some of these countries (Bangladesh and Nepal) have higher real per capita income than others not included in this category (Kyrgyz Republic and Mongolia). Together, these countries incorporate a wide variety of characteristics, although their experience in the area under review would not be representative of the experience of the contemporary developing world. Indeed, one region, Asia, and one development category, the transitional economies, are well represented. Other regions and categories have token or no representation.

[2] This quote is from the preface to the discussion papers of the ILO/SIDA case studies.

5

[3] This particular direction of the employment-growth linkage has not featured prominently in the case studies. The focus has usually been on the reverse direction of the relationship, the effect of growth on employment and labour productivity.

[4] This analytical framework is more fully discussed in Khan (2001).

[5] The estimated equation is as follows:

Log HC = −2.526 − 1.012Log Y + 3.635 Log Gini:

(−1.744) (2.055)

where HC is headcount index of poverty, Y is per capita PPP$ income and Gini is the Gini index of per capita expenditure distribution. The figures in parentheses are t-values. The adjusted R^2 is 0.204. The coefficient of Y is significant at 11.2 per cent, while the coefficient of Gini is significant at 6.7 per cent. The problem with the data is that most of the PPP$ income estimates are based on indirect methods of projection, rather than direct price information; to the best of my knowledge, no adjustment is made for the possibility of different PPP deflators for different expenditure groups in estimating the Gini ratio.

[6] In the case of China, this has been demonstrated by actual simulation by Khan and Riskin (2001). In other cases, this is strongly suggested by the case studies.

[7] While the ILO/SIDA case study on Bangladesh does not take a clear position on this issue, later work by the same authors confirms this hypothesis, though not as strongly as the UNDP case study. According to the authors of the ILO/SIDA case study, overall employment growth in Bangladesh consisted of slow growth of formal employment and faster creation of informal employment, especially in the RNF sector.

[8] As noted in Khan (2001: Annex), in the case of Uganda, this may largely be a statistical quirk. The evidence for Bolivia is also puzzling.

[9] Of these nine countries, the Indonesian experience is only considered for the post-crisis period. As briefly noted above, pre-crisis Indonesia, combining rapid growth with inequality not increasing, was unlike any of the following three categories.

[10] This criticism is of questionable validity. It is difficult to argue that, in China, the rate of aggregate credit expansion was not rapid enough or the average cost of credit was too high. The case study may, of course, be right that small borrowers were at a disadvantage due to market failure and to bureaucratic interference in credit allocation, in which case, further liberalization of credit, by itself, would be of little help.

[11] The idea that the gross output elasticity of employment in manufacturing is a reasonably reliable indicator of the system of incentives guiding decisions about technological choice may underlie the regression analysis made by Islam (2004), which shows that, for a sample of 23 countries, growth in per capita GDP and the gross output elasticity of employment in manufacturing both have significantly positive effects on poverty reduction. The underlying assumption must be that these incentives determine employment growth throughout the economy.

REFERENCES

Beresford, Melanie, and others (2004). The macroeconomics of poverty reduction in Cambodia. Processed, UNDP, Beijing.

Demeke, Mulat, and others (2003). Growth employment, poverty and policies in Ethiopia: An empirical investigation. Issues in employment and poverty discussion paper (IEPDP) 12, International Labour Office, Geneva.

Griffin, Keith (ed.) (2002). Growth, Inequality and Poverty in Armenia. Processed, UNDP, Yerevan.

Griffin, Keith (ed.) (2003). *Poverty Reduction in Mongolia*. Asia Pacific Press at the Australian National University, Canberra.

Islam, Rizwanul (2004). The nexus of economic growth, employment and poverty reduction. issues in employment and poverty discussion paper (IEPDP) 14, International Labour Office, Geneva.

Islam, Inayatul (undated). Poverty, employment and wages: An Indonesian perspective. Recovery and Reconstruction Department, International Labour Office, Geneva.

Jemio, Luis Carlos, and others (2003). Employment-Poverty linkages and policies: The Case of Bolivia. Issues in Employment and Poverty Discussion Paper (IEPDP) 11, International Labour Office, Geneva.

Kabananukye, Kabann I.B., and others (2004). Economic Growth, employment, poverty and pro-poor policies in Uganda. Issues in Employment and Poverty Discussion Paper (IEPDP) 16, International Labour Office, Geneva.

Khan, A. R. (2001). Employment policies for poverty reduction. Issues in Employment and poverty Discussion Paper (IEPDP) 1, International Labour Office, Geneva.

Khan, A. R. (2004). Growth, inequality and poverty: A comparative study of China's experience in the periods before and after the Asian crisis. Issues in Employment and Poverty Discussion Paper (IEPDP) 12, International Labour Office, Geneva.

Khan, A. R. (2005). Growth, employment and poverty: An analysis of the vital nexus based on some recent UNDP and ILO/SIDA studies. Processed 26 February, Economics Department, University of California, Riverside.

Khan, A. R., and Carl Riskin (2001). *Inequality and Poverty in China in the Age of Globalization*. Oxford University Press, New York.

Khan, A. R., and Binayak Sen (2006). The structure and distribution of personal income and poverty reduction: A case study of Bangladesh during the 1990s. In James Boyce, Stephen Cullenberg, Prasanta Pattanaik and Robert Pollin (eds.), Human Development in the Era of Globalization: Essays in the Honour of Keith B. Griffin. Edward Elgar, Cheltenham, UK and Northampton, MA, USA.

Osmani, S. R., and others (undated). The macroeconomics of poverty reduction: The case study of Bangladesh. Processed, UNDP, New York.

Pham Lan Huong and others (2003). Employment poverty linkages and policies for pro-poor growth in Vietnam. Issues in Employment and Poverty Discussion Paper (IEPDP) 9, International Labour Office, Geneva.

Rahman, Rushidan Islam, and K. M. Nabiul Islam (2003). Employment poverty linkages: Bangladesh. Issues in Employment and Poverty Discussion Paper (IEPDP) 10, International Labour Office, Geneva.

Sundaram, K., and Suresh K. Tendulkar (2002). The working poor in India: Employment-poverty linkages and employment poverty options. Issues in Employment and Poverty Discussion Paper (IEPDP) 4, International Labour Office, Geneva.

UNDP (2002). The macroeconomics of poverty: A case study of the Kyrgyz Republic. Processed, UNDP, New York.

UNDP (undated). The macroeconomics of poverty reduction in Indonesia. Processed, UNDP, New York.

UNDP (undated). The macroeconomics of poverty reduction in Nepal. Processed, UNDP, New York.

Weeks, John, and others, The macroeconomics of poverty reduction: The sase study of Vietnam, seeking equity within growth. Processed, UNDP, New York.

World Bank, (2003). *World Development Indicators, 2003.* World Bank, Washington, DC.

World Bank, (2004). *World Development Indicators, 2004.* World Bank, Washington, DC.

7

Generating Rural Employment in Africa to Fight Poverty[†]

JANVIER D. NKURUNZIZA

Africa is the only region where poverty has risen over the last three decades. This is in sharp contrast with the world trend which shows a substantial reduction in poverty. The poverty rate in Africa in 2003 is significantly higher than in South Asia, the second poorest region of the world. This makes poverty the key development challenge in Africa, and there is international consensus that eliminating it is the overriding objective of development efforts in the continent.

Employment is arguably the most important channel through which poverty in Africa will be reduced. Whether Africans are wage earners or self-employed, they earn a living from their labour. This is particularly important because of the limited alternatives they have. In many instances, particularly in rural Africa where poverty is concentrated, labour is the sole asset held by the poor. Employment income has several advantages over assistance to the poor, such as food aid, financial and in-kind assistance. Employment income is more reliable because it depends on the decision of the poor to work where employment is available. Secondly, employment income preserves the dignity of the poor as it rewards their efforts. Thirdly, employment income helps the poor to be independent, permitting family livelihood obligations to be met.

In this regard, the observed unemployment, underemployment and low returns to labour in Africa can be considered immediate causes of poverty. Hence, policies encouraging growth and employment creation are expected to be "essential for any poverty reduction strategy" (World Bank, 2000: 99). This view is supported by cross-country empirical evidence showing that expanding remunerative employment reduces the incidence of poverty (Islam, 2004).

The scope of the impact on poverty of growth through employment goes beyond the income dimensions of poverty. Employment-intensive growth increases the consumption potential of the population, especially food consumption, thus reducing malnutrition, which is particularly rampant in poor rural communities. Moreover, the additional resources generated by growth can be used to improve the accessibility of basic services essential for decent living, such as education and health.

There are several non-income dimensions of poverty, however, including those related to the capabilities of poor people, which cannot be addressed by economic growth alone. For instance, the 'human development' dimension of poverty can be addressed by enhancing the employability of poor people through better nutrition, health, training and education. Where low human development is because of unequal distribution of resources within a society, greater equity is the solution. Meanwhile, improving governance can contribute to alleviating the exclusion, marginalization and insecurity of poor people. Special targeting policies are also required in certain cases. For example, the gender dimensions of poverty may be addressed by targeting employment opportunities for women. Similarly, the spatial aspect of poverty is best tackled by targeting marginalized areas in development policies.

This chapter focuses on rural employment, since poverty is most rampant in Africa's rural areas, and proceeds as follows. The second section provides some key facts about poverty and unemployment in Africa to put the discussion of rural employment in context. The third section argues that employment is the missing link between the relatively high rates of economic growth observed in Africa over the last decade and poverty reduction. The fourth section discusses different ways of generating rural employment, and the fifth section offers conclusions.

POVERTY AND UNEMPLOYMENT IN AFRICA

Although this chapter is about employment, it is important to keep in mind that the high rates of poverty in Africa make employment creation even more urgent. For the poor, employment is not a way of fulfilling professional ambitions; it is a way of earning a living for survival. Empirical microeconomic studies of poverty in Africa identify unemployment as one of its key determinants. However, it is difficult to find similarly detailed quantitative analyses of the determinants of unemployment because of the scarcity of reliable employment data in Africa. This section discusses the key characteristics of poverty and unemployment in Africa using available data.

Scale of Poverty in Africa

Despite a steady increase in real gross domestic product (GDP) in Africa over the last ten years, Figure 7.1 shows that Africa is the only region where poverty has been rising in the last three decades.[1]

Poverty (as measured by the headcount ratio) stagnated at high levels in sub-Saharan Africa, while it declined in other parts of the world. In 2003, about 46 per cent of the sub-Saharan Africa population lived on less than $1 a day – slightly more than in 1980 and 1990. At the global level, however, the share of the population living on $1 a day declined from 40 per cent in 1980 to 20 per cent in 2003. The $1 a day headcount ratio in sub-Saharan Africa now exceeds the next poorest region, South Asia, by about 17 percentage points. Thus, while East, South-East and South Asia and North Africa are broadly on track to meet the Millennium Development Goal (MDG) of halving poverty by 2015, there has been little progress in sub-Saharan Africa towards achieving it (UN, 2004). The high rates of poverty incidence are illustrated in Table 7.1.[2]

Table 7.1 shows that growth rates vary from a high of 69 per cent in Mozambique to a low of 7.6 per cent in Tunisia. For 8 out of the 22 countries in the table, the rates are higher than 50 per cent, implying that the majority of the population is poor in those countries. Even, at the country level, however, the national average hides a dichotomy between rural and urban areas. The mean difference between incidence rates in urban and rural areas was 19.6 percentage points during 1995–2000. As a result, poverty in Africa is largely rural, as illustrated in Figure 7.2.

FIGURE 7.1
$1 a day poverty headcount, by region, 1980–2003
(percentage of population)

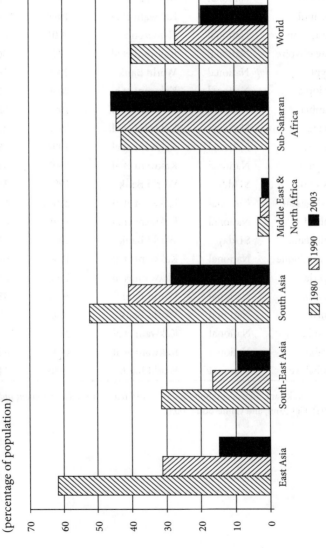

Source: ILO (2004c).

TABLE 7.1
Rates of poverty in a sample of African countries

Country	Line	Source	Survey year	Head-count
Botswana	$1/day	World Bank	1993	23.5
Burkina Faso	National	Kakwani et al.	1998	52.6
Burundi	National	Kakwani et al.	1998	61.2
Cameroon	National	Cameroon	2001	40.2
Côte d'Ivoire	National	Kakwani et al.	1998	36.7
Egypt	National	World Bank	2000	16.7
Ethiopia	National	Kakwani et al.	2000	40.9
Gambia	National	Kakwani et al.	1998	62.2
Ghana	National	Kakwani et al.	1998	43.6
Guinea	National	Kakwani et al.	1994	38.1
Kenya	National	Kakwani et al.	1997	49.7
Lesotho	$1/day	World Bank	1995	36.0
Madagascar	National	Kakwani et al.	2001	62.0
Malawi	National	Kakwani et al.	1998	63.9
Mauritania	$1/day	World Bank	2000	25.9
Mozambique	National	Kakwani et al.	1996	68.9
Nigeria	National	Kakwani et al.	1996	63.4
Tanzania	National	World Bank	2001	35.7
Tunisia	National	World Bank	1995	7.6
Uganda	National	Kakwani et al.	2000	48.2
Zambia	National	Kakwani et al.	1998	66.7
Zimbabwe	National	World Bank	1996	34.9

Sources: Kakwani, Soares and Son (2005); World Bank, *World Development Indicators* (2004), CD-Rom; and Cameroon (2003).

FIGURE 7.2
Africa: Rural-urban differentials, various years (percentage points)

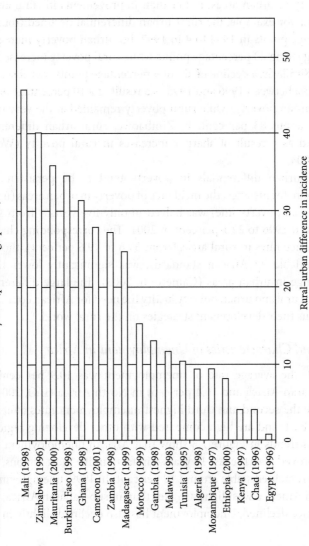

Rural–urban difference in incidence

Note: Data from household surveys, which were not conducted in the same years in every country. Data refer to national (urban, rural and total) poverty lines.
Source: World Bank (2004).

There are large inter-country, rural-urban differentials, ranging from 0.8 percentage points in Egypt in 1996 to 45.8 percentage points in Mali in 1998; 40.1 percentage points in Zimbabwe in 1996 and 35.8 percentage points in Mauritania in 2000. Rural-urban differentials are generally high, regardless of incidence rates. When they have declined, it has been mostly the result of sharp hikes in the incidence of poverty in urban areas, rather than improvements in rural areas. In Kenya, for example, the rural-urban differential declined from 18 percentage points in 1994 to 4 in 1997, but urban poverty increased by a staggering 20 percentage points while rural poverty increased by only 5. Similarly, a decline of about 9 percentage points was observed in Zambia between 1996 and 1998 as a result of a 10 percentage point rise in urban poverty, while rural poverty remained at the very high level of about 83 per cent. In Zimbabwe, rural-urban differences increased as a result of sharper increases in rural poverty (World Bank, 2004).

Rural-urban differentials in poverty tend to be persistent. In Cameroon, for instance, the incidence of poverty in urban areas (using the national poverty line) was halved in only five years – from 41.4 per cent in 1996 to 22.1 per cent in 2001. The corresponding change in incidence rates in rural areas (from 59.6 to 49.6 per cent), though commendable by African standards, was significantly lower than the change in urban areas (Cameroon, 2003). The large differences between rural and urban poverty justify the need for African countries to refocus their development strategies on the rural world.

Level and Characteristics of Unemployment in Africa

In 2003, the average rate of unemployment was 10.9 per cent in sub-Saharan Africa and 10.4 per cent in North Africa (ILO, 2004a). They are the second and third highest unemployment rates after the Middle East, and are high compared with other developing regions. Regional trends in Figure 7.3 show that African unemployment has not improved over the last 10 years – in fact, unlike most regions, the rate has remained stable around 10 per cent. In 1999, unemployment in South America was slightly higher than in sub-Saharan Africa, but it has since declined. Unemployment has also declined slightly in the

Middle East and North Africa, but is still higher than in sub-Saharan Africa.

FIGURE 7.3
Unemployment rates by region, 1995–2004 (per cent)

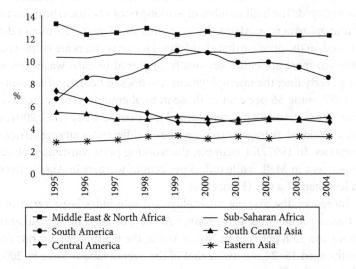

Source: Data from Tarantino (2003)

Although high compared with other regions, Africa's unemployment rate in Figure 7.3 seems unrealistically low for several reasons. First, the collection of employment data in Africa is fraught with difficulty. Many countries do not report information, reporting countries give incomplete data, and not all the reported information is comparable across countries.

Comparing Employment Data in Africa

Labour indicators (ILO, 2005a; 2005b) may not be comparable across economies for several reasons, including definitional differences, source differences as well as seasonal variations. Moreover, the reported rate does not take into account the large number of discouraged workers. Searching for a job is costly and is undertaken only when there is a relatively high probability of finding one. In many African countries, the demand for jobs is so high relative to supply that many job seekers consider it is a waste of time to seek employment. This is particularly the case in rural areas where the supply of jobs is much lower than in urban centres. In cities, the problem of discouraged workers is thought to affect educated people because they have expectations of high-paying formal jobs. These discouraged workers are not counted as unemployed. The high number of working poor confuses the measure of unemployment in Africa. The computation of unemployment rates is based on the premise that all informal sector workers are employed, although most are either seasonally employed or earn wages below the poverty line; the unemployment rate does not convey this reality. In 1997, some 56 per cent of those in total employment earned less than $1 a day, and 89 per cent earned less than $2 a day (ILO, 2004c). These regional averages mask significant differences among African countries. In 1997, for example, the working poor constituted about 75 per cent in Mali, while only 3 per cent of workers in Algeria lived on less than $1 a day (Figure 7.4).

Moreover, the average unemployment rate hides large variations between gender and age groups. At 21 per cent in sub-Saharan Africa and 22.8 per cent in North Africa, the unemployment rate for youths aged 15–24 was twice that of the overall labour force in 2003 (ILO, 2004b). These youth unemployment rates were the second and third highest in the world after the Middle East, and barely changed between 1993 and 2003. In 2003, unemployed youth as a share of total unemployed was 63 per cent in sub-Saharan Africa, even though youths made up only 33 per cent of the labour force. Furthermore, in 2003, the youth-to-adult unemployment ratio of 3:5 in sub-Saharan Africa meant that young people were much more likely than their counterparts to be unemployed.

Female unemployment rates are higher than male unemployment rates in North Africa but lower in sub-Saharan Africa, and also generally underestimated. The gender gap in favour of women in sub-Saharan Africa does not reflect the dire situation of women in the labour force because female unemployment is underestimated for a number of reasons. First, social norms tend to require women to declare themselves as housewives only involved in unpaid domestic work, which excludes them from inclusion in the labour force. Second,

FIGURE 7.4

Africa: Working poor, rate by country, 1997 (per cent)

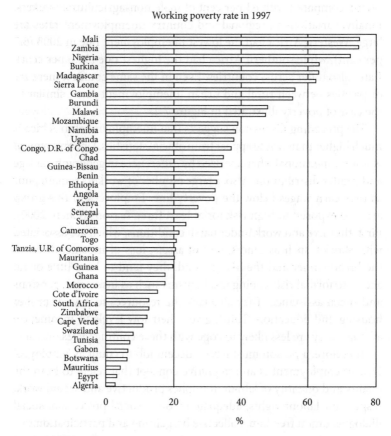

Source: Majid (2001)

women are more likely to be discouraged workers in the context of limited opportunities because men are usually favoured. Third, the criterion requiring availability for employment during the reference period penalizes women more than men because they need more time to make the necessary arrangements, before starting a job, such as arranging for care of children or elderly relatives or other household affairs. Female unemployment rates in Africa also mask the fact that female workers are mostly in informal employment, where they are more likely to be among the working poor. In sub-Saharan Africa, 84 per cent of female non-agricultural workers are in the informal sector, compared with 63 per cent of male non-agricultural workers. Finally, variations in regional and country unemployment rates are large. Western Africa had the lowest unemployment rate in 2003 (6.7 per cent), while southern Africa had the highest rate (31.6 per cent). Rates also differ across countries. Even in the same country, there are disparities between rural and urban unemployment rates, similar to the case of poverty illustrated in Figure 7.2.

The preceding discussion suggests that unemployment in Africa is much higher than would appear from official statistics. Unemployment is multidimensional, characterized by differences in geographical, age and gender distribution. Also, a large number of workers remain poor as they earn wages below the poverty line. Employees in this group are also exposed to high risk for at least three reasons (Chen, 2000). First, they live and work under harsh conditions, which are associated with shocks, such as illness, loss of assets, loss of income, death of the breadwinner and the like. Second, they tend to have little or no access to formal risk-coping mechanisms such as insurance, pensions and social assistance. They also lack the resources to pay for proper housing and education. Third, given their low levels of income, on average, they are less likely to cope with these contingencies.

Therefore, a person must have a decent job to count as 'employed'. Decent employment is an integrative concept that refers to both the quality and quantity of labour. It implies productive and secure work, respect for labour rights, adequate income, social protection, social dialogue, union freedom, collective bargaining and participation.

Economic Growth, Employment and Poverty Reduction

Despite recovery in the rates of economic growth in Africa over recent years, growth has failed to generate much employment (Figure 7.5). The real rate of economic growth has increased steadily from about 2.5 per cent in 1998 to 4.8 per cent in 2005 (UNECA, 2005). However, employment creation has remained stable at 3 per cent, with a slight decline between 2001 and 2003.

FIGURE 7.5

Sub-Saharan Africa: Economic growth and employment growth

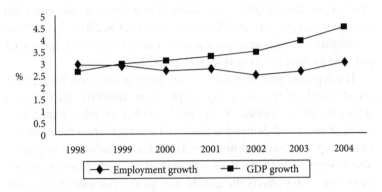

Source: UNECA calculations based on Tarantino (2003).

The high levels of poverty in Africa have not been reduced much because employment intensity in the growth process in the continent is weak. The next section reviews evidence in the Poverty Reduction Strategy Papers (PRSPs) of 21 African countries to determine the role of employment in the fight against poverty.

Weak Employment Intensity in the Growth Process

It seems paradoxical that a number of Africa's fastest growing economies have some of the highest poverty rates. Several factors help explain this. First, many currently fast-growing economies, such as Chad and Equatorial Guinea, have been very poor, implying they will need sustained high levels of growth to have a noticeable impact on poverty. For instance, it would take ten years for a country with GDP per capita of $150 growing at an average real growth rate of 7 per cent per annum to double its GDP per capita to $300. Using the $1/day poverty line many people in the country would remain poor even after doubling their income. Secondly, if the benefits of growth are not equally distributed, many people will remain poor despite growth. Thirdly, the more jobs created by the growth process the greater the impact on poverty reduction. In Africa, the high growth rates observed in oil-exporting countries have originated from capital-intensive enclave industries that have few or no links to the rest of the economy, and hence, have created few jobs. On average, non-oil-exporting countries had a growth rate of 2.9 per cent in 2003 and 3.8 per cent in 2004 – much lower than those in oil-producing countries (5.4 per cent in 2003 and 5.3 per cent in 2004). In 2005, oil economies recorded an average growth rate of 6.1 per cent against 4.1 per cent for non-oil economies (UNECA, 2005).

The degree of employment intensity in the growth process depends on demand in sectors using employment-intensive technologies (Osmani, 2003). Moreover, the total number of jobs created as a result of increased demand is likely to be higher when the economy has strong inter-sectoral linkages. In addition, the source of growth also matters. Whether job growth emanates largely from the public or private sector affects the quality and quantity of jobs created. The trends in the commodity terms of trade, and the extent to which labour benefits from higher terms of trade, are also important determinants of employment intensity in growth (see Osmani, 2003).

The impact of economic growth on employment depends on which sectors lead the growth process. When growth is spurred by labour-intensive sectors that employ a significant share of the labour force, such as smallholder agriculture, its effect on employment and poverty is greater than when concentrated in capital-intensive sectors, such as mining. In Ethiopia, for example, relatively slow growth in the labour-intensive agricultural sector accounted in part for the limited impact of growth on employment in the post-reform years of the 1990s. Agriculture grew by only 1.9 per cent, while manufacturing, which is largely capital-intensive, grew by 5 per cent a year over 1992/93 to 1999/2000 (Demeke, Guta and Ferede, 2003). In Uganda, by contrast, high growth in the labour-intensive agricultural sector contributed to a decline in unemployment – from 56 per cent in 1992 to 35 per cent in 2000.

The impact of economic growth on employment also depends on the extent to which the economy consciously adopts labour-friendly techniques across all sectors. In the past, policymakers in many African countries have favoured capital-intensive techniques, or have failed to promote employment-friendly technologies. Kenya, for example, used tractors and heavy-duty machines, instead of less-mechanized techniques, such as ox-drawn ploughs and hand tools, in the agricultural sector during the 1980s (Khan, 1997). Large machines were exempt from import duty and sales taxes and were classified in the less restrictive import category, while ploughs and hand tools were subject to high import duty and placed in the most restrictive import category. These policies have displaced labour from large farms and discouraged small farms, which are more productive and labour intensive.

It is necessary, therefore, to promote technologies that maximize employment without unduly compromising productivity. In the agricultural sector, for instance, ensuring access to basic inputs, such as seeds and fertilizer, infrastructure, such as roads and irrigation, and research and development through extension services, can have a favourable impact on the productivity of small farms. In Mozambique, failure to promote labour intensity in either the composition of output across sectors or the choice of technology within sectors is undermining the country's objective to reduce the poverty rate from 70 to 50 per cent by 2010 despite high economic growth.

The employment-generating effects of growth are more likely to be magnified in economies characterized by strong inter-sectoral linkages because they create jobs, both directly and indirectly, by stimulating demand in related sectors of the economy. For instance, promoting agro-industries is likely to create additional jobs, both within and outside the agricultural sector, by stimulating the demand for agricultural commodities to sustain the agro-industries and by increasing the demand for workers to staff them.

The quality and quantity of jobs created through growth will be influenced by the public and private sectors' roles in driving the growth process. In many African countries, the government sector accounts for a large share of the economy because the private sector is repressed. However, large government employment has been associated with low wages, high fiscal deficits and low per capita income. Sustainable employment growth will therefore require credible reforms aimed at improving the overall efficiency of the public sector to ensure that job growth is associated with rising productivity. Indeed, when public enterprises are overstaffed, increasing productivity may require downsizing, at least in the short run, which conflicts with the objective of employment creation.

Another factor that affects the employment intensity of growth is the terms of trade. Favourable external terms of trade in labour-intensive sectors have a positive effect on the performance of these sectors and consequently improve the quality and quantity of employment. Uganda's high agricultural growth was driven by favourable trends in the terms of trade in general and the prices of cash crops in particular. Coffee, for example, benefited from the boom in prices that took place in the world market. The export price of coffee rose from $0.86 per kilogram in 1991–1992 to $2.55 in 1994–1995 (Demeke, Guta and Ferede, 2003). Improvements in the terms of trade will translate into higher returns for labour and improve the livelihoods of workers only if the benefits are passed on to producers. This was the case in Uganda, where producer prices as a share of the world price of coffee increased by at least 50 per cent between 1991 and 1997 thanks to a more liberalized marketing regime. Unfortunately, many African countries have a long tradition of subjecting agricultural exports to low producer prices, which constrains productivity and therefore discourages production and employment (IFAD, 2001).

For poor people to take advantage of rapid growth and high employment creation, however, they must be employable; otherwise, they face barriers to entry in the job market, either as wage earners or entrepreneurs. They will not take advantage of employment opportunities if they lack the appropriate human capital in the form of health and education; if access to market opportunities created by economic growth is limited; if restrictive labour regulations affect their entry into the labour market; or if they are victims of discriminatory attitudes which limit their opportunities, including gender discrimination and unequal access to assets.

Weak Employment Content of Poverty Reduction Strategy Papers

As decent employment is a major route out of poverty, it should be at the heart of the poverty battle in Africa. If policymakers accord employment creation a central role in the fight against poverty, this should be reflected in the poverty reduction strategies of African countries. As of October 2004, 21 African countries had full PRSPs and 9 had interim PRSPs. The following analysis focuses on the full PRSPs and their respective annual progress reports. It assesses only the degree to which decent employment is reflected in the PRSPs, not whether the employment goals are translated into action (see Table 7.2).

TABLE 7.2
Breakdown of 21 full Poverty Reduction Strategy Papers (PRSPs) in Africa by employment content
(share of positive answers to employment-related questions)

Low (0–33 per cent)	Medium-low (34–50 per cent)	Medium-high (51–66 per cent)	High (67–100 per cent)
Chad	Benin	Tanzania	
Gambia	Burkina Faso		
Guinea	Cameroon		
Mauritania	Djibouti		
Mozambique	Ethiopia		
Niger	Ghana		
Senegal	Kenya		
	Madagascar		
	Malawi		
	Mali		
	Rwanda		
	Uganda		
	Zambia		

Source: UNECA (2005)

Of the 21 countries with a full PRSP, 17 have an identifiable core section on employment. The absence of an employment section in the PRSPs of the other four countries, however, is not necessarily indicative of weak employment content as the assessment is based on the extent to which employment issues are reflected in all sections of the PRSPs. Table 7.2 lists the countries in Africa with a full PRSP by the employment content of their poverty reduction strategies, which is expressed as a share of positive answers to a set of 116 questions covering diagnosis of the employment situation; policies for creating employment opportunities; policies for improving decent employment; group, regional and sectoral targeting for employment purposes; and quantification of the impacts of policies on different dimensions of employment. The questions analyze only the explicit employment content of the PRSPs and do not assess the intensity of the effect of employment policies. The questions do not assess implementation issues either.

None of the 21 countries had high employment content, and only Tanzania, at the top of the ranking, had a rating above 50 per cent. Most of the full PRSPs have either medium-low or low-employment content, leading to the conclusion that the overall employment content of the full PRSPs is weak. This finding contrasts with several political declarations made by African leaders over the last three decades on the centrality of employment creation in the process of economic development.[3] The issue is, therefore, how to translate these declarations into action.

Creating Rural Employment in Africa

Poverty in Africa is largely a rural phenomenon. With 70 per cent of poor Africans living in rural areas, increasing rural employment and income is crucial to fight the scourge of poverty. An increase in rural incomes would likely not only improve the living standards of the rural poor, but would also drive the structural transformation of the whole economy. Structural transformation is a process by which the relative contribution of non-agricultural sectors to the overall economy rises as agriculture's share declines in relative terms. In absolute terms, however, agriculture continues to grow and contribute to overall economic growth. Agricultural productivity growth and increased farm incomes are prerequisites for structural transformation. Increased farm incomes lead to derived demand for non-farm products, which leads, in turn, to the growth of small- and medium-size enterprises (SMEs) in rural villages, small towns and larger urban areas.

There are four main policy actions that could help Africa to successfully transform its economies in a way that stimulates growth, creates employment and reduces poverty: achieving population growth rates compatible with development objectives; developing agricultural links to the industrial and service sectors; facilitating the growth of non-farm job-creating SMEs; and, above all, finding new sources of funding to invest massively in the rural economy.

Agricultural transformation and sectoral links

Agriculture is the main source of income for 90 per cent of the population in Africa and is vital to ensuring food security for the urban population. Yet, the state of agriculture in Africa is so poor that the sector can no longer feed the growing population. Some 200 million Africans are undernourished despite commercial food imports of $15–$20 billion a year and about $2 billion in food aid per year (UNECA, 2005). Many Africans in the agricultural sector, who are either self-employed or wage earners, are the poorest people in the world, mainly because of the poor performance of African agriculture. It is also severely undercapitalized, resulting in low total and factor productivity, compared with Asia and Latin America. One of the key reasons explaining the neglect of the agricultural sector is that rural farmers, dependent on the sector, have poor political representation. As a result, politicians focus their interventions on the needs of urban elites, who represent a powerful political force (Bates, 1983).

For example, between 1996 and 2001, Cameroon halved its urban poverty rate from 41 to 22 per cent. The corresponding rates for rural areas were 60 and 50 per cent, respectively. This illustrates that poverty-reduction policies focused on the needs of urban populations. In Burundi, although 99 per cent of the poor live in rural areas, with 90 per cent of the population depending on agriculture, this sector received only 0.68 per cent of credit from the economy between 2003 and 2005. Commerce, concentrated in urban centres, accounted for 72 per cent of total credit during this same period. Between 1980 and 2004, although the share of the population depending on agriculture remained high, at around 90 per cent (see Table 7.3), the share of agriculture in GDP was reduced almost by half, from 54 to 29 per cent (Nkurunziza, Ndikumana and Nzobonimpa, 2006). A similar situation is observed in most African countries where the agricultural sector is not of direct economic interest to the ruling elites. Therefore, rather than simply being an economic problem, agricultural decline and poverty have a political dimension.

As a result, the positive trends towards democratization, decentralization and improved governance in Africa bring hope for greater participation of formerly excluded stakeholders in policy and public sector programme decision-making and implementation, with a positive impact on employment creation. Macroeconomic and sectoral policies in Africa are on a path of positive evolution as well, creating better incentives for the development of private sector initiatives. Africa must harness existing and emerging opportunities to foster agricultural development in order to create the needed jobs for its population. In this light, recent land reforms demonstrate that many African governments realize the importance of providing access to land and security of tenure to increase both wage and self-employment (see Table 7.3).

TABLE 7.3
Addressing land-related challenges to increase job creation

Land-related challenge	Examples of policy responses
Security of tenure	• Côte d'Ivoire's rural land plan seeks to identify and map all existing rights in order to give them legal status • Cameroon's 1974 land ordinance rescinds legal recognition of customary and communal tenure rights and imposes land titling as the only means of acquiring private ownership • Uganda's 1995 constitution transfers title from the state straight to landholders
Conflict management	• Niger's 1986 rural code seeks to resolve land tenure conflicts

Decentralization of land administration	• Land boards were established in Botswana (now also in Namibia and Uganda); rural councils in Senegal; land commissions in Niger; community trusts and communal property associations in South Africa; and land committees in rural Lesotho • Public participation in decision-making through local institutions improved • Lesotho's 1998 land regulations require land committees to revoke an allocation in the event the recipient refuses to adopt soil conservation measures
Land use development and agricultural productivity	• Niger's 1986 rural code seeks to resolve land tenure conflicts • The Swynnerton Plan of Kenya supported African agriculture through agricultural research programmes, credit schemes, transfer of new technology and introduction of high value crops and new institutions • Ethiopia's agricultural development-led industrialization seeks to increase the productivity of smallholder farmers by dispensing fertilizers and improved seeds, establishing credit schemes and providing support services
Equitable redistribution to reduce landlessness	• Niger's 1986 rural code seeks to resolve land tenure conflicts • Redistributive land reform policies seek to give more land to landless blacks in Malawi, Namibia, South Africa and Zimbabwe • Mozambique's 1998 land law recognizes the right to land through occupation on the part of rural families, based on oral testimony
Development of land information system	• Kenya's tenure reforms sought to establish a well-maintained registry that could be used to monitor land transfers and distribution

Source: UNECA (2004).

At the regional level, the Comprehensive Africa Agriculture Development Programme (CAADP), adopted by the New Partnership for Africa's Development (NEPAD), has provisions relating to job creation in the rural economy. The Programme's targets are that by the year 2015, Africa should have attained an average annual growth rate of 6 per cent in agriculture; developed dynamic domestic and regional agricultural markets; become a net exporter of agricultural products by improving market access and integrating farmers in the market economy; achieved a more equitable distribution of income; become more involved in agricultural science and technology development; and used better natural resource management techniques (NEPAD, 2004).

At the international level, Africa has not been able to take advantage of the opportunities offered by globalization because of its low productivity and inefficiencies. However, there is no doubt that it offers hope for African rural farmers through new market opportunities. A few African countries, such as Mauritius and Morocco, where productivity levels are comparable to those in other developing regions, have been able to tap into the opportunities brought about by globalization. To be able to export, firms need to reach a minimum level of competitiveness. Encouraging the creation of efficient and labour-intensive firms in Africa seems to be the right policy to develop the export sector. How this objective is to be achieved depends, to a large extent, on the nature of the incentives put in place to create a favourable environment for investment and production.

Revolutionary developments in information and communication technology have drastically reduced the cost of processing and transmitting information and, therefore, facilitated access to information about agricultural technology, improved early warning systems, market opportunities, prices and demand. If the necessary capacities are built, increased access to information technology will offer new opportunities for agricultural education, agricultural research and agricultural extension, in addition to conveying information on markets, transport options, road conditions, weather and employment opportunities.

Development of Rural Non-Farm Sector

The rural non-farm sector integrates farming into national and international value chains, helping to transfer value addition to rural areas in the early stages of economic development (Start, 2001; Davis and Bezemer, 2003). During the first phase, rural non-farm activities are closely linked to agriculture. Rural non-farm enterprises are mainly located in the countryside and related to the provision of agricultural inputs and services, crop processing and distribution. A dynamic agricultural sector is therefore associated with more rural non-farm activity.

In the second stage of rural non-farm sector development, rural-urban links become stronger, with workers commuting from rural areas to small towns for employment, and agro-industries grow rapidly, although farming is still important. The third stage sees greater emphasis on rural-urban links, more employment in non-agricultural activities and a move towards commercial agriculture. Sub-Saharan Africa is in the first, early stage of rural non-farm growth, while Latin America and East Asia are in the second and third stages respectively (Gordon and Craig, 2001).

The rural non-farm sector provides employment for the landless poor. About 60 per cent of the landless poor in Asia and 30 to 50 per cent in sub-Saharan Africa depend on rural non-farm employment for their livelihoods (Ellis, 1998). However, Demeke, Guta and Ferede (2003) explored links among growth, employment and poverty reduction, and found that although the rural non-farm sector alleviates destitution because it is a refuge for poor people, it cannot eradicate poverty on its own. Only households with adequate resources can have access to high- return rural non-farm activities. Some have even argued that the rural non-farm sector actually works best for those with resources and education, i.e., the ones who need it least (Reardon and others 1998). Therefore, if poverty reduction and equity are intended outcomes of interventions in the rural non-farm sector, it is also important to focus on increasing opportunities for wage employment by encouraging the development of small- and medium-size enterprises. Unlike self-employment, wage employment helps to close the gap between poor and wealthier households. Integrating poor people into the labour market can be a viable strategy for both income generation and equity.

Lessons from the study by Park and Johnston (1995) of the early stages of development of the Taiwan Province of China suggest that small- and medium-size enterprise growth responds to rural demand, especially if related to rural consumption (e.g., food and beverages, tobacco manufacturing, textiles, wood, non-metal furniture and transportation equipment) or if it triggers technological links (e.g., metal workshops and enterprises for simple agricultural tools and spare parts). At later stages of development in the rural non-farm sector, enterprises and industries that produce more complicated equipment for other markets may be viable. In the initial stages, however, productivity-led growth based on labour and land-saving techniques enables broad-based farm and non-farm cash income growth; this also fosters rural demand links and poverty reduction.

The rural non-farm sector not only has the potential to increase agricultural wages by adding value to agricultural products, but it also has the capacity to increase rural wages through direct employment because of high labour productivity relative to the farm sector. Indeed, rural Africans derive about 42 per cent of their income from rural non-farm activities – a high share, considering that only about 10 per cent of the rural labour force is employed in the rural non-farm sector (Haggblade, Hazell and Reardon, 2002). Indeed, there is a strong link between African agriculture and the rest of the economy, with growth multipliers of 1.5–2.7 per cent in Africa, compared with 1.5–2.4 per cent for Asian countries (Spencer, 1995). This means that a $1 increase in rural income would translate into a $1.50–$1.70 increase in income for other sectors, mainly through expenditure and consumption links among agriculture and other sectors, leading to growth and job creation in the non-farm sectors. For every job created through increased agricultural production, two to three jobs are created in the non-farm sector.

Experience based on Asia's green revolution and partial success in Africa shows that agricultural development is crucial to the development of rural non-farm activities and employment. However, it is also true that growth in the rural non-farm sector fuels and facilitates agricultural growth. So far, Africa and its development partners have failed to recognize and adopt strategies that take note of the complementarities between agricultural and industrial development. Table 7.4 illustrates the potential of rural non-farm employment creation in Africa. Currently, Africa has the smallest proportion of jobs created in the rural non-farm sector, but it is in one of the highest income categories.

To derive maximum advantage from rural non-farm activities, it is necessary to understand what determines participation in the sector. Gordon and Craig (2001) cite five types of capital as crucial to participation. In addition to growth in the agricultural sector, human, social, physical, financial, and natural capital are important factors.

Human and social capital: Skills, knowledge and health are the key elements of human capital needed to pursue different types of livelihood strategies, while social capital includes networks, relationships and trust, which rural people draw on in search of livelihood opportunities. Education increases one's ability to interact with key people who are important to rural non-farm business opportunities. Only 26 per cent of African women are engaged in rural non-farm activities (see Table 7.4), perhaps because women are disadvantaged in terms of most factors key to job entry, including education, finance and time.

Financial capital: Financial resources, such as savings, credit, remittances and pensions, are important for engaging in economic activities, whether in farm or non-farm sectors. Without adequate financial capital, households have to remain in activities which have fewer barriers to entry and, unfortunately, are poorly remunerated. Access to credit, of reasonable size and duration, is vital. Without credit, ownership of assets (such as cattle) becomes important for investing in rural non-farm activities. Microfinance schemes, with assistance from non-governmental organizations and donors, have proven useful in increasing access to credit. In a study of four African countries, Bagachwa and Stewart (1992) found that in 30 to 84 per cent of rural industries, poor access to credit limited business development.

TABLE 7.4
Involvement in rural non-farm employment (percentages)

Region	Share of income from rural non-farm activity	Share of rural workers in rural non-farm activity	Share of women in total rural non-farm workforce	Share of rural non-farm workers in manufacturing	Share of rural non-farm workers in trade and transport	Share of rural non-farm workers in other activities
Africa	42	10	26	24	22	24
Asia	32	24	20	28	26	32
Latin America	40	35	27	20	20	27
Eastern Europe	44	47	37	38	20	27

Source: Haggblade, Hazell and Reardon (2002).

Physical capital: Basic infrastructure (including transport, communications, energy and water) complements individually-owned production equipment and buildings in the development of rural non-farm activities. The availability of rural non-farm jobs is associated with good infrastructure, high market density and high population density, particularly in rural towns (Reardon and others, 1998). In addition to facilitating rural non-farm sector growth by reducing transaction costs, roads, electricity and telecommunications infrastructure enhance rural town development (Ellis, 1998). Infrastructure also makes technological progress possible. For example, electrification of rural towns introduces new activities, such as welding, refrigeration, entertainment, etc., that are impossible in the absence of electricity. The development of rural towns, in turn, facilitates local inter-sectoral links. Rural towns are also employment centres for commuters from rural farms and provide services for farm workers, such as retail shops, restaurants, petrol stations and entertainment centres. Rural towns are where agro-processing usually takes place, and are important as intermediate marketing centres, linking rural remote areas to more developed markets elsewhere.

Natural capital: Natural resource endowments, including land, water, wildlife and minerals, help to determine the nature of rural non-farm activities. Activities such as timber processing, fishing, mining, construction and tourism depend on the resource endowments of a certain area. Natural resource endowments need other factors if they are to facilitate rural non-farm activities.

Revitalizing Investment in the Rural Economy

The rural economy in Africa is grossly undercapitalized. One of the key factors explaining this state of affairs is the retrenchment of the state in the economy and the dramatic reduction in overall long-term investment over the last two decades. To help address this situation, Nkurunziza, Ndikumana and Nzobonimpa (2006), explore a number of proposals – summarized below – that could be implemented to mobilize funding for the development of the rural economy. These are: (1) establishment of a credit guarantee scheme for rural farmers;

(2) creation of a long-term investment fund using the excess liquidity of banks, insurance companies, and other large corporations; (3) revitalization of development banking; (4) helping the development of microfinance; (5) adopting a financial sector charter aimed at encouraging the state, financial institutions and the private sector at large to contribute more to rural development.

High risk in rural areas, especially in the agricultural sector, is one of the main reasons why rural farmers do not have access to credit. One way to overcome this constraint would be to establish a farmers' credit guarantee scheme. The scheme would allow farmers to borrow at relatively low interest rates to buy agricultural inputs and to make repayments once they have sold their harvest. This scheme would have the added advantage of increasing monetization of the rural economy by encouraging farmers to sell at least part of their output to reimburse the loans. The funds used to run the scheme could come from the government or from multilateral and bilateral donors. Obviously, once the funds have been mobilized, the success of such a scheme would largely depend on its proper management.

The idea of creating a long-term investment fund using the excess liquidity of banks, insurance companies and other large corporations was first proposed by Nyamoya and Nkeshimana (2005) in the context of Burundi. These two bankers realized that the banking sector in the country had huge idle liquidity that could be mobilized for long-term investment. The problem of over-liquidity of the banking sector in Africa appears to be a general phenomenon. Eyeffa (2006) shows that banks in Cameroon, Central African Republic, Chad, Equatorial Guinea and Gabon prefer to hold cash resources rather than investing, mainly because of high risk. In 2003, for example, cash resources held by commercial banks in these five countries were more than 100 per cent higher than the legally required amount. This situation appears paradoxical as the same banks have very high levels of credit rationing.[4] The same situation is observed at large private and semi-public corporations which do not reinvest their large profits. Developing an incentive mechanism to properly mobilize these idle funds could provide fresh resources to fund long-term productive rural projects. As it is risk that induces these corporate investors to hold cash, this mechanism would need to have provisions protecting investors to limit the level of risk associated with such investments in rural projects.

The basic objective of development banking in many African countries is to foster development by according credit to development projects not attractive to commercial banks. These sectors include rural farming and non-farming activities, which have the highest potential for employment creation. Development banking in many countries has failed, and should be revitalized, refocusing on its original mandate. Development banks could make employment creation in rural areas their key criterion for credit allocation; they should have ample resources that would allow them to lend with long-term maturities. Such resources could come partly from government resources and partly from the donor community.

Microfinance has become an increasingly important source of funding for many rural African households and entrepreneurs over the last two decades. Nowadays, this form of lending has gone a long way to fill the vacuum left by traditional commercial banking, particularly in rural communities. Until recently, however, microfinance has not been given appropriate consideration by the state or the donor community, despite its importance to those left out by the traditional banking system. Countries should fully appreciate the role of microfinance in collecting savings and allocating credit in rural areas, and consider increasing the resource base of these institutions through the creation of a microfinance fund.

Finally, it is clear that these initiatives would require the concerted efforts of the government, the private sector and the donor community to be implemented.

CONCLUSIONS

Millions of unemployed and underemployed Africans need higher paying jobs to achieve a decent standard of living. This will require a structural transformation of African economies. In the long-term, many African countries will need to reduce their current fertility rates to levels compatible with their development objectives. Given that most African economies are agriculture dependent, reforms should start in the agricultural sector to make it the engine of growth. These reforms should involve several actions, including harnessing technology by strengthening agricultural research and extension; developing and managing water resources at both national and regional levels, with a view to increasing the amount of land under irrigation; catalyzing land reforms to provide access to and security of land rights, and hence, facilitate private investment in land; and developing and facilitating access to markets, particularly by deepening marketing reforms, increasing infrastructure and information systems, facilitating regional integration and pushing for increased access to international markets.

In view of the negative effect of the HIV/AIDS pandemic and other illnesses, such as malaria and tuberculosis, on production, Africa will need to improve its healthcare, water provision and sanitation systems to have a healthier population. Gender disparities, the marginalization of women in the labour market, and the greater vulnerability of women and children to poverty, will also need to be addressed.

Rural employment cannot only rely on the development of the agricultural sector. Development policies will need to foster activities that enhance the links between agriculture and other sectors, including a vibrant rural non-farm sector. Rural development policies should exploit the complementarities between agriculture and rural non-farm activities to sustain growth in the agricultural sector and to extend the growth effects in agriculture to other parts of the economy. The rural non-farm sector is therefore needed to achieve broad-based economic growth capable of providing employment to the majority of Africans in rural areas and reducing poverty.

To facilitate the growth of the rural non-farm sector, efforts to transform agriculture should be accompanied by incentives for market-oriented production of goods and services as well as for growth of rural towns. These incentives could include facilitating the growth of rural financial institutions to mobilize savings and provide credit. Other incentives could include education and vocational training, promotion of market links, building infrastructure (for example, feeder roads, electricity and water), encouraging participatory management of natural resources, and providing a favourable business environment through supportive macroeconomic and fiscal policies.

To achieve these objectives, new sources of funding will be needed. This chapter has put forward proposals to mobilize funding for the rural economy. These are: creating a farmers' credit guarantee scheme that would allow better access to credit; establishing a long-term investment fund using the excess liquidity of banks, insurance companies and other large corporations; reinvigorating development banking by ensuring ample resources to carry out its objective of funding development projects, particularly in rural areas; and assisting the development of microfinance to complement the traditional banking sector.

The development of Africa's rural areas is both an economic and political imperative. Rural economies have been neglected for a long time because rural populations do not have the same political influence as urban elites. As most African countries are becoming more democratic, it is expected that resource allocations, particularly in terms of public and private investments, will reflect the demographic and, indeed, economic weight of the rural sector.

Notes

[†] This chapter is based on UNECA (2005).

[1] The concept of poverty is often based on income or consumption measures of welfare. However, well-being is broader than income or consumption; it encompasses the environment that people need to lead a fulfilling life (UNDP, 2004). This environment includes education, health, freedom and social participation as well as income and consumption. The comparative data used in this chapter reflect the income or consumption dimensions of poverty.

[2] It is difficult to find comparable rates of poverty covering the same period for a representative sample of African countries. The rates given in table 7.1 are the most recent available statistics, covering 22 countries, and were collected from different sources. Given the problems surrounding the quality of household data on which these statistics are based, as well as the methodological complexities required to compute national poverty lines (see Kakwani, Soares and Son, 2005), the information in table 7.1 should be interpreted as indicative. On the limitations of poverty analysis based on monetary poverty lines, see Edward (2006).

[3] In 1979, the Lagos Plan of Action for the Economic Development of Africa, 1980–2000, noted that the lack of productive employment was a key factor in explaining high levels of poverty in Africa. It called for a number of measures, including more effective use of the continent's human resources. More recently, African leaders at the highest political level have adopted several declarations on employment promotion, including the 1991 Declaration on Employment Crisis in Africa, adopted by the 27th Ordinary Session of

the Assembly of African Heads of State and Government; the 1994 African Common Position on Human and Social Development in Africa, adopted at the World Summit for Social Development; the 2002 Declaration and Framework for Action on Youth Employment; and the 2004 Plan of Action for the Implementation of the African Union Declaration on Employment Promotion and Poverty Alleviation in Africa. The Treaty Establishing the African Economic Community, the Constitutive Act of the African Union and the New Partnership for Africa's Development have important provisions on promoting employment, developing human resources and fighting poverty. All these initiatives consider employment promotion the linchpin of poverty reduction strategies in Africa. But the long list of political declarations contrasts with the lack of tangible results in terms of employment creation in Africa over the years.

4 See Eyeffa (2006) and Nkurunziza, Ndikumana and Nzobonimpa (2006) for detailed explanations on this paradox.

REFERENCES

Bagachwa, M., and T. Stewart (1992). Rural industries and rural linkages in sub-Saharan Africa: A survey. In Frances Stewart, Sanjaya Lall, and Samuel Wangwe (eds). *Alternative Development Strategies for Sub-Saharan Africa*. Macmillan, London.

Bates, Robert (1983). *Essays on the Political Economy of Rural Africa*. Cambridge University Press, Cambridge, UK.

Cameroon, Republic of (2003). Poverty Reduction Strategy Paper. Yaoundé.

Chen, Martha (2000). Risk, insurance, and the informal economy. Workshop on Risk, Poverty, and Insurance: Innovations for the Informal Economy, 6 September. Human Development Network Social Protection and Financial Sector Development Department, World Bank, Washington, D.C.

Davis, J.R., and D.J. Bezemer (2003). Key emerging and conceptual issues in the development of the rural non-farm economy in developing countries and transition economies. NRI Report 2755. Natural Resources Institute, Chatham, U.K., Department for International Development, London, and the World Bank, Washington, D.C.

Demeke, M, F. Guta, and T. Ferede (2003). Growth, employment, poverty and policies in Ethiopia: An empirical investigation. Discussion Paper 12, International Labour Office, Geneva.

Edward, P. (2006). The ethical poverty line: A moral quantification of absolute poverty. *Third World Quarterly*, 27 (2): 377–393.

Ellis, F. (1998). Survey article: Household strategies and rural livelihood diversification. *Journal of Development Studies* 35 (1): 1–38.

Eyeffa, S. E. (2006). La mobilisation et la collecte de l'épargne en Afrique centrale. Paper presented at the Forum on 'Investment Promotion in Central Africa', 19–21 June, Brazzaville, Republic of Congo.

FAO (2005). *FAOSTAT*. Food and Agriculture Organization, Rome

Gordon, A., and C. Craig (2001). Rural Non-Farm Activities and Poverty Alleviation in Sub-Saharan Africa. NRI Policy Series 14, Natural Resources Institute, Chatham, U.K.

Haggblade S, P. Hazell and T. Reardon (2002). Strategies for Stimulating Poverty-Alleviating Growth in the Rural Non-Farm Economy in Developing Countries. EPTD Discussion

Paper 92, International Food Policy Research Institute, Environment and Production Technology Division, Washington, D.C.

ILO (2004a). *Global Employment Trends, 2004.* International Labour Office, Geneva.

ILO (2004b). *Global Employment Trends for Youth, 2004.* International Labour Office, Geneva.

ILO (2004c). *World Employment Report, 2004–2005.* International Labour Office, Geneva.

ILO (2005a). *Key Indicators of Labour Market.* [www.ilo.org]. International Labour Office, Geneva.

ILO (2005b). *LABORSTA database.* [http://laborsta.ilo.org]. International Labour Office, Geneva.

IFAD (2001). *Rural Poverty Report, 2001: The Challenge of Ending Rural Poverty.* International Fund for Agricultural Development, Rome.

Islam, R. (2004). The nexus of economic growth, employment and poverty reduction: An empirical analysis. Issues in Employment and Poverty, Discussion Paper 14, Recovery and Reconstruction Department, International Labour Office, Geneva.

Kakwani, N, F. V. Soares and H. H. Son (2005). Conditional cash transfers in African countries. Working Paper No. 9, UNDP, International Poverty Centre, Brasilia.

Khan, A.R. (1997). Reversing the decline of output and productive employment in rural sub-Saharan Africa. Issues in Development, Discussion Paper 17, Recovery and Reconstruction Department, International Labour Office, Geneva.

Kirk, D., and B. Pillet (1998). Fertility levels, trends, and differentials in sub-Saharan Africa in the 1980s and 1990s. *Studies in Family Planning* 29 (1): 1–22.

Majid, N. (2001). The size of the working poor population in developing countries. employment strategy department, International Labour Office, Geneva.

NEPAD (New Partnership for Africa's Development) (2004). Implementing the comprehensive Africa agricultural development programme (CAADP) and restoring food security in Africa. African Partnership Forum Meeting, October 4 to 7, Washington, DC.

Nkurunziza, J, L. Ndikumana and O. Nzobonimpa (2006). Promoting a development oriented financial system in Burundi. Paper prepared for the African Economic Research Consortium (AERC), Nairobi.

Nyamoya, P., and L. Nkeshimana (2005). Project de création d'un fonds d'investissement. Document de Travail No. 01, ABEF, (April).

Osmani, S.R. (2003). Exploring the employment nexus: Topics in employment and poverty. United Nations Development Programme, New York, and International Labour Office, Geneva.

Park, A, and B. Johnston (1995). Rural development and dynamic externalities in Taiwan's structural transformation. *Economic Development and Cultural Change* 44 (1): 181–208.

Reardon T, K. Stamoulis, M.E. Cruz, A. Balisacan, J. Berdegue and B. Banks (1998). Rural non-farm income in developing countries. In *The State of Food and Agriculture 1998: Part III.* Food and Agriculture Organization, Rome.

Spencer, D.S.C. (1995). Past trends and future prospects for agricultural development in sub-Saharan Africa. Paper presented at the Workshop on Agricultural Transformation in Africa, September 26 to 29, Abidjan.

Start, D. (2001). The rise and fall of the rural non-farm economy: Poverty impacts and policy options. *Development Policy Review* 19 (4): 491–505.

Tarantino, G.C. (2003). Imputation, estimation and prediction using the key indicators of the labour market (KILM) data set. Employment Strategy Department, International Labour Office, Geneva.

UN (2004). Implementation of the United Nations millennium declaration. United Nations, New York.

UNAIDS (2004). *UNAIDS: 2004 Report on the Global AIDS Epidemic*. Joint United Nations Programme on HIV/AIDS, Geneva.

UN (2004). *World Urbanization Prospects: The 2003 Revision*. Population Division, Department of Economic and Social Affairs, United Nations, New York.

UN (2005). *World Population Prospects: The 2004 Revision*. Department of Economic and Social Affairs, United Nations, New York.

UNDP (2004). *Human Development Report: Statistics*. United Nations Development Programme, New York. http://hdr.undp.org/statistics/data/excel/hrd04_table_14.xls

UNECA (2001). The State of Demographic Transition in Africa. ECA/FSSDD/01/10. United Nations Economic Commission for Africa, Addis Ababa.

UNECA (2003). Report of the workshop on identification and assessment of African Green Revolution indicators and design. ECA/SDD/GRW.STI/01. United Nations Economic Commission for Africa, Addis Ababa.

UNECA (2004). *Scoring African Leadership for Better Health*. United Nations Economic Commission for Africa, Addis Ababa.

UNECA (2005). *Economic Report on Africa, 2005: Meeting the Challenges of Unemployment and Poverty in Africa*. United Nations Economic Commission for Africa, Addis Ababa.

World Bank (1997). *World Development Report, 1997: The State in a Changing World*. Oxford University Press, New York.

World Bank (1998). *World Development Indicators, 1998*. World Bank, Washington, DC.

World Bank (2000). *Can Africa Claim the 21ˢᵗ Century?* World Bank, Washington, DC.

World Bank (2004). *World Development Indicators, 2004*. World Bank, Washington, DC.

8
Labour Market Flexibility and Decent Work

GERRY RODGERS*

Debates on labour market flexibility are not new, although the term itself only became popular in the 1980s. Historically, the evolution of labour markets has been marked by periods when market forces dominated thinking and policy, alternating with periods when there was a spread of institutions to provide representation or regulate outcomes. Polanyi's analysis of the development of the capitalist system in the latter part of the 19th century and the early part of the 20th century drew particular attention to the tensions which arise when economic relationships are separated from their social context, and it is certainly true that much labour market regulation reflects efforts by governments and other actors to address the consequent need for coherence between economic and social goals and relationships.

Flexibility tends to become a metaphor for unfettered markets. Yet, there is no such thing, for markets, whether for labour or for anything else, function effectively only because they are surrounded by a set of institutions which generate common rules, reflect the interests of participants and guide behaviour. This is all the more so in the market for labour, which is in reality a social institution, not only supporting work and production, but also impacting on representation, social integration and the personal goals of its participants. So, one must start by being wary of simplified arguments about the role of labour market institutions.

In industrialized countries, labour market flexibility was part of the strategy proposed by the OECD in its 1994 *Jobs Study* – which regarded higher job creation in the US compared with Europe as due to greater flexibility in the former – and both the World Bank and the IMF have often taken a similar view. The 2005 *World Development Report*, for instance, argued that labour market deregulation would improve the investment climate, while the IMF has taken the position, in discussions on policy coherence among international organizations, that labour market flexibility is key to employment creation. However, other views can also be found in World Bank publications, while the OECD's views have evolved, and its 2004 *Employment Outlook* calls for a more pragmatic approach to labour market reform.

At the risk of oversimplifying the discussion, changing views of labour market flexibility can be interpreted as reflecting changes in the model of growth and development. In a Keynesian world, where technical change and aggregate demand drive growth, labour market institutions and regulation reflect a social compromise among social actors, which stabilizes economic relationships. This was the dominant pattern in industrialized countries in the period after the Second World War up to the early 1970s. When this model broke down, macro-economic policy shifted towards a more restrictive monetarist stance, emphasizing control of inflation and supply side incentives. In such a world, micro-flexibility is essential to generate economic adjustments.

The constituents of the ILO – workers, employers, governments – have quite different views of this issue. Not surprisingly, employers favour flexibility more than workers. World Bank surveys in a fairly large number of countries found 34 to 38 per cent of firms reporting that employment protection legislation is a moderate or major obstacle for them. Equally unsurprising, workers tend to be sceptical of the benefits of flexibility. And the positions of governments vary widely. So there is no agreed ILO position on this issue, despite its obvious importance for the ILO's decent work agenda.

THE FORMS OF FLEXIBILITY

The flexibility of a labour market might be defined as its ability to adapt and respond to change (Rubery and Grimshaw, 2003). Several different dimensions of flexibility are identified in the literature:

Employment protection. Employer freedom to hire and fire is at the heart of debates on flexibility. Employment protection measures, of course, have a double effect, reducing both inflows to and outflows from employment, so the net impact on employment and unemployment is ambiguous a priori. However, reducing these flows overall is likely to limit firms' ability to adjust to changing circumstances. Levels of protection vary widely across OECD countries (Figure 8.1). In most countries alongside the protection of regular, standard jobs a variety of temporary or otherwise less protected employment statuses are also a widely used means of flexibility.

Wage flexibility. A variety of institutions and regulations may limit wage variation, including minimum wage regulation, trade union activity and the extent to which there is coordinated wage bargaining.

Internal or functional flexibility. This largely concerns the ability of firms to organize and reorganize internal processes of production and labour use in the interests of productive/dynamic efficiency, e.g. through the flexibility of working time, job content, skill needs or technical change.

Supply side flexibility: While attention tends to focus on flexibility in labour demand, there are important issues on the supply side too. Workers may demand flexibility in working time to meet work and family needs, or the portability of rights and entitlements which would permit mobility between jobs.

A central element of the debate on flexibility concerns the relative importance of adaptability and security. Both firms and workers need both. Insofar as labour market flexibility implies a lessening of control of workers over their employment, it may affect both perceived and real security. However, attitudes to flexibility and security to a significant degree reflect social preferences. Some societies give a greater value to mobility and others to stability. Even at this simple level, there is no universal formula. A more sophisticated understanding of the importance of flexibility and stability for enterprises, and the different forms of security demanded by workers, is called for.

The Effects of Flexibility and Inflexibility

There is a widespread argument today that can be paraphrased as follows: The slow and inadequate growth of employment around the world reflects labour market institutions which provide a disincentive to job creation. Highly regulated labour markets were easier to maintain in relatively closed economies, where competitive pressures were less. But globalization has sharply increased the range and intensity of competition, and more adaptable production systems and labour markets are essential if firms are to survive in the new global economy. Conventional economic models support this argument. In such models, where wages and conditions of work adjust more rapidly to market forces, full employment is much more easily attained.

So essentially, the argument is that in a globalized economy, flexibility is a precondition for employment creation. How far is this position supported by the evidence? It is an issue on which a great deal of work has been undertaken in OECD countries in particular. The results are surprisingly muddy.

First, the relationship between employment protection and aggregate employment or unemployment is weak. Different studies show varying results. Baker and others (2005) show that the direct relationship between employment protection and unemployment is insignificant (Figure 8.2), and this is confirmed by more sophisticated multivariate analyses. Baccaro and Rei (2005) find the same result in virtually all of a wide range of specifications, including corrections for a variety of possible econometric and substantive biases. Other authors report varying results depending on the specification of their models. The OECD *Employment Outlook* (2004) concludes, on the basis of extensive empirical work, that employment protection does not clearly lead to higher unemployment, although it was found to be associated with lower employment rates. But Baccaro and Rei's work does not support the latter conclusion either.

On the other hand, the OECD finds that employment protection legislation may change the distribution of employment. While prime age males benefit, younger people and women seem to be disadvantaged. This is plausible, in so far as employment protection reduces inflows to employment of labour market entrants, though other research, e.g. by Schmitt and Wadsworth (2002), finds little evidence that the more flexible US and UK labour markets performed better for marginal groups. There is also some evidence to support the proposition that stricter protection of regular jobs is associated with higher levels of temporary and other non-standard contracts. Such non-standard employment relationships have been growing, on the whole, over the last twenty years, and a considerable literature has emerged on labour market segmentation and 'insider-outsider' tradeoffs, with varying interpretations of the causal relationships.

On wage flexibility, the evidence for an adverse effect on employment of minimum wages is also weak in OECD countries. There must be some level of minimum wages that would have such an effect, but within the observed range the effect seems to be modest. Another rather consistent finding of research in OECD countries is that coordinated wage bargaining does not have an adverse effect on unemployment (Figure 8.3). In fact, multivariate analysis suggests that the relationship with employment is positive. Since decentralized wage bargaining is sometimes seen as an important aspect of labour market flexibility, this is an interesting result. It reflects the importance of social dialogue in the debate on flexibility, a point to which I will return. On the other hand, Baccaro and Rei (2005) find union density to have a positive impact on unemployment, in the absence of bargaining coordination, and argue that this may come from the impact on wage levels.

Functional and organizational flexibility within firms may well be more important than labour market flexibility as such, but situations are diverse and evidence correspondingly anecdotal. National models for the organization of production vary widely, and local and specific factors are usually involved. The growth of global production systems is probably the most significant factor here, introducing flexibility and adaptation through new sourcing arrangements which by-pass national policies.

An important issue concerns the relationship between employment stability, skill development and productivity. Auer, Berg and Coulibaly (2004) show that employment tenure has a positive effect on productivity at the firm level, at least up to a certain length of tenure. There is a great deal of case study material which shows that job stability is important for training – obviously longer tenure increases the returns to investment in job specific training. Other research suggests that longer job tenure is associated with greater innovation, where this is knowledge intensive, presumably because of the importance of on the job learning. More innovative firms tend to offer somewhat longer tenure to their workers than less innovative firms. Figure 8.4 also shows that changes in tenure across industrialized countries are positively associated with labour productivity growth. But there are considerable variations in job tenure between countries, suggesting there are many possible institutional frameworks. And Auer, Berg and Coulibaly (2004) find tenure is negatively correlated with employment rates, hinting at a productivity-employment trade-off. All of this illustrates the complexity of the analysis of labour market flexibility, since institutions and their roles differ from country to country, making the cross-country analyses discussed above particularly unreliable.

On the supply side, there is wide variation across countries in the degree to which workers can move flexibly between enterprises, maintaining pension and other rights, adapt working time to family needs, and so on. Not much research addresses the implications for growth and employment, but the experience of Scandinavian countries, where such policies are most advanced, suggests that the synergies can be positive. These countries have, on the whole, high employment rates with low and flexible working hours, which contribute to goals of gender equality and permit varying strategies through the life cycle.

On the whole, it would be risky to draw strong policy conclusions about the impact on employment of labour market flexibility on the basis of this literature. There is much that remains unclear, or dependent on local factors, in this complex relationship between labour market institutions and employment performance.

And although there is no consensus in the literature, the case can readily be made that aggregate demand conditions are more powerful predictors of employment outcomes than labour market regulation. After all, even in less flexible economies job creation and destruction is fairly large (20 per cent of jobs per year in France) so large adjustments do occur all the time. Schmitt and Wadsworth (2002), for instance, argue that in both the US and the UK, employment growth can be largely traced to macro-economic policy, and that labour market flexibility has mainly helped to increase inequality. Baker and others (2005) reach similar conclusions.

The evidence cited thus far comes mainly from the industrialized world. What can be said about developing countries?

The first and most obvious point is that most developing country labour markets are in reality highly flexible because of the presence of a large informal economy. Production systems very frequently straddle the formal and the informal, there are informal workers in formal enterprises and informal enterprises delivering goods and services to formal markets. This does not mean that the informal economy is unregulated – even when laws are not fully enforced, they have an indirect effect, and there is a great deal of informal social regulation.

But it does mean that the discussion of labour market flexibility in low income countries cannot reasonably be separated from discussion of informality. It is true that there is a widespread assumption, much as in industrialized countries, that part of the employment problem lies in overregulated formal sectors which promote dualism and reduce employment levels. As noted above, the World Bank's *World Development Report 2005* takes the line that developing country labour markets are widely overregulated, and that this has an adverse effect on investment and growth. They argue that this is true of minimum wages, working time and employment protection, among others.

But the data base for such conclusions is much weaker than in industrialized countries, and hard evidence on the real impact of regulation on employment growth is scarce. It is true that if the minimum wage is set far too high, either it will be ignored or it will constrain employment creation. But in fact the evidence, such as it is, does not point to minimum wages as a major constraint on employment growth. On the contrary, in many countries it plays an important stabilizing role. The 1996–1997 *World Employment Report* argued that observed minimum wages in most developing countries were unlikely to have a serious adverse effect on employment, while real wages tended to move in line with productivity, and to be rather flexible. More recent ILO work has reached similar conclusions. A recent literature review (Devereux, 2005) concluded that carefully designed minimum wage policies do help to reduce poverty. Much depends on the interpretation and application of such policies, making it difficult to compare country experiences.

The recent experience of Argentina and Chile is consistent with the view that labour market flexibility was not the main factor driving employment growth. In Argentina, for instance, the flexibility policies put in place in the 1990s appeared to lower employment elasticities rather than raising them (Marshall, 2004), so that rapid GDP growth was accompanied by rising or stagnant unemployment. In Chile in the 1990s, on the other hand, the gradual re-regulation of the labour market was consistent with continued employment growth up to the Asian Financial Crisis (ILO, 1998). Recent work by the Asian Development Bank also argues that while some labour reforms are needed, labour policies are not the main cause of increasing unemployment and persistent underemployment in Asia (ADB 2006).

In Latin America, more systematic work by Marquez and Pages (1998) is interesting in that it mirrors to some extent the findings in industrialized countries – employment protection legislation does reduce job turnover, and is associated with greater self-employment (which can be interpreted as an indicator of dualism), and perhaps less wage employment, for younger and older workers at least, but not necessarily with lower employment overall. In other words, the distributional implications may be more important than the aggregate impact. On the whole, while employment protection is strong in Latin America, job turnover is high and tenure low, an inconsistency which is hard to explain unless it simply reflects poor implementation of the legislation.

In those situations, the real issue is the construction of universal policies and institutions. We should note that the influence of formal regulation reaches deep into the informal economy – minimum wage legislation, for instance, clearly affects informal wages even when it is not fully enforced. We should also note that there is little evidence that reducing the levels of protection of the formal economy is likely to help to reduce informality. But there may be institutional strategies in which a more flexible approach to the formal economy is part of a universal strategy in which there are also more serious efforts to construct viable frameworks of regulation that embrace the informal.

In that context, the work of Galli and Kucera (2003) shows that countries with stronger civic rights (basically freedom of association) have a higher share of formal employment. So such rights may well play an important part in constructing a coherent policy response.

Labour Institutions and Social Models

We have seen that the empirical evidence is mixed. But this should not really be a surprise. Labour market flexibility or rigidity is in general only one aspect of a broader social model. In reality, labour market institutions are or can be ways of accommodating different interests and achieving sustainable results. Different combinations of policies and institutions may achieve similar goals. In Europe, the debate on the future of the social model has made it clear that there are a number of quite different routes being taken in different countries. Table 8.1, taken from work by Peter Auer, suggests one typology, in which high employment protection and expenditures on labour market policy complement or substitute for each other in different countries. Recently the 'Danish model' of flexicurity, in which low employment protection is combined with effective income protection and labour market policy to provide occupational or career security, has received particular attention. But there are different ways of combining flexibility and security, and the Swedish and Finnish approaches provide another, different example, embracing high public expenditure on social services, flexibility for enterprises, labour market security for workers, and an egalitarian framework of values in which all actors have both rights and responsibilities (Lefebvre and Méda, 2006).

The basic issue is to find a balance between employment protection provided at the level of the firm (or the public sector), and social protection and income security provided at the societal level. When a firm is embedded in broader institutions of social protection, it is much easier to achieve a negotiated flexibility at the enterprise level, than where the worker is exclusively dependent on the firm – unless, as was the case in Japan, the firm itself plays this broader role (Dore, 1986). Workers likewise need flexibility in order to take advantage of new labour market opportunities, and that too has implications for the design of institutions for protection – for it may be that the best way to increase security will be to increase the portability of rights between jobs, in a framework of 'protected mobility'.

THE GOAL OF DECENT WORK: FLEXIBILITY, SECURITY AND DIALOGUE

How does these issues relate to the ILO goal of decent work? In reality, the decent work agenda constitutes a framework for social policy which integrates many of these elements. Each country has its own social goals and institutions, but there are broad goals which are widely shared: the importance of access to productive employment for all; security of work and income, and in the workplace; respect for core rights at work, including freedom from coercion and discrimination, and freedom of association; and a democratic process of negotiation and social dialogue by which these goals are set and achieved. This concerns the dignity of work and gender equality in work, and the role of work in social integration and personal development. These are all elements of a decent work agenda.

Achieving decent work calls for a coherent set of policies for employment promotion and protection, for security and income support, for the promotion of equality in opportunity and access, for rights at work – but also for competitive and effective production systems, in which adaptability and innovation are key. It involves not only public action, but also representative institutions through which social actors can express their views and participate in decisions. It is precisely this combination of institutions and policies which constitutes a social model. And because work is in many ways the point of articulation between economic and social goals, it makes sense to build coherence in economic and social policy on this foundation.

Within that framework, the issue of flexibility can be adequately addressed only by considering its multiple effects and the packages of measures of which it might be part. If there are tradeoffs, e.g., between security and employment, it is necessary to find institutional and policy frameworks which can address both. For instance, if employment protection legislation is an important source of security, and has little overall effect on employment, but has an impact on labour market segmentation or exclusion, a coherent approach will require complementary active measures aimed at promoting employment for excluded groups. Weakening employment protection overall may undermine other goals without necessarily improving labour market opportunities.

While a wide variety of approaches may work in different situations, one important lesson from successful experiences in both Europe and elsewhere is the essential nature of broad participation and social dialogue in the process. Institutions which involve tradeoffs among objectives and the different interests of different groups cannot be easily imposed from above. They need to be constructed by the actors concerned, if they are to achieve legitimacy and stability. Representative organizations of workers and employers have played a vital role in many countries in achieving solutions in the common interest.

In the end, labour market regulation is about what society you want to create – economic success is only part of the picture. Within efforts to achieve decent work, the flexibility of employment relationships is part of a much wider balance. The real issue lies in constructing the institutions that can achieve that balance.

TABLE 8.1
Employment security or labour market security?

	High labour market policy spending	Low labour market policy spending
High Employment Protection	France Germany	Japan, Portugal, Greece, Italy, Spain
Low Employment Protection	Denmark, Belgium, (Netherlands), Finland, (Ireland)	United States United Kingdom

Source: Auer (2006).

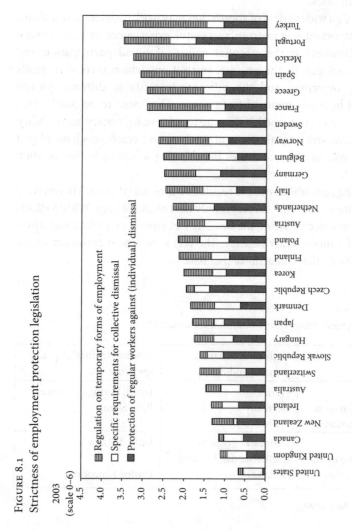

FIGURE 8.1
Strictness of employment protection legislation

2003
(scale 0–6)

■ Regulation on temporary forms of employment
□ Specific requirements for collective dismissal
▨ Protection of regular workers against (individual) dismissal

Source: OECD (2004).

FIGURE 8.2

Labour market institutions and unemployment: Employment protection

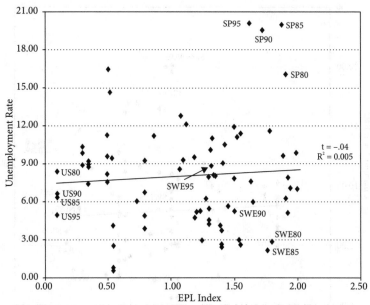

Source: Baker and others (2005).

FIGURE 8.3
Labour market institutions and unemployment: Bargaining coordination

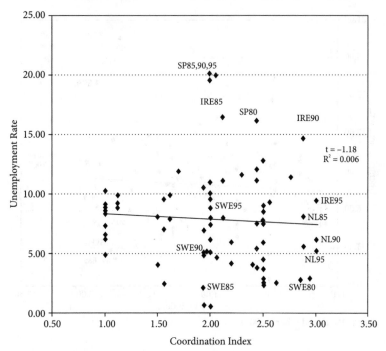

Source: Baker and others (2005).

FIGURE 8.4

Change in job tenure and labour productivity growth, 1992–2002

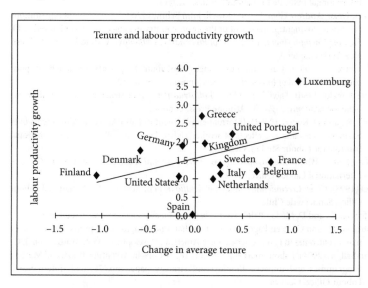

Source: Auer, Berg and Coulibaly (2004).

NOTES

* The views expressed here are personal and do not commit the International Institute for Labour Studies or the International Labour Office. Thanks are due to Peter Auer for helpful comments.

REFERENCES

Asian Development Bank (2006). *Labor Markets in Asia: Issues and Perspectives.* Palgrave Macmillan, Hampshire.

Auer, Peter (2006). Protected mobility for employment and decent work: Labour market security in a globalized world. *Journal of Industrial Relations* 48 (1), February: 21–40.

Auer, Peter, Janine Berg, and Ibrahim Coulibaly (2004). Is a stable workforce good for the economy? Insights into the tenure-productivity-employment relationship. Employment strategy paper no. 2004–15, International Labour Office, Geneva.

Baccaro, L., and D. Rei (2005). Institutional determinants of unemployment in OECD countries: A time series cross-section analysis (1960–98). Discussion paper 160, International Institute for Labour Studies, Geneva.

Baker, Dean, Andrew Glyn, David Howell, John Schmitt (2005). Labor market institutions and unemployment: Assessment of the cross-country evidence. In David Howell (ed.), *Fighting Unemployment: The Limits of Free Market Orthodoxy*. Oxford University Press, New York: chapter 3.

Devereux, S. (2005). Can minimum wages contribute to poverty reduction in poor countries? *Journal of International Development* 17: 899–912.

Dore Ronald (1986). *Flexible Rigidities: Industrial Policy and Structural Adjustment in the Japanese Economy, 1970–80*. Athlone Press, London.

Galli, R., and D. Kucera (2003). Informal employment in Latin America: Movements over business cycles and the effects of worker rights. Discussion Paper 145, International Institute for Labour Studies, Geneva.

ILO (1996). *World Employment 1996/1997: National Policies in a Global Context*. International Labour Office, Geneva.

ILO (1998). *Chile: Crecimiento, empleo y el desafío de la justicia social*. International Labour Office, Santiago de Chile.

Lefebvre, A., and D. Méda (2006). *Faut-il brûler le modèle social français?* Seuil, Paris.

Márquez, G., and Carmen Pagés (1998). Ties that bind: Employment protection and labor market outcomes in Latin America. Inter-American Development Bank, Washington, DC.

Marshall, A. (2004). Labour market policy and regulations in Argentina, Brazil and Mexico: Programmes and impacts. Employment strategy paper, no. 2004/13, International Labour Office, Geneva.

OECD (2004). *Employment Outlook*. Organisation for Economic Co-operation and Development, Paris.

OECD (1994). *Jobs Study: Evidence and Explanations*. Organization for Economic Co-operation and Development, Paris.

Polanyi, Karl (1944). *The Great Transformation*. Beacon Press, Boston.

Rubery, Jill, and D. Grimshaw (2003). *The Organization of Employment*. Palgrave, London.

Schmitt, J., and J. Wadsworth (2002). Is the OECD jobs strategy behind US and British employment and unemployment success in the 1990s? CEPA working paper, no. 2002–06, Center for Economic Policy Analysis, New School University, New York.

World Bank (2005). *World Development Report, 2005*. World Bank, Washington, DC.

9

How Employment and Workers Rights can be Made Complementary[†]

ROBERT BOYER

The current concern about development with decent work has to be appraised in historical retrospect. Back in the 1960s, the so-called Golden Age for developed countries, the institutionalization of workers' rights and the constitution of an extended welfare state proved to be compatible with a fast and rather stable growth. At that time, dynamic efficiency and social justice were more frequently perceived as complementary rather than contradictory.

Since the 1970s, however, the slowdown of growth and the emergence of mass employment have put into question this virtuous configuration. What was thought of as an asset has turned out to be viewed as a liability. In this context, experts have convinced many Governments that most, if not all, labour-market institutions had to be reformed because they generated various rigidities detrimental to job creation and innovation. The strategies of 'flexibilization' of labour markets have been generalized and concern not only wage formation, employment legislation and welfare, but also work organization. During this second epoch, most analysts have perceived a trade-off between economic efficiency and social justice.

The pressure to reform labour contracts and welfare in developed countries has been reinforced by the process of globalization: multinational corporations have delocalized significant segments of the value chain towards emerging countries, especially in Asia. These countries were supposed to enjoy a definite competitive edge, associated with low wages, high labour-market flexibility and, for some of them, fast growth of their domestic markets. Consequently, the relative decline of old industrialized countries was partially attributed to the rigidity of their labour-market institutions, whereas the surge of emerging countries benefited from highly flexible labour markets. Thus, during the 1990s, more and more worker security-enhancing devices have been perceived as detrimental to job creation, growth and innovation.

The core message of this chapter is that this period might be over, for at least three main reasons. First, the old labour-market theory, based on symmetric information, has been replaced by more realistic hypotheses that take into account the specificity of the capital-labour nexus, which is both a market contract and a subordinate relationship. Therefore, low wages and poor working conditions are no more an optimum for firms, given the endogeneity of work intensity, commitment and productivity. For instance, a fair labour contract that warrants a form of security – employment stability, access to unemployment benefits, right to training and further education – might be superior both for firms and individuals compared with a typical competitive adjustment of wages to the ongoing equilibrium value. The chapter proposes to detect the various mechanisms according to which security-enhancing welfare may improve simultaneously the financial performance of a firm and the welfare of the workers.

A second line of argument builds upon the results of various comparative analyses of the performance of the member countries of the Organization for Economic Cooperation and Development (OECD) during the last decade. Whereas the countries that had more fully deregulated their labour market were supposed to be the best performers in terms of job creation, innovation and growth, a surprising finding focuses upon the quite remarkable configuration of small social democratic economies (Finland, Denmark and Sweden). Generous income security is associated with the wide freedom granted to firms concerning employment decisions. This exchange of a form of security against the capacity for adjustment is part of a compromise that delivers very good macroeconomic outcomes. Similar to the Golden Age, the security of workers is no longer in contradiction with the flexibility of firms. This 'flexicurity' model is an alternative to the flex-flexibility, typical workfare based upon an absolute search for flexibility in all the components of the labour contract (employment, hours, wages, social benefits, unemployment compensation, skills and competence, etc.).

A last reason is specific to developing countries. A decade ago, the implementation of the Washington Consensus was supposed to promote high-speed growth, near full-employment and the progressive eradication of poverty. Nowadays, it is clear that the link between fast growth and the subsequent improvement in labour standards is far from mechanical. Of course, the poverty rate has been significantly reduced in large countries such as China and India, but it is not a widely observed phenomenon. Furthermore, a new branch of development theory stresses that basic rights might well be a precondition for successful growth strategies, and not only the long-term automatic outcome of economic reforms in the direction of efficiency. Similarly, empirical investigations recurrently show that low wages and poor working conditions are not necessarily the key factors governing the localization of multinationals. Consequently, the crucial issue might be expressed in the following manner: what kind of workers' security could benefit development, and how could the required securities be implemented?

The chapter builds upon these three lines of analysis in order to detect how the reactivity to macroeconomic shocks, globalization and technical change can be made compatible with the implementation of some securities for the workers of developing countries.

Contemporary Economic Theories: A Reappraisal of the Labour Flexibility/Security Debate

The issue of decent work, and more generally workers' security, is closely linked to the broader question of the function and the impact of the welfare state. Actually, few frameworks take into account both the 'theoretical' and actual size of a welfare system and analyse the long-run impact of social security. By chance, the renewed interest for growth theory and the recent concern for institutional analysis entitles a third way, that this chapter tries to follow.

The Inadequacy of the Pure Competitive Model in Assessing the Impact of a Security-enhancing Welfare State

After World War II, the issue of social security used to be analysed within a macroeconomic framework, put forward by the Keynesian breakthrough: in a sense, the Beveridge Plan was conceived as a complement to a full-employment programme. Nowadays, the intellectual scheme governing economic policy decisions is strongly embedded into a microeconomic analysis of the rational choice of agents facing a system of prices, incentives and uncertainties (Council of Economic Advisers, 1998). Thus, implicitly at least, Partial or General Equilibrium Theory is frequently used to assess the impact of the social benefits and collective coverage of risk typical of welfare. If one adopts the old microeconomic theory, where information is perfect and no externality prevails, then ineluctably any welfare system will introduce a distortion departing from a pure and perfect competitive equilibrium that is simultaneously a Pareto optimum. This is specially so if one considers some form of collective control over employment or collective coverage of individual risk. Under this framework, any welfare measure is always costly in terms of economic efficiency: this trade-off should be arbitrated by the democratic system, but the economist is clearly on the side of efficiency and efficacy (Figure 9.1).

Such an approach is largely unsatisfactory and in some instances erroneous. First of all, modern economic theory does not confirm the generality of the convergence of a 'tâtonnement' process toward equilibrium. It has been argued convincingly that the two welfare theorems actually relate to a perfectly planned economy and not at all to a fully decentralized market economy (Benassy, 1982). If, then, information is made imperfect and the economy is subjected to stochastic disturbances, it has been proved that a fully rational economic agent who would react instantaneously to the price signals exhibited by the market would be worse off than a prudent agent who had adjusted his strategy smoothly (Heiner, 1988). Of course, not adjusting at all would lead quasi certainly to the bankruptcy of the agent: the maximum speed of adjustment is not optimum any more. This is a first and quite general rationale for the inverse U-shaped performance curve of Figure 9.1.

FIGURE 9.1

Why competitive equilibrium theory is not suited for assessing the security provided by welfare systems

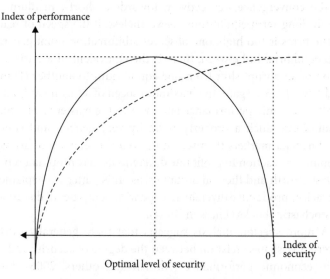

The market view: security introduces a distance with respect to the general equilibrium that is a Pareto optimum.

The institutionalist view:
• Full security may contradict the requirements of a capitalist economy.
• No security at all may create instability in labour contracts and industrial relations.
• In between, some security may be optimum for economic performance as well as for welfare.

Many other models suggest a similar result about the optimality of an intermediate level of adjustment and of flexibility. For instance, a very simple multi-sector model describing income distribution and effective demand formation shows that the same inverse U-shaped curve is observed with respect to the speed of adjustment of employment to its (neo-classical) efficient level (Boyer and Mistral, 1982). The reason is simple: what is gained at the micro level in terms of productive efficiency can be lost at the aggregate level by a negative impact upon effective demand. More general models inspired by modern classical theory put forward the role of the correction of various disequilibria (on the product market via inventories, on the labour market via hiring, and on the financial market via investment) in the convergence, respectively, towards a short-, medium- and, finally, long-term equilibrium. Nevertheless, if the speed of reaction of the firms is too high, one observes a bifurcation point generating two equilibria. In between, there is the equivalent of a crisis, in the sense of an abrupt shift from one equilibrium to another (Dumenil and Lévy, 1993). Again, the maximum speed of adjustment is adverse to the economic performance and even to the existence of a market equilibrium. Such a property is finally very general and concerns too financial markets themselves: up to a threshold, too fast capital mobility in reaction to profit rate differentials may propitiate a period of fast growth and then an abrupt crisis. This pattern is explained by the lack of productive diversity to cope with new types of disturbances or stochastic shocks (Eliasson, 1984).

A more specific analysis suggests that there generally exists an inverted U-shaped relation between the degree of security and long-term economic performance (Altman and others, 2006). First, a basic level of security allows individuals to take risks, for instance, to invest in education, launch a business or try new methods or imagine new products, all actions that are at the origin of growth. Second, the existence of a safety net mitigates the adverse effects of hardship because the assistance in terms of finance, education or training helps in overcoming the temporary setbacks that go along with a constantly evolving economy. A third benefit of a modicum of security is especially important during a period of globalization and fast technical change: an adequate level may lessen the demand for protectionism and Malthusian policies that would hamper growth. The very process of creative destruction calls for some form of security for the industries and jobs adversely affected by the restructuring of the economy.

Thus, neither total insecurity nor complete security is good for long-term growth. Consequently, the issue is to find out what the optimum degree and form of security should be, given the parameters of each economy. There is no rationale for seeking maximum flexibility and, conversely, a significant reactivity in the labour market is not necessarily in contradiction with decent work, defined as the right to basic security. These general results are especially important for the assessment of welfare systems because they basically deliver a form of insurance and a smoothing of adverse events. From a theoretical point of view they may (or may not – but this is an empirical issue) contribute to macroeconomic performance.

The Need to Take into Account Externalities Associated With Various Forms of Security

The previous reasoning was questioning the hypothesis of full information in an uncertain world and was claiming that a form of insurance and smoothing of disturbances might improve macroeconomic performance. But there is a second justification for extended welfare and public intervention, i.e., the existence of positive or negative externalities that cannot be internalized via private insurance or incentives directed towards the private sector (WHO, 2000: 55). The argument can be developed, made more specific and can closely conform to the various forms of security analysed by the Socio-economic Security Programme (ILO, 2004b) (Figure 9.2).

- Traditionally, public authorities may promote income security in reaction to the adverse outcome of pure market logic upon poverty and social inequalities. One form of this security is the imposition by law of a minimum wage. For this intervention to be effective and binding, conventional micro theory concludes that the less-paid workers will be priced out of the market, provoking then unemployment. It is, however, only a partial-equilibrium result since such a measure has a global impact upon the total wage bill, hence the level of effective demand. Have recent careful studies not concluded that the recent hikes in the American minimum wage have finally benefited employment, contrary to the expectation of a typical neo-classical analysis? This short, medium-term impact might be completed in the long run by the incentive that the absence of a downward flexibility of wage exerts upon the direction and intensity of labour-saving innovations. On aggregate, the impact might be positive – and has actually been during the Golden Age (Boyer, 2000).

- A second form of income security, the unemployment insurance system, has also some impact upon the speed of adoption of technological and organizational change. Whereas most of the analysts focus upon the negative side of the social contribution associated with the payment of unemployment benefits, i.e., less employment, a medium, long-term view introduces a positive factor: when workers are sure to be somehow compensated for the job destruction associated with technical change, the related restructuring is more easily accepted. Some European comparisons made during the early 1980s, confirm this (Boyer, 1988). Conversely, when such compensation is absent (in contemporary Russia, for instance (Touffut, 1999)), the benefits from technical change are not clearly perceived by the workers, who tend to protect the existing technologies, closely associated with the conservation of their jobs. Thus macro solidarity is better than micro egoism for the diffusion of innovations.

- Voice-representation security is present when, for instance, collective rights are granted to unions for representing workers; negotiating with firms may have the same dual impact. On one side, a form of oligopolistic power is thus introduced into the functioning of the labour market that may create a negative effect upon the level of employment in compensation for the higher wage. On the other side, the voice given to representatives of the workers may enhance commitment, and the ability to introduce new technologies or redesign the organization of the firm to the mutual benefit of the entrepreneurs and the workers (Freeman and Medoff, 1984).

- Life security is a still another component of workers' security. It can be extended from accident and illness at work to health care in general. Now, more and more, some theoreticians of economic development (Chenery and Srinivasan, 1988; Todaro and Smith, 2005) admit that the level of health is an important factor in the quality and size of the labour supply and, by extension, in the productivity of workers. Even for developed countries, the welfare gains associated with the extension of life expectation and the reduction of morbidity may have overtaken gains as they are

Final.

FIGURE 9.2
How various securities may enhance dynamic efficiency

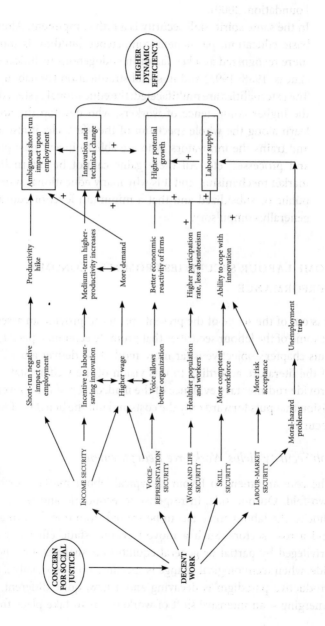

measured by conventional national accounting methods (Lasker Foundation, 2000).

- In the same spirit, skill security is a fifth component. Along with basic education, permanent competence building is more and more recognized as a key factor in endogenous technical change (Lucas, 1988; 1993) and in social stratification (Bénabou, 1996). The externalities are multifaceted: the educational system delivers the higher competence of workers, who develop the ability to learn along the whole spectrum of the life cycle; it also detects and trains the innovators, who are able to invent new products and processes, etc. All these gains cannot be internalized by market mechanisms, and it is why many educational systems are public or subsidized and that a minimum level of education is generally compulsory.

SOME LABOUR SECURITIES PROMOTE ECONOMIC PERFORMANCE

It is out of the scope of the present chapter to provide an assessment of some of the labour securities that promote economic performance. This chapter's objective is far more modest: to deliver a brief survey of the literature according to this vision of the welfare state. Let us provide rudimentary evidence of the inadequacy of the conventional vision that puts forward only the costs and not the benefits of workers' security.

Job Security Helps Workforce Redeployment

The core argument in favour of typical labour-market flexibility is two-fold. On one side, in response to economic and technological shocks, the labour force has to be shifted from one firm to another and across sectors. Such a move warrants static efficiency that is privileged by partial or general equilibrium analyses. On the other side, when technological change is speeding up – especially if an old, productive paradigm is decaying and a new, quite different, one is emerging – an intensive shift of workers has to take place from the mature to the sunrise industries. The question is why workers should accept these structural changes. The reason would be only if their ex post long-term welfare could be improved, and if the transition costs were reduced by an adequate public redistribution of the benefits associated with productivity increases and product differentiation.

An international comparison suggests that job security is quite beneficial to the acceptance of change and the move from bad to good jobs (Figure 9.3). Of course, the relationship is not that simple.

FIGURE 9.3
Selected European countries:
Quality of job prospects and insecurity, 1995–2000 (percentages).

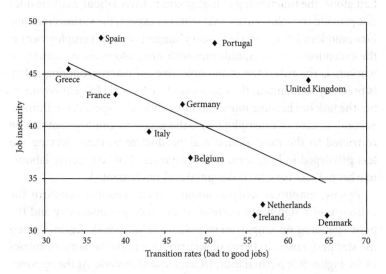

Note: Transition rates from low-quality to good-quality jobs are measured in percentages and are based on a European Commission survey conducted during 1995–1996. Jobs are categorized depending on pay, productivity, job security, training opportunities and career prospects. Job insecurity data measures the percentage of workers who are unsure of a future with their employer even if they perform their job well.
Sources: European Commission, 2002. Data for 2000 based on the International Survey Research database, various years.
Source: ILO (2004a: 206).

On the one hand, Ireland, Netherlands and Denmark do combine job security and very high transition rates from obsolete to emerging jobs. On the other hand, the United Kingdom of Great Britain and Northern Ireland defines a second configuration whereby a high level of insecurity induces significant mobility. This is an important caveat for any temptation to single out one particular best-way model. Institutional economics explain why: there exist different complementarities between the nature of competition, the organization of the labour market, the generosity of the welfare, and the direction and intensity of innovation (Aoki, 2001; Amable, 2003).

Labour-market Policies can Reduce Job Insecurity

Left alone, the functioning of highly competitive labour markets does not provide the job security that workers expect, for various reasons. First, modern labour-market theory suggests that full employment is the exception and the equilibrium with unemployment or scarcity of workers is the rule. One of the objectives of macroeconomic policy is precisely to maintain the economy close to quasi full employment, but the task has become more and more difficult, especially in Europe. Second, in case of unemployment, the access to employment can be restricted to the most skilled and productive workers, leaving the less privileged in long-term unemployment. It is why active labour-market policies have to be designed and implemented.

Precise, empirical analyses among OECD countries confirm the existence of a significant correlation between job insecurity and the poor spending on employment policies (Figure 9.4). Again, among the star performers in terms of security, one finds the same countries as for Figure 9.3: Netherlands, Ireland and Denmark. At the opposite end, the United Kingdom and the United States of America, as well as the Republic of Korea (South Korea) and Japan, are characterized by a low degree of intervention in the functioning of the labour markets and quite high job insecurity.

FIGURE 9.4

Selected OECD countries:
Job insecurity and spending on labour market policies, 2000.

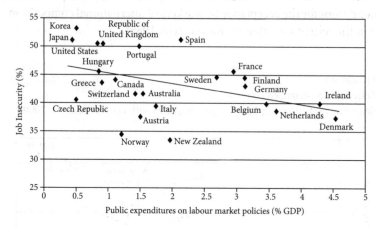

Sources: OECD, 2002; International Survey Research database, various years.
Source: ILO (2004a: 207).

Small, Open Economies have More Active Employment Policies

Conventional economic theories generally suggest that small and very open economies need greater flexibility than medium-sized or large countries. Basically, they should be price takers, and thus unable to finance the extra costs associated with a generous welfare state promoting workers' security. This stylized fact is not at all confirmed by international comparisons among OECD countries. At one extreme, large and not so open economies, such as the US and Japan, do not spend large amounts for employment policies. At the other extreme, Finland, Sweden, Netherlands and Belgium combine a large openness to world trade with a major influence on labour-market policies (Figure 9.5).

Political economists provide a quite appealing interpretation of this situation. When the welfare of citizens is highly dependent on successful integration in the international division of labour, simultaneously some major risks do occur due to the fast and frequently unexpected variations in the demand, exchange rate and price in the international economy. Therefore, according to a long historical process, these small, open economies have found that extensive welfare and redistributive tax systems are the permissive conditions for the acceptance by workers of international competition and the related uncertainty (Katzenstein, 1985).

FIGURE 9.5
Selected industrialized countries:
Spending on labour-market policies increases with openness, 1970–2000

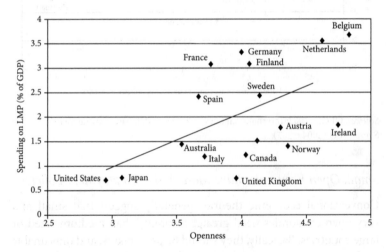

Note: Openness index ix calculated as the natural log of the average ratio of exports plus imports to GDP during 1971–1999.
Sources: OECD, 2004; Dar and Amirkhalkhal, 2003
Source: ILO (2004a: 190).

Active Welfare Policy may be Complementary to Innovation Policy

One could expect that the economies with the most intensive redistribution via welfare should be lagging in terms of macroeconomic performance. On the contrary, it is surprising to find out that the countries with the leaner welfare benefits are not necessarily at the forefront of technological innovation and that most of the small, open economies with extensive welfare have been faring quite well during the last decade (Denmark, Finland, Sweden, etc.), with total factor productivity increases rivalling the so-admired American 'New Economy' (Figure 9.6). The recent research, carried out under the aegis of OECD to explain why growth rates differed so much during the 1990s, has shown that these European economies are already operating under the virtuous circle that is assumed to be typical of a Knowledge-Based Economy (KBE) (Bassanini, Scarpetta and Visco, 2000; OECD, 1999; Guellec, 2000).

FIGURE 9.6
Change in multi-factor productivity growth and change in business research and development intensity

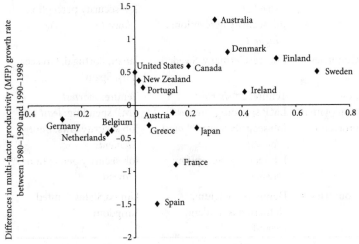

Source: Bassanini A., S. Scarpetta and I. Visco (2000: 27)

A Whole Spectrum of Configuration for Workers' Security

Thus, international comparisons falsify the conventional hypothesis of a single best way for the organization of welfare. A priori, one should observe a very large variety of ways, combining income security, voice-representation security, life security and skill security. Actually, the existing configurations are less diverse, probably due to the existence of complementarity as well as some major incompatibilities between these various forms (Table 9.1).

TABLE 9.1
Employment or employability protection?
A typology of OECD countries during the late 1990s and early 2000s

	High social protection	Low social protection
High employment protection	Tenure: 2nd longest LMP spending: 2nd greatest Job security laws: 2nd strictest Job security perception: 2nd highest	Tenure: longest LMP spending: 2nd least Job security laws: strictest Job security perception: lowest
Countries	France, Germany, Sweden	Japan, Portugal, Greece, Italy, Spain
Low employment protection	Tenure: 2nd shortest LMP spending: greatest Job security laws: 2nd most lenient Job security perception: highest	Tenure: shortest LMP spending: least Job security laws: most lenient Job security perception: 2nd lowest
Countries	Denmark, Belgium, Netherlands, Finland, Ireland	United States, United Kingdom

Source: ILO (2004a: 209).

Basically, for developed countries, two major tools have been used in reaction to workers' demands and the nature of insecurity. On the one hand, some Governments might be tempted to protect existing jobs, and this is employment security stricto sensu. Typically, Mediterranean European countries belong to this model. On the other hand, social partners might prefer to accept intensive job destruction and creation in return for a safety net that provides high income security for the displaced workers in response to competition, technical change or crisis. Again, the small, open economies previously mentioned, Denmark, Belgium, Netherlands, Finland and Ireland, belong to this configuration. Two composite cases exist. A third group, composed of the US and the United Kingdom, simultaneously exhibits low social protection and very weak employment protection. A hybrid configuration combines both high social coverage and employment protection: France, Germany and Sweden.

Thus, this brief survey of the links between labour-market flexibility and workers' security in OECD countries delivers an important message: according to economic specialization, degree of opening and the nature and history of social political demands, various mixes of flexicurity can be observed.

DEVELOPING COUNTRIES' SPECIFIC CONDITIONS

A priori, many structural conditions differ between developed and developing countries. Therefore, it is not a surprise if the configuration of flexicurity cannot be copied easily, even among closely linked European countries (Boyer, 2006).

Constraints and Opportunities Regarding Productive Employment and Decent Work

The objectives of productive employment and decent work should be universally valid, but bearing in mind the specific features of different groups of countries their achievement calls for quite contrasted institutions, mechanisms and ways of achieving them (Ghai, 2002). Basically, if the need to compete via product differentiation and innovation is an incentive to flexicurity in the context of high-employment rates in the formal sector, by contrast, most developing countries suffer from two structural obstacles to the diffusion of decent work and security. First, an impressive labour surplus leads to the domination of informality regarding, for example, the absence of labour contracts and the legal status of an activity, as well as the avoidance of taxes. It is especially so for the rural sector, which is largely associated with the domination of agriculture. Consequently, the implementation of ILO standards is highly problematic for developing countries which specialize in the production and export of primary commodities.

Second, collective action in favour of workers' security is made difficult because Governments and public administrations have neither the resources nor the ability or legitimacy to implement economy-wide labour standards. Similarly, workers' unions are difficult to organize, or even do not exist in the informal sector.

Furthermore, developing countries experience a larger macroeconomic volatility than industrialized economies, in the context of low-income levels that make insurance for workers difficult to finance. The pro-cyclicality of public budgets is another hindering factor. Paradoxically, financial globalization, which was supposed to help poor countries to alleviate economic downturns, seems, until now, to have had the opposite impact, i.e., it has created new sources of crises, especially for Asian countries. This has been quite detrimental because these crises have reduced long-term growth of poor countries (Cerra and Saxena, 2005). The number and severity of these constraints may suggest that the strategy proposed by ILO is hopeless for developing countries. Some (modest) countervailing forces are, however, pointed to in the literature.

- It is at first difficult to consider that the relative security granted to the small number of workers employed in the formal sector is the reason for the lack of protection of informal workers. The argument may apply to OECD countries, where a large sector protected by labour laws is complemented by atypical labour contracts that bear most of the required flexibility in reaction to uncertainty. In developing countries, however, the ocean of flexibility of informal work is not the necessary complement of the rare islands of relative security: the high flexibility is the direct consequence of the productive structures, the nature of demand, and, eventually, the style for macroeconomic policy. The diversity of informal work has be recognized and carefully analysed (Chen, 2006), and the complex relations between the formal and informal sectors should be understood before addressing the issue with a strategy of progressive formalization of informal work.

- Given the pressures towards more flexibility even for previously protected workers, the distance between formal and informal employment could be reduced by progressive steps in granting some rights to informal workers, compatible with the employment decisions of entrepreneurs. The long-term goal could thus be to open a path in the direction of "a single regime with qualified tolerance and minimum floors" (Tokman, 2006). Symmetrically, a simplification of property titles and a form of de jure recognition of de facto property could help in fostering entrepreneurship, thus creating more wealth and alleviating poverty and insecurity (De Soto, 1986). In both cases, the recognition of rights may foster production and employment.

- The low level of surplus available for accumulation is a strong incentive to allocate scarce resources to the more productive investments. The formation of human capital, in education and health, appears as a powerful lever in the promotion of development since it delivers more competences and life security (Todaro and Smith, 2005). This is, simultaneously, the input and the output of the process of development: quality of life and work security do evolve along with growth.

- Macroeconomic instability – either typically domestic or implied by the vagaries of the world economy – should be an incentive to search for mechanisms providing one form of security or another to people, and especially workers. This need is fulfilled, however, only if collective action allows for the design of the equivalent of insurance mechanisms: business associations, workers' unions, non-governmental organizations (NGOs) and civil servants are required to discuss, negotiate and agree to build the various components of a welfare state. Actually, the more open the developed economies, the larger the spending on welfare, including active labour-market policies (see Figure 9.5 "supra"). This process took nearly a century, and is continuing in response to the structural changes of the last decades. It should not be a surprise, therefore, if poor countries experience similar difficulties in building their welfare states in the epoch of trade liberalization, financial globalization and productive paradigm shifts. The organization of collective actors as well as the effectiveness and legitimacy of the State are among the discriminating variables. This might well be a convincing explanation why national trajectories differ so much between Africa (Nkurunziza, 2006) and Latin America (Pagès, 2003), or even within East Asia (Kwon, 2006).

Employment Diagnosis: A Method for Drawing a Dividing line Between Flexibility and Security

Quite rightly, the UN/DESA Development Forum on Productive Employment and Decent Work stressed that productive employment was the primary component of any pro-labour policy. This chapter tries to show that the maximum flexibility is generally far from the optimum in terms of economic efficiency. The issue is then to determine what should be the most convenient flexibility/security mix compatible with the objective of job creation. The answer cannot be derived from pure theory, since the precise structural conditions have to be analysed in each national, regional or local context. In a sense, this is a drastic reversal with respect to the legacy of the so-called Washington Consensus, according to which the same general menu was supposed to fit all domestic contexts.

The question is whether the relevant tools are available to make such an analysis. The long experience of development economics has recently provided quite an interesting and stimulating method to cope with the diversity of developing as well as developed countries. The growth diagnostics approach (Hausmann, Rodrik and Velasco, 2005) proposes systematic review of the multipliers associated with the relaxation of the various constraints inhibiting economic activity and this is an important tool in the design of economic policy and reform of economic institutions. In some instances, a policy that delivers quite impressive results in one country may be inefficient or, worse, detrimental to growth in another. For instance, the authors find that a sound macroeconomic policy is far from being a sufficient condition for growth since the long-term trajectory is shaped by factors quite different from those that would shape the short-term equilibrium. In other words, static efficiency – frequently associated with price flexibility – has to be distinguished from dynamic efficiency, i.e., the ability to improve, cumulatively, productivity and the standards of living of an entire population.

It might be useful to rejuvenate a macroeconomic theory that was quite enlightening in the 1980s in order to propose an analytical framework that would transcend the opposition between Keynesian and neoclassical conceptions of the determinants of employment (Benassy, 1982). Actually the so-called disequilibrium theory exhibits a series of determinants of employment. Unemployment is Keynesian if the limiting factor is effective demand; classical if low profitability limits hiring; and Marxist if the scarcity of productive capacity is the origin of low employment. When applied to developing countries and to the analysis of the links between employment and various forms of workers' security, this framework delivers three major lessons (Figure 9.7).

- In many cases, the issue of labour-market institutional reform might be irrelevant, since the disequilibrium originates from totally different factors: an overvaluation of the domestic currency, an excessively high interest rate due to the lack of credibility of economic policy or bad management of firms, etc. In such a context, the search for wage flexibility, for example, may deliver second-order results, since this is not the relevant constraint on growth. Too often, in the 1990s, financial disequilibria have triggered excessive downgrading of workers' security in terms of wages, work intensity, welfare, etc.

- In some instances, employment levels can increase by strengthening precise forms of workers' security. For instance, if unemployment is Keynesian, more income security for workers has a positive impact both on employment and profit rate. Similarly, when firms are limited by a scarcity of skills, a policy developing workers' competences simultaneously improves macroeconomic performance and promotes welfare, and possibly reduces income inequality. In this case, there is a complementarity between employment levels and the form of worker security. Nevertheless, this is not necessarily the case, and the mix between flexibility and security has to be tuned to the precise local situation at a given historical period.

FIGURE 9.7
A growth diagnostics approach to employment creation

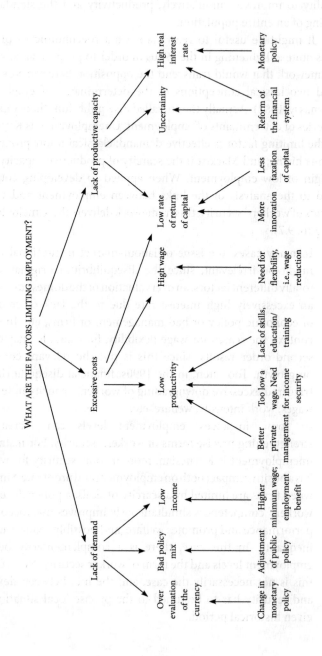

Within a third configuration, labour flexibility might be required to increase productive employment if, for instance, classical unemployment is the main source of macroeconomic disequilibria. Alternatively, some collective agreements can codify automatic indexation to inflation and productivity, and this configuration might appear unable to react effectively to new macroeconomic shocks. This case was quite frequent in the 1970s and 1980s, but nowadays the majority of developing countries are suffering from the opposite disequilibrium: productivity increases mainly feed profit increases and relative prices decline, but wages increase only marginally. The likelihood of classical unemployment is now quite small in most developing countries.

Consequently, each country has to find its own mix between security and flexibility. At this level of generality, there are configurations that fulfil the same objective as the flexicurity model, but with totally different institutional settings, since productive structures, social values and political choices differ significantly from one country to another. Even within the same national economy, the coexistence of defensive flexibility can be observed in some clusters – i.e., via wage reduction and work-intensity increase – along with offensive flexibility in others, where the building of individual and collective competence is the main answer to technical change and the evolution of world competition (Vijayabaskar, 2005).

Some Few Developing Countries do Succeed

In the light of the previous arguments, it will come as no surprise that the global index of economic security, elaborated by the ILO Socio-economic Security Programme, shows that the majority of best performers do belong to OECD (ILO, 2004b: 277). The only exceptions are four Eastern and Central European countries; this can be interpreted as a legacy of the order, inherited from the Soviet-type regime, where the State was warranting strong security to workers in exchange for compliance with political authorities.

No developing countries are part of the group of pacesetters, but Mauritius, South Africa, Costa Rica and Chile, as well as Estonia, Lithuania and Slovakia, belong to this group: in terms of outcomes these countries are quite successful in spite of a poor score on inputs and processes governing worker security.

The majority of other countries belong to a fourth group, characterized by less effective security and low institutional mechanisms to obtain it. Most African countries are part of this group, as well as some Latin American countries. China and India are present in this group too, and this is an important finding: per se high growth is not sufficient to promote worker security. Nevertheless, growth generates many imbalances and social unrest that implicitly at least raise the issue of the implementation of decent work.

CONCLUSION

This chapter has tentatively challenged the conventional wisdom that the dynamism of employment is always contradictory to the enforcement of some forms of security for workers. Three major arguments can be mobilized.

1. Contemporary theorizing has drastically changed, and economists now recognize the specificity of the wage-labour nexus, by contrast with typical market relations. Consequently, minimum security is required for good economic performance by firms and national economies. Other social sciences do stress the ethical and moral values associated with labour, and thus provide strong justifications for the implementation of basic securities for individuals.

2. A comparative analysis of OECD countries shows that the extended security promoted by welfare systems has not been detrimental to growth, innovation and job creation. On the contrary, small, open social democratic economies display a clear complementarity between security and economic performance, equity and dynamic efficiency. The need for inclusive welfare is clearly perceived by some fast-growing Asian countries, such as South Korea and China.

3. Developing countries cannot immediately catch up with the emerging standards of flexicurity but, quite pragmatically, they should look for the forms of worker security that are

compatible with sustainable development. A priori, many different configurations might coexist in response to economic specialization, social values and political choices.

The epoch of the Washington Consensus is fading away and the idea that 'the same size fits all' is probably over. These are clear incentives for a new generation of research, and for innovative policies to sustain the current hope and strategy that has recently emerged in Latin America: 'growth with equity'.

Notes

† This chapter is abridged from 'Employment and Decent Work in the Era of "Flexicurity"', DESA Working Paper No. 32, revised from a paper of the same title prepared for the UN/DESA Development Forum on 'Productive Employment and Decent Work', held at the United Nations headquarters, New York, on 8 and 9 May 2006.

References

Altman, Roger, Jason Bordoff, Peter Orszag and Robert Rubin (2006). *An Economic Strategy to Advance Opportunity, Prosperity and Growth*. Brookings Institution, Washington, DC.

Amable, Bruno (2003). *The Diversity of Modern Capitalisms*. Oxford University Press, Oxford.

Aoki, Masahiko (2001). *Toward a Comparative Institutional Analysis*. MIT Press, Cambridge, MA.

Bassanini, Andrea, Stefano Scarpetta and Ignazio Visco (2000). Knowledge, technology and economic growth: Recent evidence from OECD countries. Processed, Economics Department, OECD. Prepared for the 150th Anniversary of the National Bank of Belgium, 'How to Promote Economic Growth in the Euro Area', Brussels, May 11–12.

Bénabou, Rolland (1996). Heterogeneity, stratification, and growth: Macroeconomic implications of community structure and school finance. *American Economic Review* 86 (3): 584–609.

Bénassy, Jean-Pascal (1982). *The Economics of Market Disequilibrium*. Academic Press, Boston.

Boyer, Robert (ed.) (1988). *The Search for Labour Flexibility*. Clarendon Press, Oxford.

Boyer, Robert (2000). The French welfare: An institutional and historical analysis in European perspective. CEPREMAP Working Paper no. 2000–07, Centre d'Etudes Prospectives d'Economie Mathematique Appliquees a la Planification, Paris.

Boyer, Robert (2006). *La flexicurité danoise. Quels enseignements pour la France*. Opuscule CEPREMAP, Editions de l'ENS, Paris, http://www.cepremap.ens.fr/depot/opus/OPUS2.pdf

Boyer, Robert, and Jacques Mistral (1982). *Accumulation, Inflation, Crises.* Presses Universitaires de France, Paris (1st édition, 1978).

Cerra, Valerie, and Sweta Chanan Saxena (2005). Growth dynamics: The myth of economic recovery. IMF Working Paper No. 05/147, International Monetary Fund, Washington, DC.

Chen, Martha Alter (2006). Rethinking formalisation of the informal economy: Who, what, why, and how. Prepared for the UN/DESA Development Forum on 'Productive Employment and Decent Work', United Nations, New York, May 8 and 9.

Chenery, Hollis, and T.N. Srinivasan (eds.) (1988). *Handbook of Development Economics.* Vol. I. Elsevier Science Publishers B.V., Geneva: 40–71.

Council of Economic Advisers (1998). *Economic Report of the President, 1998.* US Government Printing Office, Washington, DC.

de Soto, Hernando (1986). *El otro sendero: La revolucion informal.* Instituto libertad y Democracia, Lima.

Duménil, Gérard, and Dominique Lévy (1993). *The Economics of the Profit Rate: Competition, Crises, and Historical Tendencies in Capitalism.* Edward Elgar, Aldershot, UK.

Eliasson, Günar (1984). Micro heterogeneity of firms and the stability of industrial growth. *Journal of Economic Behavior and Organization* 5 (3–4): 249–274.

Freeman, Richard B., and D. Medoff (1984). *What do Unions Do?* Basic Books, New York.

Ghai, Dharam (2002). Decent work: Concepts, models and indicators. Discussion Paper No. 139, International Institute for Labour Studies, Geneva.

Guellec, Dominique (2000). Economic growth in Europe: Entering a new era. Presentation at the Deutsch-Französisches Wirtschaftspolitisches Forum, Bonn, 17 and 18 January.

Hausmann, Ricardo, Dani Rodrik and Andrès Velasco (2005). Growth diagnostics. Processed, John Kennedy School of Government, Harvard University, March.

Heiner, H. (1988). Imperfect decisions and routinized production: Implications for evolutionary modelling and inertial technical change. In Giovanni Dosi Christopher Freeman, Richard Nelson, Gerald Silverberg and Luc Soete (eds). *Technical Change and Economic Theory.* Pinter, London: 147–169.

ILO (2004a). *World Employment Report, 2004–2005.* International Labour Office, Geneva.

ILO (2004b). *Economic Security for a Better World.* International Labour Office, Geneva.

Katzenstein, Peter J. (1985). *Small States in World Markets: Industrial Policy in Europe.* Cornell University Press, Ithaca.

Kwon, Huck-Ju (2006). Transforming the development welfare states in East Asia. Processed, Sung Kyun Kwan University, Seoul.

Lasker Foundation (2000). *Exceptional Returns: The Economic Value of America's Investment in Medical Research.* Albert and Mary Lasker Foundation, New York. http: www.fundingfirst.org

Lucas, Robert (1988). On the mechanisms of economic development. *Journal of Monetary Economics* 72, July: 3–42.

Lucas, Robert (1993). Making a miracle. *Econometrica* 61 (2): 251–272.

Nkurunziza, Janvier (2006). Generating rural employment in Africa to fight poverty. Prepared for the UN/DESA Development Forum on 'Productive Employment and Decent Work', United Nations, New York, May 8 and 9.

OECD (1999). *The Knowledge-Based Economy: A Set of Acts and Figures.* Organisation for Economic Co-operation and Development, Paris.

Pagès, Carmen (2003). *Good Jobs Wanted: Labor Markets in Latin America.* Inter-American Development Bank, Washington, DC.

Todaro, Michael P., and Stephen C. Smith (2005). *Economic Development*. 9th edition. Pearson Education, Harlow, UK.

Tokman, Victor (2006). Integrating the informal sector in the modernization process. Prepared for the UN/DESA Development Forum on 'Productive Employment and Decent Work', United Nations, New York, May 8 and 9.

Touffut, Jean-Philippe (1999). Stabilité, transformation et émergence des modes de coordination dans la Russie post-soviétique. PhD thesis, October, Ecole des Hautes Etudes en Sciences Sociales (EHESS), Paris, and Université Lomonosov, Moscow.

Vijayabaskar, M. (2005). Governance of flexible accumulation in clusters: Can it create "decent work" in low income region. Processed, Madras Institute of Development Studies, Chennai.

World Health Organization (2000). *Annual Report*. Oxford University Press, Oxford.

10

Rethinking the Informal Economy: Linkages with the Formal Economy and the Formal Regulatory Environment

MARTHA ALTER CHEN

Since it was 'discovered' in Africa in the early 1970s, the informal economy has been subject to interpretation and debate and has gone in and out of fashion in international development circles. Despite the debates and critiques, the informal economy has continued to prove a useful concept to many policymakers, activists, and researchers because the reality it captures – the large share of economic units and workers that remain outside the world of regulated economic activities and protected employment relationships – is so large and significant. Today there is renewed interest in the informal economy worldwide. This re-convergence of interest stems from two basic facts. First, despite predictions of its eventual demise, the informal economy has not only grown in many countries but also emerged in new guises and unexpected places. Second, despite continuing debates about its defining features, supporting informal enterprises and improving informal jobs are increasingly recognized as key pathways to promoting growth and reducing poverty.

This chapter explores the relationship of the informal economy to the formal economy and the formal regulatory environment. It begins with a comparison of the earlier concept of the 'informal sector' with a new expanded concept of the 'informal economy' and a discussion of the size, composition, and segmentation of the informal economy broadly defined. The second section discusses the linkages between the informal economy and the formal economy, on one hand, and the formal regulatory environment, on the other. The concluding section suggests why and how more equitable linkages between the informal economy and the formal economy should be promoted through an appropriate policy and regulatory environment.

THE INFORMAL ECONOMY

The recent re-convergence of interest in the informal economy has been accompanied by significant rethinking of the concept, at least in some circles. The rethinking about the informal economy, summarized below, includes a new term and expanded definition; recognition of its segmented structure; and a revised set of assumptions about its defining features. This section concludes with a summary of available statistics on women and men in the informal economy broadly defined.

New Term and Expanded Definition

In recent years, a group of informed activists and researchers, including members of the global research policy network Women in Informal Employment: Globalizing and Organizing (WIEGO), have worked with the International Labour Organization (ILO) to broaden the earlier concept and definition of the 'informal sector' to incorporate certain types of informal employment that were not included in the earlier concept and definition (including the official international statistical definition). They seek to include the whole of informality, as it is manifested in industrialized, transition and developing economies and the real world dynamics in labour markets today, particularly the employment arrangements of the working poor. These observers want to extend the focus to include not only *enterprises* that are not legally regulated but also *employment relationships* that are not legally regulated or protected. In brief, the new definition of the 'informal economy' focuses on the nature of employment in addition to the characteristics of enterprises. It also includes informal employment both within and outside agriculture.

Under this new definition, the informal economy is comprised of all forms of 'informal employment' – that is, employment without labour or social protection – both inside and outside informal enterprises, including both self-employment in small unregistered enterprises and wage employment in unprotected jobs.

Key Features of the Informal Economy

What follows is a discussion of key features of the informal economy broadly defined, including: its significance and permanence, the continuum of employment relations within it and its segmented structure. The discussion ends on the issue of its legality or illegality as there is a widespread misconception that the informal economy is somehow illegal or is the equivalent of the underground, or even criminal, economy.

Significance and permanence: The recent re-convergence of interest in the informal economy stems from the recognition that the informal economy is growing; is a permanent, not a short-term, phenomenon; and is a feature of modern capitalist development, not just traditional economies, associated with both growth and global integration. For these reasons, the informal economy should be viewed not as a marginal or peripheral sector but as a basic component – the base, if you will – of the total economy.

Continuum of economic relations: Economic relations – of production, distribution and employment – tend to fall at some point on a continuum between pure 'formal' relations (i.e., regulated and protected) at one pole and pure 'informal' relations (i.e., unregulated and unprotected) at the other, with many categories in between. Depending on their circumstances, workers and units are known to move with varying ease and speed along the continuum and/or to operate simultaneously at different points on the continuum. Consider, for example, the self-employed garment maker who supplements her earnings by stitching clothes under a sub-contract, or shifts to working on a sub-contract for a firm when her customers decide they prefer ready-made garments rather than tailor-made ones. Or consider the public sector employee who has an informal job on the side.

Moreover, the formal and the informal ends of the economic continuum are often dynamically linked. For instance, many informal enterprises have production or distribution relations with formal enterprises, supplying inputs, finished goods or services either through direct transactions or sub-contracting arrangements. Also, many formal enterprises hire wage workers under informal employment relations. For example, many part-time workers, temporary workers and homeworkers work for formal enterprises through contracting or sub-contracting arrangements.

Segmentation: The informal economy consists of a range of informal enterprises and informal jobs. Yet there are meaningful ways to classify its various segments, as follows:
- Self-employment in informal enterprises: workers in small unregistered or unincorporated enterprises, including:
  o employers
  o own account operators: both heads of family enterprises and single person operators
  o unpaid family workers
- Wage employment in informal jobs: workers without worker benefits or social protection who work for formal or informal firms, for households or with no fixed employer, including:
  o employees of informal enterprises
  o other informal wage workers such as:
    ♦ casual or day labourers
    ♦ domestic workers
    ♦ unregistered or undeclared workers
    ♦ some temporary or part-time workers[1]
  o industrial outworkers (also called homeworkers).

From recent research findings and official data, two stylized global facts emerge about the segmented informal economy. The first fact is that there are significant gaps in earnings within the informal economy: on average, employers have the highest earnings; followed by their employees and other more 'regular' informal wage workers; own account operators; 'casual' informal wage workers; and industrial outworkers. The second is that, around the world, men tend to be over-represented in the top segment; women tend to be over-represented in the bottom segments; and the shares of men and women in the intermediate segments tend to vary across sectors and countries. These twin facts are depicted graphically in Figure 10.1.

FIGURE 10.1
Segmentation of the informal economy

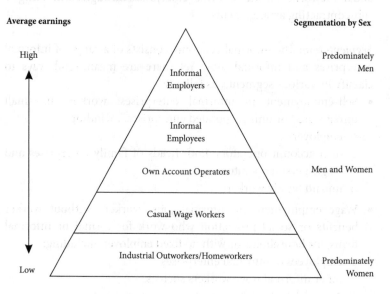

Note: *The informal economy may also be segmented by race, ethnicity, caste, or religion.

The net result is a significant gender gap in earnings within the informal economy, with women earning less on average than men.[2] An additional fact, not captured in Figure 10.1, is that there is further segmentation and earning gaps within these broad status categories. Women tend to work in different types of activities, associated with different levels of earning, than men – with the result that they typically earn less even within specific segments of the informal economy. Some of this difference can be explained by the fact that men tend to embody more human capital due to educational discrimination against girls, especially in certain societies (e.g., in North India and Pakistan). This difference can also be explained by the fact that men tend to have *better tools* of the trade, operate from *better work sites/ spaces* and have *greater access to productive assets and financial capital*. In addition, or as a result, men often produce or sell a *higher volume* or a *different range* of goods and services. For instance, among street vendors in some countries, men are more likely to sell non-perishables while women are more likely to sell perishable goods (such as fruits and vegetables). In addition, men are more likely to sell from push-carts or bicycles while women are more likely to sell from baskets, or simply from a cloth spread on the ground.

Legality or Semi-Legality

Previously, there was a widespread assumption that the informal sector was comprised of unregistered and unregulated enterprises whose owner operators choose to avoid registration and, thereby, taxation. While it is important to understand informal employment in relation to the legal framework in any given country, this is far from being the whole story.

- There is a distinction between illegal *processes or arrangements* and illegal *goods and services*. While production or employment arrangements in the informal economy are often semi-legal or illegal, most informal workers and enterprises produce and/or distribute legal goods and services. Admittedly, one part of the informal economy – the criminal economy – operates illegally and deals in illegal goods and services. But it is only a small part of a larger whole that is, for the most part, not illegal or criminal.
- Many owner operators of informal enterprises operate semi-legally or illegally because the regulatory environment is too punitive, too cumbersome or simply non-existent. Also, many informal activities do not generate enough output, employment or income to fall into existing tax brackets.
- Most owner operators would be willing to pay registration fees and taxes if they were to receive the benefits of formality (enjoyed by registered businesses). For instance, street vendors who now pay a mix of legal and illegal fees would welcome the security that comes with being legally recognized (Chen, Vanek and Carr, 2004; Chen and others, 2005).

- It is important to note that, in the case of informal wage work, it is usually not the workers but their employers, whether in formal or informal firms, who are avoiding registration and taxation.

More fundamentally, most informal workers associate operating outside the legal regulatory framework with costs rather than benefits. Most self-employed and wage workers in the informal economy are deprived of secure work, worker's benefits, social protection and representation or voice. The self-employed must take care of themselves and their enterprises as well as their employees (if they hire others) or unpaid contributing family members (if they run a family business). Moreover, they often face competitive disadvantage vis-à-vis larger formal firms in capital and product markets. Informal wage workers also have to take care of themselves as they receive few (if any) employer-sponsored benefits. In addition, both groups receive little (if any) legal protection through their work or from their governments. As a result of these and other factors, a higher proportion of the informal workforce than of the formal workforce is poor.

Table 10.1 summarizes the key differences between the old and new views of the informal economy.

TABLE 10.1
Old and new views of the informal economy

The old view	The new view
The informal sector is the traditional economy that will wither away and die with modern, industrial growth.	The informal economy is 'here to stay' and expanding with modern, industrial growth.
It is only marginally productive.	It is a major provider of employment, goods and services for lower-income groups. It contributes a significant share of GDP.

(contd)

TABLE 10.1 *(contd)*

The old view	The new view
It exists separately from the formal economy.	It is linked to the formal economy – it produces for, trades with, distributes for and provides services to the formal economy.
It represents a reserve pool of surplus labour.	Much of the recent rise in informal employment is due to the decline in formal employment or to the informalisation of previously formal employment relationships.
It is comprised mostly of street traders and very small-scale producers.	It is made up of a wide range of informal occupations – both 'resilient old forms' such as casual day labour in construction and agriculture as well as 'emerging new ones' such as temporary and part-time jobs plus homework for high tech industries.
Most of those in the sector are entrepreneurs who run illegal and unregistered enterprises in order to avoid regulation and taxation.	It is made up of non-standard wage workers as well as entrepreneurs and self-employed persons producing legal goods and services, albeit through irregular or unregulated means. Most entrepreneurs and the self-employed are amenable to, and would welcome, efforts to reduce barriers to registration and related transaction costs and to increase benefits from regulation; and most informal wage workers would welcome more stable jobs and workers' rights.
Work in the informal economy is comprised mostly of survival activities and thus is not a subject for economic policy.	Informal enterprises include not only survival activities but also stable enterprises and dynamic growing businesses, and informal employment includes not only self-employment but also wage employment. All forms of informal employment are affected by most (if not all) economic policies.

Women and Men in the Informal Economy

Compiling statistics on the size, composition and contribution of the informal economy is hampered by the lack of sufficient data. While many countries have now undertaken a survey on employment in the informal sector, very few countries undertake these on a regular basis. Furthermore, only a handful of countries have collected data to measure informal employment outside informal enterprises. In addition, the available data are not comprehensive. Many countries exclude agriculture from their measurement of the informal sector while others measure only the urban informal sector. In most developing countries, however, a majority of the informal workforce may well be in agriculture. There are also a number of problems that limit the international comparability of data. However, in the absence of reliable data collected directly, various indirect methods to estimate the size and composition of the informal economy can be used. What follows is a summary of main findings from the most recent and most comprehensive set of estimates of the informal economy in developing countries, including its gender dimensions, using indirect methods where necessary.[3]

Size of the Informal Economy

Informal employment broadly defined comprises one-half to three-quarters of non-agricultural employment in developing countries: specifically, 48 per cent in North Africa; 51 per cent in Latin America; 65 per cent in Asia; and 72 per cent in sub-Saharan Africa. If South Africa is excluded, the share of informal employment in non-agricultural employment rises to 78 per cent in sub-Saharan Africa; and if comparable data were available for other countries in South Asia in addition to India, the regional average for Asia would likely be much higher.

Some countries include informal employment in agriculture in their estimates. This significantly increases the proportion of informal employment: from 83 per cent of *non-agricultural* employment to 93 per cent of *total* employment in India; from 55 to 62 per cent in Mexico; and from 28 to 34 per cent in South Africa.

Informal employment is generally a larger source of employment for women than for men in the developing world. Other than in North Africa, where 43 per cent of women workers are in informal employment, 60 per cent or more of women non-agricultural workers in the developing world are informally employed. In sub-Saharan Africa, 84 per cent of women non-agricultural workers are informally employed compared to 63 per cent of men; and in Latin America the figures are 58 per cent of women in comparison to 48 per cent of men. In Asia, the proportion is 65 per cent for both women and men.

Composition of the Informal Economy

As noted earlier, the informal economy is comprised of both self-employment in informal enterprises (i.e., small and/or unregistered) and wage employment in informal jobs (i.e., without secure contracts, worker benefits or social protection). In developing regions, *self-employment* comprises a greater share of informal employment outside of agriculture (and even more inside of agriculture) than wage employment: specifically, self-employment represents 70 per cent of informal employment in sub-Saharan Africa, 62 per cent in North Africa, 60 per cent in Latin America and 59 per cent in Asia. If South Africa is excluded, since black-owned businesses prohibited during the apartheid era have only recently been recognized and reported, the share of self-employment in informal employment increases to 81 per cent in sub-Saharan Africa.

Informal *wage* employment is also significant in developing countries, comprising 30 to 40 per cent of total informal employment (outside of agriculture). Informal wage employment is comprised of employees of informal enterprises as well as various types of informal wage workers who work for formal enterprises, households or no fixed employer (see definition above).

LINKS WITH THE FORMAL ECONOMY AND FORMAL REGULATORY ENVIRONMENT

A key issue in the debates on the informal economy is whether and how the informal economy and formal economy are linked. However, these debates have tended to blur the distinction between the formal economy and the formal regulatory environment and the relationship of the informal enterprises and informal workers to each. But it is important to distinguish between the:

- *formal economy*: comprising regulated economic units and protected workers
- *formal regulatory environment*: comprising government policies, laws, and regulations

This section of the chapter discusses the linkages between informal enterprises and workers and, respectively, the formal economy and the formal regulatory environment. In real life, of course, it is often hard to know what is driving what: as large formal registered enterprises are often involved in 'setting' formal policies and regulations; and formal policies and regulations are often biased towards formal registered firms to the disadvantage of both informal enterprises and informal wage workers.

The Formal Economy

Over the years, the debates on the informal economy crystallized into three dominant schools of thought regarding the informal economy: dualism, structuralism, and legalism. Each of these has a different perspective on how the informal and formal economies are linked. The dualists argue that informal units and activities have few (if any) linkages to the formal economy but, rather, operate as a distinct separate sector of the economy; and that informal workers comprise the less-advantaged sector of a dualistic labour market (Sethuraman, 1976; Tokman, 1978). Unlike the dualists, structuralists see the informal and formal economies as intrinsically linked. To increase competitiveness, capitalist firms in the formal economy are seen to reduce their input costs, including labour costs, by promoting informal production and employment relationships with subordinated economic units and workers. According to structuralists, both informal enterprises and informal wage workers are subordinated to the interests of capitalist development, providing cheap goods and services (Moser, 1978; Portes, Castells and Benton, 1989). The legalists focus on the relationship between informal entrepreneurs/

enterprises and the formal regulatory environment, not formal firms. But they acknowledge that capitalist interests – what Hernando de Soto calls 'mercantilist' interests – collude with government to set the bureaucratic 'rules of the game' (de Soto, 1989).

Given the heterogeneity of the informal economy, there is some truth to each of these perspectives. But the reality of informal employment is more complex than these perspectives would suggest. What follows is a summary of various ways in which informal enterprises and workers are linked to formal firms.

Informal Enterprises and Formal Firms

Few informal enterprises, except perhaps some survival activities, operate in total isolation from formal firms. Most source raw materials from and/or supply finished goods to formal firms either directly or through intermediate (often informal) firms. Sourcing and supplying of goods or services can take place through *individual transactions* but are more likely to take place through a *sub-sector network* of commercial relationships or a *value chain* of sub-contracted relationships.

To understand the linkages between informal enterprises and formal firms it is important to consider the nature of the production system through which they are linked. This is because the nature of the linkage – specifically, the allocation of authority (over the work situation and the outcome of work done) and economic risk between the informal and formal firm – varies according to the nature of the production system. For instance, a garment maker might produce for the open market (with some authority and all of the risk) or for a supply firm linked to a multinational company (with little authority but much of the risk in the form of non-wage costs, rejected goods, and delayed payments). Types of production systems include:

- *individual transactions*: some informal enterprises or own account operators exchange goods and services with formal firms in what might be characterized as open or pure market exchange (in the sense of independent units transacting with each other). In such cases, the more competitive firm in terms of market knowledge and power – as well as the ability to adjust if the transaction does not proceed – controls the exchange or transaction.

- *sub-sectors*: many informal enterprises or own account operators produce and exchange goods and services with formal firms in what are called sub-sectors, networks of independent units involved in the production and distribution of a product or commodity. In such networks, individual units are involved in transactions with suppliers and customers. The terms and conditions of these transactions are governed largely by the more competitive firm in specific transactions (as above) but also by the 'rules of the game' for the sub-sector as a whole, which typically are determined by dominant firms in the sub-sector.

- *value chains*: some informal enterprises and own account operators and, by definition, all industrial outworkers produce goods within a value chain. The terms and conditions of production in value chains are determined largely by the lead firm: a large national firm in most domestic chains and a large trans-national corporation in most global value chains. However, the major suppliers to whom the lead firm sub-contracts work— also often formal firms—also help determine the terms and conditions of work that they sub-contract to informal firms and workers down the chain.

In sum, in the manufacturing sector in particular, informal enterprises are quite likely to have linkages with formal firms. But these commercial relationships are not likely to be regulated, although this differs context to context. In the provision of services, such as catering, transport, and construction, there is greater possibility of de-linking from formal firms.

Informal Workers and Formal Firms

Historically, the 'employment relationship' has represented the cornerstone – the central legal concept – around which labour law and collective bargaining agreements have sought to recognize and protect the rights of workers. Whatever its precise definition in different national contexts, it has represented 'a universal notion that links a person, called the employee (frequently referred to as 'the worker') with another person, called the employer to whom she or he provides labour or services under certain conditions in return for remuneration' (ILO, 2003).

The concept of employment relationship has always excluded those workers who are self-employed. Increasingly, some wage workers have found themselves to be, in effect, without legal recognition or protection because their employment relationship is either:

- *disguised*: the employment relationship is deliberately disguised by giving it the appearance of a relationship of a different legal nature. For example, the lead firm in a sub-contracting chain may claim that it has a 'sales-purchase' – or commercial – relationship with those who produce goods for it, rather than a sub-contracted employment relationship. In Ahmedabad City, India, many bidi traders now claim that they sell tobacco and other raw materials to those who produce bidis (hand-rolled cigarettes) and buy the finished bidis from them. This is because the bidi-rollers are trying to leverage employer contributions to a retirement fund from the bidi traders.

- *ambiguous*: the employment relationship is objectively ambiguous so there is doubt about whether an employment relationship really exists. This is the case, for instance, with street vendors who depend on a single supplier for goods or sell goods on commission for a distributor.

- *not clearly defined*: the employment relationship clearly exists but it is not clear who the employer is, what rights the worker has, and who is responsible for securing these rights. For example, in value chain production, it is not clear who the real employer is: the lead firm, the supply firm, or the sub-contractor? Similarly, in the case of temporary work, it is not clear who the real employer is: the agency that supplies temporary workers or the firms that hire them on a temporary basis? Or in the case of day labourers or seasonal labourers in agriculture and construction, whether the labour contractor or gang master is the employer?

Under each of these employment relationships, workers tend not to be protected under labour law or collective bargaining agreements: in brief, they are informally employed. It is important to note that, in many such cases, the employer seeks to disguise the employment relationship or avoid definition of who is responsible; and that the employer in question may well represent a formal firm, not an informal enterprise (ILO, 2003).

Beginning in the 1980s, formal firms in some developed countries began to favour flexible labour relationships. This form of labour market segmentation took place in the interest of flexible specialized production, not in response to rising wage rates or labour costs (Piore and Sabel, 1984). Also increasingly since the 1980s, many formal firms in developed countries have decided to sub-contract production to workers in developing countries: some of whom are relatively protected (e.g., those who work in call centres) while others are not protected (e.g., many of those who work in assembly factories). Production under this form of labour market segmentation takes place in developing countries where labour costs are low and there is no real threat of rising wages due to legislation or unionization. In producing countries, there is often further segmentation between the core semi-permanent workforce and a peripheral temporary workforce that is mobilized during peak seasons and demobilized during slack seasons (what has been called a 'permanent temporary workforce'). Depending on the context, the effect is to shift uncertainty from permanent employees to 'permanent temporary' employees or from 'permanent temporary' employees to industrial outworkers.

In sum, many formal firms prefer informal employment relationships, in the interest of flexible specialized production, global competition, or (simply) reduced labour costs. The related point is that formal firms choose these types of informal employment relationships as a means to avoiding their formal obligations as employers. In such cases, it is the formal firm not the informal worker that decides to operate informally and enjoys the 'benefits' of informality. This reality points to the need to re-examine the notion that informal employment is 'voluntary' from the perspective of informal wage workers, not just of the self-employed.

The Formal Regulatory Environment

The three dominant schools of thought also view the relationship between the informal economy and the formal regulatory environment in different ways. In regard to informal enterprises, dualists pay relatively little attention to government regulations per se but focus instead on government provision of necessary support services: notably, credit and business development services. In regard to informal wage workers, some dualists subscribe to the neo-classical economics notion that government intervention in labour markets leads to wage rigidities which, in turn, lead to more informal employment. The legalists believe that government deregulation would lead to increased economic freedom and entrepreneurship among working people, especially in developing countries (de Soto, 1989). However, the founder of the legalist school – Hernando de Soto – recently advocated one form of regulation: namely, the *formalization* of property rights for the informal workforce to help them convert their informally-held assets into real assets (de Soto, 2000). In marked contrast, the structuralists see a role for government in regulating the unequal relationships between 'big businesses' and subordinated informal producers and workers: they advocate the regulation of commercial relations in the case of informal producers and the regulation of employment relations in the case of informal wage workers.

Over-Regulation

As noted earlier, the legalists have focused on excessive regulations that create barriers to working formally. However, over-regulation may raise barriers and costs not only to operating formally but also to operating informally. Consider the case of gum collectors in India. Following the nationalization of the forests in India, gum and other forest products came under the control of the National and State Forest Departments with the result that trading these products requires a government license. Although there is a thriving open market for gum that includes textile and pharmaceutical companies, those who collect gum must sell gum to the Forest Development Corporation; to sell in the open market requires a special license. Most gum collectors – except those who can afford to obtain a license – must sell to the Forest Development Corporation for below market prices (Crowell, 2003).

Consider also the case of salt makers in India. The cheapest way to transport salt within India is via railway. Historically, small salt producers have not been able to transport their salt by train because of a long-standing government regulation that stipulates that salt farmers need to own a minimum of 90 acres of land to be eligible to book a train wagon. Given that most small salt farmers lease land from the government or local landlords, most small salt farmers are not eligible to use rail transport. Because they have to use private transport, small salt farmers face high transportation costs and, therefore, remain less competitive than larger salt farmers (Crowell, 2003).

Deregulation

As part of economic restructuring and liberalization, there has been a fair amount of *deregulation*, particularly of financial and labour markets. Deregulation of labour markets is associated with the rise of informalization or 'flexible' labour markets. It should be noted that workers are caught between two contradictory trends: *rapid flexibilization* of the employment relationship (making it easy for employers to contract and expand their workforce as needed) and *slow liberalization* of labour mobility (making it difficult for labour to move easily and quickly across borders or even to cities within the same country) (Chen, Vanek and Carr 2004).[4] Labour advocates have argued for *re-regulation* of labour markets to protect informal wage workers from the economic risks and uncertainty associated with flexibility and informalization.

Lack of Regulation

The regulatory environment often overlooks whole categories of the informal economy. A *missing* regulatory environment can be as costly to informal operators as an *excessive* regulatory environment. For example, city governments tend to adopt either of two stances towards street trade: trying to eliminate it or turning a 'blind eye' to it. Either stance has a punitive effect: eviction, harassment, and the demand for bribes by police, municipal officials and other vested interests. Few cities have adopted a coherent policy – or set of regulations – towards street trade. Rather, most cities assign the 'handling' of street traders to those departments – such as the police – that deal with law and order (Bhowmik, 2004; Mitullah, 2004).

The different perspectives on regulation outlined above are appropriate for the specific components of the informal economy to which they refer: the legalists focus on informal *enterprises* (and informal *commercial* relationships); labour advocates focus on informal *jobs* (and informal *employment* relationships); and those concerned about street vendors focus on the regulation of *urban space* and *informal trade*. Arguably, for each component of the informal economy, what is needed is *appropriate regulation*, not complete deregulation or the lack of regulation.

Promoting More Equitable Linkages

Given that the informal economy is here to stay and that the informal and formal economies are intrinsically linked, what is needed is an appropriate policy response that promotes more equitable linkages between the informal and formal economies and that balances the relative costs and benefits of working formally and informally. While the focus here is on the role of government, there is a role for all stakeholders, including for formal firms in promoting socially responsible corporate practices and for organizations of informal workers in policy making.

Reflecting the schools of thought outlined above, policymakers have taken differing stances on the informal economy: some view informal workers as a nuisance to be eliminated or regulated; others see them as a vulnerable group to be assisted through social policies; still others see them as entrepreneurs to be freed from government regulations. Another perspective sees the informal workforce as comprising unprotected producers and workers who need to be covered by labour legislation. Subscribing to one or another of these, policymakers have tended to over-react to the informal economy, trying to discourage it altogether, to treat it as a social problem or to promote it as a solution to economic stagnation.

But at the core of the debate on the informal economy is the oft-repeated and greatly misunderstood question of whether to 'formalize' the informal economy. However, it is not clear what is meant by 'formalization'. To many policymakers, formalization means that informal enterprises should obtain a license, register their accounts, and pay taxes. But to the self-employed these represent the costs of entry into the formal economy. What they would like is to receive the benefits of operating formally in return for paying these costs, including: enforceable commercial contracts; legal ownership of their place of business and means of production; tax breaks and incentive packages to increase their competitiveness; membership in trade associations; and statutory social protection. But what about informal wage workers? To them, formalization means obtaining a formal wage job – or converting their current job into a formal job – with secure contract, worker benefits, and social protection.

Taking into account the different meanings of formalization, the feasibility of formalizing the informal economy is unclear. First, most bureaucracies would not be able to handle the volume of license applications and tax forms if all informal businesses formalized. Second, most bureaucracies would claim that they cannot afford to offer informal businesses the incentives and benefits that formal businesses receive. Third, recent trends suggest that employment growth is not keeping pace with the demand for jobs – there simply are not enough jobs to go around, especially given the very sharp rise in the proportion of people who are of working age in many countries. Finally, available evidence suggests that employers are more inclined to convert formal jobs into informal jobs – rather than the other way around.

The formalization debate should be turned on its head by recognizing, first, that formalization has different meanings for different segments of the informal economy and, second, that it is unlikely that most informal producers and workers can be formalized – although efforts should be made to do so. Further, the formalization debate needs to take into account the benefits due to informal enterprises if they operate formally and to wage workers if they get a formal job; and the costs of working informally for both the self-employed and the wage employed. The policy challenge is to decrease the costs of working informally and to increase the benefits of working formally.

NOTES

[1] Those temporary and part-time workers who are covered by labour legislation and statutory social protection benefits are *not* included in the informal economy.

[2] For a detailed analysis of available statistics on the gender segmentation of the informal economy and the linkages between working in the informal economy, being a woman or man, and being poor, see Chen and others (2004).

[3] This section draws from an ILO statistical booklet prepared by Martha Chen and Joann Vanek that includes data compiled by Jacques Charmes for anywhere from 25-70 countries, depending on the specific estimate, as well as case studies for India, Mexico, South Africa and OECD countries (ILO 2002). Data available since 2002 were supplied by Jacques Charmes.

[4] Liberalization of labour markets implies (a) wage flexibility, (b) flexibility in contractual arrangements, and (c) limited regulation in terms of the conditions under which labour is exchanged. It should be noted that international labour mobility is often excluded from discussions of labour market flexibility.

REFERENCES

Bhowmik, S. (2004). Survey of research on street vendors in Asia. Processed, Women in Informal Employment: Globalizing and Organizing (WIEGO), Cambridge, MA.

Chen, M.A., J. Vanek and M. Carr (2004). *Mainstreaming Informal Employment and Gender in Poverty Reduction: A Handbook for Policy-Makers and Other Stakeholders.* Commonwealth Secretariat, London.

Chen, M.A., J. Vanek, F. Lund, J. Heintz with R. Jhabvala and C. Bonner (2005). *Progress of the World's Women 2005: Women, Work, and Poverty.* United Nations Development Fund for Women (UNIFEM), New York.

Crowell, D.W. (2003). *The SEWA Movement and Rural Development: The Banaskantha and Kutch Experience.* Sage Publications, New Delhi.

de Soto, Hernando (1989). *The Other Path: The Economic Answer to Terrorism.* Harper Collins, New York.

de Soto, Hernando (2000). *The Mystery of Capital: Why Capitalism Triumphs in the West and Fails Everywhere Else.* Basic Books, New York.

ILO (2003). *Scope of the Employment Relationship: Report IV, International Labour Conference, 91st Session.* International Labour Office, Geneva.

Mitullah, W. (2004). A review of street trade in Africa. Processed, Women in Informal Employment: Globalizing and Organizing (WIEGO), Cambridge, MA.

Moser, C.N. (1978). Informal sector or petty commodity production: Dualism or independence in urban development. *World Development* 6: 1041-1064.

Piore, Michael, and Charles Sabel (1984). *The Second Industrial Divide*. Basic Books, New York.

Portes, Alejandro, Manuel Castells and L.A. Benton (eds) (1989). *The Informal Economy: Studies in Advanced and Less Developed Countries*. Johns Hopkins University Press, Baltimore.

Sethuraman, S.V. (1976). The urban informal sector: Concept, measurement and policy. *International Labour Review* 114 (1): 69-81.

Tokman, V. E. (1978). An exploration into the nature of the informal-formal sector relationship. *World Development* 6 (9/10): 1065-1075.

11
Modernizing the Informal Sector

VICTOR E. TOKMAN*

There is general agreement over the need to pay attention to the informal sector because of its importance to employment and poverty issues. There are also an increasing number of programmes aimed at supporting similar informal activities in highly diverse national contexts. This consensus is backed through the adoption, at the highest level, of policy measures that are meeting with growing acceptance and, sometimes, the active support of social actors, in particular among entrepreneurial and trade union organizations. Such a stand is also based on evidence to the effect that policies to promote the informal sector are viable and profitable, even during economic downswings, and have international financial support.

Nevertheless, to the extent that it fails to embrace a shared strategic vision, this is a limited consensus that hinders the effectiveness of policies implemented in this area. While often adequate on an individual basis, they are insufficient and produce limited effects by failing to respond to a more comprehensive approach.

The lack of a shared approach is related to the absence of a common definition of the informal sector, which has grown increasingly complex since it was first described in a pioneering ILO report on Kenya in 1972. Along with the heterogeneous nature of informal economic activities, different perceptions lead to different strategies. These are reviewed in the first section. Too great an emphasis on the regulatory perspective has identified informality with illegality and labour precariousness. In spite of their ties to informality, however, the two categories are conceptually different. The second section is devoted to these subjects and, particularly, to the precariousness of the employment relationship. Lastly, the third section explores strategic options to regulate the informal sector, tracing the features of a different approach to formalizing informal activities, to facilitate their full integration in the modernization process. For the purpose of this chapter, the latter concept is defined as the most dynamic part of the economy operating under a common regulatory framework.

FACTS AND CONCEPTS

Interpretations and Trends

The notion of the informal sector was brought forward in a 1972 ILO report on Kenya (ILO, 1972), following a 1971 paper (Hart, 1973). They highlighted that the problem of employment in less-developed countries is not one of unemployment but rather of employed workers who do not earn enough money to make a living. They are 'working poor'. This conceptual interpretation was based on their opposition to formality and their lack of access to the market and productive resources.

This was followed by several contributions (see Tokman, 1978). One perspective is guided by the logic of survival. Informal sector activities are the result of pressure exerted by a labour surplus for jobs, when good jobs, usually in the modern sectors, are scarce. The result is that people seek low-productivity, low-income solutions by producing or selling anything that may provide for their survival.

Another rationale associated with globalization and changes in the international division of labour, points to productive decentralization (Portes, Castells and Benton, 1989). To deal with an increasingly unstable demand, modern enterprises adapt to the new environment by introducing more flexible productive systems and decentralizing productive and labour processes, which allow them to cut production costs and to externalize demand fluctuation.

Other research efforts attach growing importance to the informal sector's operation beyond the prevailing legal and institutional frameworks (de Soto, 1986). However, the issue of whether this feature is the cause or the consequence of informal activities has not yet been settled. An even more recent evolution in the concept placing the emphasis on the employment relationship has led the ILO (2002) to extend informality from the sector to the overall economy.

Efforts to explain the informal sector have shifted focus throughout the years. The logic of survival has also been, and continues to be, a major factor in the development of informal activities. There is a growing presence of new activities generated by the logic of decentralization, particularly in a context of rapid economic opening, and the extra-regulatory behaviour has become an important aspect for analysis and policy. The increase in precarious labour, partly promoted by labour reforms, is also a major factor in the ongoing discussion.

Independent of the interpretation adopted, the characteristics of the informal sector are similar: small, unsophisticated technologies, low capital requirements per worker, and a distinction between micro- and large-sized enterprises in terms of capital requirements. Additional features include limited sharing of the property of the means of production, and a majority of waged workers labouring without contracts and protection.

The importance of the informal sector as a source of new jobs is unmistakable. By 2003, this sector was providing about half of total urban employment[1]. Moreover, its share in the labour market continued to grow steadily. Out of every 100 new jobs created since 1980, around 60 have been informal ones. The current process of growing informality is undergoing a transformation in that micro-enterprises are showing the highest rate of growth. An increasing number of these enterprises are becoming a valid job-creation option regarding income, although they are still far from offering acceptable conditions in terms of job stability and labour and social protections.

The growing importance of informality in the 1980s is clear and marks a break with the three preceding decades. Between 1950 and 1980, approximately four out of every ten new jobs were created by the informal sector; i.e., the equivalent of two thirds of its contribution during the adjustment. This behaviour was determined by two factors: the withdrawal of the public sector as a net employer, and downsizing measures implemented by large-sized enterprises. The public sector conducted its own adjustment process, as part of policies aimed at reducing the fiscal deficit and promoting privatization. Meanwhile, large-sized enterprises dealt with the economic opening by increasing productivity, basically at the expense of employment.

Public employment decreased in relative and, in some countries, even in absolute terms. During the 1990s there was some recovery, but only 15 out of every 100 new jobs were generated by large-sized enterprises, that is, one third of their contribution before the adjustment process. In fact, the rapidly expanding segment of micro-enterprises arose from the need to provide the jobs that large-sized enterprises failed to create (Figure 11.1).

In addition, subcontracting and decentralization of production and work processes to reduce costs contributed to the enlargement of the informal sector at the expense of labour protection.

FIGURE 11.1
Latin America: Employment generation by sector, 1950–2000 (Origin by sector of each 10 new jobs)

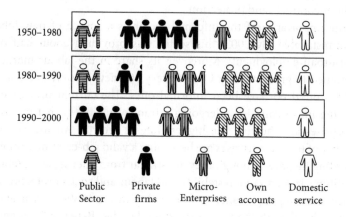

Source: Tokman, V.E. (2001b)

Alternative Strategies

The interpretations discussed above suggest different strategic courses of action. The main approach of this chapter is to seek ways and means to incorporate the informal sector into the process of modernization that to varying degrees is currently underway in Latin America; this is an alternative way of designing a survival support strategy, conceived as a policy to fight poverty with a welfare bias. While the informal sector embraces survival activities that have no chance of converging with the mainstream of a country's economy, it also includes a large number of activities whose growth is dependent on the ability to incorporate them fully into the overall economic system.

This important objective would help to turn support for the informal sector into a source of self-sustained growth behaviour no longer tied to permanent governmental support. On the other hand, an equally important objective such as poverty alleviation through the support of survival strategies that do not promote income expansion tends to perpetuate inequality and segmentation. Emphasis should, therefore, be placed on moving towards integration. By doing so, the orientation of a variety of institutions created to support informal activities could also be clarified. Presently, these agencies are torn between welfare interventions and productive initiatives that often lead to conflicting actions and, worse yet, inter-agency strife.

Integration of the informal sector into the process of modernization may be achieved through different but complementary means. Prevailing policies to this effect generally favour a three-pronged approach. The first consists of providing support to foster the productive development of micro-enterprises by facilitating their access to market and productive resources. The tools used more frequently for those purposes are credit programmes, as well as training and promotional programmes to seek access to more dynamic markets by strengthening organizational skills and marketing practices.

The second approach involves the social welfare of informal workers. At this level, policy options tend to get mixed with poverty-alleviation policies. It should be kept in mind, however, that the family unit and the small-scale productive unit always become entangled. Labour and family relations merge in a workshop or small business. Capital goods, such as means of transport, are investment capital, to the extent that they are used for business purposes. However, they are also consumer goods used for private purposes, which renders them family assets too. Resource fungibility makes the absence of social protection an obstacle to good economic performance. In other words, when the uninsured owner–worker gets sick the micro-enterprise collapses. Thus, mutually complementing policies implemented from a social welfare perspective have externalities capable of generating a positive interaction with the productive development of the poor.

Lastly, a third course of action focuses on the regulatory framework. Informal activities are not caused by regulatory inadequacies but rather by the failure of the economic system to create enough productive employment. However, the fact that regulatory improvements favour the integration of informal activities into the modernization process cannot be ignored. This debate has evolved in the last few years, resulting in a substantial narrowing of the gap which had existed between those who argued in favour of the simplistic notion that legislative or procedural changes are enough to overcome the existing problems and those who denied the role of regulatory arrangements relating to the economic system.

While recognizing the relevance of the first two courses of action discussed above, this chapter addresses the latter. It attempts to deepen a strategy aimed at altering the regulatory framework in a manner conducive to the integration of the informal sector.

FORMALIZATION AS A MEANS OF INCLUSION

Informality and Illegality

A generally accepted interpretation of the genesis of informal activities is rooted in their operating beyond the prevailing regulatory systems. In other words, these activities do not comply with legal or administrative requirements. A more positive view suggests that exclusion has to do with the lack of access to development policies, in particular to credit programmes, training and the marketplace. This approach to the informal sector emphasizes lawlessness as a feature and tends to deal with it as an area devoted to underground activities.

Actual conditions in the marketplace are not as unequivocal as it would appear. The informal sector is not a 'black market' operation, and the modern sector is not as law-abiding as could be expected – grey areas prevail, as it were. Informal activities were previously described as the result of limited compliance with legal and procedural requirements, going from complete illegality to full compliance

(Tokman, 1992; Tokman and Klein, 1996). What prevails, however, is a middle ground where certain registration prerequisites are met, while tax obligations are neglected and haphazard compliance with labour law is commonplace. This situation is also found in modern activities, particularly in countries where fiscal discipline is poor and inspection capabilities are limited. Obviously, total illegality is non-existent, but limited legality is significant.

FIGURE 11.2
Informality and illegality (per cent of informal units by levels of illegality)

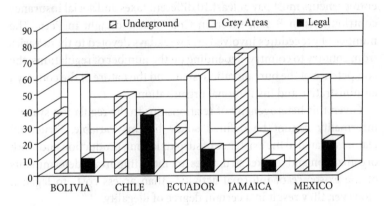

Source: Tokman, V.E. and E. Klein (1996) and Tokman V.E. (1992)

On the other hand, data on the informal sector around 1997 show that micro-enterprises making limited contributions to finance labour benefits reached 65 per cent in Peru (only 6.4 per cent was in full compliance, while 28.6 per cent failed to make any payments), 70 per cent in Brazil and 57 per cent in Chile (Tokman, 2001b). The proportion of micro-enterprises that paid some taxes is significantly higher: 94 per cent in Peru in 1996; in Chile, where some 70 per cent of the micro-enterprises employing five or less workers, and 96 per cent of those employing five or more workers, paid income tax and value added tax (VAT) in 1990; in Ecuador, where 78 per cent of small micro-enterprises and 94 per cent of larger micro-enterprises paid income tax, while 54 per cent and 81 per cent respectively paid

VAT. Moreover, close to 80 per cent of Ecuadorian micro-enterprises paid some municipal taxes. However, a significant proportion of the micro-enterprises operating in all these countries, and a majority in some of them, failed to comply fully with labour and tax laws.

ILO research also confirmed the high cost of formality. To bring a micro-enterprise in line with regulations, micro-entrepreneurs must go through a number of different administrative procedures: at least 11 are required in Brazil, nine in Peru, six in Colombia, and four in Chile. Obviously, each of these procedures, such as applying for a licence to start a business or requesting sanitary clearance, entails a large amount of paperwork and bureaucracy. In addition, micro-entrepreneurs must pay at least 10 different taxes and social insurance contributions in Brazil, seven in Colombia and eight in Peru. The number of procedures involved and weekdays devoted to them varies from country to country, depending on the number of regulations, the competence of the bureaucratic system and the nature of the country's administrative and institutional organization.

Given this heterogeneity of relationships to the regulation system, informality cannot be defined solely by this variable. Structural features related to the existence of surplus labour, production and work organization and market structures are more important determinants of the existence of informal activities than access costs to legality. However, they result in a certain degree of illegality.

Informality and Labour Precariousness

Labour relations have become more precarious since the mid 1980s. This results not only from a transformation in the employment structure, but also from the introduction of labour reforms in search of more flexible employment relationships, to gain the competitiveness required to operate in a more open national and world economy. They were geared to gain efficiency, without taking due account of the costs involved in terms of the effects on labour and social protection. These reforms constituted a second generation in the economic reforms package. They were justified by a diagnosis of the existence of too much rigidity in the labour market. In addition, a decentralization process resulted in increased interrelationships between enterprises of different sizes.

The main modality adopted by the labour reforms was the introduction of atypical labour contracts of a different nature, but possessing more flexibility than the indefinite-term contract with full protection that constituted the predominant contract. This was consistent with the objective of job stability. Promotional labour contracts of different sorts were introduced, such as fixed-term, temporary and part-time contracts, as well as contracts specifically tailored to youths, women and unemployed head of households, among others. In some cases, like Peru, in addition to the introduction of these new contracts, the externalization of the labour process was promoted by allowing the creation of workers' cooperatives or 'services' to supply labour to enterprises. These new contractual forms provide less stability and allow for employment adjustments by firings in an easier and less costly manner in relation to the previous contracts. In some cases, though not in the majority, the atypical contracts are exempted, partially or entirely, from honouring some labour obligations.

The scarce and fragmented data available shows the importance and expansion of workers under atypical contracts and those without any contract. The growth of these contracts is clear during the first half of the 1990s and, although the data is not entirely comparable, it shows that the process continued in Peru, where workers without contracts or with atypical contracts reached 74 per cent by 2000, and in Chile, where the percentage reached 45 per cent. By 2002, on average for 11 countries with information from household surveys, workers without contracts amounted to 47 per cent, while those with contracts that are not for an indefinite term reached 21 per cent (Tokman, 2006).

The legal and explicit recognition of the employment relationship is crucial because it constitutes a prerequisite for the recognition of the rights to labour and social protection. Recent data on coverage of pensions show that workers with written contracts are covered six times more than those without contracts. Furthermore, waged workers in micro-enterprises moving to a formal enterprise of larger size increase their probability of being covered by pensions from 24 to 66 per cent (Tokman, 2006).

The result has been that, together with labour contracts diversification, there has been an increase in workers without any contract. The latter situation does not recognize any legal obligation, while the former, in some cases, diminishes or dilutes the level of obligation but maintains its legality. This is partly the consequence of the failures in labour legislation to adapt to new forms adopted by the labour relationship, and partly because of the weakness of labour inspection in most countries. It could also be the reading of employers of the signs of flexibility associated with the labour reform discourse, which had underlined the rigidities, accompanied by permissiveness of inspection in a weak labour institutional environment. Beyond flexibilization, the discourse and the reforms transmitted a message, willingly or not, of deregulation.

Thus, undeclared and precarious work, usually associated with informality, builds up in the labour market. Informality, illegality and precariousness have become synonymous. Unprotected and precarious labour is not only found in the informal sector but also in formal enterprises or in production chains, introduced to reduce costs and gain flexibility. This led the ILO to widen the informal sector concept, introduced at the beginning of the 1970s, incorporating a new concept: the informal economy. The latter includes the informal sector, but adds all the workers occupied, directly or indirectly, by formal enterprises.

The International Conference on Labour Statistics held in 1991 agreed to define the informal sector to identify its contribution to the GNP, usually omitted from national accounts. It was agreed that the sector should be defined according to the characteristics of the productive units that perform these activities (entrepreneurial approach), rather than by the characteristics of the persons involved or their occupational position (labour approach). This was consistent with the concept of the informal sector introduced by the ILO in 1972. The new concept, as approved by the International Labour Conference in 2002 (ILO, 2002) – considering that the former approach does not capture all dimensions of informal employment – recommends that workers should be classified as formal or informal according to their labour status. It does not propose to eliminate the concept of the informal sector but rather to extend it to the informal economy.

In this connection, work posts were selected as the unit of analysis and added to the unit of production previously considered informal.

The main innovation is the inclusion as informal of all workers, independently of where they work, whose employment relationship is not subject to labour legislation standards, taxes, social protection and other labour benefits (vacations, sick leave, firing indemnity, etc.). This mostly means the addition to the informal sector of all unprotected labour working in enterprises of more than five workers. Statistically, the urban informal economy implied an expansion of the informal sector from 46 to 57 per cent in Mexico and from 31 to 36 per cent in Chile, around 2003.[2]

The use of atypical contractual arrangements in formal enterprises is a regular practice and results in a reduction of labour protection. This trend does not necessarily denote informality, however, but rather the application of new labour laws or ambiguous labour legislation, or simply law evasion. The loss of protection since the 1990s can be significant, as suggested by differences in pensions coverage: In 2002, 86 per cent of workers with indefinite term contracts were covered, compared to only 57 per cent of those under other types of contracts (Tokman, 2006).

The ILO, consistent with the recognition of a significant and increasing use of unprotected labour, has promoted the adoption of new international labour instruments (conventions and recommendations) aiming at protecting working rights. A proposal for a new labour standard failed to pass in 1998, and ILO was asked to analyze in depth the nature of the employment relationships. The process finished at the recent International Labour Conference held in June 2006, with a recommendation that advises governments to "effectively establish the existence of an employment relationship", to "combat disguised employment relationships", "to ensure standards applicable to all forms of contractual arrangements including those involving multiple parties" and "to establish who is responsible for the protection contained". The adopted recommendation did not receive, however, the full support of the ILO constituency, denoting that the substantive discussion about the potential existence of trade-offs between employment and protection is not yet settled.[3]

While the effort made to advance the clarification of the employment relationship aiming at a review of the labour regulations to ensure protection should be appreciated, its contribution to dealing with informality is not obvious. A first conceptual observation refers to the combination of two units of analysis, unit of production and work post, and their relationship with access to labour and social protection. In fact, the latter is made in a partial manner since those working in the informal sector are, by default, considered as unprotected labour. This does not reflect the prevailing situation as informality cannot be taken as synonymous with unprotected labour because some workers in the informal sector do have access to protection. In 2002, 18 per cent of those persons occupied in the informal sector had coverage for old age pensions. There are differences within them as only 6 per cent of the self-employed are covered, compared to 22 per cent of workers in micro-enterprises.[4]

However, for the majority of those employed in the informal sector the lack of access to labour and social protections is the result of the informal nature of small-scale economic activities. Only in micro-enterprises do these concepts tend to represent a single phenomenon of informality. As can be seen in Figure 11.3, more than 90 per cent of workers in micro-enterprises in Mexico and Peru are without written contracts, or are in precarious contracts; the percentage is 87 per cent in Ecuador; and, even in a more formalized country like Chile, it reaches 56 per cent. The concentration of self-employment, undeclared and precarious labour in the informal sector results in lower protection. Only 18 per cent of those employed are covered by social security, compared to 68 per cent of coverage in the formal sector.

The starting point for integration into the regulatory system is the inability of informal entrepreneurs to comply with the requirements and to shoulder the cost involved in becoming formal. A study conducted in Peru (Tokman, 2001b) estimated that only 35 per cent of the micro-enterprises employing five or less workers and 60 per cent of those employing between six and ten workers could comply with the whole package of social insurance contributions. It was also estimated that full compliance would represent over a 50 per cent cut in the profits of 75 per cent of these enterprises. The proportion of compliant micro-enterprises would significantly drop under 35 per cent, however, if the burden of complying with income and other taxes were to be added. For this group the trade-off is not only one of employment and protection but rather one of employment and public welfare.

FIGURE 11.3
Precarious and undeclared labour in micro-enterprises

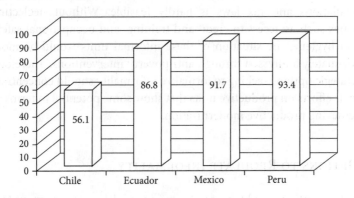

Source: Tokman, V.E. and D. Martinez (1999).

Apart from considering the conceptual differences, it is also important to deepen strategic options to integrate the informal sector into the regulatory system as a means of achieving fuller participation in the modernization process. The starting point is recognition of the inability of informal entrepreneurs to comply with legal requirements and to shoulder the costs of becoming formal. Regardless of the various factors involved, this situation shows an unbalanced relationship between requirements and possibilities, and calls for a different approach if the goal is to advance the formalization process as a tool to achieve integration in the modern sector.

Given the existence of grey areas and segmentation within the informal sector, the question arises as to whether a differentiated set of regulations responding to the specific characteristics and capabilities of this economic sector and its different segments should apply. Before dealing with this issue and undertaking the design of strategic options to regulate informality, the chances of each informal segment accomplishing a successful process of modernization should be assessed.

Available empirical evidence about productivity and income in the segment of productive units that respond to survival strategies shows that they would accomplish very little through productive modernization. Most of them are family units in which regular labour relations have no place, and which operate at such low levels of productivity and income that compliance with administrative regulations and tax laws is hardly feasible. Without neglecting issues such as access to credit and training, and occupational safety and hygiene, the situation of these informal units would be more adequately addressed through anti-poverty interventions. Therefore, strategic options seeking to formalize informality should concentrate their efforts on productive units that show some potential in terms of achieving productive modernization.

Options to Regulate Informality

A first option would be to design an ad hoc regulatory system different from existing regulatory schemes that apply to activities and individuals occupied in more organized sectors. This would involve the adoption of dual or preferential regimes. This approach is opposed on fiscal, commercial and, above all, on labour grounds. Distinctions sanctioned by law hamper fiscal oversight both with regard to micro-enterprises and large-sized enterprises, by causing 'sliding' for tax evasion purposes (Revilla, 1999). Furthermore, limitations imbedded in special regimes often become obstacles to the growth of the micro-enterprises involved. In the labour field, the implementation of preferential schemes would entail that, depending on the size of the enterprises, workers would no longer be treated equally before the law. Therefore, for reasons that mainly take into account the labour dimension of this issue, a single system would be preferable, even acknowledging that full compliance with existing legal requirements is impossible, at least during a transition period (ILO, 1991).

It should be emphasized that the preference for single systems has to do with special comprehensive regimes, but it does not exclude the implementation of de facto differential tax procedures, such as a non-taxable basic income, simplified tax declarations or tax estimations based on presumptive income, nor does it exclude either the implementation of credit programmes at preferential interest rates. Even objections raised regarding labour issues depend on the nature of the affected rights. For instance, it is generally acceptable to introduce a distinction in collective bargaining to best address the peculiarities of small productive units.

The single regime proposition also generates a variety of options open to the implementation of different policies. The first one argues that to accept a de facto dual situation without enforcing penalties entails a certain degree of tolerance, as well as the adoption of a different promotional rationale for the informal sector while other economic sectors are being penalized. This is one of the courses of action usually followed in the field of labour rights, where legal requirements become goals and progress towards greater compliance is an area subject to monitoring and oversight. All this should be qualified by the respect due to certain fundamental labour rights whose enforcement is required, regardless of the nature of the activity or labour relationship involved, to the extent that these are labour-related human rights, notably, freedom of association and collective bargaining, forced labour, non-discrimination and eradication of child labour. This option may be described as a "single regime with qualified tolerance and a minimum floor"[5].

A second, non-exclusionary, strategic option consists in adapting formalization requirements to bring them closer to the capabilities of informal entrepreneurs, insofar as the costs of formality and formalization procedures and machinery are concerned.

The cost of legalizing informal activities may be cut down, without affecting the 'single regime' perspective, provided that the reduction is universal. This is the current stand in the labour field, where the flexibility and reduction of non-salary labour costs sought by the modern sectors to improve competitiveness should also lead to the abatement of obstacles to the integration of informal activities. The same thing may take place in the fiscal area because of reduced taxation or increased emphasis on informal activities. Unlike current trends in the labour area, present tendencies in the fiscal area go in the opposite direction, as expanding tax collection becomes a major priority and taxation increasingly relies on VAT.

Simplifying bureaucratic procedures is another way of bringing down access barriers. Numerous measures have been adopted to implement simplified registration regimes, both in terms of unifying registries and administrative steps towards compliance. Current trends point to the implementation of a single-registry, single-window regime. This approach would minimize the cost of formalization, but its feasibility has not yet been tried. Creating a single authority would facilitate the dissemination of information and avoid overlapping and contradictory regulations, administrative procedures and oversight efforts. However, this field is littered with obstacles, from bureaucratic vested interests to technical demands raised by oversight and enforcement actions. This situation may present the opportunity in some fields of combining interventions by institutions with different objectives to follow a unified procedure. The cost involved for the micro-entrepreneurs would be less than in the present multiple agency inspections.

Lastly, there is room for action regarding the mechanisms for formalization. An increasingly popular device, first suggested by de Soto (1995), is the recognition of property titles as a mechanism to have access to credit. The proposed innovation seeks to simplify the release of a legal property title and to adapt it to prevalent conditions of de facto ownership. This course entails disregarding contractual prerequisites and providing proof of property using alternative means of recognition, such as long-term usufruct, calling on witnesses (preferably neighbours when housing or land are involved) and having boundaries recognized by third parties when there are conflicts of interest. Thus, entitlement responds to a major obstacle to having access to credit, since collateral requirements, which usually involve assets, represent a further hurdle to a sector where 'property' is not formalized.

An additional formalization tool, which could be modified for the same purpose, is the recognition of labour relationships. In Peru, for instance, 90 per cent of labour contracts in informal activities are not written, although this is an indispensable prerequisite to have access to the benefits of employment promotion laws. Nevertheless, a verbal contract entered into by mutual agreement could be accepted as an alternative, without having to stretch the existing regulations. A note in the employer's monthly book may provide proof of the labour relationship, by calling witnesses to attest to it or to the performance of a regular work schedule, or by showing proof that salaries have been paid. All of this would help to 'formalize' the labour relationship, as a first step to entering into regulated relations.

Street vendors deserve special treatment through the implementation of a strategy capable of reconciling the public's right to enjoy public spaces and the right of street vendors to have a stable, income-generating occupation. While these activities must be regulated within a single legal, fiscal and labour framework, the relevant formalization and modernization strategy must also take into account the peculiarities of this sector. First, access to land through ownership or leasing, for the purpose of setting up commercial activities in compliance with municipal regulations; secondly, rendering the supply of available urban land compatible with the public transportation system, to provide the public with adequate access to shopping areas; thirdly, encouraging street vendors to organize both at the market level and also at a higher level, to improve the rate of return of their investment by developing economies of scale.

The separation of assets between the individual and the entrepreneur (also a very important step to micro-entrepreneurs), is usually conducted by creating firms of a diverse legal nature and diverse degrees of complexity. Requirements associated with this simple but crucial change to the patrimonial responsibility of micro-entrepreneurs entail a monetary cost, as well as compliance with a series of regulations that render this enfranchising step towards formality a difficult one. This process could be simplified by conferring legal status to the entrepreneur along with the business licence (Fuentes, 1997).

From Informality to Economic Citizenship

Previously discussed options lead to a different vision of formalization as a tool to ease the integration of informal activities in the modernization process. The extension of formalization is not warranted from the point of view of the organized sectors; rather, for the benefits that access to formality may bring about to foster the development of informal activities and the people occupied in this economic sector.

Oversight campaigns targeting informal activities are often justified by the need to widen the tax base, cut down evasion and punish illegality. While these are important objectives per se, it is also well known that these campaigns usually do not yield the expected results. (According to SUNAT, every additional sol collected in Peru entails an administrative cost of 0.75.) Actually, the importance of the integration of an informal activity as a tax-paying entity is that its first consequence consists in meeting a basic business requirement, such as producing accounting information. If the entrepreneur fails to do so he is deprived of a key tool of modern management, a requirement to achieve full economic citizenship.

The same happens with the recognition of labour contracts, an area where the goal should not be so much to punish illegality as to create citizens who are ready as workers to gain access to labour protection, or embrace the logic of business, as would be the case of micro-entrepreneurs who have to adapt to formal labour relationships. Having to respect certain labour rules is conducive to more modern management standards.

A similar argument may be advanced regarding the recognition of ownership titles for the purpose of gaining access to credit or to a patrimonial division between the individual and the business, brought about by receiving the legal right to subscribe contracts. As far as street vendors are concerned, stopping police harassment and assuring a stable and lawful place of business reduces the cost of informality and may also provide access to new markets and productive resources.

Micro-enterprises present a paradox. Large enterprises are shifting strategies to improve competitiveness and increase productivity by adopting more flexible productive systems to smooth supply-side fluctuations, producing goods upon request and getting closer to customers before and after delivering the goods. This is the kind of approach traditionally followed by small businesses. A new opportunity is therefore opening up.

To take advantage of it, however, micro-entrepreneurs must radically alter their behaviour by going through a process of cultural change. They must move from individualistic ways of doing business, driven by the imperative of succeeding by any means in an extremely competitive environment, to a culture that seeks the benefits of pooling productive resources and associating with other producers in an effort to gain access to the marketplace. Previous ways of relating to customers should change too, and new forms of communicating with different actors should be explored. From working on an individual basis and being barred from credit in an environment in which he or she usually entertains a personal relationship with customers, the entrepreneur must start producing for a market in which customers are faceless, request good quality, expect timely services and expect professionalism. The informal sector operates in flexible ways but it is culturally unprepared to produce for demanding markets.

In order to have access to credit, informal micro-entrepreneurs must undergo a cultural change that involves establishing and nurturing relationships within the banking system. Likewise, dealing with state institutions requires learning to take advantage of existing programmes designed to assist entrepreneurs, and not being intimated by ministerial and other public authorities. They must also get acquainted with the ways and means of collective representation, when securing benefits and concessions is the result of social efforts. Usually, micro-entrepreneurs or their workers do not join business or trade union organizations. After all, it was not so long ago that these organizations stopped seeing them both as disloyal competitors, and started to make efforts to integrate them and accommodate their concerns, mainly as a result of a quest for greater representation.

The present proposal is indeed addressed to the ongoing cultural change. It seeks to foster new attitudes and behaviour to favour the development of the micro-enterprises and of those who labour in them in an environment more conducive to success. Formalization may be the gateway to full economic citizenship as a prerequisite to competition in the marketplace. It entails rights as well as duties. The proposed views alter previous priorities. Rights should be emphasized over duties, because the former are tools for development and progress. Enfranchisement may inspire 'virtuous circles' leading to the expansion of the regulatory framework and to the creation of new conditions to allow citizens to comply with their duties, while also benefiting from them. Such a context would provide incentives to turn informal businesses into the main force behind formalization efforts.

Lastly, the present strategy faces at least two limitations that it is unlikely to overcome on its own. The first one is represented by a segment of survival activities that would gain very little from formalization. The second is that the effects of formalization will not come automatically and may become insufficient to integrate informal activities into the modernization process. Therefore, complementary measures should be taken to secure the benefits of enfranchisement. Entitlement requires financial institutions to make adjustments to acknowledge the value of property. To have access to safe places of business of their own, street vendors need marketplace support, credit and advice. The recognition of legal status as a corporate, labour and fiscal subject must go along with educational efforts to learn to take advantage of administrative and productivity accounting books, patrimonial division and more formal labour relationships. Special machinery and financing may also be necessary to facilitate the transition period.

NOTES

[1] This chapter builds on several earlier papers (Tokman, 2001a and 2001b). It updates the conceptual discussion and facts about informality.

[2] The informal sector is defined as including the self-employed with less than 13 years of education, unpaid family members, employees and employers in establishments of less than five employees and domestic servants (Tokman, 2004).

[3] This estimate refers only to the urban informal economy. If informality in rural areas is included, as suggested by the ILO in 2002, the increase is from 57 to 65 per cent in Mexico.

[4] The employers in the ILO, on the basis of the need for further analysis on the subject in 1998, obtained a postponement and the commitment of the secretariat to undertake further studies and to resubmit it in 2003 for a general discussion. However, in 2006, they still voted against the adoption of the recommendation on this subject.

[5] A special case in the differentiation of the informal economy and sector are home workers, mostly women, who are included in the informal sector because of their unit of production characteristics. But if their work results in a product or service as specified by the employer, and unless this person has the degree of autonomy and economic independence necessary, it should be considered as a decentralized labour relationship and treated similarly to other wage earners, taking into account the special characteristics

of home work. This entitles them to the right of association in an organization of their own choosing and of labour protection. The responsibility for complying with this obligation should be shared between employers and intermediaries, if they exist. The situation of home workers is guided by the ILO Convention 177 of 1996. Unfortunately, up to 2005, only four countries have ratified this Convention (Albania, Finland, Ireland and Netherlands).

6   The recent experience in the negotiations of the Free Trade Agreements between several Latin American countries and the United States of America has expanded this minimum floor, contained in the ILO Declaration of 1998, by adding working conditions (minimum wages, health and safety and hours of work) to discipline, including trade sanctions.

REFERENCES

de Soto, Hernando (1986). *El otro sendero: La revolución informal.* Instituto Libertad y Democracia, Lima.

de Soto, Hernando (1995). Por qué importa la economía informal? In V.E. Tokman (ed.). *El sector informal en América Latina: Dos décadas de análisis.* Consejo Nacional para la Cultura y las Artes, México: 275–86.

Fuentes, S. (1997). ¿Como formalizar a los informales? In E. Chávez, A.M. Yañez, C. Luna, R. De la Flor, S. Fuentes, M. Robles (eds). *Perú: El sector informal frente al reto de la modernización.* International Labour Office, Lima: 274–63.

Hart, K. (1973). Informal income opportunities and urban employment in Ghana. *Journal of Modern African Studies* 11 (1): 61–89.

ILO (1972). *Employment, Income and Equality: A Strategy for Increasing Productive Employment in Kenya.* International Labour Office, Geneva.

ILO (1991). *Dilemma of the Informal Sector.* Report of the Director-General presented at the 78th International Labour Conference, International Labour Office, Geneva.

ILO (2002). *Decent Work and the Informal Economy.* Report of the Director-General presented to the 90th International Labour Conference, International Labour Office, Geneva.

Tokman, V.E. and Martinez, D. (1999). *Flexibilización en el márgen: la reforma del contrato de trabajo,* in Martinez, D and Tokman, V.E. (eds)1999. *Efectos de las reformas laborales: entre el empleo y la desprotección,* Chapter 1, International Labour Office, Lima.

Portes, Alejandro, Manuel Castells, and L.A. Benton (1989). *The Informal Economy: Studies in Advanced and Less Developed Countries.* The Johns Hopkins University Press, Baltimore.

Revilla, A. (1999). La modernización del sector informal y las cargas tributarias y administrativas a las empresas en el Perú. Documento de Trabajo 92, International Labour Office, Lima.

Tokman, V.E. (1978). An exploration into the nature of informal-formal sector relationships. *World Development* 6: 1065–1075.

Tokman, V.E. (1992). *Beyond Regulation: The Informal Sector in Latin America.* Lynne Rienner Publishers, Boulder.

Tokman, V.E. (2001a). Integrating the informal sector into the modernization process. *SAIS Review* 21 (1): 45–60.

Tokman, V.E. (2001b). *De la informalidad a la modernidad*. International Labour Office, Santiago.

Tokman, V.E. (2004). Las dimensiones laborales de la transformación productiva con equidad. Serie Financiamiento del Desarrollo 150, CEPAL, Santiago.

Tokman, V.E. (2006). Inserción laboral, mercados de trabajo y protección social. Serie Financiamiento del Desarrollo 170, CEPAL, Santiago.

Tokman, V.E., and E. Klein (eds) (1996). *Regulation and the Informal Economy: Micro-enterprises in Chile, Ecuador and Jamaica*. Lynne Rienner Publishers, Boulder.

12
Changing the Paradigm in Social Security: From Fiscal Burden to Investing in People

MICHAEL CICHON, KRZYSZTOF HAGEMEJER,
JOHN WOODALL

Since the mid-1980s, national social security systems in many countries have come under pressure from several directions. Social security or social protection systems (also often called the 'welfare state') can be understood as a set of institutions, measures, rights, obligations and transfers whose *primary goals* are to guarantee access to health and social services; and to provide income security to help cope with certain significant risks in life (*inter alia,* loss of income due to invalidity, old age or unemployment) and prevent or alleviate poverty.

From a global legal perspective, social security has been recognized as a right of people. Universally negotiated and accepted legal instruments that describe social security as a fundamental societal right, and grant this right to every human being, include Article 22 of the Universal Declaration of Human Rights and Article 9 of the International Covenant on Economic Social and Cultural Rights. Social security as a human right is an explicit part of the International Labour Office's (ILO) mandate, and is enshrined in a series of ILO Conventions, most prominently the Social Security (Minimum Standards) Convention, 1952 (No. 102), which became the blueprint for the European Code of the Social Security and other regional instruments. Social protection or social security is one of the pivotal pillars of the ILO's Decent Work Agenda (see ILO, 1999). Without social security, people are working and living unprotected, in material insecurity, and without access to health and social services. Without social security, neither work nor lives can be decent.

Many industrialized market economies explicitly accepted the right to social security and developed extensive systems providing various social transfers as an inherent part of the post-World War II environment of high economic growth, but such systems have come under strain in the more recent conditions of reduced growth, which seem likely to continue for the foreseeable future.

The aim of this chapter is to recapitulate the role of social security in economies and societies, to identify new challenges, and to discern the policy responses which will be needed to allow the ILO to assist its member States to optimize their national systems of social security within an overall Decent Work framework.

Social Security for Decent Work and Decent Societies

Social Security Coverage

In the major market economies the historical developmental patterns of social security coverage have mirrored developments in labour markets. Coverage began to increase following the European Industrial Revolution as formal wage and salary employment in industry increased and the workforce migrated from rural areas into towns.

The coverage ratios of public social security systems in the developing world are low. This does not mean that people living there have no access to certain social security arrangements. Traditional modes of social protection, i.e., largely family and community support systems, still cover wide sections of developing country populations. For many decades, it was assumed that the levels and patterns of public vs. private social transfers in the industrialized countries would – with a time lag of perhaps several decades – be achieved in the countries of the developing world. However, for the present, the vast majority of all social transfers in these societies are still done through private informal arrangements, and progress towards greater coverage through public systems remains slow. Between a half and two-thirds of all workers work outside any formal contractual arrangements or registration of economic activity. Moreover, there remain many so-called formal sector workers who lack effective coverage by public social security systems.

Consequently, national social security or social protection systems need to reach out beyond the boundaries of formal contractual employment. Decent working conditions cannot remain a privilege for a few formal sector workers. Many governments try to provide some access to health care or income support to individuals who cannot work or who can only find work in low paying jobs. Some countries have addressed the problem with the provision of 'universal benefits' covering the entire population (e.g., the National Health Service in the United Kingdom or the universal pension schemes in some OECD countries and in some developing countries such as Namibia and Botswana), while others rely on specific measures, possibly administered by non-government organization, for the so-called informal economy (such as micro-insurance schemes in Africa and Asia).

Social Impact

Social security systems providing social transfers are the key instruments for the abolition and prevention of poverty, which are more direct and faster than the 'trickle down' effects of economic growth. The International Financial and Actuarial Service of the ILO conducted a study to estimate the resources needed, at the global level, to address the problem of ongoing poverty in this way. A hypothetical package of minimum social provision was devised for this purpose, comprising basic education, access to basic health care and income transfers in case of need. The results indicate that a mere two per cent of global GDP is needed to provide such a minimum package of benefits to all the world's poor. Most of these resources can be raised nationally, although some transfers (between countries) are needed at the global level to help the poorest countries, with GDP per capita close to or below the global poverty line, cope.

There is clear evidence from Europe and other OECD countries that social transfers have successfully reduced poverty and social insecurity (Cichon and others, 2004: 37–41). Figure 12.1 shows the net estimated effect of public transfers and taxes on poverty rates (as measured by the poverty head count index, perhaps the clearest indicator of income inequality) in OECD countries, i.e., in countries with fairly extensive social transfer systems and well developed tax systems. The effects are nothing less than dramatic. Tax and transfer systems have reduced the risk of poverty by at least about 10 percentage points, the approximate figure for the US and to a high of around 30 percentage points in Sweden.

FIGURE 12.1
Pre-tax-and-transfer vs. post-tax-and-transfer poverty rates in selected OECD countries, 1990s

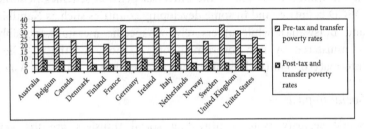

Source: Förster and Pellizari. (2000: Figure 5.1)

It is not possible to draw such clear-cut conclusions in relation to developing countries since the overall volumes of social transfers are comparatively small. However, some basic social protection transfers, such as basic non-contributory pension schemes, have proven to be potent means in the fight against poverty. A variety of countries have introduced universal pension schemes in recent years, and while they have mostly provided benefits at modest levels, their poverty-reducing effects for whole families have been very positive. Benefits are provided for the old and disabled, but in practice, benefits provided for individuals – whose status in their families is often significantly enhanced by their receipt of a cash income – effectively support whole families. Redistribution of cash incomes within the household means that more families become able to finance school fees, medicines, etc. (e.g., HelpAge International, 2004). Positive experiences come from countries as diverse as Brazil, Mauritius, Namibia, Nepal and South Africa. The ILO's International Financial and Actuarial Service has calculated that provision of such a basic package of social transfers in most countries would cost between 1 and 2 per cent of GDP, roughly representing between 5 and 10 per cent of national budgets (Pal and others, 2005). Implementing such a package could represent a first step in a broader attack on deep-rooted and chronic 'pockets' of poverty found in many countries.

Social transfers also have a marked impact on income equality, which is an indicator of social cohesion. Evidence from the Luxembourg Income Study of the mid-1990s (before the recent wave of reforms) shows the combined tax-and-transfer systems in OECD countries reduce income inequality by between 40 and 50 per cent in countries including Belgium, France, Germany and Sweden, and by between 20 and 30 per cent in countries such as Australia, Canada, the United Kingdom and the United States (Ruiz-Huerta, Martinez and Ayala 1999). Prominent observers of inequality in Europe and OECD since the mid-1990s, including Smeeding (2002) and Atkinson (2003), attribute the increasing inequality within societies, as measured by the rising Gini coefficients, to changes in governments' tax and transfer policies. Analysing the impacts of globalization and public policy on income equality, Atkinson (2003: 25) concludes "we must not lose sight of policy. Changes in tax and transfer policy have played a major role in the increasing inequality in a number of countries. To a considerable extent the development of inequality in disposable incomes – what matters to our citizens – lies in our own hands."

One may then ask why the reduction or containment of social expenditure is a pre-occupation of policy makers in many countries around the world. The answer lies in the trade off between economic growth and the extent of national social expenditure, i.e. the belief that social security leads to lower growth and welfare losses; this is critically appraised in the next section.

The Growth vs. Equity Trade-off: A Critique

National social protection systems and their perceived effects on economic performance have been subject to intense policy debates in many countries over recent decades. On the one hand, some experts claim that social systems redistributing up to 35 per cent of a country's GDP are no longer affordable. Social protection expenditure at and beyond this level is seen as an impediment to growth, with negative effects in both the short- and long-term. Others hold the opposite view and consider well managed social protection to be a genuine productive factor. Cichon and others (2004: 121) recently concluded: "Once all the arguments are on the table, the outcome of the theoretical debate on the potential positive versus negative economic effects of the welfare state appears to be a draw." For the policy analyst and the decision-maker, an inconclusive debate is of limited value. However, proof that social transfers have a direct positive impact on growth is not needed for policy formulation. For that purpose it is enough to recognize that substantial levels of social transfers simply and economic growth can co-exist, and that these transfers making the economic growth more equitable serve to strengthen its sustainability.

Global economic growth over recent years has not been translated into an equally fast decline of poverty or social insecurity. At the same time, social insecurity has been increasing in many countries as social protection levels are reduced. Since about the mid-1970s, i.e. after the first oil price crisis, countries with well-established social security systems entered a period of *welfare state containment*. Major welfare states such as Austria, Germany, France, the Netherlands and others, broadly maintained social expenditure even when facing new demands for benefits (e.g. due to increased unemployment), as measured by the percentage allocation of GDP, at the levels reached in the mid-1970s. Contrary to the expected outcome of such policies, growth rates did not increase until the end of the 1990s.

Nevertheless, countries continue to implement policies designed to contain public social expenditure. The reasons for doing so usually concern the fiscal affordability of social security systems – in poor and rich countries alike. This is based, in turn, on the need to keep their taxes and public spending at low levels, so as to be competitive in the global economy (low social security contributions and other low taxes will help to bring in foreign investments and allow exports to remain cheap) and to keep work incentives high. Additional fears are triggered by the expected consequences of ageing on the level of taxes and contributions.

Some believe that too much security, particularly income security, undermines people's incentives to work, be inventive and productive. But the truth is likely to be the opposite: the less secure we feel, the more averse we will be to taking enterpreneurial or economic risk. Studies reveal that poor people are risk averse. Rationally risk-averse individuals will take risks only if the potential loss is relatively small compared to his or her wealth. Wealth provides security, and more can be risked. Social security substitutes wealth for many people. A rational individual will also take additional economic risk if he/she is relatively well protected against other risks he/she has to cope with, like sickness or disability. Those who have no access to relevant protection mechanisms against numerous social risks will tend to avoid taking any additional economic risks, as they have to focus on protecting themselves against the first. The poor have practically no access to hedging instruments, which richer people can use to hedge economic risks they may face.

But how much social security is affordable? OECD countries spend between 10 and 30 per cent of GDP on social security – usually between one-third and half of total public expenditure. Countries at the same level of economic development differ significantly in how much they spend on social security. The size of the social security system is obviously shaped mainly by prevailing political attitudes towards redistribution rather than by stringent 'economic laws'. Affordability is a function of social willingness to finance social transfers through taxes and contributions. Social security systems, which perform in a way approved by much of the general public, are usually also affordable, whatever their size. Systems which perform badly, from the point of view of the general public, usually lose support and acceptance, and may become unaffordable, even if relatively small in fiscal terms.

A recent statistical analysis by the ILO's Social Security Department confirms that investing in equity and security through social transfers is clearly not incompatible with economic performance and that the equity/equality vs. growth trade-off is probably an outdated belief. Figure 12.2 shows a strong positive correlation between social expenditure (per capita of the population) and labour productivity (GDP per hour worked) in the OECD.

FIGURE 12.2
Correlations between per hour productivity and social expenditure per capita
in OECD countries, 2001

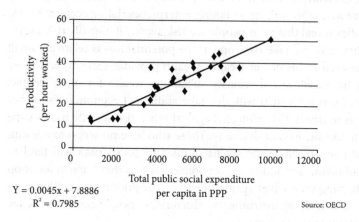

Y = 0.0045x + 7.8886
R^2 = 0.7985

Source: OECD

Source: ILO calculation based on data from OECD (2006) on-line databases.

The correlation between 'simple' per-capita (per worker) productivity and social expenditure (per capita) is also positive but less tight. While the nature of the actual causality behind this correlation needs further research, one conclusion is obvious: High productivity and high social expenditure can co-exist, and hence, an extensive social security system is not incompatible *per se* with a highly productive economy. The widely presumed trade-off does not hold.

MAIN CHALLENGES TO SOCIAL SECURITY SYSTEMS

The demographic, economic and social environments within which national social security systems are operating are obviously rapidly changing. These changes pose obvious challenges for societies and their social transfer systems.

Global Demographic Transition

Global demographic change is the single most important challenge to the viability of national social protection systems. The key indicators for the demographic stress on national social transfer systems are dependency rates. The demographic environment of a social protection system, which includes the morbidity structure of the population with which the health system has to cope, co-determines the *system dependency ratio* – that is to say, it influences the ratio of the number of beneficiaries (i.e. transfer recipients) in the system to the number of people financing these transfers or earning the national income from which transfers have to be financed. Demography is not the exclusive determining factor, as governance too has a marked impact on dependency. Demographic factors (ageing as expressed by dropping fertility and mortality rates, morbidity and mortality) determine, to a large extent, the potential number of beneficiaries and financiers of the national social protection system, thus explaining the *pure demographic dependency* ratio. Demographic factors do not explain the full extent of system dependency: the economy also determines the number of unemployed, while national law, a governance factor, also influences the number of people who are retired and of those receiving education, influenced, for example, by legal provisions governing the minimum number of years of compulsory schooling or of studies requirement for the first university degree.

All other determinants – economic development and governance factors – being equal, ageing is the most important influence on pension schemes, which are, in turn, the biggest expenditure items in national social protection systems. That impact is especially strong in mature systems with a high proportion of the elderly covered by social security. However, demographic projections suggest that while developed regions are substantially 'older' than less developed ones, the pace of ageing is actually much faster in the developing world. So, if the less developed countries have pension systems with universal coverage (which they do not, with a few exceptions like Botswana, Brazil, Namibia and South Africa), in relative terms, they face an even more serious ageing problem between 2000 and 2050 than the schemes in more developed parts of world.

However, there is still reason to believe that the global demographic transition is manageable. Should the OECD countries be able to manage their own demographic transitions, they might even be able to create some fiscal space for the alleviation of poverty or health problems in other parts of the world (*inter alia* in regions with high prevalence of HIV/AIDS). The key indicator for Europe's alleged 'demographic catastrophe' in social security has always been the old-age dependency rate. However, that problem might not be as big as it may seem to be. The reason seems quite simple. Figure 12.3 shows that in rapidly ageing Western Europe, the increase of the retirement age or the extension of the *de facto* working life is probably a solution for most pension schemes. Calculations using a relatively simple model show that increasing demographic burdens can be contained by measures that increase labour force participation. An increase in the labour force participation rate of the 15 to 64 years age group through various measures such as increased labour force participation rates for women to levels slightly below those of men, increased overall rates due to earlier entry into the labour force, and most importantly, a gradual increase of the *de facto* retirement age from 60 today to 65 (simulated here between 2011 and 2021), should mean that the old-age demographic dependency rate can be kept at the present level for the next five decades.

Not all of the potential increase of labour force participation and the increased retirement age may be achievable in practice. The difference will have to be made up by immigration if the overall level of standard-of-living is to be maintained in ageing societies. In any case, the ageing problem of societies cannot be reduced to a pension problem. Overall and per capita GDP growth rates are at risk when populations' age and employable labour forces shrink. The European Commission (2005: 11) conceded that ageing under status quo conditions may act as a brake to economic growth, bringing it down, on average, from 2.0–2.5 per cent per annum to half that rate. Achieving increased labour force participation rates for all aged over 18 is imperative for maintenance of the standard of living in ageing societies. Migration can help maintain a stable dependency rate, but will only provide partial relief. Maintenance of a sufficiently large endogenous labour force remains crucial (see: Cichon, Léger and Knop, 2003). Creating suitable jobs for older workers remains the real challenge for ageing societies and remains a key policy tool for disarming the 'ageing crisis'.

FIGURE 12.3

Estimated old age system dependency rates in Western Europe without (DR1) and with (DR2) increased retirement age, 2004–2050

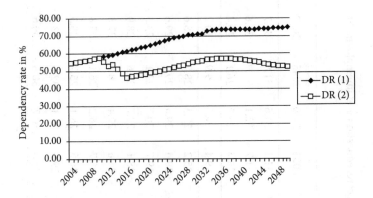

Source: ILO Financial and Actuarial Service estimates.

However, even if – in the worst of all scenarios – the management of the demographic challenge was to fail generally, the effects on the sustainability of national social transfer systems even in countries with highly developed systems might be less dramatic than commonly assumed. The European Union's latest projections of the cost of the most important social security benefits as a result of ageing populations are presented in Table 12.1. There are obvious problem cases, but on average, cost increases by less than four percentage points of GDP over a period of 45 years appear to be rather benign and manageable.

CHANGES IN HEALTH, SOCIETY AND THE LABOUR MARKET

Public Health Issues

New public health threats are rapidly changing the demographic environment in which some national social protection systems operate, particularly in developing countries. In addition to expected pandemics of other infectious diseases, the HIV/AIDS pandemic is

TABLE 12.1
EU 15 and 25: Projections for public spending on pensions, health, long-term care, education and unemployment benefits, 2004–2050

	2004	2005	2010	2015	2020	2025	2030	2035	2040	2045	2050	Change 2004–50
Belgium	25.4	25.3	25.1	25.5	26.6	28.2	29.9	31.1	31.6	31.8	31.7	6.3
Denmark	26.8	26.8	27.0	27.9	28.6	29.5	30.8	31.7	32.1	31.9	31.6	4.8
Germany	23.7	23.4	22.5	22.2	22.9	23.8	24.7	25.4	25.7	26.1	26.4	2.7
Greece	8.9	8.9	8.7	8.7	8.7	8.9	9.1	9.4	9.7	9.9	10.2	1.2
Spain	20.1	20.0	19.7	19.6	20.4	21.7	23.4	25.2	27.3	28.7	28.6	8.5
France	26.7	26.6	26.7	26.9	27.6	28.1	28.6	29.4	29.6	29.7	29.6	2.9
Ireland	15.5	15.2	15.4	16.3	17.1	18.0	18.8	19.7	20.7	22.1	23.3	7.8
Italy	26.2	26.2	25.7	25.6	25.9	26.4	27.3	28.1	28.7	28.6	28.0	1.7
Luxembourg	19.5	19.5	19.4	20.5	21.6	23.5	25.0	26.6	27.4	28.1	27.8	8.2
Netherlands	20.9	20.5	20.6	21.5	22.4	23.4	24.7	25.7	26.2	26.1	25.8	5.0
Austria	25.2	24.9	24.2	24.0	24.2	25.2	26.0	26.5	26.1	25.7	25.3	0.2
Portugal	23.8	24.2	24.2	24.9	26.3	27.1	28.0	29.5	31.1	32.6	33.6	9.7
Finland	25.4	25.2	25.6	26.5	27.7	28.8	30.1	30.8	30.7	30.6	30.6	5.2

TABLE 12.1 (contd)

	2004	2005	2010	2015	2020	2025	2030	2035	2040	2045	2050	Change 2004–50
Sweden	29.6	29.2	28.2	28.3	28.6	29.5	30.9	31.7	31.9	31.7	31.8	2.2
United Kgdm	19.6	19.6	19.4	19.5	19.9	20.7	21.8	22.5	22.9	23.2	23.6	4.0
Cyprus	16.4	16.4	16.5	16.7	17.6	18.8	20.5	21.9	23.4	25.0	28.2	11.8
Czechoslovakia	19.3	19.3	18.8	18.6	19.2	20.0	21.0	22.4	24.1	25.5	26.4	7.2
Estonia	17.1	17.5	16.5	15.4	15.1	15.0	14.8	14.6	14.3	14.3	14.4	–2.7
Hungary	20.7	20.9	21.0	21.3	22.3	22.9	23.5	24.7	26.4	27.4	27.7	7.0
Lithuania	16.0	16.0	15.3	14.8	15.1	15.7	16.3	16.6	16.8	17.0	17.4	1.4
Latvia	17.5	16.9	14.6	14.1	14.6	15.5	16.0	16.2	16.2	16.1	16.2	–1.3
Malta	18.2	18.2	19.1	19.7	20.4	20.5	20.0	19.5	19.2	18.9	18.5	0.3
Poland	23.7	23.4	20.2	18.1	17.9	17.7	17.6	17.5	17.3	17.1	17.0	–6.7
Slovakia	16.2	16.5	15.4	14.9	15.3	15.8	16.5	17.1	17.7	18.3	19.1	2.9
Slovenia	24.2	24.2	24.0	24.5	25.5	27.0	28.6	30.2	31.7	33.0	33.8	9.7
EU25	23.4	23.3	22.7	22.7	23.2	24.0	24.9	25.8	26.4	26.7	26.8	3.4
EU15	23.5	23.3	22.9	23.0	23.5	24.4	25.4	26.3	26.8	27.1	27.2	3.7

Source: Economic Policy Committee(2006: Annex, Table 1-1)
* Total expenditure for Greece does not include public pension expenditure.
EU15 – 15 member states before 2004. EU25 – 25 member states 2004–2006.

the most prominent problem. The expected extent of the pandemic has been accounted for in the above global dependency figures, but will nonetheless pose substantial problems in some regions. In some regions of Africa, the infection rate is estimated to have reached almost 40 per cent. This probably means that within the next five to ten years, at the latest, 40 out of every 100 people alive today will have died, unless there is spectacular medical progress and – perhaps more importantly for Africa – if the cost of drug treatment does not go down. A crisis of this magnitude must have a dramatic effect on the costs of any national social protection scheme. It is probably fair to say that HIV/AIDS is likely wipe out all the financial and fiscal space for the improvement of social protection that growth in Africa could have produced under normal conditions. However, while less prominent and limited to the poorest regions of the world, malaria has an even more dramatic effect on population and morbidity structures with which developing country health systems have to cope. Ways and means have to be found to improve the access of whole populations to basic health services and essential drugs. Social and community based health insurance schemes can extend the revenue base of the health sector and thus help finance improved access to care.

Employment Effects of Globalization

Domestic and export markets in almost all countries in the global economy are experiencing ever tougher global competition. The former Soviet Republics, the countries of Central and Eastern Europe, as well as large parts of China and India, have joined the global labour market since the early 1990s, with relatively low labour costs, while effectively doubling its size. High technology communication as well as fast and cheap means of transport facilitate global production chains, but also the movements of goods, services and people (ILO, 2006: 23-24). The result is that technologies, as well as workplaces and skills become obsolete at an ever increasing pace. The directly measurable effect of workplace migration is smaller than the actual rate one would assume (the average unemployment rate in OECD increased from 6.1 per cent in 1990 to about 6.9 per cent in 2004). Only about half a million jobs in developing countries produce goods and services for consumption in the developed world. However, the indirect and perceived effects on job security seem much higher. In the longer run, global competition will be much less about lower absolute labour costs, but rather about productivity and social infrastructure facilitating economic activity and boosting productivity, including social security systems.

Migration and Family Composition

The ILO estimates that at the beginning of the new century, about 175 million people worldwide lived outside their country of birth or citizenship; including about 90 million migrant workers (ILO, 2006: 26). At the same time, people are migrating from rural to urban areas. Globally, the share of rural employment in total employment fell by three percentage points, or about 90 million workers, to about 43 per cent between 1994 and 2004. Together with migrating dependents, the total number of persons moving from rural to urban areas might already be about 200 million a decade. These figures will increase dramatically due to rural-urban migration in China. Internal and external migration is influenced by a variety of reasons ranging from national or international conflicts and natural disasters to unemployment and poverty. In many cases, however, only one family member migrates, seeking security or income in better paid jobs in urban areas or in other countries. This compounds the disruptive effects of HIV/AIDS and other diseases on family coherence and structures. In many cases, migrants remain excluded from the mainstream in society with all the associated risks for their own health and well-being, as well as the risks for the receiving societies. Integrating migrants into national social security systems is one way of integrating them into the new countries or cities they choose to live in. At the same time, their remittances can help provide some social security for their families.

Informalization of Labour Markets and Economies

ILO (2006: 28) states that the 'dual economy model' nurtures expectations that assume – drawing on the experience of industrialized countries – that most rural agricultural workers would move to urban manufacturing jobs. Hence, there would be a gradual movement towards formalization of largely informal agricultural labour. That pattern of development does not hold true any longer. Manufacturing has ceased to be a major sector of employment growth in many regions and the rural and urban movements of labour are largely absorbed by informal petty trade. The share of informal employment in total urban employment is 48 per cent in North Africa, 72 per cent in sub-Saharan Africa, 51 per cent in Latin America and 65 per cent in Asia (ILO, 2006: 28). Traditional social insurance systems have limited reach to those in the informal sector.

Globalization and the New Uncertainty

Increased economic integration since the last decades of the twentieth century has coincided with rising income inequality in most countries and increasing unemployment among the low-skilled. The impact of internationalization on wages and employment reduces the national tax base and the capacity of national governments to extend social protection. Critics of the welfare state have argued that increased openness creates difficulties in raising sufficient revenues, and therefore requires a downsizing of the welfare state. There is some evidence that countries are currently engaged in tax competition, although perhaps much less than might be expected. In the case of tax competition triggered by globalization, one might expect declining capital tax rates and rising labour and consumption tax rates. In a number of OECD countries, average tax rates on labour have increased, as the substantial decline in the tax base has been responsible for the rise in tax rates on labour incomes. Average effective tax rates have been raised to compensate for the shrinking tax base.

According to the economic paradigm prevailing since the 1980s, expenditure reductions, even in the face of new social security needs triggered by the need for adjustments in the face of globalization, seemed to be the way to reduce fiscal pressure on national tax bases. Consequently, while only growing gradually in developing countries, the level of social security in industrialized market economies is declining. The cost-containment policies of the last decades are taking their toll. Health care systems are excluding services and increasing out-of-pocket outlays, unemployment benefits and other cash benefits are declining.

Paradigmatic pension reforms have changed established systems from defined-benefit schemes to at least partially defined contribution schemes or notionally defined contribution schemes. Parametric reforms changed benefit formulas, reduced pension adjustments and increased retirement ages. Both types of reforms directly or indirectly seek to 'off-load' some of the fiscal burden for financing income security for old age, disability and in case of the loss of the breadwinner, from public or quasi-public budgets to private resources.

There was a strong belief in some quarters that the reforms converting widespread defined-benefit pension schemes, financed on a pay-as-you-go basis, into pre-funded defined contribution schemes, will help ensure the availability and affordability of pension schemes. On the one hand, there was hope that such reforms would prevent contribution rates and other costs of pension systems growing as a result of ageing populations: unless people contribute longer and retire later, benefits will go down, keeping the overall costs of pensions more or less constant. On the other hand, there was also a strong belief that such reformed systems, closely linking amounts contributed with future benefits and relegating re-distributive components to social assistance schemes would provide very strong incentives to contribute, even on a voluntary basis. Such systems were thus seen as a major instrument to increase coverage of all those not covered, particularly the self-employed. Privatization of the management of funds was supposed to strengthen these incentives: by providing higher rates of return and also by gaining more public confidence than allegedly bankrupt public schemes.

The Chilean pension reform introduced at the beginning of the eighties was the first attempt to follow this new paradigm. The World Bank's (1994) *Averting the Old Age Crisis* announced this new pension policy paradigm as globally relevant. Numerous ILO studies of reformed pension systems, particularly in Latin America[1] and in the transition economies of Central and Eastern Europe[2], over recent years confirm that the reformed pension schemes: may reduce income security in old age of those covered; may reduce effective coverage of the previously covered population; and are not meeting expectations to increase coverage heightened by rising national savings rates.

While some reforms have clearly improved the fiscal sustainability of some pension schemes, a number of ILO concerns have since been echoed by the World Bank's Independent Evaluation Group (IEG). The IEG evaluation of World Bank assistance to pension reforms concluded *inter alia*: "There is little evidence that privately funded pillars have succeeded in increasing national savings or in developing capital markets . . . " and " . . . the Bank's preoccupation with fiscal sustainability tended to obscure the broader goal of pension policy, that is, to reduce poverty and improve retirement income adequacy within a fiscal constraint" (World Bank, 2005: xvi–xvii). Some countries in Europe introduced or considered introducing reforms similar to those in Latin America, aimed mainly at reducing the future costs of pensions to public budgets and hoping that such systems would encourage later retirement. The ILO studies mentioned above also point to high administrative costs and expected low replacement rates, especially for women or other persons with short, broken careers and lower incomes or those who – like the self-employed – are only obligated to contribute minimally. The resulting revenue reductions are now leading to reducing benefit levels, resulting in added uncertainty for those hardest hit by global and national adjustment processes.

Unlike the demographic challenge, the potential detrimental effects of global tax competition on the level of social security in some countries are less easily managed. This requires international agreements and recognition that social security and reduced inequality would reduce the resentment that exacerbates social unrest and security problems. The means to address these problems are missing.

Between Universalism and Pluralism: The Changing Pattern of Solidarity

Nonetheless, there is increasing recognition of the role of social security as an investment in poverty alleviation. There is growing support for a new social security developmental paradigm based on the introduction of basic universal benefits. The World Commission on the Social Dimensions of Globalization has promoted the idea of a socio-economic floor for the global economy (ILO, 2004c). The global community has already assumed some responsibility for the provision of basic services in some developing countries. In Ghana and Tanzania, for example, direct budget support from donors already accounts for substantial proportions – i.e., 40 and 50 per cent respectively – of the national health budgets.

Some say that acceptance of the concept of solidarity is deteriorating as many social protection schemes have broken down into smaller and smaller risk pools (right down to the financing of risks by individual accounts). Others observe that the commonly accepted notion of solidarity is simply changing, now focusing more on the attainment of basic security for more, rather than equal security for a few. In any case, on the basis of the newly developing notion of solidarity, social security systems are becoming more pluralistic. Pension schemes are turning into systems where basic public provision of income security mechanisms are topped up by social insurance or privatized savings arrangements where benefits have a much closer link to earned insured income, which, in turn, are topped up by voluntary or mandated arrangements. The consequence is a wide range of different income levels at retirement among different population groups.

In health care, the second biggest expenditure rubric in overall national social expenditure, pluralistic health systems have emerged where state provision of basic services is complemented by social health insurance schemes and community-based schemes. The World Health Assembly of May 2005 explicitly acknowledged the role of social health insurance schemes in national health systems (WHO, 2005).

Community-based schemes have sprung up everywhere in the developing world, mostly in Africa and parts of Asia. The total coverage of such mutual help schemes is estimated to be about 40 million persons. There is certainly room for further growth and qualitative improvements of governance in these schemes. However, they cannot constitute or substitute a universal basic layer of security based on national solidarity. Nevertheless, these insurance schemes can create an efficient quality-enhancing payer–provider relationship in the health sector. In addition, public subsidies for the poor and underwriting of bad risks have to be created with a central national or international agency to ensure the long-term viability of the scheme. The new health insurance law in Ghana, for instance, has given legal force to this principle. Community-based insurance schemes have the potential to increase the overall resource base for social security, and hence, the fiscal space for the government. It is also *de facto* one way of indirectly taxing the informal economy, or of making those in the informal economy contribute to some degree of state financing. It is thus a step toward the 'formalization' of the informal economy and including its participants in some form of national solidarity arrangement. Community-based schemes may also play an even more important role where nation states fail.

CHANGING THE SOCIAL SECURITY PARADIGM

A comprehensive policy response is needed to address the above challenges. This policy response has to be developed at the community, regional, national and international level and requires a change in attitude towards social security. It also requires a developmental vision for social security that can be applied to countries at different stages of development.

Changing Attitudes: From Social Cost to Investment in People

The ILO (2001: 2) has always maintained that "social security – if properly managed – enhances productivity by providing health care, income security and social services. [. . . .] it is an instrument for social and economic development . . . . It is noted that while social security is a cost to enterprises, it is also an investment in, or support for people. With globalization and structural adjustment policies, social security becomes more necessary than ever." Social security – or in a larger sense, social protection (including social transfers, but also safe and fair conditions of work, private social safety nets, etc.) – is one of the main pillars of the decent work concept.

The adaptation of national labour markets to the challenges of demographic transition, new health hazards, global migration, changing family structures, changing values and globalization cannot proceed without investments in well designed social transfers that:

- maintain the productivity of workforces (notably ageing workforces) through investments in health care that, *inter alia*, combat new global health risks;
- facilitate adjustments in employment, *inter alia*, through facilitating training, retraining and job search, and facilitating the integration of migrants;
- achieve fair distribution of the proceeds of globalization, and hence, generate more acceptance of global processes of social change;
- help maintain social peace and global security that are prerequisites for stable long-term economic growth, hence creating the material basis for enhanced welfare for all.

It is difficult to see how the above can be done without investments in the building and reform of sound, properly managed and governed social security institutions.

Building a Global Vision: Towards Universal Coverage

The ILO is presently developing a coherent country-specific policy vision of effective and efficient national social security systems that countries at different levels of development can afford. The model has to be:

(a) flexible, to accommodate national circumstances; and
(b) progressive, i.e. it has to permit a gradual build-up of more comprehensive systems as societies mature (in an economic sense);
(c) accept the benefit levels and entitlements defined by ILO minimum standards (e.g. Convention No. 102) as an ultimate minimum level of protection.

We believe that social security in the poorest countries can start with the following basic elements:

(a) Access to basic health care through pluralistic national systems that consist of public tax-financed components, social and private insurance components and community-based components linked to a strong central system.

(b) A system of family benefits that permits children to attend school.

(c) A system of self-targeting basic social assistance (cash-for-work programmes) that helps to overcome abject poverty for the able-bodied.

(d) Developing a system of basic universal pensions for old age, invalidity and survivorship that effectively supports whole families.

The following section shows that even in the poorest developing countries – contrary to widely held perceptions – some level of social protection is affordable and desirable. As countries mature economically, higher levels of protection can gradually be achieved. The key objective is universality, i.e., achieving some social security as a right for all, the core mandate of the ILO's ongoing Campaign for the Extension of Social Security Coverage.

Universality does not mean uniformity. It is not realistic to believe that all societies can – left to their own devices – achieve the same level of social protection, even if the correlation between GDP levels and per capita social spending is weak. National social security systems inevitably have to grow with the fiscal space made available by increasing GDP. Systems address priority needs in such a way that the level of security can be augmented as economic development progresses. Within an overall national resource envelope, at different stages of development, contributions and taxes allocated for priority social security expenditures have to be defined. In developing countries, they should be prioritized with respect to their contributions to achieving an acceptable level of health, and to the reduction of poverty and social insecurity.

AFFORDABILITY AND IMPACT OF BASIC SOCIAL PROTECTION IN LOW-INCOME COUNTRIES IN SUB-SAHARAN AFRICA

It is widely presumed that low-income countries cannot afford social protection, but this is not true. A number of examples show that basic social protection programmes are feasible and can have a marked effect on reducing poverty. ILO has demonstrated that basic social protection benefits are not out of reach of low-income countries in sub-Saharan Africa, even though some international assistance may be necessary (Pal and others, 2005). Seven countries were included in this study, namely Burkina Faso, Cameroon, Ethiopia, Guinea, Kenya, Senegal and Tanzania.

A wide basic social protection package was assessed, including a universal old-age and invalidity pension, universal access to basic education, universal access to basic health care and a universal child benefit. Reflecting the methods used in the Millennium Development Goal indicators and other major international reports, the model assesses the cost of a universal old-age and invalidity pension at US$0.50 (PPP) per day, UNICEF primary education costs, per capita health care costs (according to the Commission for Macroeconomics and Health) and a child benefit of half the level of the universal pension.

The results in the case of Tanzania (Figure 12.4) show that the total expenditure for a basic social protection package over the next three

FIGURE 12.4
Projected basic social protection expenditure as share of GDP, Tanzania, 2005–2034

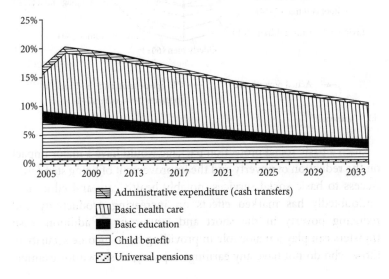

decades is projected to increase from 16.8 per cent of GDP in 2005 to 20.2 per cent in 2007, and would then drop to 10.3 per cent of GDP in 2034. A more modest approach to pension and child benefit levels (i.e., to a level of 30 per cent respectively 15 per cent of GDP per capital) and health care (i.e., to an infrastructure level as in Namibia), would reduce cost dramatically, i.e., perhaps by about 10 percentage-points. That level could probably be financed after some phase-in period entirely by domestic resources.

FIGURE 12.5
Reduction of the poverty rate through universal cash transfers: Simulated poverty rates of Tanzania

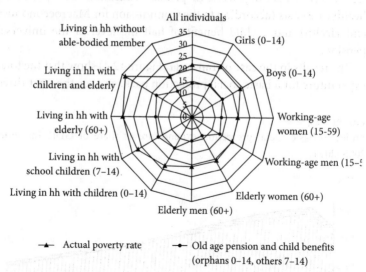

hh – household

Such a basic social protection package would have a major impact on the reduction of poverty and the improvement of living standards. Access to basic social services, notably health care and education, undoubtedly has marked effects on increasing productivity and reducing poverty in the short and long run. In addition, cash transfers can play a major role in providing basic income security to those who do not have any earnings capacity, as shown for example in a GTZ-sponsored pilot project in the Kalomo district of Zambia (see Schubert, 2004). Recent ILO micro-simulations for the case of Tanzania (Gassman and Behrendt, 2006) show that the combination of basic universal old-age pensions and child benefits to school children and orphans under the age of 14 would reduce overall poverty rates by about one-third (see Figure 12.5).

Stepping up efforts to provide basic social protection is a viable way to reduce poverty and insecurity for countries in sub-Saharan Africa, specifically with a view to achieve the first Millennium Development Goal by 2015. The results of recent ILO research have shown that this can be both affordable and effective. This is a commitment which each individual nation needs to make, and some African countries have already committed themselves to enhancing social protection in their national poverty reduction strategies. Nevertheless, many countries cannot achieve this without external support for at least some time to come.

By Way of Conclusion: Accepting Global Responsibility

If the global community embraces globalization on the one hand, and sets global goals in the social sphere on the other hand, it has to organize the global economy and global society in such a way as to enable nation states to achieve nationally and internationally defined policy objectives. It would mean searching for ways in which the global community can protect the fiscal space of national states to finance social transfers. This can be done in two complementary ways:

First, by setting and finding ways to implement social rights and global minimum standards for social transfers addressing poverty and social insecurity and to halt the race to the bottom – when it comes to curbing social rights and social spending – at a decent level. ILO social security standards and core labour standards can be seen as beginning a financing global process to protect the of social security systems. In the context of a revival of a rights-based approach to social security, new and wider instruments defining and defending a 'global social floor' have to follow.

Second, the global community can also increase the fiscal space of national governments through global support for sound anti-poverty policies. The international community has just begun to accept that responsibility. PRSPs, debt relief and ODA through budget support may signal a new beginning. More needs to be done. A suitable fund may be needed to support the creation of sound national social transfer schemes.

Some sceptics may not believe that social security is a prerequisite for growth; the evidence is strong that good economic performance and sound social security can co-exist. It is clearly evident that these schemes reduce poverty and inequality and help people adapt changing circumstances on their own. In the end, what matters is people – and people are better off with social security.

NOTES

[1] See, for example, ILO (2005), ILO (2004a), Arenas de Mesa and Benavides Salazar (2003), Bertranou (2001), Bertranou and Arenas de Mesa (2003), ILO (2004b), Bertranou, Solorio and Ginneken (2002), Nitsch and Schwarzer (1996).
[2] See Fultz (2004), Fultz, Ruck and Steinhilber (2003), Fultz (2002), Fultz and Ruck (2000), Hagemejer (1999), Cichon, Hagemejer and Ruck (1998).

REFERENCES

Arenas de Mesa, A., and P. Benavides Salazar (2003). *Protección social en Chile – Financiamiento, cobertura y desempeño 1990-2000*. International Labour Office, Santiago.

Atkinson, A.B. (2003). *Income Inequality and the Welfare State in a Global Era*. J Douglas Gibson Lecture, School of Policy Studies, Queen's University, Kingston.

Bertranou, F.M. (ed.) (2001). *Cobertura previsional en Argentina, Brasil y Chile*. International Labour Office, Santiago.

Bertranou, F.M., C. Solorio, and W. van Ginneken (eds) (2002). *Pensiones no contributivas y asistenciales Argentina, Brasil y Chile, Costa Rica y Uruguay*. International Labour Office, Santiago.

Bertranou, F.M., and A. Arenas de Mesa (eds) (2003). *Protección social, pensiones y género en Argentina, Brasil y Chile*. International Labour Office, Santiago.

Cichon, M., K. Hagemejer, and M. Ruck (1998). *Social Protection and Pension Systems in Central and Eastern Europe*. International Labour Office, Budapest.

Cichon, M., F. Léger, and R. Knop (2003). White or prosperous: How much migration does the ageing European Union need to maintain its standard of living in the 21st century? Processed, International Labour Office, Geneva.

Cichon, Michael, Wolfgang Scholz, Arthur van de Meerendonk, Krzysztof Hagemejer, Fabio Bertranou, and Pierre Plamandon (2004). *Financing Social Protection*. International Labour Office, Geneva.

Economic Policy Committee (2006). The impact of ageing on public expenditure: projections for the EU25 member states on pensions, health care, long-term care, education and unemployment transfers (2004-2050). Report prepared by the Economic Policy Committee and the European Commission (DG ECFIN), European Economy special report no. 1/2006-Annex, European Commission, Brussels.

European Commission (2005). European values in the globalized world. Communication from the Commission to the European Parliament, the Council, the European Economic and Social Committee and the Committee on the Regions, European Commission, Brussels.

Förster, Michael F., and Michele Pellizzari (2000). Trends and driving factors in income distribution and poverty in the OECD area. Labour Market and Social Policy occasional paper no. 42, Organisation for Economic Co-operation and Development, Paris.

Fultz, Elaine (ed.) (2002). *Pension Reform in Central and Eastern Europe*. (Vol. 1: *Restructuring with privatization – Case studies of Poland and Hungary*; Vol. 2: *Restructuring of public pension schemes – Case studies of Czech Republic and Slovenia*). International Labour Office, Budapest.

Fultz, Elaine (2004). Pension reform in the EU accession countries: Challenges, achievements and pitfalls. *International Social Security Review* 57 (2): 3–24.

Fultz, Elaine, and Markus Ruck (2000). *Pension Reform in Central and Eastern Europe: An Update on the Restructuring of National Pension Schemes in Selected Countries*. International Labour Office, Budapest.

Fultz, E., Markus Ruck, and S. Steinhilber (eds) (2003). *The Gender Dimension of Social Security Reform in Central and Eastern Europe: Case Studies of the Czech Republic, Hungary and Poland*. International Labour Office, Budapest.

Gassmann, F., and C. Behrendt (2006). Cash benefits in low-income countries: Simulating the effects on poverty reduction for Tanzania and Senegal. Issues in Social Protection discussion paper 15, International Labour Office, Geneva.

Hagemejer, Krzysztof (1999). The transformation of social security in Central and Eastern Europe. In K. Müller, A. Ryll and H.-J. Wagener (eds). *Transformation of Social Security: Pensions in Central-Eastern Europe*. Physica-Verlag, Heidelberg and New York: 31–58.

HelpAge International (2004). *Age and Security: How Social Pensions Can Deliver Effective Aid to Poor Older People and Their Families*. HelpAge International, London.

ILO (1999). *Decent Work*. Report of the Director General, International Labour Conference, 89th Session, International Labour Office, Geneva.

ILO (2001). *Social Security: A New Consensus*. International Labour Office, Geneva.

ILO (2004a). *Valuación actuarial del Sistema Integrado de Jubilaciones y Pensione sal 31 de diciembre de 2001. Servicio de Actividades Financieras, Actuariales y Estadísticas, Programa InFocus sobre Respuesta a la Crisis y Reconstrucción*. International Labour Office, Buenos Aires.

ILO (2004b). *El sistema de pensiones en Chile en el contexto mundial y de América Latina: Evaluación y desafíos*. Ponencias del Seminario Internacional, Oficina Internacional del

304 • Towards Full and Decent Employment

Trabajo, Ministerio del Trabajo y Seguridad, Social Fundación Chile 21, International Labour Office, Santiago.

ILO (2004c). *World Commission on the Social Dimension of Globalization: A Fair Globalization – Creating Opportunities for All.* International Labour Office, Geneva.

ILO (2004d). *A Fair Globalization. The Role of the ILO.* Report of the Director-General on the World Commission on the Social Dimension of Globalization, International Labour Conference, 92nd Session, International Labour Office, Geneva.

ILO (2005). *Prospectiva de la previsión social: valuación financiera actuarial del Sistema Integrado de Jubilaciones y Pensiones 2005–2050.* Serie de publicaciones de la secretaria de Seguridad Social, AÑOF, Ministerio de Trabajo, Empleo y Seguridad Social y Servicio de Actividades Financieras, Actuariales y Estadísticas de la OIT, International Labour Office, Buenos Aires.

ILO (2006). *Changing Patterns in the World of Work.* Report of the Director General, International Labour Conference, 95th Session, International Labour Office, Geneva.

Nitsch, M., and H. Schwarzer (1996). Recent development in financing social security in Latin America. Issues in Social Protection Discussion Paper 1, International Labour Office, Geneva.

OECD (2005). OECD statistics on-line. Data on productivity per hour worked from: 'OECD estimates of labour productivity for 2005' at http://www.oecd.org/dataoecd/28/17/36396820.xls (accessed on 20 October 2006); Data on public social expenditure per capita from 'Total public social expenditure, per head, at current prices and current PPPs, in US dollars' at: http://www.oecd.org/dataoecd/54/2/35055715.xls (accessed on 20 October 2006)

Pal, K., C. Behrendt, F. Léger, M. Cichon, and K, Hagemejer (2005). Can low income countries afford basic social protection? First results of a modelling exercise. Issues in Social Protection Discussion Paper 13, International Labour Office, Geneva.

Ruiz-Huerta, Jesús, Rosa Martinez, and Luis Ayala (1999). Earnings inequality, unemployment and income distribution in the OECD. LIS working paper no. 214. Luxembourg Income Study, New York.

Schubert, B. (2004). *Social Cash Transfers - Reaching the Poorest: A Contribution to the International Debate Based on Experience in Zambia.* Deutsche Gesellschaft für Technische Zusammenarbeit, Eschborn.

Smeeding, T.M. (2002). Globalization, inequality and the rich countries of the G-20: Evidence from the Luxembourg Income Study (LIS). LIS Working paper no. 320, Luxembourg Income Study, Sydney.

WHO (2005). Sustainable health financing, universal coverage and social health insurance. Resolution WHA58.33 adopted at the World Health Assembly, 48th Session, World Health Organization, Geneva.

World Bank (1994). *Averting the Old Age Crisis: Policies to Protect the Old and Promote Growth. World Bank Policy Research Report.* World Bank, Washington, DC.

World Bank (2005). *Pension Reforms and the Development of Pension Systems: An Evaluation of World Bank Assistance.* World Bank, Washington, DC.

13
Transformative Social Policy

THANDIKA MKANDAWIRE

Recent United Nations Research Institute of Social Development (UNRISD) research has highlighted the *developmental* role of social policy, even as it addresses issues of intrinsic value such as social protection, equality and social citizenship, and calls for rescuing social policy from the residual role it was assigned during much of the 1980s and 1990s.

Social Policy

Social policy is state intervention that directly affects social welfare, social institutions and social relations. It involves overarching concerns with redistribution, production, reproduction and protection, and works in tandem with economic policy in pursuit of national social and economic goals. Social policy does not merely deal with the 'causalities' of social changes and processes; it is also a contribution to the welfare of society as a whole.

Social policy may be embedded in economic policy, when the latter has intended welfare consequences or reflects implicit or explicit socioeconomic priorities, such as reducing politically unacceptable levels of unemployment or producing the human skills for development. But most elements of social policy are explicit, such as direct government provision of social welfare through, for example, broad-based education and health services, subsidies and benefits, social security and pensions, labour market interventions, land reform, progressive taxation and other redistributive policies. Social policy can also be used to transform gender, racial and other social relations – through, for example, 'affirmative action', antidiscrimination legislation and laws pertaining to marriage and the family. Social policies can also be deployed to regulate existing or to produce new social institutions and norms. Thus an important feature of social policy is the establishment and enforcement of standards and regulations that shape the role of non-state actors and markets in social provisioning.

UNRISD research has highlighted the developmental role of social policy, even as it addresses issues of intrinsic value such as social protection, equality and social citizenship. The research also offers arguments for rescuing social policy from the residual role it was assigned during much of the 1980s and 1990s.

This Research and Policy Brief presents some of the key lessons from the UNRISD research. How these lessons are absorbed or translated into national policy will, of course, depend on national contexts. Furthermore, the complex interplay among the various policies suggested by these lessons must be borne in mind, as must the importance of context and the historical circumstances of each country.

LESSONS FROM THE RESEARCH

The Multiple Tasks of Social Policy

Value-driven arguments for social policy must work in tandem with instrumental ones. Social policy must deal with four major concerns: distribution, protection, production and reproduction. It must be concerned with the redistributive effects of economic policy, protecting people from the vagaries of the market and the changing circumstances of age, enhancing the productive potential of members of society, and reconciling the burden of reproduction with that of other social tasks, as well as sharing the burden of reproduction.

Different welfare regimes have placed different weights on each of these. Thus, while one may speak of 'distributionist' or 'productivist' welfare states, one has to recognize that such descriptions merely capture positions on a continuum. Because considerable complementarities and synergies generally exist among these goals, the pursuit of only one of these goals to the exclusion of others can cause problems that might undermine the pursuit of the chosen goal. Thus, for example, a focus only on the distributive functions of social policy would ultimately be economically unsustainable. This has been the fate of the 'populist' regimes whose exclusive focus on distribution often led to inflation and stagnation that ultimately left the poor worse off. Similarly, a purely productivist approach to social policy would encounter political opposition, producing political instability that would undermine the growth objective. And finally, a policy regime focused on protection would fail on both grounds, and it would not cope with the dynamics of demography.

In general, 'late industrializers' (such as countries of Northern Europe and East Asia) have given greater weight to the productive or developmental aspects of social policy than did pioneer industrializers like the United Kingdom. Indeed, this focus has been the *differentia specifica* of 'developmental welfare states'. However, partly as a response to globalization, to pressures for competitiveness and to the ascendancy of ideologies much more inclined against redistribution, there is a growing bias even in the developed countries toward a productivist role. This is evidenced by the shift of welfare regimes toward what have been referred to as 'social investment' and 'workfare states'.

Ideologies

Ideologies are important to social policy because they determine the underlying motives and norms for a number of policy measures: are they an aspect of social rights, or are they social privileges accorded by an authoritarian or paternalistic regime? State elites are often motivated by a particular kind of ideology: to provide the national community with a kind of 'moral good' which may include 'nation-building', 'self sufficiency', 'social cohesion', 'socialism', 'solidarity' or 'mutual responsibility'. It is ideologies that determine the weights attached to various costs and benefits of social interventions, that underpin the moral entitlements of individuals to social support and that shape the purpose of social policy to empower citizens or to pacify them.

Social Policy and Poverty

Social policy in developing countries is not only about poverty eradication. Historically, social policy has had other objectives, such as national or social cohesion and equity. Indeed, in a number of countries that have successfully dealt with poverty within a relatively short period of time, the relief of poverty was not even the most explicit motive for the introduction of social policies. In the Nordic or East Asian countries, for example, 'poverty reduction' per se was not one of the main pillars of their social policies. The point is not to dethrone 'poverty' from the policy agenda, but rather to stress that the factors that may eventually reduce poverty are not those that address its proximate causes, nor are they the most obvious ones like targeting the poor.

Late Industrialization and Social Policy

Social policy is not something to engage in only after reaching a certain development threshold; nor is it an exclusive domain of advanced welfare states: social policy is a key instrument for economic and social development. There is some kind of 'Gerschenkron thesis' for social policy whereby late industrializers have tended to adopt certain welfare measures at much earlier phases in their development than did the 'pioneers'.

This is partly in order to handle the 'social questions' that arise with rapid industrialization. In addition, both 'learning effects' and 'contagion' can lead to leapfrogging and a much earlier adoption of certain 'technologies' – including social policy – at much earlier stages of development than a linear view of development would suggest. The implication is that quite a number of welfare measures can be introduced at fairly low levels of income in response to both normative and functionalist imperatives to use social policies for distributive, protective and proactive ends.

The Instrumental Value of Social Policy

Social policy is not only an expression of normative values, but can also serve as a major transformative instrument in the process of development. The great challenge is how to mobilize the instrumental value of social policies without undermining the intrinsic value of the goals being pursued.

Social policy can contribute to capital accumulation through 'forced' savings collected as social insurance funds. In some late industrializers pension funds were crucial in financing major infrastructure projects, such as the electrification of Finland. Social policy also contributes to the formation of human capital by ensuring the education and the health of the population and by improving the efficiency of labour markets, for example, and other markets for social provision. It ensures the legitimacy of the political order and contributes to political stability. It contributes to 'social capital' by enhancing social cohesion and resolving social conflicts.

Not only does social policy contribute to the 'supply side' of development; it also affects the demand side by influencing the levels and structures of demand.

Finally, social policy can be one of the 'focusing devices' of technological change by providing the human capital wherewithal for technological innovation and adaptation, as well as by sanctioning or disallowing certain technologies.

Labour Markets

Labour market policies are an extremely important arena for addressing issues of poverty and development. Labour markets are not simply institutions for the static efficient allocation of existing labour resources, but they are also the site for the realization of basic civil and social rights though what the International Labour Organization calls 'decent work'. Moreover, they perform the developmental role that is often obscured by the preoccupation with market clearance: as noted above, they can be sources of savings through contributory schemes such as pensions, and they can also resolve coordination problems and address 'market failures' in the production of human capital by creating investment incentives for both employers and employees. It is also in the labour market that reconciling production and reproduction clearly emerges as a social concern of developing economies, in addressing the need to facilitate women's labour force participation (through the provision of public childcare services) which, apart from being a social right, can also produce positive macroeconomic effects (it uses the human capital investments made through female education, it has multiplier effects by creating a demand for various caring services, and so on).

Not surprisingly, a common feature of all the development success stories has been their intervention in labour markets, or the pursuit of 'active labour market policy', to use current parlance. While such policies are generally implemented at the micro level, they have great macroeconomic effects on inflation, growth and distribution. The extension of social policies to larger sections of the population has often been accompanied or facilitated by greater formalization of employment. Informalization has tended to undermine the construction and financing of social protection measures (such as pensions) and acted as a major source of social exclusion in many developing regions, including even more developed ones like Latin America.

In the process of development, labour markets are some of the most politically explosive ones. The importance of what the Germans referred to as the 'social question' in the process of industrialization often expresses itself most sharply in this market. It is also state policies in the labour market that often most vividly distinguish authoritarian and democratic states in terms of the rights of labour to organize itself.

The Gendered Nature of Social Policy

Social policy is always filtered through social institutions – families and communities, markets, the care economy; health and education systems, the public sector – that are 'bearers of gender'. It is thus always gendered not only because it shapes how society cares for its young, old and frail, but also because it affects the participation of women and men in both household and non-household economic activities.

A core aspect of any economy is the 'care economy'. How problems of care are addressed by social policies not only colours the texture of society but also fundamentally determines the lives of women by either broadening their capabilities and choices, or by confining them to so-called traditional roles. It also affects both the pattern and rate of economic development.

Leaning Toward Universalism

For poor countries there is a strong case for leaning toward universalistic policies when addressing issues of poverty. In many of the late industrializers that confronted problems of social dislocation and poverty, it became obvious that where poverty was widespread, targeting was unnecessary and administratively costly.

Targeting is fraught with such problems as information asymmetries, incentives distortion and moral hazard. In addition, the process of identifying the poor opens up space for discretion and arbitrariness, and subjects the recipient of support to stigmatization and invasive processes. Thus the 'universalism' guiding social policy in many countries was in fact dictated by underdevelopment – targeting was simply too demanding in terms of available skills and administrative capacity.

One potent criticism levelled against many social security systems in developing countries is that they are 'segmented' and only benefit the few, in the formal sector. This argument has been used to advocate for targeted social policy in favour of the poor. Historically, however, the foundation of many of today's most successful universalistic welfare states was such 'stratified universalism', or exclusive voluntary provision of social services to members. In most late industrializers – such as Germany and Japan, for example – welfare entitlements were directed at those parts of the workforce that were most crucial for economic growth, best organized, and thus politically most powerful: skilled industrial workers.

However, late industrializers tended to climb the ladder toward universalism much faster than the pioneers of industrialization. The political regime in place conditioned the speed with which universalism spread. In contrast, structural adjustment programmes and Poverty Reduction Strategy Papers, driven by a targeting rationale, begin by dismantling the exclusive rights of formal labour on the grounds that this will lead to greater labour market flexibility and will attract donor funds for pro-poor policies.

Macroeconomics and Social Policy

In the successful developmental experiences, macroeconomics gave special attention to economic growth and structural changes as instruments for the social objective of eradicating poverty and improving social welfare. In the 1980s, macroeconomics was detached from these social moorings, becoming increasingly socially blind. Economic policies and the instruments chosen to implement them were no longer constrained by social objectives, such as protecting people's incomes or eradicating poverty. Instead they were almost exclusively assigned the tasks of reducing the twin deficits, containing public debt and inflation, liberalizing product and factor markets, privatizing state assets, and liberalizing external trade and capital flows.

The ability to achieve rapid poverty reduction depends critically, inter alia, on the nature of the development, social and macroeconomic policies adopted to promote rapid growth and equitable income distribution. While scholars and policy makers of different economic persuasions generally agree on the broad lines of suitable pro-poor development and social policies, the nature of macroeconomic policies consistent with poverty reduction remains controversial, and the discord has intensified with the liberalization of international capital movements.

Tellingly, the countries that have achieved rapid poverty reduction and are poised to reach the Millennium Development Goal of halving extreme poverty – China, India, Viet Nam and a few others – mostly adopted macroeconomic policies that differed markedly, or at least in part, from those promoted by the neoliberal approach. These countries adopted policies in consonance with their local structures and institutions.

The International Environment for Social Policy

National-level social policy is pursued within an international context, and this global environment impinges on social policy in various ways. It can set limits on which instruments can be used in the pursuit of social goals. It can, through the provision of resources (including finance, ideas and norms), facilitate the design and implementation of social policies in developing countries. Consequently, it is important to design global economic and governance structures as if the social values pursued by social policy actually matter. This was one of the central features of the Keynesian Bretton Woods international regime that permitted nation-states to pursue their welfare and developmental policies while engaging in greater economic interaction with other states. Social policy is imperative for strategically opening up economies not only because it provides the human capital necessary for enhancing competitive capacity, but also because it provides the necessary protection for citizens from the vagaries of global markets.

Democracy and Social Policy

There is no simple one-to-one relationship between political regime and social policy. Many democracies have not done well with respect to some of the central preoccupations of social policy, while far-reaching social policies have been implemented by authoritarian regimes. In the latter contexts social policy has been largely dependent on the ideological predilections of the ruling elite or bureaucracy, often to 'buy peace' or to carry out the mandate of the popular movements that may have placed them in power. However, democracy provides more space for the social articulation of interests and has, over the years, been used by social movements to push for social policies. Consequently, while one may not witness radical redistributive policies under a democratic regime, one does not find the kind of egregious neglect of social policies that can occur in an authoritarian regime.

A strong case can be made that social policy and how poverty is dealt with affect the development of democracy. They can contribute to its consolidation as well as enhance its quality by improving the security of the overwhelming majority of citizens, improving social solidarity (a cornerstone of citizenship), weakening clientelistic social relations, and enhancing the capacity of citizens to participate in public life as autonomous actors. In other words, social policy may impact the political system and democracy through social cohesion. However, all this depends on the nature and effectiveness of social policy and the political perceptions around it.

State Capacity

Policy choices must be aligned with institutional capacity. The state is a key institution as an organizer, if not necessarily a provider, of social protection and provisioning. States that are well institutionalized are better able to translate political commitments into effective social policies and delivery systems. Social policies are demanding in terms of the quality of social institutions they require, as well as in terms of financial resources, efficiency, transparency and integrity. 'Capacity' refers not only to the direct provision by the state of social services through public expenditure, but also to the state's ability to regulate and stimulate non-state actors in the fulfilment of requirements in social sectors. The necessary capacity is not only administrative or technocratic, but even more importantly political, in terms of building the necessary consensus or social pacts for the coordination of otherwise segmented and conflicted initiatives.

Much commercialization of service provision is premised on the regulatory capacity of the state, the responses of the bureaucracy to the new policy regime, and the development and performance of the private sector. In many cases the industrialized countries are looked to as examples, and their experiences are assumed to be equally applicable to developing countries. However, the more developed the market, the greater the regulatory capacity of the state. Consequently, just because deregulation has worked in the industrialized countries does not mean it can work in the less developed countries. Liberalization in countries with weak markets may demand of the state a regulatory capacity that it simply does not have. In many cases this has led to inefficient monopolistic markets without the redistributive imperatives of state enterprises, producing both inefficiency in production and inequity in access to social services. These effects have been compounded by the general weakening in capacity of the public sector labour force, as well as by its wanton retrenchment.

Increasingly, service provision is being transferred to non-governmental organizations. Experiences with voluntary service provision suggest that there are often difficulties in scaling up to the national level activities that work at the micro level. Voluntarism tends to entail inherent institutional limits to coverage. In any case, the juxtaposition between voluntary and compulsory insurance schemes can be misleading. In many cases compulsory social insurance programmes tended to emerge either when the very broadest pre-existing voluntary movements pushed for them or when a weak pre-existing movement proved entirely unable to meet the demands for running the system. In addition, the success of a voluntaristic approach depends crucially on the institutionalization of such basic rights as the right to organize, as well as on the administrative capacity of both the state and voluntary organizations.

Financing Social Policy

The instruments for financing social policy must be fiscally prudent and compatible with other social goals, including equity and efficiency. Many regimes have ultimately foundered on the basis of a macroeconomic populism that paid scant attention to this delicate balance or confined itself to 'give but not take' policies.

Most populist policies and programmes ultimately fail because they do not ensure fiscally responsible financing. Successful welfare regimes have also tended to be higher tax regimes. More conservatively inclined regimes have reduced state capacity for social provisioning by reducing taxes on the rich.

In many countries mineral rents make up a major source of revenue. There is also considerable evidence that such wealth is misused and that these resources are not used effectively for social development. Some have construed this to suggest that a 'resource curse' befalls all countries richly endowed with mineral resources. But there are cases confounding the hypothesis, and these need to be better understood.

Social Movements and Social Pacts

Social movements and social contestation are important determinants of social policy. Such movements have affected social policies in direct and indirect ways. In the most direct way, social mobilization has placed certain items on the policy agenda. In many cases, elite understanding of what is required to pre-empt or forestall social unrest may have driven social reform. Social pacts have played an important role in shaping social policies in a number of countries, especially in democratic ones.

A Diversity of Instruments

A wide range of instruments may be used to reach certain universal goals. Even in 'models' that are, for heuristic or comparative purpose, identified as 'welfare regimes' (for example, the Nordic countries), there are substantial differences in instruments used and paths traversed over time.

Instruments have included fiscal policy, land reform, social legislation, classical welfare measures, regulation of the private sector, and so on. The choice of instruments and the dominance of one set of instruments over others is often the result of a complex interplay of forces – political compromises, ideological predispositions, institutional structure, and responses to the economic and political environment – the combination of which may be unique to each country. The political feasibility of a particular set of policies is determined by a country's history and reflects the constellation of social forces. This speaks against one-size-fits-all approaches. Societies must be allowed more room and more instruments for devising policies appropriate to their circumstances.

Policy Regimes

Social policy should be formulated within a policy regime framework that includes social policy, economic policy and political regimes. An important determinant of the success of social policies is the recognition of sectoral affinities or synergies between institutions located in different spheres of the political economy. In such situations, the structure and direction of movements in one sector complement those in the others.

14
Protecting Workers, Creating Jobs: Rethinking Social Protection in Developing Countries

CARMEN PAGÉS

This short chapter argues that around the world, workers face high risk of unemployment that cannot be easily mitigated by market mechanisms. As such, it becomes the responsibility of the State to develop and administer instruments, programs and policies to protect workers against that risk. Workers in developing countries are especially affected, but their governments are ill equipped to deal with it. We will assess the relative merits/costs of different instruments, and discuss options to improve protection against unemployment risk in developing countries. The first part of the chapter presents recent data on unemployment risk in developed and developing countries. The second part examines and assesses the typical configuration of programs and policies to protect workers against unemployment in developing countries before considering options for improvement.

Market Economies Generate Substantial Unemployment Risk for Workers

Over the last ten years, there has been considerable research around the world that suggests that market economies in developed and developing countries generate substantial unemployment risk for workers. Across sectors, and across countries, job turnover is very high. Firm level data suggest that regardless of whether an economy is in recession or expansion, between 7 and 20 per cent of jobs, depending on the country, are destroyed in a given year. In turn, between 8 and 20 per cent of the jobs get created in a given year.

FIGURE 14.1
Average share of jobs created and destroyed on average in a year

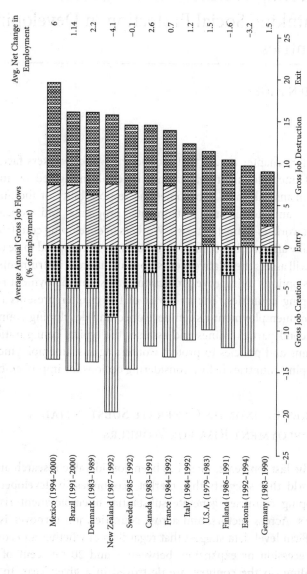

Source: OECD Employment Outlook 1996, Davis and Haltiwanger (1999), Kaplan, Gonzalez and Roberts (2003) and Menezes-Filho et al (2003).

It is important to point out that more than one third of job creation and destruction is associated with the death and birth of firms. So job destruction occurs, not only because existing firms are shedding labour, but also because of the death of existing firms. Around the world, turnover levels are higher in smaller and younger firms, and also in sectors intensively using unskilled labour. Another important finding is that most of the turnover is not related to macro-shocks or recessions, but rather to firm-specific shocks. This implies that at any given point in time, within a given sector, no matter how narrowly defined, there are firms that are being created and firms that are expanding and, simultaneously, there are firms that are shrinking or dying (Davis and Haltiwanger, 1999; IADB, 2003). This implies that the risk of unemployment is present at all times, during recessions as well as expansions, although it increases in times of aggregate economic distress due to higher risk of dismissal, longer duration of unemployment, and quite possibly, reduced earnings in new jobs (Beaudry and Pagés, 2000; IADB, 2003)

The unemployment risk caused by constant churning is even larger in developing countries. This is because they tend to have a larger proportion of employment in small firms and in industries that are intensive in the use of unskilled labour. Second, although macroeconomic shocks are not the main cause of high turnover, they do have an effect, and many developing countries tend to experience larger and more frequent shocks. Third, there is a greater prevalence of unregistered or informal jobs. The evidence suggests that informal jobs tend to be even more unstable than formal jobs (see Figure 14.2).

Thus, while the rates of job creation and job destruction presented in Figure 14.1 are estimated from firm-level data for formal firms, the data presented in Figure 14.2, estimated from household surveys, indicates that the probability of transiting from a job to unemployment is always higher for those in jobs in the informal sector (proxied here by those jobs in which employers do not register workers with Social Security).[1]

What is the source of this risk? Research suggests that economic growth and turnover are both associated with a dynamic process by which the most productive firms expand and less productive firms

FIGURE 14.2
Probability of becoming unemployed
Probability of being unemployed is conditional on being employed in a formal or an informal job a year earlier.

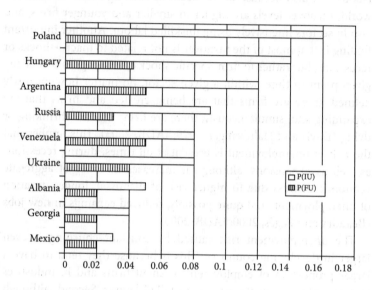

Source: Duryea and others (2006)
Note: In this data, a formal job is defined as one in which the worker is affiliated to Social Security through the job.

contract or exit the market. Figure 14.3 presents a decomposition of productivity growth into four components:

- the share due to the productivity growth of existing firms,
- the share due to the reallocation of employment across existing firms,
- the share due to the entry of new firms, and
- the share due to the exit of firms.

About a third of labour productivity growth comes from the exit of less-productive firms. So, quite importantly, not only economic recessions, or periods of restructuring associated with unemployment, but also the process of growth itself, generate risks.

FIGURE 14.3
Job reallocation: An important source of productivity growth
Decomposition of productivity growth in four components

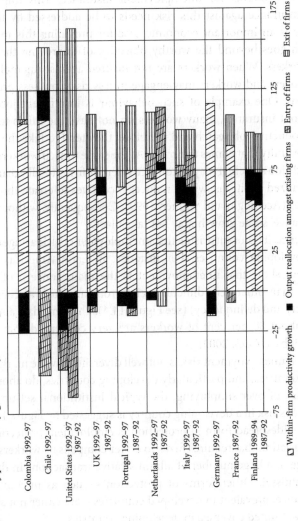

Source: Scarpetta, Hemmings, Tressel and Woo (2002), and IADB (2003).

DEVELOPING COUNTRIES POORLY EQUIPPED TO INSURE WORKERS AGAINST UNEMPLOYMENT RISK

There is no country in the world that has been able to produce a private market for unemployment insurance. This implies that any insurance against this risk needs to be addressed by the state. There is an important economic case for providing this insurance, which goes beyond the worthy objective of improving the welfare of workers. When workers are not insured against unemployment, employers and workers may engage in less risky, but less productive actions. One example of such behaviour is insufficient job search. Without insurance, many workers do not have the funds to engage in productive job search and therefore, they tend to take the first job opportunity that comes their way. At the same time, if workers engage in little job search, it may become costlier for firms to fill vacancies for specialized positions, which reduces incentives to create those types of jobs (Acemoglu and Shimer, 1999). Consequently, without proper insurance, some growth may not take place.

Hence, it is not surprising that unemployment risk is a huge concern in developing countries. For instance, in Latin America, opinion surveys show that unemployment is the main concern of people, more than other very difficult social problems (such as corruption, poverty and delinquency) (see Figure 14.4). The same data also shows that about 80 per cent of workers are very concerned about losing their jobs. (IADB, 2003)

So if unemployment risk is not well diversified by the market, what can countries, and particularly developing countries, do about it? At the risk of over-simplifying, the typical institutional set-up to deal with this risk in a developing country is suggested by Figure 14.5: The most widespread form of protection is employment protection, that is, legislation that requires firms to either compensate workers or/and engage in a large number of administrative transactions in the event of dismissal. Other forms of protection – such as unemployment insurance, prevalent in developed countries – are either not available or have limited coverage in developing countries.

FIGURE 14.4
Unemployment: Main source of concern for Latin Americans
Percentage of respondents that point to a given issue as their main problem (more than one response allowed)

Unemployment
Corruption
Poverty
Delinquence/Insecurity
Employment Instability
Low wages
Terrorism/Political Violence
Low quality of Education
Inflation
Lack of opportunities for youth
Drug Consumption
Human Rights Violations
Health Problems
Drug traffic
Housing problems
Transport
Environment
Racial Discrimination
0%
5%
10%
15%
20%
25%

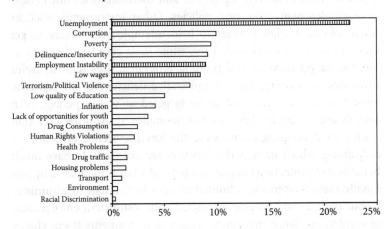

Source: Latinobarometer (2001)
Note: Average of responses for 17 countries of Latin America.

FIGURE 14.5
Typical labour market institutional set-up in developing countries (Latin America & South Asia)

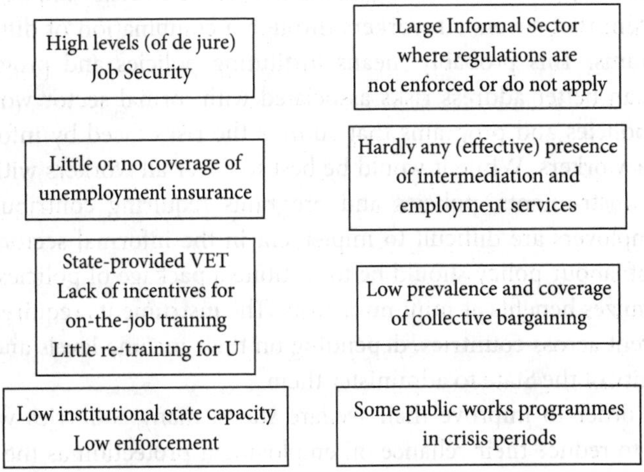

High levels (of de jure) Job Security
Large Informal Sector where regulations are not enforced or do not apply
Little or no coverage of unemployment insurance
Hardly any (effective) presence of intermediation and employment services
State-provided VET Lack of incentives for on-the-job training Little re-training for U
Low prevalence and coverage of collective bargaining
Low institutional state capacity Low enforcement
Some public works programmes in crisis periods

On the other hand, developing countries are characterized by having a large percentage of employment in the unregistered or informal sector. This implies that a large share of the labour force is not covered by labour legislation and therefore does not benefit from employment protection policies. Other instruments, such as active labour market policies to help unemployed workers to get jobs, are not very developed. Thus, while most countries have some intermediation services and training programs, they tend to suffer from lack of coverage and administrative deficiencies. In addition, most training services tend to be targeted at young people, with very little training available for the unemployed. Another common feature in developing countries is the low prevalence of collective bargaining, which implies that workers are not likely to have much benefits and protections negotiated beyond what is mandated by law. Finally, there is often a very limited capacity by the State to administer labour policies and programs coupled with insufficient enforcement of regulations. Since this configuration of instruments is not clearly sufficient to protect workers against unemployment, some countries have instituted emergency programs of public works to help workers cope with crises (Márquez, 2000).

In sum, the typical constellation of programs and policies available in developing countries constitutes a highly fragmented, inefficient and insufficient welfare state. Developing countries need to rethink their policies to protect workers against unemployment risks and develop a system that covers all workers through a combination of different programs. This probably means instituting policies and programs that can better address risks associated with formal sector workers and policies and programs that address the risks faced by informal sector workers. While it would be best to cover all workers with the same instruments, policies and programs requiring contributions by employers are difficult to implement in the informal sector. The aim of labour policy should be to institute a package of policies that maximizes benefits at minimum costs. The instruments required are different across countries, depending on their income levels and the capacity of the State to administer them.

In order to improve their welfare states, many countries would need to reduce their reliance on employment protection as the only instrument to provide income security to workers. While measuring the level of benefits of such legislation across countries is not easy, a World Bank index indicates that at least judging by the text of the law, employment protection legislation is more protective of workers in countries with lower per-capita income (see Figure 14.6). This is not so surprising once we bear in mind that such legislation constitutes the only form of income protection available to workers in many low-income countries, as instruments available in higher income economies are normally not available in the development world.

The main advantage of employment protection over other policies is that it does not require much administrative capacity from the State. Thus, unlike unemployment insurance, employment protection legislation does not require a contribution collection and payment system since firms make payments directly to workers. In addition, there is no need to verify whether a worker is unemployed. Still, employment protection requires enforcement by the State, which cannot be taken for granted. The former implies that employment protection may be one of the few viable instruments in some countries. Still, in that case, the levels need to be adjusted to avoid employment costs. In countries where EPL is very stringent, for instance, in India, where large firms are virtually prohibited from dismissing workers, employment protection legislation has been shown to have adverse effects on job creation (Besley and Burgess, 2004; Ahmad and Pagés, 2006). This research shows that excessive employment protection reduces the creation of formal sector jobs because it reduces the pace of entry of new firms. It also increases the size of the informal sector. There is also evidence that employment protection legislation creates problems in sectors of activity that require high flexibility. One good example is the textiles and garments sectors for which demand is quite volatile. This implies that these sectors would need to adjust continually to demand fluctuations. Since EPL restricts adjustment, it imposes a larger operations cost on these sectors. Research shows that the share of employment in these sectors is smaller than it would otherwise be with less protective legislation (Micco and Pagés, 2006). The research also suggests that EPL biases the creation of employment against young workers and women (Bertola Blau and Khan, 2002; Montenegro and Pagés, 2004)

Finally, another problem associated with employment protection is that firms are required to make payments to workers at times of economic distress. Payments from firms that go out of business are, in many instances, difficult to enforce. The former discussion emphasizes that while employment protection might be a valid instrument when better alternatives are not available, it needs to be improved upon. Oliver Blanchard (2002) characterized employment protection legislation as the most rudimentary form of insurance. One way to improve upon the current system is to ensure that firms make regular contributions to a reserve fund (either to individual firm reserve funds, or to a collective fund). Such reserves ensure that severance can be paid, even in the event firms go out of business. It also ensures that firms do not have to raise funds during periods of distress. In countries where the state has greater administrative capacity, switching from EPL to some form of unemployment insurance – as done in Chile – may improve workers' security and reduce costs in terms of employment and output.

FIGURE 14.6
Average Employment Protection by Level of Income

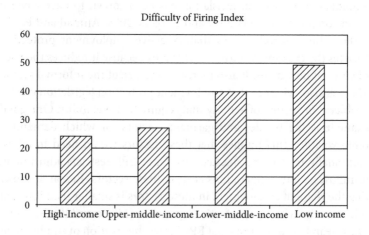

Source: World Bank (2004)

Another family of instruments widely used in a number of countries in Latin America and worth considering are unemployment insurance savings accounts (UISA). With this type of instrument, employers contribute a given percentage of workers' incomes into specially set-up individual workers' unemployment insurance savings accounts. Such funds are then made available to workers at the end of the employment relationship, regardless of the reason for termination (i.e., both in case of involuntary dismissal or voluntary resignation).[2] This mechanism protects workers by forcing them to save part of their disposable income in the event of possible unemployment. The main advantage of this tool is that it requires less administrative capacity than unemployment insurance, although it needs a relatively well-functioning capital market. The main disadvantage is that it does not pool risks across workers. Each worker has to save for his or her own unemployment, but it may be worth considering when insurance is not available[3].

Countries also need to invest in providing better job intermediation services for unemployed workers and improving the provision of training. Finally, public works need to be made permanent as unemployment risk is not only a feature of crises. The size and coverage of the program can be adjusted to the overall unemployment rate, but some form of public work programs ought to always be in place to provide a form of insurance against unemployment to the poorest workers, who are normally not covered by formal protection schemes. Combined with some worker training and job search assistance, they can become a useful form of unemployment insurance targeted at the poorest workers.

Making progress towards a better welfare state requires courage to change the status quo. It also requires experimentation and learning, as there is no scheme that fits all countries. Countries should start small, and carefully evaluate new initiatives. Such a measured approach could go a long way in protecting workers against unemployment risk.

NOTES

[1] It should be pointed out that such figures do not distinguish between workers who quit voluntarily and workers who are laid off from their jobs. However, it is clear that regardless of the cause, many more informal workers

[2] An exception is found in Brazil, where the funds in the individual accounts are only available if a worker is involuntarily laid-off.

[3] Another important shortcoming of both employment protection and UISAs is that they do not insure workers against the risk of *extended unemployment*. Thus, both instruments provide a fixed amount that depends on the past tenure of workers, but not on the duration of unemployment. Instead, UI tends to last for a number of months (in many cases, up to an upper limit). This implies that more resources are transferred to workers experiencing longer unemployment.

REFERENCES

Acemoglu, D., and R. Shimer (1999). Efficient unemployment insurance. *The Journal of Political Economy* 107: 893–928.

Ahsan, Ahmad, and Carmen Pagés (2006). Helping or hurting workers? Assessing the effects of de jure and de facto labor regulation in India. Processed, World Bank, Washington, DC.

Blanchard, Olivier (2002). Designing labor market institutions. Paper presented at the conference 'Beyond Transition: Development Perspectives and Dilemmas', April 12–13, Warsaw.

Beaudry, Paul, and Carmen Pagés (2001). The cost of business cycles and the stabilization value of unemployment insurance. *European Economic Review*, 45 (8), August: 1545–1572.

Besley, Timothy, and Robin Burgess (2004). Can labor regulation hinder economic performance? Evidence from India. *Quarterly Journal of Economics* 119 (1): 91–134.

Bertola, Giuseppe, Francine D. Blau and Lawrence M. Kahn (200 2). Labour market institutions and demographic employment patterns. NBER Working paper no. 9043, National Bureau of Economic Research, Cambridge, MA.

Botero, Juan, Simeon Djankov, Rafael La Porta, Florencio Lopez-de-Silanes, and Andrei Shleifer (2004). The regulation of labor. *Quarterly Journal of Economics* 119 (4): 1339–1382.

Davis, S., and J. Haltiwanger (1999). Gross job flows. In O. Ashenfelter and D. Card (eds). *Handbook of Labor Economics*, Volume 3. North-Holland, Amsterdam.

Duryea, Suzanne, Gustavo Marquez, Carmen Pagés and Stefano Scarpetta (2006). For better or for worse? Job and earnings mobility in nine countries. Forthcoming in Susan M. Collins and C. Graham (eds). *Brookings Trade Forum, 2006*. Brookings Institution Press, Washington, DC.

Inter-American Development Bank (2003). *Good Jobs Wanted: Labor Markets in Latin America*. Inter-American Development Bank, Washington, DC.

Kaplan, D., G. Martínez González, and R. Robertson (2003). Worker- and job-flows in Mexico. Processed, Instituto Tecnológico Autónomo de México (ITAM), Instituto Mexicano del Seguro Social (IMSS) and Macalester College.

Márquez, Gustavo (2000). Labor markets and income support: What did we learn from the crises? Research Department Working Paper WP-425, June, Inter-American Development Bank, Washington, DC.

Micco, Alejandro, and Carmen Pagés (2006). The economic effects of employment protection: Evidence from international industry-level data. Processed, World Bank, Washington, DC.

Montenegro, Claudio, and Carmen Pagés (2003). Who benefits from labour market regulations? Chile, 1960–1998. NBER Working Paper no. 9850, National Bureau of Economic Research, Cambridge, MA.

OECD (1996). OECD Employment Outlook. Organisation for Economic Co-operation and Development, Paris.

Scarpetta, Stefano, Philip Hemmings, Thierry Tressel, and Jaejoon Woo (2002). The role of policy and institutions for productivity and firm dynamics: Evidence from micro and industry data. economics department working paper no. 329, Organisation for Economic Co-operation and Development, Paris.

World Bank (2004). Doing Business 2004. World Bank, Washington, DC.

15

Transforming the Developmental Welfare States in East Asia[†]

HUCK-JU KWON

This chapter attempts to explain changes and continuity in the developmental welfare states in Korea and Taiwan within the East Asian context. The welfare states[1] in these two economies have undergone significant changes since the Asian economic crisis of 1997–1998. These changes seem to counter the neo-liberal argument that market driven globalization renders the welfare state of marginal importance in economic life (e.g., Beck, 2000; Ohmae, 1995). There have been counter-arguments to this assertion, but the analysis is fairly based on European experience (e.g., Pierson, 1998). The welfare reforms in Korea and Taiwan have also strengthened state institutions and the welfare state in particular amid instability and flexibility in the globalized market. Nevertheless, political and economic dynamics in these countries differ from those in European countries. What are the underlying dynamics of such reform and are there policy implications in the development context? To answer these questions, it is necessary to adopt a developmental perspective as well as a social policy approach, since social policy in these countries has been established as part of the overall framework of economic development.

Through this unified approach, this chapter will argue that the welfare reforms in Korea and Taiwan have pointed toward a socially inclusive welfare state while maintaining their developmental credentials. This chapter will first elaborate two strands of welfare developmentalism in order to capture the changing nature of the welfare state in East Asia. It will then explain why and how the welfare states in Korea and Taiwan underwent policy reform, drawing on a proposition derived from the concept of the developmental welfare state. In order to put the analysis in the East Asian context, this chapter will, where appropriate, refer to the experiences of Singapore and Hong Kong, where the welfare state remain largely unchanged. Lastly, this chapter will reflect policy implications of the East Asian experience in the wider context of economic and social development.

The success of the rapid economic development in these two countries was due largely to the developmental state, which played a strategic role in the process of industrialization (see Johnson, 1982; White, 1988; Woo-Cumings, 1999). However, it was not just economic policy but also social policy that was institutionalized so as to be able to play a part in the overall strategy for economic development. Hort and Kuhnle (2000:167–168) showed that East Asian countries introduced the first social security programmes at lower levels of socio-economic development than the European countries. This suggests that East Asian countries adopted the social welfare programmes as policy instruments for economic development. Goodman and White (1998: 17) highlighted the characteristics of the East Asian welfare states that were incorporated in the state developmental strategy: a development ideology that subordinated welfare to economic efficiency, discouraged dependence on the state, promoted private source of welfare, and diverted the financial resources of social insurance to investment in infrastructure.

EAST ASIA AND TWO STRANDS OF WELFARE DEVELOPMENTALISM

This preoccupation with economic development led to the welfare state being predominantly composed of social insurance programmes for industrial workers, in which people were required to pay contributions prior to entitlement to social benefits. As a result, only selected groups of people had access to social protection, while leaving the vulnerable section of the population outside the system. To avoid a demand for universal entitlement, the state did not provide funding for the welfare programmes, but enforced the rules, formal and informal, which regulated the payment of contributions for social benefits by companies and their employees. The social insurance programmes were operated by quasi-governmental agencies, working at arms-length from the government, but not, strictly speaking, a part of the government.

Because of the selectivity of the system, the East Asian welfare state had its inevitable downside. Since social policy programmes covered mainly industrial workers, the welfare states tended to reinforce socioeconomic inequalities. Kwon (1997) pointed out that the lion's share of redistribution through social policies went to high-income earners, reflecting the fact that wage earners in large-scale businesses and state sector employees were the first group of people covered by social policy programmes. The vulnerable people in society not only suffered because of their difficult situation but were also stigmatized by being excluded from the welfare state. The authoritarian government maintained a regressive welfare system and suppressed dissenting voices. These characteristics of the East Asian welfare state are well summarized by the notion of the developmental welfare state, where elite policy makers set economic growth as the fundamental goal, pursue a coherent strategy to achieve it, and use social policy as an instrument for attaining that goal (Gough, 2001).

Of course, the concept of the developmental welfare state[2] is a theoretical construct, aimed at capturing its distinctive features. The welfare states in individual East Asian economies have evolved as their socio-economic structures have changed, for example, through the process of democratization and industrialization. National Health Insurance in Korea, for instance, was extended to cover the entire population in 1988–1989. In Taiwan's case, National Health Insurance was introduced in 1995 with a central management system. The democratization of politics played an important part in these changes, resulting in similar, but different health systems in Korea and Taiwan. Singapore developed a welfare state that was anchored in a Central Provident Fund, and Malaysia implemented its New Economic Policy, which aimed mainly to redistribute economic resources along ethnic lines while developing its own Employees Provident Fund. Hong Kong recently established a similar mandatory provident scheme, in addition to welfare programmes, predominantly based on the idea of public assistance by the state. These welfare states originated during British colonial rule and were influenced in subsequent periods by nation-building efforts. Given the fact that they took such different paths, however, the developmental aspect of these welfare states is as strong as in their counterparts in Northeast Asia.

The developmental welfare state was tested in terms of its effectiveness as a social protection system during the Asian economic crisis of 1997–1998, which exposed its weaknesses. For example, during the economic crisis in Korea, one of the hardest-hit countries, it was very clear that the welfare state could not cope with the sudden rise in unemployment, because it had been based on the assumption of full employment and therefore, minimal support for the unemployed. While the economy grew fast, the number of the unemployed was small, and those who were unemployed relied on their families or on their savings as a safety net. During the economic crisis, the welfare state that had focused on workers employed in the formal sectors did not help those who lost their jobs.

As in Taiwan and Singapore, the public assistance programmes, which were based on a very low level of means-tested criteria, were not available to them in times of need. In response to this situation, the Korean government launched a range of temporary public works projects and extended the Employment Insurance Programme. After the worst phase of the economic crisis had passed, a new public assistance programme, the Minimum Living Standard Guarantee, was introduced. This programme recognized entitlement to benefits as a social right and raised the level of benefits according to the relative concept of poverty, which is an important departure from the welfare rationale of the past. In Taiwan the Employment Insurance Programme, which functioned mainly as unemployment insurance, was first introduced in 1999 in response to the rise in the unemployment rate since the late 1990s. National Health Insurance, introduced in 1995, had already signalled a new direction for the welfare state development. It was a universal programme, covering the entire population, and the government contributed a part of the funding, not only for public employees but also for farmers and the self-employed.

Considering that the developmental welfare state is based on the idea of discouraging people from dependence on the state, while providing necessary benefits for those working in the productive sectors, these welfare reforms reflect important changes. How do we explain these changes? Are these changes in the developmental welfare state pointing in a new direction that will lead to a different path from that of the past? Kwon has raised the question whether the welfare state in East Asia is moving beyond welfare developmentalism (Kwon, 2002). Changes have taken place not only in social welfare programmes, but also in the politics of social policy. Highlighting changes in the politics of social policy in which different groups of social actors are actively engaged in social policy making, Wong uses the notion of 'mainstreaming social policy' in politics (Wong, 2004). However, Kwon and Wong remain cautious on whether the clear shift, using Titmuss' term, to the institutional welfare state has not taken place. A simple answer of 'no' to the question of the shift needs to be equally tentative, since there have been important changes in the developmental welfare state.

In contrast to Korea and Taiwan, the governments in Singapore and Hong Kong did not carry out major reforms in social policy. There has been no major reform in the Central Provident Fund in Singapore. Although the Mandatory Provident Fund was introduced in 2000, there was no big shake-up of the welfare state in Hong Kong. On the contrary, the Hong Kong government tried to check the expansion of the welfare state after the hand-over in 1997 (Pearson, 2003). The welfare state in Singapore and Hong Kong shows strong continuity. What are the underlying factors of these different responses among the East Asian countries?

To capture these changes and continuities, it is necessary to elaborate the concept of the developmental welfare state, especially its political, economic and social aspects. It is important to recognize that the developmental use of social policy is not particularly new, if one looks back to the history of the welfare state. The most notable example is Bismarck's social policy in the 1880s (Rimlinger, 1971), which sought to facilitate industrialization through social insurance programmes, and at the same time to undermine political support for the socialist movement in Prussia. Bismarckian social policy did not attach equal importance to the intrinsic goals of social policy such as human well-being, social justice and redistribution. Social policy was only conceived as instrumental to economic and political objectives.

In this respect, the welfare states in East Asia are clearly in line with the Bismarckian concept.

There has also been another strand in the developmental use of social policy. An early example of this type is the Scandinavian experiment with active labour market policy in the 1930s (Dahl, Dropping and Lodemel, 2001). While providing income maintenance, this policy was intended to provide the recipients with the necessary skills that would enable them to enter the labour market, to make their own living and subsequently to contribute to economic development. This strand of welfare developmentalism was further elaborated by the United Nations and its specialized agencies in the late 1960s and 1970s. For example, in 1966, the United Nations Economic and Social Council passed a resolution in which it emphasized the interrelated character of economic and social factors and the importance of incorporating social development into economic development in order to achieve a better standard of living.

This resolution was developed in more detail by a group of experts on social policy. The chairman of the group of experts was Gunnar Myrdal, who argued for a unified approach to social and economic planning in developing countries. The group criticized the tendency in economics to draw a distinct line between economic and social phenomena, separating social development from economic development (UNDESA, 1971: 4). It argued that social factors, such as excessive concentration of wealth and income, inequalities in educational opportunities and inegalitarian social and power structures, impede development and should be dealt with by social policy. In other words, economic development requires social policy.

The experts went on to propose four principles of social policy, which could be regarded as the core of the second strand of welfare developmentalism: (1) to leave no important section of the population outside the scope of change and development; (2) to make it a principal objective to activate a wider sector of the population and to ensure its participation in development; (3) to accept and aim at social equity as being morally important, as well as a significant element in increasing long-term economic efficiency; and (4) to give high priority to the development of human potential, especially that of children, by preventing malnutrition during their early years and by providing health services and equal opportunities (UNDESA, 1971: 11).

This UN initiative, however, failed to have a significant impact on policy making due to the worldwide economic recession in the 1970s. The ascendancy of neoliberalism in the 1980s also prevented this strand of welfare developmentalism from influencing development thinking. Yet, some scholars continued their research on ways in which economic development and social development could go hand-in-hand (see Midgley, 1982; Midgley, 1995), and some of the UN agencies such as United Nations Development Programme (1990) and the United Nations Research Institute for Social Development, (2000) have attempted to reinvigorate the idea of welfare developmentalism.

The key principles of the second strand of welfare developmentalism are productivism, universal social investment and democratic governance (which will be referred to as 'inclusive welfare developmentalism'), while the Bismarckian strand has features of productivism, selective social investment and authoritarianism (referred to as 'selective welfare developmentalism'). If the welfare states in East Asia fall under the selective type of the developmental welfare state, will the recent changes transform the welfare state in Korea and Taiwan into the inclusive type? What are the driving forces for such a transformation, if such transformations have really taken place? What are the institutional advantages and drawbacks that Korea and Taiwan have experienced in the process of change?

Before we try to answer these questions, it is necessary to make it clear what we mean by the development state, since the developmental welfare states, either selective or inclusive, are in fact discussed in the context of the developmental state with particular attention to social policy. We define a developmental state as a state that plays a strategic role in economic development with a bureaucracy that is given sufficient scope to take initiatives and operate effectively (Johnson, 1999). Here, economic development is given priority over other spheres of public policy, and the national economy as a whole has priority over the comparative advantage of particular industries. This is a minimalist definition, compared to the conventional one, which also carries with it a heavy load of economic, political and social implications.

Although the developmental state has shown an affinity with authoritarian politics, we do not assume that the developmental state is intrinsically opposed to democracy, just as the leading commentators have never denied the possibility of democratic politics within the developmental state (Johnson, 1999; White, 1998; White, 1988).[3] We also do not assume that the welfare state within such a paradigm should be a selective one. However, our minimal definition suggests that the overarching economic goal defines the nature of the welfare state. Of course, this link is not automatic, but is intermediated by the politics of each country. The hypothesis arising from our conception of the developmental state is that once the overarching goal of economic policy is reset, other public policies including social policy will be readjusted in line with the new policy paradigm.

In the remaining part of this chapter, we will argue that the shift in the overall goal of economic policy from extensive growth based on cheap labour to economic competitiveness based on high quality products, which was hastened by the Asian economic crisis, brought about new definitions of developmental social policy in Korea and Taiwan, and created enough room to accommodate political demands for greater social rights. This is an interesting contrast to Singapore and Hong Kong, where the paradigm of economic policy was not reset and the politics did not undergo major changes. This explains why these two welfare states remain essentially the same as before the economic crisis in these two countries.

CHANGES IN ECONOMIC STRUCTURE AND REDEFINING DEVELOPMENTAL SOCIAL POLICY

Based on their data analysis of the West European countries, Huber and Stephens (2001) argue that there is a clear link between the production regime and the welfare regime that a country may have developed. They also argue that countries with different production regimes tend to respond to economic challenges with different social policy reforms. Of course, the link is not automatic and it depends on the intermediate political process.

Such links have been equally evident in the developmental welfare state in East Asian countries since social policy has been used as an instrument for economic development strategies. In order to identify the developmental nature of social policy in Korea and Taiwan, it is necessary to examine the ways in which economic development was pursued. In this context, we will examine the question as to whether some social policy programmes, such as unemployment insurance, which had been regarded as hampering economic development, were now understood as developmental as economic restructuring took place.

Even though the state played a strategic role in the economic development of all the East Asian countries examined in this chapter, the role of the state in different countries was not exactly the same. In Korea and Taiwan, the state deliberately intervened in the economic decision making of firms to facilitate industrialization of the whole economy, rather than just certain sectors with comparative advantages. The economic development in both countries was set as an overarching goal of public policy. This was related partly to the nationalist zeal of the authoritarian leaders – Park Chung-Hee in Korea and Chiang Kai-shek in Taiwan – who first embarked on the economic development plan in the two countries. It is fair to say that not only these political leaders, but also bureaucrats and the public in general regarded economic development as an overarching imperative in order to put their countries on an equal footing with the West (Haggard, 1988).

More importantly, the authoritarian governments in both countries attempted to legitimise their rule by economic development. This is why Korea and Taiwan took the road to economic development through state intervention, instead of letting the market do the job. Amsden (1989) argued that the Korean state had intervened in the market mechanism and deliberately distorted market prices in order to compete internationally. This is not a unique experience in the history of economic development. What made the Korean case different was the discipline the state exercised over big business, known as *chaebol*.[4] The Korean state imposed performance standards on private firms, and once these standards were met, the state provided various kinds of subsidy, for example low-interest capital, allowing businesses to enter new markets or consolidate their monopoly status.

The other side of the industrial policy in Korea during the period of rapid economic growth was the harsh suppression of trade unions and labour movements. Political suppression was not, however, the only measure used to ensure industrial stability and workers' loyalty. The Park government and the following authoritarian governments established a range of policies to enhance the welfare of industrial workers. This is why major social insurance programmes started with large-scale firms such as Industrial Accident Insurance, National Health Insurance and the National Pension Programme (Kwon, 1999). A cheap but well-trained labour force was an essential requisite for the export-oriented industrialization strategy. In this context, as Yi and Lee (2003) argue, vocational training and occupational welfare programmes for workers were promoted by the state, which private firms perceived as orders rather than guidelines from the state. These occupational welfare benefits were very often workplace-based and consequently non-transferable, so that workers' loyalty to firms was ensured.

The role of the state in Taiwan during the period of rapid economic growth is similar to that of Korea. Wade (1988: 54) explains that the aim of government intervention was not to encourage firms to maximise profitability based on current comparative advantage, but rather to control the composition of national investment so that Taiwan could establish a flexible and integrated production structure. What was different in Taiwan was that the share of the large conglomerates in the economy was smaller than in Korea and such conglomerates were concentrated in the state-controlled strategic industries, such as the China Petroleum Corporation. A large share of economic production was undertaken by small- and medium-sized enterprises. These firms were run by families: the head of the family was often the owner/manager and the other family members worked for wages (Hsiung, 1996).

Given the strong authoritarian state, the trade union movements were weak and not perceived by the state as a threat to the economic development plan. Labour Insurance, which was one of the first major social insurance programmes during the development period, was targeted mainly toward industrial workers in large-scale firms, and the state sector workers were among those first covered by health insurance programmes. Within these overall economic strategies, social protection for vulnerable people in society was left to families. Some social insurance programmes, such as unemployment insurance, were never on the agenda since they were perceived as discouraging the work ethic and encouraging dependency on the state. It is also important to note that women were doubly burdened in the export-oriented industrialization in both Korea and Taiwan, since they were the main providers of cheap labour for industry as well as of welfare for their families.

In Singapore and Hong Kong, social development was not a priority, and as in Taiwan and Korea it was subordinated to the overall economic development strategy. Nevertheless, their strategies were different from those pursued by Korea and Taiwan during the period of rapid economic growth. This resulted in a different structure of the welfare state. Singapore also set economic development as the overriding goal for society. Initial conditions soon after independence in 1954 were not favourable for Singapore to undertake industrialization projects because of her neighbours such as Indonesia and Malaysia, which were not altogether friendly to Singapore (Singapore was separated from the Malaysian federation in 1965), the multi-ethnic composition of the population, and the volatility of politics.

The economic strategy of the People's Action Party was to build a sound infrastructure, to ensure workforce compliance, provide generous tax incentives, and allow international capital to completely own their business operations (Chua, 2003). In contrast to the strategy of Korea and Taiwan to build a national economy with a vertical integration of industries, Singapore attempted to build an international platform for industrialization, and left international capital to carry out its own business instead of giving it guidelines and punishing it if it did not follow them as in Korea and Taiwan. The Central Provident Fund was central to this economic policy. Initially established by the British colonial government to provide lump-sum retirement pensions (Kwon, 1998), it was used as an effective way of capital mobilization. One of the important innovations which the Singapore government cleverly devised, was to link the Central

Provident Fund to housing policy. Chua explains that the Central Provident Fund was a vital part of the capital formation of Singapore through its housing programmes. He also points out that improved housing conditions through the Central Provident Fund provided permanent shelter, improved sanitation and health conditions, and enhanced well-being, which then led to increasing labour productivity (Chua, 2003: 10).

It is, however, important to recognize that this seemingly virtuous circle was based on three very authoritarian policies: the Land Acquisition Act of 1966, the Industrial Relations Act of 1968 and the Internal Security Act of 1958. The Land Acquisition Act allowed the government to acquire any piece of land it deemed necessary, which was an effective nationalization of land; the Industrial Relations Act severely curtailed the trade union movements; and the Internal Security Act allowed the government to detain anyone it saw as opposing social stability for extendable two-year terms of detention.

Hong Kong pursued a very similar industrialization strategy to that of Singapore during the period of rapid economic growth, although the British colonial government had never explicitly declared that it had implemented an industrialization policy. In a way, it is fair to say that Hong Kong was the pioneer of industrialization strategy through the building of an international entrepôt for trade and finance with some export-oriented industries. What was different in Hong Kong was that it did not have a provident fund like Singapore. The provident funds in the British colonies were introduced as part of the decolonization process, which was why it was discussed under the last British Governor in Hong Kong, Chris Patten, towards the end of the British governance in Hong Kong. What was very similar in Hong Kong and Singapore was that housing policy was central to social policy as an instrument of economic development. The Housing Authority of the colonial government built numerous rental and home ownership estates. Hong Kong also built comprehensive social assistance programmes which were introduced under the auspices of the governor David Wilson (Hong Kong Government, 1991). These programmes were financed by public revenues. In other words, the state was the main provider in financing welfare programmes, which was unique in East Asian welfare states.

TABLE 15.1
Key indicators in four East Asian countries

		1996	1997	1998	1999	2000
Korea	GDP growth rate	6.7	5.0	−6.7	10.9	8.8
	Unemployment rate	2.0	2.6	6.8	6.3	4.1
Taiwan	GDP growth rate	6.1	6.7	4.6	5.4	5.9
	Unemployment rate	2.6	2.7	2.7	2.9	3.0
Singapore	GDP growth rate	7.6	8.5	0.1	5.9	9.8
	Unemployment rate	3.0	2.4	3.2	4.6	4.4
Hong Kong	GDP growth rate	11.6	10.5	−6.6	−2.9	
	Unemployment rate	2.8	2.2	4.7	6.3	5

Source: Asian Development Bank (2002)

Despite such differences in economic strategy, East Asian countries were very successful during the 1970s, 1980s and the first part of the 1990s. These developmental strategies were challenged to a great extent as these countries became exposed to global competition. This was manifested during the Asian economic crisis. As Table 15.1 suggests, the four countries were equally influenced by the economic crisis, and serious rethinking in economic policy took place in Korea and Taiwan, while Singapore and Hong Kong basically continued the strategy for the international entrepôt of trade and finance. Although it was inevitable that Singapore and Hong Kong would be affected by the international economic downturn, there seemed no other viable alternatives for them to the current economic strategy of remaining as a centre of international trade and finance, given the deepening of global economic integration.

It is true that there has been a critical re-examination of the existing economic paradigm in Singapore and Hong Kong. Both countries now emphasize the importance of building a high-tech and knowledge-based economy, but such new emphasis is still in line with the existing framework of economic development. Social policy responses to the economic crisis in Singapore and Hong Kong were also within the selective form of the developmental welfare state.

During the economic crisis, the Singapore government lowered the employer's contributions to the Central Provident Fund from 20 to 10 per cent, as in 1986. Hong Kong introduced the Mandatory Provident Fund in 2000, but it was a pension fund just like the Central Provident Fund. In other words, there were no fundamental changes in the developmental welfare state.

In contrast, Korea and Taiwan suffered from the structural problems behind the headline indicators. In fact, they were already identified before the Asian economic crisis. As for Korea, its international competitiveness rapidly decreased during the 1990s. As Park (2001) shows, the average increase in wage was 14.3 per cent, while labour productivity increased by 10.4 per cent during the 1990s. As we pointed out, Korean firms provided various company welfare benefits to their workers in order to maintain their loyalty. Furthermore, the life-time employment and seniority-based remuneration system remained an implicit contract between employers and employees. Such company welfare benefits were arranged on the basis of low wages and weak trade unions. However, once trade unions were allowed to mobilize workers and successfully increase the level of wages from the late 1980s, the existing formula of company welfare benefits could not be sustained.

Considering that Korea's economic growth was mainly based on cheap labour costs, the loss of international price competitiveness raised a fundamental question about the existing economic strategy and the developmental welfare state. This was also prompted by China and other East Asian developing countries encroaching on the traditional Korean market. The Korean government saw that the country would need to develop a high-technology based economy with a flexible labour market, and in 1990 launched the 'Seven-Year Development Plan for High-Tech Industry'. The aim of this plan was to bring high technology into the Korean economy and make it competitive (Ahn, 1998: 134). The Korean government also set in place institutional arrangements necessary for structural adjustment. The inevitable corollary of structural adjustment was to lay off workers and staff in sectors that were no longer competitive. In this context, the Employment Insurance Programme, which included job-training schemes as well as unemployment benefits, was introduced in 1995.

This led to a new definition of 'developmental social policy' in Korea and a significant change in social policy: providing benefits to those who are not working and training them outside companies. What remains essentially the same is the state's effort to utilize social policy as an instrument of economic policy. The other side of the coin was to reform the labour market so that employers could lay off their workers if necessary. This was harder to do because Korea had become democratic and the bureaucrats could no longer rely on the authoritarian power of the president in passing the controversial programmes through the National Assembly.

Taiwan also faced a problem of high labour costs. Before martial law was lifted, trade unions in Taiwan were controlled by the state. Once this oppressive law was lifted in 1987, trade union movements and the Taiwan Labour Front in particular, started to mobilize workers. They demanded political freedom and higher wages, and the number of strikes increased sharply (Chen, Ko and Lawler, 2003). The response from the government was to promote a capital- and skill-intensive industrial structure instead of a labour-intensive one. As in Korea, Taiwan made significant progress on this front, notably in the information technology (IT) industry.

The Taiwanese employers, however, responded to the rising cost of labour in other ways as well. They started to move their operations to mainland China. As Chen (2003) reports, Taiwanese investment in China increased sixteen times during the period from 1991 to 2001. It is true that capital mobility increases as global economic integration deepens. For the Taiwanese entrepreneurs, either in a labour- or capital-intensive industry, China provided an excellent investment opportunity as a cheap labour supplier and an enormous market. This, in turn, led to an increase in unemployment in Taiwan.

The unemployment rate was low by international standards, but for the developmental welfare state, which was based on full employment without unemployment insurance, it posed a serious challenge. Further, it emerged that the unemployed were typically male workers from the manufacturing sectors, and that they tended to remain unemployed in the longer term. This suggests that the selective form of the developmental state could not serve the need of the Taiwanese economy. Since the Taiwanese economy escaped the domino effect of the financial crisis because of its huge foreign reserves, policy change was less dramatic than in Korea. This does not mean that changes in social policy were less significant in Taiwan, which also introduced unemployment insurance with a training programme package in 1999.

DEMOCRATIC POLITICS AND INCLUSIVE SOCIAL POLICY

It would be misleading to assume that the politics of the developmental welfare state would automatically produce public policy decisions required for economic development, particularly when it was undergoing democratization. The new understanding of 'developmental' social policy needed to find its meaning in practice through the political process. At the beginning, however, the Korean government attempted to adjust social policy according to the new set of economic goals without building broad political support. For example, in March 1997, the Kim Young-sam government passed a bill to revise the Labour Standard Law through the National Assembly behind locked doors without opposition members, which had been a typical tactic of the authoritarian government to pass the bills it wanted. It aimed to reform the labour market in order to make it easier for employers to lay off workers. The opposition party, then led by Kim Dae-jung, strongly opposed the bill, as did the public. The then governing party, at the last minute, halted the provision of lay-offs in the bill for two years in an effort to gain wider support. This raised serious doubts about the ability of the state to carry through its economic reform under democratic politics, which then sparked a chain reaction of financial crisis at the end of 1997.

The economic crisis produced a surprise winner in the presidential election at the end of 1997: the long-time opposition leader, Kim Dae-jung. It gave the Korean government another opportunity to carry out labour market reform. In February 1998 the President-elect Kim Dae-jung established a tripartite committee, the Employees-Employers-Government Committee, to forge a social consensus for reform. It is worth noting that the Korean Confederation of Trade Unions, which had been subject to harsh suppression by the government, participated in this committee as did the Korean Federation of Trade Unions. In other words, this committee was able to produce a broad-based social consensus for reform (Kwon, 2003a). The committee agreed to the labour market reform, but also recommended that the government implement a package of social protection measures for the unemployed, which was later called the 'Master Plan for Tackling Unemployment'. The Master Plan included, *inter alia*, the swift extension of the Employment Insurance Programme, the implementation of public works projects, and the reinforcement of employment services (see Table 15.2). The training schemes within the Employment Insurance Programme were put into full operation. Yi and Lee argue that policy emphasis shifted from job security to job capability of workers, according to their recipient-centred analysis of the labour market policy (Yi and Lee, 2003).

TABLE 15.2

The extension of the unemployment benefits (benefit coverage*)

	1997	1998	1999	2000
Korea	7.8	26.34	33.1	33.3
Taiwan	n.a.	n.a.	13.9	35.9

* benefit coverage refers to proportion of people receiving unemployment benefits among the unemployed.

Source: *Korea Statistical Yearbook* and *Employment Insurance Review* (Korea); *Statistical Yearbook* of the Republic of China and Council of Labour Affairs (http://dbsi.cla.tw/stat/)

Since, unlike Korea, Taiwan was not hit by the economic crisis, the policy response was less urgent, but built in a similar way on social consensus initiated by the new government. In 2000, the opposition candidate of the Democratic Progressive Party, Chen Shui-bian, was elected to the presidency. During the campaign, Chen unveiled his labour policies, which departed from the traditional KMT line: further autonomy for the trade union movements; re-examination of the privatisation policy of state-owned enterprises; and labour-management conferences (Chen, Ko and Lawler, 2003). After the election, the DPP government convened the first 'National Economic Development and Consultation Conference' in 2001. The conference agreed to reform the three basic labour laws, which were under review at the time of writing this chapter (Lin, 2003). After this conference in 2003, the Employment Insurance Programme integrated the existing, but fragmented unemployment benefit and training schemes in 2003 after this conference. In a nutshell, the unemployment insurance programme, which was the last programme the developmental welfare state would consider for introduction, became a centrepiece of the system in the newly defined 'developmental' welfare state in Korea and Taiwan.

Although a shift in economic strategy in Korea and Taiwan brought about the new understanding of 'developmental' social policy, it is not the whole story. Under the politics of democratization, there emerged advocacy coalitions who pressed their agenda for inclusive social policy. It is also important to note that these new advocacy coalitions did not suddenly take on social policy as the opportunities arose. For many years, there had existed advocacy coalitions that pursued the goal of an inclusive social policy and attempted to change the developmental welfare state in Korea and Taiwan. Their roles in social policy making have often been mentioned in passing in the existing literature of comparative social policy, since these actors often failed to achieve their policy outcomes under authoritarian politics.

At first, these advocacy coalitions did not have a very clear idea about inclusive social policy or a coherent political strategy to be able to pursue policy outcomes. I have explained that in Korea, the advocacy coalition for an inclusive health insurance system did not have a clear idea about social justice, and argued that they had to compromise their positions under the authoritarian politics from the early 1960s until the late 1980s (Kwon, 2003b). Their first serious attempt in 1988 to integrate the health care system, which would have included the self-employed and farmers under one national health insurance, failed because President Roh vetoed the integration bill initiated by the opposition party. As the advocacy coalition, which initially comprised policy experts, extended their network to the grassroots civil societies, bureaucrats and politicians, their ideas and political strategy also became coherent. In 1998, when the Kim Dae-jung government came to power, this group of people successfully seized key positions in the government and were able to integrate National Health Insurance in Korea in 2000. Nevertheless, integration reform was not a clear-cut victory for the advocacy coalition, since the financial integration was not completed, while the administration side of integration was. This was partly due to the antiquated tax system and strong objections from the opposition party in the National Assembly.

Another major breakthrough towards an inclusive social policy was also made by basically the same advocacy coalition: the reform of the public assistance programme. During the economic crisis, the existing public assistance programme based on a strict means-test idea did not help the poor. The advocacy coalition was able to introduce the Minimum Living Standard Guarantee, which recognized the right of every citizen to a decent living as a social right. It abolished the so-called family test to provide cash benefits to those who have non-poor family members and increased the level of benefits based on the concept of relative poverty (Kwon, 2003a). It is worth noting that the reform of the programme was also part of Kim Dae-jung's political strategy to win a majority in the National Assembly in the 2000 general election. The new public assistance programme also includes a range of workfare and training programmes as well as cash benefits. The catchword, 'productive welfare state', used by the Kim Dae-jung government for the general election (Presidential Office, 2000), summarized the nature of welfare reform after the economic crisis.

National Health Insurance was also an important part of democratization politics in Taiwan. Once *Tangwai* (meaning 'outside the party') was allowed as a political party as the Democratic Progress Party in 1986, the DPP fought elections (initially local elections) on a platform of democratization, Taiwanization and social welfare (Lu, 1992). In fact the DPP's social welfare manifestos turned out to be more effective than those of Taiwanization in local elections, as some DPP candidates were successful with policy for old-age allowances. It was also true that a majority of the Taiwanese wanted to avoid the issue of Taiwanization because of military warning from Beijing. In this context, the KMT, the then governing party, decided to introduce National Health Insurance in 1995, five years earlier than planned.

Before the introduction of the universal health insurance programme, only public sector employees, school teachers and employees in the large-scale firms were covered by the various social insurance programmes. Farmers had their own health insurance from 1989, but the majority of the population was not covered by any public health insurance. As the DPP began to address the issue, the KMT did not have a choice other than to introduce the National Health Insurance (Hwang, 1995), which covered the whole population, with the government providing funding for the self-employed, informal sector workers and farmers. It was an important departure from the selective form of the developmental welfare state in Taiwan. Nevertheless, the KMT government placed an important conditionality on the new National Health Insurance. The government was required to review the administrative and financing arrangement within five years after its introduction (Ku, 1998). In particular, a multiple carrier system would be considered against the current single carrier system.

The KMT government had already started to prepare the National Health Insurance reform as early as 1997. The Department of Health drew a policy draft for a health system of multiple insurance carriers. The proposal failed to go through the legislative process contrary to the KMT government's intention in 1999. It was partly due to the factional split of the KMT in the run-up to the Presidential election, but Wong (2004) points out that the citizens' advocacy coalition, the 'NHI coalition', was an active player in the efforts to resist reform. The coalition successfully argued that the multi-insurance carrier reform would bring NHI back to a selective and fragmented system.

While the democratic politics in Korea and Taiwan accommodated new 'developmental' social policies and initiated a universal healthcare system, politics in Singapore and Hong Kong were relatively stable. Whether Singapore's 'guided' democracy is democratic or not has been a controversial issue for some time. Nevertheless it is important to recognize that the Singapore government has enjoyed what Chua calls performance legitimacy from the population (Chua, 2003). Despite the hand-over of sovereignty to China, Hong Kong's politics remains absorbed by the administration. This seems to be the case with an exception of the period in which Chris Patten attempted to introduce quasi-democratization before the hand-over. Given the political stability, and since there has been no major shift in economic strategy in Singapore and Hong Kong, it was not necessary to the economic and social policy paradigm that proved to be successful in achieving what it aimed: a platform for a global city of trade and finance, as Ramesh (2003) explains. It is worth noting recent protest over the introduction of an anti-subversion law in Hong Kong that showed a growing pressure for democratization of politics in Hong Kong, but it is not very clear whether this will lead to a significant democratic reform. It is also worth noting that the overall size of the welfare state has grown in response to structural factors such as the ageing of the population in Hong Kong and Singapore.

Concluding Remarks

This chapter has argued that the recent reform of the developmental welfare state in Korea and Taiwan was mainly due to the shift in the overall goal of economic policy from extensive economic growth to economic competitiveness. The economic crisis in 1997–1998 made the reform of the structural weakness of the economy inevitable. This chapter explained how the welfare state that had focused on those working in the large-scale firms now began to protect those not working, including the poor and the elderly as well as the unemployed, in line with the economic changes. Within the new social protection schemes, training programmes as well as unemployment benefits were predominant. In other words, the emphasis was placed on the protection of the job capability instead of the job security of workers.

The reform in economic and social policy had to be carried out through democratic politics. The newly elected governments in Korea and Taiwan were able to forge a social consensus through tripartite committees. Through the opportunities arising from the change of governments, the advocacy coalitions for inclusive social policy successfully achieved their social policy agenda instead of just accommodating economic changes. National Health Insurance, as well as public assistance programmes, in both countries was made more inclusive. In short, the change in the overall goal of economic policy, and a shift toward democratic politics resulted in making the developmental welfare state more inclusive in Korea and Taiwan.

What remains unchanged is that the social policy is developmental, while social inclusion is now considered an equally important social policy goal. In contrast, the developmental welfare states of Singapore and Hong Kong have remained largely unchanged in their underlying principle. This chapter has argued that despite the adverse effects of the Asian economic crisis, Singapore and Hong Kong maintained the overall strategy of economic development through international trade and finance, a strategy that seems appropriate as global economic integration continues. In terms of politics, the administration still absorbs the politics, and there are no serious political challenges to the prevailing order.

The move toward an inclusive developmental welfare state does not mean that the welfare state has become as inclusive as in the Scandinavian countries. There is a whole range of areas of social policy that needs to be improved in terms of social inclusion. Despite the changes, the developmental welfare state is still gender biased. For example, in Korea, the National Pension Programme, the Employment Insurance Programme and Industrial Accident Insurance should include all workers whether they are regular or temporary. In practice, however, less than half the temporary workers are covered by these programmes while most regular workers are within the schemes. Considering that the number of temporary workers has increased and that they are more likely to be women, they are not equally protected by the programmes. In Taiwan, the government created a number of low-paid jobs for the wives of middle-aged men who had lost their jobs. Although the jobs may have compensated for a part of the lost family income, they were likely to double the women's burden: the women now had to work both outside and in the home.

In the areas of social services and social care, there has been little improvement compared to those of public assistance, pension, health care and unemployment. Caring for chronically ill people, the bedridden elderly and the disabled fell mostly to families, which in turn, meant the women. The absence of improvement in these areas of social policy showed that the welfare state in Korea and Taiwan still places stronger emphasis on development than on social inclusion. It is also clear that the improvement of social protection depends to a great extent on political mobilization as in the case of health care, which has been the centre of political debates in Korea and Taiwan.

In the wider context of economic and social development, the recent experiences of Korea and Taiwan counter the assertion that social protection should come as an after-thought of economic development. More socially inclusive welfare states helped these two countries to come out of the economic crisis without much adverse social effects such as a sharp rise of poverty or serious worsening of income inequality. It will be useful for the development debate if the idea of the developmental welfare state be explored in the context of other developing countries against the tendency that separates social protection from economic development.

In terms of policy implications, in addition to the inclusive welfare reform after the economic crisis, I would like to emphasize that Korea and Taiwan had developed social policy institutions in an incremental fashion for quite some time, which proved to be a basis for the inclusive reforms, and that those social forces which had had frustrating experiences persevered in pursuing their social agenda. Of course, not everything is rosy in Korea and Taiwan. For instance, levels of unemployment remain relatively high compared to those in the past, and the governments in Korea and Taiwan have struggled to finance the welfare states due to the expansion of the programmes. Nevertheless, considering that economic development has been set as a trade-off with social protection and democracy in the development context, the Korean and Taiwanese experiences show that it is possible to achieve democracy, economic development and social inclusion at the same time.

Notes

† This chapter was originally prepared as part of the UNRISD project on 'Social Policy in a Development Context'. The author is grateful to Thandika Mkandawire, Shahra Razavi and Justin MacDermott for insightful discussions during the preparation of the chapter and has also benefited from comments by Sarah Cook, Chua Beng Huat, Ito Peng, Joe Wong, Ilcheong Yi and M Ramesh at a Bangkok workshop in June 2003 and Evelyn

Huber and John Myles at the Research Committee C 19 Conference in August 2003. A slightly revised version has been published in *Development and Change* 36 (3). The usual caveats apply.

[1] The welfare state refers here to the set of social policies and institutions that aim to protect citizens from social contingencies, poverty and illness, but it does not necessarily mean that the level of well-being of citizens is achieved nor that all citizens have access to social benefits.

[2] In a similar vein, Holliday uses the term 'productivist welfare regimes' when he argues that the East Asian welfare regimes constitute a fourth welfare regime (Holliday 2000). This article uses the concept of the developmental welfare state partly because it allows us to examine the political, economic and social context of the welfare state in East Asia and partly because it enable us to draw on the rich literature of development studies that has elaborated the concept of the developmental state.

[3] White points out the socioeconomic conditions that are conducive to democracy in the developmental state: a higher level of socioeconomic development; a relatively homogenous population; a strong sense of national identity, a cohesive social structure; a society lacking in gross inequalities; a vibrant civil society; and a well-developed political party system (White 1998).

[4] A *chaebol* is a large capitalist organization, usually based on a single family having controlling interests in a variety companies, similar to the Japanese *Zaibatsu*.

REFERENCES

Ahn, H. (1998). From the active labour market policy to income maintenance: An analysis of the Korean Employment Insurance Programme. *Yonsei Social Welfare Review* 5: 125–154 (in Korean).

Amsden, A. (1989). *Asia's Next Giant: South Korea and Late Industrialization*. Oxford University Press, Oxford.

Asian Development Bank (2002). *Key Indicators in 2001: Growth and Change in Asia and the Pacific*. Asian Development Bank, Manila.

Beck, U. (2000). *What is Globalization?* Polity Press, Cambridge.

Chen, F.l. (2003). The reform of unemployment policies in Taiwan: Implications for gender and families. UNRISD workshop on 'Social Policy in a Development Context', United Nations Research Institute for Social Development, Bangkok.

Chen, S.H., Ko, J.J., and J. Lawler (2003). Changing patterns of industrial relations in Taiwan. *Industrial Relations* 42: 315–40.

Chua, B.H. (2003). Welfare developmentalism in Singapore and Malaysia. In H. J. Kwon (ed.). UNRISD Workshop on Social Policy in a Development Context. United Nations Research Institute for Social Development, Bangkok.

Dahl, E., J.A. Dropping, and I. Lodemel (2001). Norway: Relevance of the social development model for post-war welfare policy. *International Journal of Social Welfare* 10: 300–08.

Goodman, R., and G. White (1998). Welfare orientalism and the search for an East Asian welfare model. In R. Goodman, G. White and H.J. Kwon (eds). *The East Asian Welfare Model: Welfare Orientalism and the State*. Routledge, London.

Gough, I. (2001). Globalization and regional welfare regimes: The East Asian case. *Global Social Policy* 1: 163-189.

Haggard, S. (1988). The politics of industrialization in East Asia and Taiwan. In H. Hughes (ed.). *Achieving Industrialization in East Asia*. Cambridge University Press, Cambridge.

Holliday, I. (2000). Productivist welfare capitalism: Social policy in East Asia. *Political Studies* 48: 706–23.

Hong Kong Government (1991). *Social Welfare into the 1990s and Beyond*. Hong Kong Government, Hong Kong.

Hort, S., and S. Kuhnle (2000). The coming of East and South-East Asian welfare states. *Journal of European Social Policy* 10: 162–84.

Hsiung, Y.T. (1996). Blood thicker than water: Interpersonal relations and Taiwanese investment in southern China. *Environment and Planning* 28: 2241–261.

Huber, E., and J. Stephens (2001). Welfare state and production regimes in the era of retrenchment. In P. Pierson (ed.). *The New Politics of the Welfare State* Oxford University Press, Oxford: 107–45.

Hwang, Y.S. (1995). Funding health care in Britain and Taiwan. Unpublished Ph.D. dissertation, University of Newcastle.

Johnson, Chalmers (1982). *MITI and the Japanese Miracle: The Growth of Industrial Policy, 1925–1975*. Stanford University Press, Stanford.

Johnson, Chalmers (1999). The developmental state: Odyssey of a concept. In Meredith Woo-Cumings (ed.). *The Developmental State*. Cornell University Press, Ithaca.

Korea, Republic of (various years). *Korea Statistical Yearbook*. Statistics Office, Seoul.

Ku, Y.W. (1998). Can we afford it? The development of national health insurance in Taiwan. In R. Goodman, G. White and H.J. Kwon (eds). *The East Asian Welfare Model: Welfare Orientalism and the State*. Routledge, London. Kwon, H.J. (1997). Beyond European welfare regimes: Comparative perspectives on East Asian welfare systems. *Journal of Social Policy* 26: 467–84.

Kwon, H.J. (1998). Democracy and the politics of social welfare: A comparative analysis of welfare systems in East Asia. In R. Goodman, G. White and H.-J. Kwon (eds), *East Asian Welfare Model: Welfare Orientalism and the State*. Routlege, London: 27–74.

Kwon, H.J. (1999). *The Welfare State in Korea: The Politics of Legitimation*. Macmillan, London.

Kwon, H.J. (2002). Welfare reform and future challenges in the Republic of Korea: Beyond the developmental welfare state? *International Social Security Review* 55: 23–38.

Kwon, H.J. (2003a). Advocacy coalitions and the politics of welfare in Korea after the economic crisis. *Policy & Politics* 31: 69–83.

Kwon, H.J. (2003b). The reform of the developmental welfare state in Korea: Advocacy coalitions and health politics. UNRISD Workshop on 'Social Policy in a Development Context', United Nations Research Institute for Social Development, Bangkok.

Lin, C.H. (2003). Amendment of the 'Three Labour Laws': Reconsidering the Executive Yuan's 2002/05/01 Version. Council of Labour Affairs, Republic of China.

Lu, A.Y.L. (1992). Political opposition in Taiwan: The development of the Democratic Progressive Party. In T.J. Cheng and S. Haggard (eds). *Political Changes in Taiwan*. Lynne Rienner, London.

Midgley, J. (1982). *The Social Dimension of Development: Social Policy and Planning in the Third World*. John Wiley.

Midgley, J. (1995). *Social Development: The Developmental Perspective in Social Welfare*. Sage, London.

Ohmae, K. (1995). *The End of the Nation-State: The Rise of Regional Economies.* HarperCollins, London.

Park, B.G. (2001). Labor regulation and economic change: A view on the Korean economic crisis. *Geoforum* 32: 61–75.

Pearson, V. (2003). Welfare accountability and citizenship in Hong Kong: Two colonial masters. United Nations Research Institute for Social Development (UNRISD) workshop on 'Social Policy in a Development Context', Bangkok.

Pierson, C. (1998). *Beyond the Welfare State: the New Political Economy of Welfare.* Polity Press, Cambridge.

Presidential Office (2000). *DJ Welfarism: A New Paradigm for Productive Welfare in Korea.* Presidential Office, Seoul.

Ramesh, M. (2003). One and a half cheers for provident funds in Malaysia and Singapore. United Nations Research Institute for Social Development (UNRISD) workshop on 'Social Policy in a Development Context', Bangkok.

Rimlinger, G. (1971). *Welfare Policy and Industrialization in Europe, America, and Russia.* John Wiley & Sons, New York.

China, Republic of China (various years). *Statistical Yearbook of the Republic of China.* Statistical Office, Taipeh

UNDESA (1971). Unified socio-economic development and planning: Some new horizons. United Nations, New York.

UNDP (1990). *Human Development Report: Concept and Measurement of Human Development.* United Nations Development Programme, New York.

UNRISD (2000). *Visible Hands: Taking Responsibility for Social Development.* United Nations Research Institute for Social Development, Geneva.

Wade, Robert (1988). State intervention in 'outward-looking' development: Neoclassical theory and Taiwanese practice. In G. White (ed.). *Developmental State in East Asia.* St. Martin's, New York.

White, Gordon (1988). *Developmental States in East Asia.* St Martin's, New York.

White, Gordon (1998). Constructing a democratic developmental state. In M. Robinson and G. White (eds). *The Democratic Developmental State: Politics and Institutional Design.* Oxford University Press, Oxford.

Wong, J. (2004). Re-thinking development in Taiwan: Democracy and social policy. United Nations Research Institute for Social Development (UNRISD) workshop on 'Social Policy in a Development Context', Bangkok.

Woo-Cumings, Meredith (1999). *The Developmental State.* Cornell University Press, Ithaca.

Yi, I., and B.H. Lee (2003). Changing developmental characteristics in the Korean labour market policies, United Nations Research Institute for Social Development (UNRISD) workshop on 'Social Policy in a Development Context', Bangkok.

16

Labour Inspection for Decent Work and Economic Development[†]

MICHAEL J. PIORE AND ANDREW SCHRANK

Latin American economic and social policy is at a turning point: the emblem of that turn is the growing list of successful presidential candidates who have run against neo-liberalism – Hugo Chávez in Venezuela, Luiz Inácio Lula da Silva in Brazil, Tabare Vázquez in Uruguay, Néstor Carlos Kirchner in Argentina, Michelle Bachelet in Chile, and Evo Morales in Bolivia – and the near misses of populist candidates in Peru and Mexico. In many of these countries, presidential campaigns have turned into social movements that have continued after the elections, with peasant marches in Ecuador and Bolivia, enormous rallies in urban Mexico, factory takeovers in Argentina, and mobilization in the slums of Venezuela, revved up by weekly presidential addresses. The battle cry that unites these movements is a call to end the so-called Washington Consensus, with its commitment to markets as the arbiters of economic activity. The new regimes are riding a wave of discontent directed against the market, but are they simply reverting to the past practices against which the Washington Consensus was a reaction? Or are they creating something new that might temper or replace market mechanisms? And if they are innovating, what are the new institutions and how are they likely to evolve?

THE DOUBLE MOVEMENT

It is hard not to be reminded here of Karl Polanyi's *The Great Transformation*. Polanyi described the economic policies of industrial society as the product of a 'double movement'. The first movement is toward a free market, particularly in labour and land, and also in international trade. But free markets generate enormous pressures for the continual redeployment of resources, especially human resources. So Polanyi's second movement is a response, an attempt to protect society from these pressures. While the movement toward the market is guided and directed by a coherent theory and the ideology of political and economic liberalism (the Washington Consensus is but its most recent expression), the second movement is visceral, an instinctive effort to rescue society from the ravages of unfettered economic competition and the constant redeployment of resources that destroys the context in which people understand themselves and create meaning and purpose in their lives.

Our age is distinctive in offering no alternative vision of institutions or terms that might ease tensions between economic and social needs. In the past, there have been a number of visions, perhaps too many. Polanyi himself saw the makings of alternatives in Robert Owen's factory organization in the early 19th century and in the International Labour Organization in the early 20th century. Another, much more articulated vision was, of course, Marxism. When Polanyi was writing, in the 1930s, fascism also constituted an influential alternative. By the time his book was actually published, in 1944, Keynesian economics had captured the public imagination and seemed not only to complete his argument, but to provide a framework for the reconciliation of social and economic forces that avoided the twin pitfalls of Marxism and fascism. But each of these philosophies has since been discredited.

BUILDING NEW ALTERNATIVES INDUCTIVELY, FROM THE BOTTOM UP

In this unprecedented intellectual vacuum, one way to begin creating a coherent alternative would be to try to construct such a vision inductively, working from the changes that are actually happening on the ground. In studying what people are already doing locally in response to the conflict between market and social forces and identifying the particular institutions that are emerging in that process, we might find a way of working those institutions into the broader structure of the economy, using them as the starting point for an alternative model of social and economic organization. A number of domains lend themselves to this kind of inquiry, but Polanyi devoted a good deal of his attention to the construction and regulation of the labour market and to the birth of factory inspection in particular, and we therefore follow his lead.

The operation of the labour market affects workers concretely and immediately, and hence, is a flashpoint for clashes between social forces and economic exigencies. While many of the policies promoted by the Washington Consensus are only now beginning to encounter determined resistance, Polanyi's second movement has been underway for some time in the labour market – and labour-law reform therefore constitutes something of a Waterloo for the forces of neo-liberalism. In fact, the labour-law reforms anticipated by proponents of the Washington Consensus have not only been "limited to a few countries", according to Eduardo Lora and Ugo Panizza of the Inter-American Development Bank, but have arguably been more likely to expand than to curtail the scope of worker protection. For example, Brazil, Chile, Costa Rica, and the Dominican Republic have rededicated themselves to labour-law enforcement in recent years. And potentially more fundamental reforms are underway from Argentina, where they are motivated by domestic party politics, to Central America, where they are a product of transnational pressures emanating from the campaign for a US–Central America Free Trade Agreement.

The results are neither trivial nor cosmetic. In the 1990s, the Chileans hired new inspectors and thereby doubled the size of their enforcement division. And the Dominicans not only tripled the size of their own enforcement division, but simultaneously adopted new hiring criteria – including legal credentials and competitive examinations – as well as wage and employment guarantees. By the early twenty-first century, therefore, one of the Dominican Republic's least reputable regulatory agencies had been transformed into a model of administrative reform, and the island nation's inspectors were fanning out across the region to impart their lessons to their neighbours.

By examining the process of labour inspection in greater detail, we can begin to talk in a specific way about how these reforms might be reconciled with economic efficiency, what kinds of compromises it is reasonable to promote, and, most importantly, what larger project might emerge. For the past four years, therefore, we have been studying Latin American labour inspectors at a close level. We have observed and interviewed dozens of inspectors, as well as their private-sector interlocutors, in Costa Rica, the Dominican Republic, Guatemala, and Mexico; participated in conferences with inspectors from Brazil and the Southern Cone; and studied the history and practice of labour inspection in France and Spain, where Latin American labour ministries find their primary intellectual inspiration. We actually do see an emergent model for reconciling market and social forces, particularly in Mexico and Central America, where the adjustment to an open trading regime has been particularly brutal. We see hope in the street-level practices of labour inspectors in the so-called CAFTA countries of Central America and the Dominican Republic. We will argue, in fact, that the Latin approach to labour-market regulation is not only distinct from the prevailing US approach, but is also better able to reconcile the need for regulation with the exigencies of economic efficiency. Indeed, it offers the possibility for a country to shift from a strategy of competing in world markets through cost-cutting and labour exploitation to a strategy of upgrading business practices to raise productivity, reduce inventory levels, and improve quality.

Labour Inspection

Labour-inspection systems in Central and South America are basically variants of the Spanish model, which originated in France. The Spanish model is a general, or unified, system: virtually the whole of the labour code is administered by a single agency, the Inspección de Trabajo. The inspectors also enforce various provisions of private collective-bargaining contracts. In the United States, in contrast, each regulation, or type of regulation, falls under the jurisdiction of a separate administrative body (the Department of Labour's

Wages and Hours Division enforces minimum wage and overtime regulations, OSHA takes care of occupational heath and safety, ERISA covers pension regulations, and so on). And there is a separate and totally private system for the enforcement of collective-bargaining agreements.

General work-inspection agencies also operate in the Spanish model as 'street-level bureaucracies' – the line officers have considerable discretion and decision-making power and are very difficult to control and direct from above. Policemen on the beat, classroom teachers, and social-welfare case workers are typical street-level bureaucrats. In the United States, street-level bureaucracies typically arise inadvertently in regulatory agencies, when the agency is under-funded relative to its mission and the regulations it administers are too complex or too extensive to be applied literally. But in the case of Latin American labour inspection, the discretion is present by design; it gives the inspectors the capacity to adapt the system to the exigencies of particular enterprises. It also allows the inspector to judge the burden the regulations impose on the enterprise, and where this is excessive, or threatens the enterprise's very solvency, to balance particular regulations against each other and against the broader role of the enterprise in providing employment and goods and services. In the United States, where each regulation is essentially considered in isolation, there is no place in the system where the total burden is weighed.

The second characteristic that distinguishes Latin American labour-market regulation from the North American system is the fact that it is a compliance system. The United States takes the sanctioning approach: violations are punished, usually by paying a penalty, and the employer's obligation can generally be discharged in this way. In the Latin American system, the enterprise is expected to come into compliance: its obligations cannot be discharged by paying a penalty. Compliance is a process, and the inspector is empowered to work out a plan that brings the enterprise into compliance gradually over time. Penalties are viewed as an instrument designed to force compliance. But they are only one instrument, typically invoked when the violations are wilful, repeated, and deliberate. When they are inadvertent, growing out of ignorance or lack of technical background, or, as is very often the case in Latin America, the attempt to remain competitive in an increasingly inhospitable environment, the inspector operates more as an advisor or consultant than as a policeman.

DISCRETION AND FLEXIBILITY

The 'minimalist' version of the Latin model of labour inspection, and the one in the minds of the critics, uses the inspector's discretion simply to protect the worker and maintain social peace, but often at the expense of economic efficiency. For example, in Guatemala we accompanied a pair of inspectors responding to a complaint in one of the countless Korean-owned garment factories that ring the capital and, to some observers at least, constitute the visible manifestation of the metaphorical 'race to the bottom'. According to the complaint, the owners had denied a skilled machine operator his legally mandated vacation time. The inspectors visited the factory and took testimony from both sides. The Guatemalan worker described the situation; the Korean owner pleaded ignorance of the law; and the Guatemalan plant manager admitted that the worker in question had been denied his request for time off because he was at least 50 per cent more productive than the next available candidate for the job. While the inspectors were able to guarantee the worker his vacation, they did nothing to help the manager solve his impending productivity shortfall. Asked what he would do when the worker – who was quite literally on the way out the door – was on vacation, the manager looked despondent, shrugged, and said, "Slow down". In the cutthroat international garment trade, the cost of a slowdown could be enormous, not only for owners and managers, but for workers as well.

Elsewhere in Latin America, though, inspectors have recognized the potential tension between social protection and economic welfare and are using their discretion to address this problem in embryonic, but by no means unimportant ways. A number of the inspectors we interviewed in the Dominican Republic, for example, not only inform owners and managers of their legal obligations, but also disseminate information on the most efficient ways to comply with those obligations, and thereby build bridges between individual employers and publicly subsidized human-resource development programs designed to resolve the very dilemmas that emerged in the Guatemalan case.

Inspectors are in a good position to play this role because they visit a wide variety of enterprises and, perhaps better than anyone else, can compare business behaviour and disseminate best practices that reduce conflict between standards and efficiency. But unified labour inspection agencies do not rely on the experience of the inspectors alone to develop compliance plans. They usually also have specialists who play a staff function, providing expert advice when called upon by the line officers. Typically, these specialists include not only labour lawyers, but doctors, engineers, and industrial hygienists who are intimately familiar with the production process and therefore particularly adept at reconciling the needs of workers with the demands of the market. An initiative financed by the U.S. Department of Labour, called the Regional Center for Occupational Safety and Health (Centro Regional de Seguridad y Salud Occupacional, or CERSSO), has endeavoured to exploit these advantages by training more than 600 inspectors and technicians in eight different Central American and Caribbean labour ministries over the course of the past few years, and a growing body of evidence suggests that their efforts have paid off. A recent study of garment factories in El Salvador, Guatemala, and Nicaragua, for example, found that returns on safety and health investments engendered by the program ranged from four to eight times the costs of the initial interventions.

Even modest improvements, such as better lighting or noise reduction, can have a positive impact on output, absenteeism, and turnover. More substantial interventions can yield even greater payoffs. And even costly reforms can be rendered palatable if adopted throughout a given sector or labour market – thereby taking worker protection out of competition. But price signals alone will not lead employers to protect their workers. Nor will altruism. In the absence of meaningful government intervention, ignorance, self-interest, and short-term thinking will rule the day. And professional labour inspectors are therefore needed not only to block the low road, but to pave the high road as well.

The flexibility of the Latin model in particular contradicts the image of labour-market regulations as bad for business. A telling example comes from our interviews with inspectors in France, where the Latin model originated, but where it is currently under attack for its alleged rigidity. One inspector discussed his approach to the limitations on the use of temporary help and gave as an example the case of a large firm that he knew to rely excessively on temporary employees. He also knew, however, that it had an informal agreement with its unions to periodically move a certain number of temporary workers onto its permanent payroll, and in light of this agreement, he simply ignored the temporary-help violations. His reasoning, he explained, was that the goal of the temporary-help restrictions was to expand permanent employment, and he thought he would be unable to obtain more permanent jobs by enforcing the existing regulation than by tolerating the admittedly illegal informal arrangement with the union. The law, he pointed out, is a means, not an end in itself.

Other interviews in France and Spain suggest that this kind of discretion gives the system considerable flexibility over the business cycle. In applying the rules governing economic layoffs, for example, the inspectors weigh the immediate cost to workers of unemployment against the burden their continued employment poses to the viability of the enterprise, and thus jobs, over the long run. In this sense, it has some of the flexibility of the market, but does not simply mimic a market system. Both of these costs rise in a downturn, and the balance might favour easing restrictions, as it would in a market system, or it might favour tightening them.

In Latin America, of course, the chief problem is not cyclical unemployment, but adjustment to the global economy and the pressures of the international marketplace. The problem is more often ignorance than lack of flexibility. The Washington Consensus emphasized putting the firm under competitive pressure, internally through deregulation and globally by opening the economy to trade and investment. The economic theory upon which the consensus rested had very little to say, however, about the adjustment process, and the policy implicitly assumed that firms would know or learn how to respond to these pressures on their own. In reality, however, many firms were completely overwhelmed by competitive pressures. Unable to survive in the international marketplace by adjusting production and marketing techniques, they responded almost inadvertently in a blind attempt to lower costs, and this led to health and safety violations, longer hours, and the use of unqualified labour.

This is very noticeable in small family firms, where the shop is often in the household or in outbuildings directly connected to the household, and work and family roles are narrowly intertwined. Because the shop is in the household, the workspace is typically full of young children who are watched over by women also engaged in income-generating activities. But as the shop struggles to survive, the women work harder and harder, providing less supervision for the children, and the children themselves are often drawn prematurely into production. The result is both child neglect and child labour.

In larger industrial enterprises, particularly those operating directly as subcontractors for international clients, adjustment was aided by professional consultants or engineers sent from the client abroad to upgrade quality and ensure compliance with delivery schedules. But there, too, labour standards have frequently deteriorated. Recent studies of efforts by large transnational companies to monitor labour standards among their subcontractors suggest that their own business practices are heavily implicated in the deterioration of working conditions that has taken place, especially those associated with the pace of work and with working time. The transnationals wait until the last moment to place their orders, in order to keep up with the latest turn in fashion, or work from last-minute data on consumer buying, which they track daily in their stores. They then demand rapid delivery of orders that often exceed the subcontractor's capacity and can only be met by pressuring the labour force to work at an excessive pace and for inordinately long hours.

It is precisely in these areas of structural adjustment that the compliance model of labour inspection should be most effective. It gives the inspectors the power to help firms identify the business practices that are the underlying causes of their problems, and then the latitude to allow them time and space to correct them. What is needed is the expertise required to make these corrections. We have argued that part of this expertise already resides in the inspectors themselves, who see a larger range of business practices as they move from work site to work site than perhaps any other actor in the economy. They are thus already in a position to recognize best practices and spread them to non-compliant enterprises. The ability to use what is now essentially a kind of tacit knowledge, acquired inadvertently and informally, could be increased through specialized training and augmented by a growing body of research on the relationship between standards and business practices of the kind just cited. The underlying Latin model allows for additional expert support in the staff functions to which the line inspectors turn for advice and specialized assistance. And one sees traces of this model in almost all of the labour inspection organizations in Latin America.

The range of policy instruments available to the labour inspectors in promoting compliance could be broadened still further by enabling them to draw on the full gamut of programs for economic adjustment that are now housed in other parts of the government: labour-force training and education programs, financial assistance and tax credits, and industrial extension services.

New Approach

This last step crosses the threshold from a conception of labour inspection narrowly focused upon work standards to a notion of labour inspection as a much broader approach to social and economic policy. The agency then becomes a bridge between economic and social forces, at least one piece of an alternative to the Washington Consensus, or rather to the vacuum in which the reaction to the Washington Consensus is emerging.

There are actually signs of movement in precisely this direction. In Guatemala, the national labour inspectorate has established a special maquila division, which is taking an active approach to labour standards and labour relations more broadly. To facilitate a collective-bargaining agreement, for instance, inspectors have actually designed in-plant experiments on the effect of shortening the work week and lengthening the work day on labour productivity and worker satisfaction. In the Dominican Republic, as we have noted, inspectors have begun to use government training programs to facilitate compliance planning. For example, training was recently used as a key instrument in an agreement with a large Italian firm to create a cadre of skilled nationals as substitutes for illegally hired Chinese immigrants. And in Mexico, the Ministry of Labour is working with the ILO at the Volkswagen plant in Puebla to train labour inspectors to upgrade both production practices and labour standards in the company's Mexican suppliers.

These examples, it is to be emphasized, are of interest, not because of their quantitative significance. Indeed, their number is actually quite limited. But they point to the ways in which the Latin model of labour inspection might constitute the vehicle for a much broader approach to economic development – one that brings firms up to the standards imposed by their regulatory obligations, rather than bringing regulatory obligations down to the productivity levels characteristic of firms.

Moreover, they are particularly noteworthy examples because the inspectors offered technical assistance to sophisticated transnational companies that presumably had access to the best international consultants. The fact that they have emerged, even in countries with a relatively weak government apparatus, like Mexico and Guatemala, suggests that this approach is consistent with, even in some sense inherent in, the logic of the system. But before it could play this role more generally, most Latin American countries will have to combat a legacy of studied neglect in which these governmental functions have been starved for resources and qualified and well-trained personnel. Low salaries and insecure tenures constitute threats to the integrity of inspectors throughout the region, and operational resources are at best scarce. In Mexico and in most countries of Central America, for example, inspectors have neither transportation nor computer facilities of their own. They take public transportation when making inspections and write up their reports on manual typewriters. And Mexico, in particular, suffers from the draconian and arbitrary way in which the government has sought to control expenditures: the number of posts has been reduced through a system of special incentives for early retirement, but the remaining staff has been redeployed neither functionally nor geographically. The results are that federal offices, like that in Yucatán, have staff positions (doctors in occupational medicine and safety engineers) that are filled with experts, but most of the inspectors whom they are supposed to advise are gone.

Nonetheless, the effort to revitalize labour inspection has been underway in a number of Latin American countries for some time, and there is a collective fund of experience with innovative ways to upgrade personnel and to provide the missing infrastructure. In the Dominican Republic, the constraints imposed by salary structure have been circumvented by linking the careers of young inspectors informally to more lucrative positions in the private sector. In Guatemala, the labour ministry obtains educated inspectors at low cost by hiring the equivalent of law students who have yet to be admitted to the bar. And in Costa Rica, an agreement with the social-security inspectors who collect revenue, and therefore have claim to greater physical infrastructure, provides labour inspectors with transportation that their own budget does not cover. The question is, can these still dispersed efforts to revive labour-market regulation and the isolated forays into upgrading production and management be consolidated into a program that the political class can offer as an alternative to the Washington Consensus? Will it convince an electorate exasperated by the impact of 20 years of neo-liberalism that it offers real change?

ROLE OF INTERNATIONAL AGENCIES

To realize this potential would require a concerted and organized effort beyond national boundaries to articulate the broader implications of existing practice and to disseminate both the practices and the underlying model of regulation. What is called for is leadership that can play a role in developing and disseminating the new model analogous to the role played by the World Bank and the IMF in the diffusion of the Washington Consensus. The obvious agency to play this role is the International Labour Organization.

The ILO is the oldest of the UN agencies. It was founded by the League of Nations – according to Polanyi "partly in order to equalize conditions of competition amongst the nations so that trade might be liberated without danger to standards of living". It is thus older than

368 • Towards Full and Decent Employment

the UN itself. It is also unique among international organizations in having a tripartite structure in which each country is represented, not only by its government, but also by delegations composed of employers and unions. Over the years, it has promulgated a series of workplace norms and regulatory standards, and is historically the repository of expertise in how labour regulations are administered. The long list of legal norms is, in many ways, a caricature of the kind of government regulation that the Washington Consensus fought with its campaign against 'labour-market rigidities', and the debates among lawyers at meetings in Geneva often seem to validate this view. But as we have seen, the administration in the field is much more complex and subtle. And even casual contact with inspectors in the field in Latin America reveals that the ILO retains the respect and allegiance of the officials on the ground and the political appointees who supervise them, who look to the organization for advice and leadership and closely follow the pronouncements and publications that come out of its headquarters in Geneva. If it took up the challenge we are suggesting, it would have an audience.

To move in this direction, however, the ILO would have to reinforce, reemphasize, and integrate several activities in which it is actually engaged. One division of the ILO, now quite small but once considerably larger, is dedicated to labour inspection itself and offers advice on administration and comparative experiences. There are also a series of programs spread widely throughout the organization that are focused on particular business practices and their impact on employment, labour standards, and competitiveness. In this sense, the project in Mexico upgrading VW contractors is emblematic of a much larger class of activities. The ILO has been particularly active in studying the development potential of small and medium-sized enterprises. These activities have developed largely independently of the unit concerned with labour inspection, but they certainly could be integrated in a way that created the base for a systematic effort to link labour inspection and economic development.

But the ILO has not moved in this direction. Instead, it has responded to its neo-liberal critics by retreating from its historical role. It has not repudiated the accumulated body of labour standards. But it has attempted to shift the focus of the debate toward a set of 'core' labour standards, most notably against child labour and forced labour, upon which it appears possible to achieve a consensus that encompasses even its critics. It has also promoted the notion of 'decent work', a much more ambiguous concept, but one that holds the promise of rising above the bare minimum suggested by the 'core'. In the process, it has moved resources and personnel within the organization away from labour inspection and tried to reshape its external image around these new concerns.

It is almost impossible to argue with these concepts; indeed, that is the point of focusing on them. And it has in fact proved possible to find shocking examples of child labour and forced labour even in advanced developed economies, notably the United States. But these are hardly the central issues in labour-market regulation, the ones that touch the daily lives of the bulk of the labour force in an industrial society, and certainly not the ones that have triggered the political reaction in Latin America. Ironically, to play a role in the newly emergent global economy, the ILO must reclaim its core mission. Of course, nothing in all of this ensures that we can escape Polanyi's classic dilemma; perhaps in the end, we will have to choose between the social and economic. But even here, we would have to develop a new social consensus; and the tripartite structure of the ILO would appear to be a better forum for doing so than the boards of bankers and businessmen governing the World Bank and the IMF.

Notes

1. Originally published as 'Trading Up: An embryonic model for easing the human costs of free markets', *Boston Review September/October 2006*.

Contributors

Robert Boyer is senior economist at CNRS (Centre National pour la Recherche Scientifique), and Professor at EHESS (Ecole des Hautes Etudes en Sciences Sociales), in charge of the Masters program on 'The Economics of Institutions'. He is currently working at Paris-Jourdan Sciences Economiques (PSE) and Center for economic research and its applications (CEPREMAP), Paris. Boyer has been contributing to historical and institutional macroeconomics, with a special emphasis on labour market institutions, innovation systems and growth regimes, both for OECD and developing countries. He is a contributor to the 'regulation school' that investigates the long run transformation of capitalist economies and stresses the persisting diversity of national forms of capitalism. His publications in English include *Regulation Theory: The state of the art* (Routledge, 2002) and *The Future of Economic Growth* (Edward Elgar, 2004).

Martha Chen, Lecturer in Public Policy, is coordinator of the global research policy network, Women in Informal Employment: Globalizing and Organizing (WIEGO). An experienced development practitioner and scholar, her areas of specialization are gender and poverty alleviation with a focus on issues of employment and livelihoods. Before joining Harvard University in 1987, she lived for 15 years in Bangladesh where she worked with BRAC, one of the world's largest NGOs, and in India, where she served as field representative of Oxfam America for India and Bangladesh. She is the author of numerous books including, most recently, *The Progress of the World's Women 2005: Women, Work and Poverty* (co-authored with Joann Vanek, Francie Lund, James Heintz, Christine Bonner and Renana Jhabvala), *Mainstreaming Informal Employment and Gender in Poverty Reduction* (co-authored with Joann Vanek and Marilyn Carr), *Women and Men in the Informal Economy: A Statistical Picture* (co-authored with Joann Vanek), and *Perpetual Mourning: Widowhood* *in Rural India*. Chen received a PhD in South Asian regional studies from the University of Pennsylvania.

Michael Cichon works in the Social Security Department of the International Labour Office in Geneva.

Diane Elson is Professor in the Sociology Department at the University of Essex, UK, as well as Senior Scholar and Co-Director of the Program on Gender Equality and the Economy, Levy Economics Institute of Bard College, USA.

Gerald Epstein is Professor of Economics and founding Co-Director of the Political Economy Research Institute (PERI) at the University of Massachusetts. He received his PhD in Economics from Princeton University in 1981. Epstein has previously taught at Williams College and the New School for Social Research. He has also been a visiting Professor at the Johns Hopkins School for Advanced and International Studies in Bologna, Italy, and at Xiamen University in Xiamen, Fujian Province, People's Republic of China. Epstein's current research focuses on employment oriented macroeconomic and trade policies. He is the editor or co-editor of numerous books, including *Globalization and Progressive Economic Policy*, (Cambridge University Press, 1999, with Dean Baker and Robert Pollin), *Capital Flight and Capital Controls in Developing Countries* (Elgar, 2005) and *Financialization and the World Economy* (Elgar, 2005).

Krzysztof Hagemejer works in the Social Security Department of the International Labour Office in Geneva.

Rolph van der Hoeven is at the Policy Integration Department, International Labour Office, Geneva.

Jomo K. S. has been Assistant Secretary General for Economic Development in the United Nations' Department of Economic and Social Affairs (DESA) since January 2005. He was Professor in the University of Malaya, and then Visiting Professor at the National University of Singapore. Jomo was Founder Chair of IDEAs,

International Development Economics Associates (www.ideaswebsite. org), and has authored over 35 monographs, edited over 50 books and translated 12 volumes besides writing many academic papers and articles for the media. He is on the editorial boards of several learned journals.

Azizur Rahman Khan is Visiting Professor, School of International and Public Affairs, Columbia University, New York, and Professor Emeritus, Economics Department, University of California, Riverside.

Huck-Ju Kwon is Associate Professor and Chair of the Department of Public Administration, Sung Kyun Kwan University, Seoul.

Malte Lübker is in the Policy Integration Department, International Labour Office, Geneva.

Thandika Mkandawire is Director of the United Nations Research Institute for Social Development (UNRISD), was Executive Secretary for the Council for the Development of Social Science Research in Africa (CODESRIA) and is the author of many books and articles.

Janvier D. Nkurunziza works for the United Nations Conference on Trade and Development (UNCTAD) in Geneva, Switzerland. He has authored a number of articles on Burundi, Kenya and Africa. His research interests include poverty and economic growth, political economy of Africa, economics of civil wars, and applied industrial organization. He holds a DPhil in Economics from the University of Oxford, where he was affiliated with the University's Centre for the Study of African Economies. He has lived and worked in Burundi, Ethiopia, England, USA, Cameroon and Switzerland. He is a research member of the African Economic Research Consortium (AERC) and the Global Development Network (GDN).

José Antonio Ocampo was United Nations Under-Secretary-General of the Department of Economic and Social Affairs from September 2003 to June 2007. Prior to that, he served as Executive Secretary of the United Nations Economic Commission for Latin America and the Caribbean, Minister of Finance, Minister of Agriculture and in other portfolios in the Colombian Government. He holds a PhD from Yale University, has taught in several universities and published extensively on economic and social issues. He is currently a Professor at Columbia University.

Carmen Pages was Senior Labour Market Economist, Human Development and Social Protection Team (HDNSP), The World Bank, Washington, DC, and returned to the Inter-American Development Bank (IDB) in October 2006.

Prabhat Patnaik is Vice-Chairman, State Planning Commission, Kerala, India, on leave from being Professor of Economics, Centre for Economic Studies and Planning, Jawaharlal Nehru University, New Delhi. He is the author of numerous books and articles.

Michael J. Piore is the David W. Skinner Professor of Political Economy at the Massachusetts Institute of Technology (MIT). He is a labor economist, who has worked on problems ranging from immigration and low income labour markets to technological change and industrial adjustment, primarily in the United States, but also in Western Europe and Latin America. His most recent book is *Innovation: The Missing Dimension* (with Richard Lester). He is currently president-elect of the Society for the Advancement of Socio-Economics and in the process of organizing the 2008 meetings which will be held in Costa Rica. Piore and Schrank are currently collaborating on a study of the impact of CAFTA on labour market regulation under the auspices of CEPAL.

Gerry Rodgers is Director of the International Institute for Labour Studies, ILO, Geneva. He has a DPhil in Economic Development from the University of Sussex and has published widely on poverty, inequality, social exclusion, employment, labour markets, child labour, population growth and economic development, including empirical work in South and Southeast Asia, in Latin America and in Europe.

Andrew Schrank is an assistant professor of sociology at the University of New Mexico and the current co-chair of the Latin American Studies Association's Organized Section on Economics and Politics. He has worked extensively on problems of industrial development and labour in Latin America with a particular emphasis on the Dominican Republic and Mexico. He is currently completing a book on foreign investors and their local suppliers and subcontractors in Latin American export platforms. Piore and Schrank are currently collaborating on a study of the impact of CAFTA on labor market regulation under the auspices of CEPAL.

Victor E. Tokman, is an Argentine economist, with a DPhil from Oxford University, an MA from the University of Chile and several honorary doctorate degrees. He has published numerous books and articles in the employment field, particularly in relation to the informal sector. He worked at the ILO for almost three decades as Regional Director for the Americas, Director of the Employment and Development Department and Director of the Regional Employment Programme for Latin America and the Caribbean. He was also an Economic Advisor to the President of Chile, Ricardo Lagos E. from 2000 to 2006. He is presently a consultant, collaborating particularly with the Economic Commission for Latin America and the Caribbean (ECLAC), where he has published recently on labour issues related to social and labour protection as well as equity and structural change.

John Woodall works in the Social Security Department of the International Labour Office in Geneva.

Index

absenteeism, 362
adaptability and innovation, 200
affirmative action, 305
Africa, 9; banking sector, 184–85; development policies, 186; economic stagnation, 8; employment security, 225; financial and social capital, 181; fiscal deficit, 171; GDP, 160; informal economy, 234; labour market, 172, 180; natural and social capital, 183; poverty and unemployment, 8, 158–74; private sector, 171, 176, 184, 186, 187; public sector, 71; self-employment, 179; social protection, 288; wage employment, 179
ageing, 14, 285, 286, 293
agricultural employment, 7, 148, 150; in Africa, 170–71, 172, 174, 180, 184, 185–86, 242; transformation and sectoral links, 175–78; gender difference, 83; elasticity, 145, 146; labour, formalization, 292
agriculture, 8, 136, 144, 223; reforms, 148
Algeria: unemployment, 166
Argentina: economic crisis, 108; employment targeting economic policy, 106; industrialization,

115; inflation targeting, 110; labour market flexibility, 198; stable and competitive real exchange rate (SCRER), 109
Armenia: agriculture, 136; economic growth, 135; employment growth, 138; macroeconomic policies, 139, 152; poverty reduction, 135, 136, 138, 148
Asian Development Bank (ADB), 198
Asian economic crisis, 16, 198, 224, 330, 337, 342–43, 348, 351
Asian tigers, 137
Australia: social transfers, 281
Austria: welfare state, 282
authoritarianism, 332, 336, 337, 338, 339, 344, 347

Bachelet, Michelle, 356
balance of payments (BoP), 25, 56
Bangladesh: economic growth, 134–35; fiscal policy, 141; industrial transformation, 7; macroeconomic policies, 139, 140, 141, 152; poverty reduction, 138; remunerative employment, 150
Bank-Fund conditionalities, 139, 141, 152
banking sector, *see* central banks

education, educational systems, 216, 305

Employees-Employers-Government Committee, 16

employment, employment issues, 1; creation, 2, 3, 4, 5, 6, 12, 118; diagnosis, flexibility and security, 226–29; financial openness and, 38–47; effects of globalization, 288–91; generation, 6, 110, 114; growth/intensity weak in the growth process, 11, 54, 137–38, 144, 146–47, 151, 159, 169–72, 170, 197, 252; role in growth-poverty linkage, 123–53; indicators, 38; opportunities for women, 159; to population ratio, 92; and poverty reduction, 106, 123–53; protection, 192–93, 197, 199, 201, 223, 322, 324–26; legislation, 9, 192, 194, 198, 203; and skill development and productivity, 195; and unemployment, 194, 195; reallocation, 319; relationship, 204, 234, 235, 236, 244, 246–48, 250–51, 255, 262, 263, 265; risk, 10; security, 10, 222; externalities associated with various forms, 213–16; stability, 208; targeted economic program for South Africa, 106, 112–13; and workers right complimentarity, 207–31

enfranchisement, 273–74

entrepreneurship, 18

equity-efficiency trade-off, 14

Estonia: workers' security, 229

Ethiopia: agricultural employment, 170; poverty, 136; social protection, 299

European Commission (EC)/ European Union (EU), 40–41, 84, 286, 287; unemployment, 77

European Code of Social Security, 277

European Industrial Revolution, 278

European Stability and Growth Pact (SGP), 40–41

European welfare states, 14

exchange rate, 3, 6, 36, 43–45, 58, 89, 98, 105, 107, 110, 141–42, 219; competitiveness, 110; under-valuation, 111; variability, 113

export promotion, 114

export sector, 6; growth, 57–58, 68; women's employment, 89

family and community support systems, 278

fascism, 17, 357

Federal Reserve Bank of New York, 116

female career bias, 78, 80, 84, 89, 90

female labour force participation, 4, 73–74, 80, 309

female-headed household, 84

financial crises, 2–3, 20, 24, 27, 28, 29, 31–33; and employment, 34; negative effect on growth, investment and incomes, 24; labour-share, 34–38; negative effects on the labour market, 38

financial integration, 28; and financial liberalization, difference, 25; and growth, 27, 28

financial openness, 2, 3, 19, 66; crises and employment, 34; and employment, 22ff; and employment, need for greater policy coherence, 38–47;

productivity, 55–60, 62, 63, 66, 68, 365; growth, 204; protection, 258; relations, 12, 261, 268–71, 272, 274, 365; rights, 20, 214, 269; saving technologies, 4; securities promote economic performance, 216–23; shares, financial openness and financial crises, 34–38; surplus, 256, 262
labour market, 3, 47, 72, 86, 105, 172, 180, 191, 207–08, 235, 296, 309–10, 343–44, 358, 362; demand, 2, 4, 59–60, 61, 65, 68, 211; deregulation, 191; and economies, informalization, 291–92; and employment performance, 196; global, 288; growth, determinants, 55–58; interventions, 18, 19; policies, 1, 19, 127, 225, 324, 335; reforms, 9, 227, 257, 262–64; rigidities, 367; regulations, 13, 17, 20, 196, 203, 359, 363, 368; segmentation, 202, 248; and social models, 199–200, 202; supply side, 4, 77; theory, 208; and unemployment, 203
labour market flexibility, 4, 9–11, 18, 20, 207–08, 212, 219; and decent work, 191ff; flexicurity model, 199, 208, 223, 229, 230; protected mobility model, 200; and security debate, 208–13, 224–25, 250, 264; supply side flexibility, 193, 196
Lagos Plan of Action for the Economic Development of Africa, 1980–2000, 188n3
land reforms, 148, 305, 316; in Africa, 176–77, 186
Latin America, 28, 368; agricultural sector, 175; competitive and stable real exchange rate, 108;

conditionality for financial support, 28; economic and social policy, 356; employment security, 226; financial crisis, 31, 34; growth with equity, 231; inequality, 28; informal sector, 242, 243, 258–68; jobless growth, 8; labour inspection, 359, 360, 361, 363, 365; labour market flexibility, 198; pension reforms, 294; rural-urban migration, 292; rural non-farm sector, 179; social policy, 310; unemployment, 77, 322–23; unemployment insurance, 327; workers' security, 229
lawlessness, 260
learning effects, 308
legalism, 244
liberalization, 2–3, 6, 7, 17, 22, 24–31, 33, 37, 42, 44, 55, 56, 60, 61, 105, 114, 152, 225, 250, 312, 314; effects on growth, 26–27
life security, 214, 222, 225
liquidity, 39
Lithuania: workers' security, 229
Lorenz distribution curve of income, 124–25

macroeconomic, macroeconomics: instability, 225; management, 27; performance, 213, 220; policies, 2, 3, 123–24, 126–27, 105, 151, 153, 176, 192, 224, 227; employment, unemployment and gender equality, 70ff; role in determining rate and character of growth, 138–44; populism, 315; of poverty reduction, 123; shocks, 229, 319; and social policy, 310–11; stabilization,